CHARLES RENNIE MACKINTOSH

JAMES MACAULAY

COLOR PHOTOGRAPHS BY MARK FIENNES

W. W. NORTON & COMPANY :: NEW YORK :: LONDON

Charles Rennie Mackintosh
James Macaulay
Color photographs by Mark Fiennes

Copyright © 2010 by James Macaulay and Mark Fiennes

Manufacturing by Mondadori Printing, Verona
Book design by Robert L. Wiser, Silver Spring, MD
Composed in Rennie Mackintosh and Meyer Two

Library of Congress Cataloging-in-Publication Data
Macaulay, James.
     Charles Rennie Mackintosh / James Macaulay; color photographs by
Mark Fiennes.—1st ed.
          p.   cm.
     Includes bibliographical references and index.
     ISBN 978-0-393-05175-9 (hardcover)
     1. Mackintosh, Charles Rennie, 1868–1928—Criticism and
interpretation. I. Mackintosh, Charles Rennie, 1868–1928. II. Fiennes,
Mark. III. Title.
     NA997.M3M26 2010
     720.92—dc22   2009049576

W. W. Norton & Company
500 Fifth Avenue, New York, NY 10110
www.wwnorton.com

W. W. Norton & Company Ltd.
Castle House, 75/76 Wells Street, London, W1T 3QT

1   2   3   4   5   6   7   8   9   0

Frontispiece. Scotland Street School (Mark Fiennes Library)

Contents. Willow Tea Room (Culture and Sport, Glasgow Museums)

Last page. Conversazione Program

Photographic Acknowledgments (listed by illustration figures)
T. and R. Annan and Sons 1, 181–2, 222; © Hunterian Museum and Art
Gallery, University of Glasgow 2, 4, 43–4, 51, 78–9, 94, 98, 106, 113, 131, 165,
216, 227, 235–7, 240, 242–4, 246; Courtesy of the Mitchell Library, Glasgow
City Council 3, 5, 8, 10, 52, 56, 81, 85, 93, 96, 115, 122, 136, 160, 166–7, 178–9,
198; © Mark Fiennes Library 6, 7, 9, 14–6, 18–20, 30–3, 55, 68, 73, 75–6,
88–9, 109, 112, 114, 116–8, 123, 126–130, 133–5, 137, 145–7, 149, 150, 152–4,
156, 163–4, 172, 187–8, 194–6, 217–8, 229–32; Culture and Sport Glasgow
Museums 11, 34, 40, 45–7, 245; Family Collection 22–3; Courtesy of the
National Gallery of Ireland 35, 69, 70, 77, 82, 99; Vivian Carvalho 37–9,
41–2, 53, 56, 62–4, 74, 80–81, 83; 85–7, 90–2, 108, 115, 119–21, 124, 132,
161–2, 173, 175–7, 183–6, 189–90, 192–3, 197, 199–200, 203–6, 209, 219–21,
223–5; Glasgow School of Art 48–50, 95, 97, 100, 138–44, 148, 151, 168–71,
233–4; Trustees of the Macaulay Settlement 38, 101–5, 174, 191; Reproduced
courtesy of the Royal Commission on the Ancient and Historical
Monuments of Scotland 54, 201, 208; James Macaulay 57–9, 71, 226; Hornel
Library, National Trust for Scotland 65; Archive Services, University of
Glasgow 66–7, 110; Toyota Municipal Museum of Art 84; Glasgow City
Archives and Special Collections, Mitchell Library 90–2, 125, 158–9; Argyll
and Bute Council 107; Ruth Currie 208, 210; National Library of Scotland
215–6; 78 Derngate Northampton Trust 238; Private Collection 239; the
E. O. Hoppé Estate/Curatorial Assistance, Inc. 241

It has not been possible in every instance to trace the owners of copyright.
Information regarding copyright should be forwarded to the author.

IN MEMORIAM
GEORGE IAIN MACAULAY
1961 :: 2004

CONTENTS

LIST OF ILLUSTRATIONS

ACKNOWLEDGMENTS

Given the quantity of published material relating to Charles Rennie Mackintosh and his circle one may fairly ask about the need for yet another text. Yet for this author the urge to do just that was perhaps preordained. I first wrote publicly about Mackintosh forty-five years ago when there was discussion in the newspaper columns about the possible destruction of some of Mackintosh's buildings and interiors. Before then, as a child, I and my siblings would be taken to the Ingram Street Tea Room by our mother and, once seated in the Ladies' Luncheon Room with glasses of orange squash, would be instructed to look at the huge lead chimney piece and the other decorations. My mother's stepmother had some contact with the Mackintosh circle. So stories abounded and not least that they all drank, "even the women." In our family home there were numerous items from the last home of Herbert and Frances McNair as well as later acquisitions of furniture, light fittings, and paper works. To be surrounded by such objects could only be inspirational to one who would try in later years to understand Mackintosh.

In embarking on this book I was encouraged by the interest of the architectural and landscape photographer the late Mark Fiennes. Having first met when he came to Glasgow in 1992 to take photographs for *Glasgow School of Art*, we became firm friends. It was Mark, when on a trip to New York with one of his sons, who persuaded Jim Mairs of W. W. Norton to commission this book. In the years since Jim Mairs would often have cause to wonder, after one of our many lunches in the New York Yacht Club, if he would ever receive the text, albeit he had long had the engaging photographic images by Mark Fiennes secure in his office. Additional photography is by Mrs. Vivian Carvalho, Mr. Eric Gordon, Mr. Craig Laurie, and Mr. Graham Nisbet. Mr. Robert L. Wiser has devised the layout with much sensitivity and Ms. Austin O'Driscoll has sedulously edited and corrected the text as need be.

The task of compiling and researching the text has been beset by many difficulties. In these years many people have given advice and encouragement, not least members of my immediate family, Lord and Lady Vaughan and Mr. Christian Plaickner, while Lord Huntly has provided his own idiosyncratic encouragement.

I am grateful to the numerous colleagues and friends who have or have had the Mackintosh inheritance in their keeping. They include Mr. Chris Allan, Mr. Martin Hopkinson, and Professor Pamela Robertson at the Hunterian Art Gallery; Mrs. Anne Ellis at The Hill House; Mrs. Pat Douglas and Mr. Stuart Robertson, Queen's Cross Church; Mr. Jim Allan, Broughton House; Mr. Neil McVicar, Mr. David Buri, and Dr. George Rawson (librarians), Mr. Peter Trowles (curator), and Miss Adele Redhead and Miss Sarah Hepworth (archivists), Glasgow School of Art; the Rev. Dr. R. Mackenzie, Brechin Cathedral; Mr. Bill Mason, BBC; Mr. Graham Roxburgh, Craigie Hall; Mrs Dorothy Stewart, Scotland Street School; Mr. Daniel Robbins and Miss Alison Brown, Kelvingrove Art Gallery; Mrs. Margaret Harrison, University of Strathclyde; Miss Joanna Finegan, National Library of Ireland; Mr. Howard Averill, University of Toronto, Special Collections; and the staffs of the Mitchell Library, University of Glasgow Library, and the National Library of Scotland.

Professor John Blackie and Mrs. Ruth Currie supplied historical information as did Mr. Ian Begg, Professor William Brumfield, Mr. William Buchanan, Mr Alan Crawford, Miss Elaine Grogan, Mrs. Catherine Hamilton, Mr. Richard Hoppé, Mr. Stanley K. Hunter, Mr. David Ross, Dr. Gavin Stamp, Miss Fiona Sinclair, Father Anthony Symondson, Mr. F. M. Walker, Lady (Joan) Williams, the late Miss Winifred Mackenzie, who generously lent her father's travel diary (here published for the first time), and Miss Aylwin Clark. Others who gave help include Mr. Ian Alexander, Mr. Robert Coates, Dr. Elizabeth Cumming, Mr. Alan Ferdinand, Mr. Jim Hastie, the late Professor Tom Howarth, Mrs. Julie Lawson, Mr. Ivan Mavor, Mr. Marvin Sloman, the late Mrs. Ailsa Tanner and her daughter Mrs. Bridget Paling, and Mrs. Anne Paterson Wallace There were informative discussions with the late Ms. Jude Burkhauser, Mrs. Elaine Ellis, Professor Janice Helland, and Ms. Bille Wricke. Mrs. Pat Crichton lent her good offices as did Sir William Macpherson of Cluny. There were summer site visits with Mr. and Mrs. Malcolm Holzman.

Good cheer and insights were provided, and still are, around the Fireplace at the Glasgow Art Club by the late Dr. John Cunningham, Mr. Cooper Hay, Mr. Robin Hume, Dr. James Robertson, and Mr. Theo van Asperen (honorary librarian), among others. Mr. Leslie McIntyre answered early queries about the club archives, which were unearthed by Mrs. Anne Parker.

This work would not have proceeded let alone been accomplished without such good folk and many others.

James Macaulay :: Glasgow :: July 2007

harles Rennie Mackintosh (1) is an enigma. Although much has been written about his talents as an architect and an artist, as a human being he remains elusive to our understanding. Known facts about his early life are few, being no more than the occasional family reminiscence. Once he became an architect and a husband there is more account from family and friends although such enlightenment amounts in each instance to little more than limited remembrances. Nobody in the Mackintosh circle seems to have kept a diary recording the minutiae of the social scene with its chance encounters and observations on character, habits, and appearance, and whatever letters there were have long vanished, either by intent or by accident, if indeed any existed. After all what need was there for correspondence, other than the occasional holiday postcard or Christmas card, when family, friends, colleagues, and patrons for the most part resided within five or ten minutes' walking distance of one another's houses in Glasgow's confined west end? The few surviving letters of Margaret Macdonald Mackintosh, however, and the diary compiled by her husband in France, when she was in England, reveal a liveliness in writing that makes one regret the absence of more.

A missed opportunity for personal recollection was the occasion of the 1933 "Memorial Exhibition" following the death earlier in the year of Margaret Macdonald Mackintosh. Her contemporary Jessie Newbery contributed "A Memory of Mackintosh" to the catalogue's foreword in which she acknowledged his place as "one of a group of four" in whose early work "was seen the first blooming of a new style in Architecture, internal decoration and in various crafts." Even so Margaret Macdonald Mackintosh merits no attention other than as "partner and collaborator" while her sister Frances and Herbert McNair are named but with no mention of their place in the Turin exhibition. At the time of the 1933 exhibition Herbert McNair, alone of The Four, was still alive but his existence was not acknowledged nor were any of his works included in the exhibition, while Frances was represented solely by a pair of candle sconces and a couple of joint works with her sister.

Jessie Newbery, contributing from hindsight some useful information, such as the group's early knowledge of *The Studio* with illustrations by Aubrey Beardsley and by Carlos Schwabe for Émile Zola's *Le Rêve*, as well as Jan Toorop and C. A. Voysey and other professional prescriptions, says nothing of the private Mackintosh. There is some compensation, however, in the same foreword in a foreigner's description of the appearance of Mackintosh and his wife as well as the only account of their first married home in the tenement flat in Mains Street.

After 1933 there is little or nothing of substance that bears on personal reminiscence until Thomas Howarth's research got under way in the middle 1940s as he came into contact with some of those who had worked with or otherwise been associated with Mackintosh and his circle. Some of the recollections would be incorporated almost as a subtext in Howarth's 1952 publication although the absence of direct contact between John Keppie and Howarth does give food for thought.

The most useful of Howarth's correspondents was William Moyes, who had been in the office of John Honeyman and Keppie for a decade before emigrating in 1907.[1] Passing on knowledge gleaned from James Fulton, another employee, he affirmed that the *Glasgow Herald* building, Queen Margaret College, and the Martyrs' School in "the design and detail was the work of Mackintosh" while Annan's showroom and photographic studio, Pettigrew and Stephen's department store, the Paisley Library, and the Patients Building at the Victoria Infirmary "was the work of Mr. Keppie." More illuminating was the information that Mackintosh "had no hobby so far as I know and limped when he walked,"[2] which was confirmed by another correspondent. "He was a very distinguished looking gentleman, in spite his club foot and his defective eye."[3]

Mackintosh's parents were William McIntosh and Margaret Rennie. In his early years the father's occupation was given as "clerk at Central Police Chambers" until he was seconded to the chief constable's office.[4] The first family home was in Glasgow's Townhead where Mackintosh was born, in 1868,

cessive generations of the Dennistoun family by the purchase and amalgamation of a number of small estates around the core of Golfhill on which the Dennistouns erected a modest mansion in 1802.[5] From the 1850s Dennistoun was being laid out as a planned residential suburb for those with social aspirations but without the means to settle in the more affluent and salubrious west end. Around Golfhilll House there were villas, vaguely Italianate in style and below them regiments of terraces set around private squares of gardens; there were also the ubiquitous and more lucrative tenements, the older ones of blond sandstone, the newer ones, more ornate with granite pillared entrances, in the fashionable imported red sandstone.

As Dennistoun was not fully built up there was space on the southern flatlands for a showground where Buffalo Bill Cody and his troupe of cowboys, Indians, and animals would entertain eager families of Glaswegians. To the north there were the pleasure grounds of Golfhill House where William McIntosh was permitted some ground for the pursuit of his favorite hobby, the cultivation of garden flowers, especially hyacinths.[6]

The summit of Golfhill gave a view to the west of the Firpark Hill on which there loomed the statue of John Knox, a reminder of the city's staunch Presbyterianism and of William McIntosh's strict faith. At Knox's feet there were avenues of domes, vaults, and arches, which sheltered the dead. It was romantic and picturesque,

the fourth child and second son. Another seven children would follow although four would die within a span of a few years. When the family moved from the crowded Townhead it was but a short distance to the east to a larger tenement flat in Dennistoun just over the Firpark Hill from the city's medieval cathedral. Dennistoun had been created by suc- and where the Molendinar stream had tumbled between craggy banks was the cathedral to which Mackintosh would take his younger siblings "right down into the crypt," as recalled by the youngest, Nancy Mackintosh,[7] who inherited her brother's carefully composed watercolor study *Glasgow Cathedral at Sunset*. (2)

2. *Glasgow Cathedral at Sunset*, Charles Rennie Mackintosh

Mackintosh's mother died in 1885. Seven years later William McIntosh remarried. His second wife was a widow who insisted that her stepchildren address her as "madame."[8] Also in 1892 William McIntosh became a police superintendent. A new wife and promotion allowed for a better address across the river where the family settled in Regent Park Square—in reality a long, narrow, tree-shaded thoroughfare just behind "Greek" Thomson's Moray Place. The houses were two storys plus attics with a tall basement looking into spacious gardens at the front and the rear. Here, one of Mackintosh's sisters remembered helping her brother beat out patterns on the thin metal panels to decorate furniture.[9] Mackintosh lived in Regent Park Square until his marriage in 1900 to the red-haired, green-eyed Margaret Macdonald.[10]

The Macdonalds were a professional family, mostly solicitors.[11] The father of Margaret and Frances was a mining engineer in Staffordshire. When the family returned to Glasgow in 1888 they settled at Windsor Terrace, a respectable address, between the city center and the west end and in a locality that, though it backed on to the industrial hinterland of Port Dundas with its canal, basins, mills, and factories, was distinguished by the failed beginnings of some grand town planning schemes. The Macdonalds' home would have been an extremely grand tenement flat with a hall expansive enough to allow for the dancing of eightsome reels. Unlike Mackintosh's sisters, the Macdonald girls were not under the necessity of seeking immediate employ-

ment and could afford to attend classes in the Glasgow School of Art before setting themselves up, like many successful male painters, in a city center studio not so far from that of Herbert McNair.

3. *Old Sugar House, 138 Gallowgate*, William Simpson

McNair's immediate family were local bigwigs being armigerous and possessed of a family seat at Greenfield on the city's eastern outskirts. The family money had first come from the sugar trade (3) and long-established, albeit declining, interests in coal mining. However, by 1909 Herbert McNair's branch of the family was bankrupt. That was the year when Herbert and Frances McNair quit Liverpool. Back in Glasgow, with the loss of family money and with no permanent jobs, they had no recourse but to move into a main door flat, belonging to the Macdonald family, on the lower and less fashionable part of Hillhead. From then on their fortunes declined until it seems that necessity drove them to begin selling treasured possessions such as the Mermaid Cabinet and the Smoker's Cabinet to their friend John Knox for whom McNair had once designed a bookplate. For a while Herbert and Frances held posts in the Glasgow School of Art[12] but soon resigned and were without paid occupation thereafter. At the close of 1921 Frances hanged herself in her kitchen. She was forty-eight. The cause of death was recorded as a cerebral hemorrhage.

In Liverpool the McNairs seem to have been popular with their "homely way of conversing which immediately sets people at their ease."[13] Augustus John was one of those who were entertained by "this cheerful couple"[14] whose home "was a centre of much merriment and entertainment,"[15] although a disgruntled McNair once complained plaintively (4), "Confound it. I have to stay at home and mind the kid and can't go to the Xmas party."[16]

Mackintosh had his own fun at Christmas when he would wind different colored wools round the furniture in the studio drawing room, "so that the room looked like a spider's web," with each color leading to a present for a niece or a nephew. They did not care for their aunt whom the Mackintosh family considered to be "condescending and aloof."[17] Perhaps she disliked the beauty and order of her home being disturbed.

"On the second floor of a modest building in the great industrial smoky town of Glasgow there is a drawing room amazingly white and clean-looking. Walls, ceiling and furniture have all the virginal beauty of white satin.... In the still-

ness of the studio, among a bevy of plants and strewn with the novels of Maeterlinck, two visionary souls, in ecstatic communion from the heights of loving mateship, are wafted still further aloft to the heavenly regions of creation."[18]

4. Greetings Card, J. Herbert McNair

harles Rennie Mackintosh was born in Glasgow in 1868; he and his wife, Margaret Macdonald, left the city in 1914. Thus Mackintosh's time in Glasgow coincided with the period of the city's greatest prosperity as the Second City of the British empire in wealth and size.

In the decade of Mackintosh's birth the population was half a million when a hundred years previously it had been twenty-eight thousand. By the year of his departure it had peaked at a million and a quarter with immigration from the Highlands and Ireland and by incorporating within the city boundaries in 1891 neighboring small burghs, including Hillhead where Mackintosh and his wife would settle. In 1912 Partick, Govan, Shettleston, and Tollcross, the industrial and working-class zones to the west, south, and east of historic Glasgow, were absorbed, adding a further quarter of a million to the city's population which at 19.4 percent of the population of Scotland exceeded the ratio between London and Victorian England.[1] Glasgow had become the sixth-largest city in Europe, taking its place after London, Paris, Vienna, Berlin, and St. Petersburg, all imperial capitals.

Glasgow is the preeminent Victorian city in Britain. One informed commentator writing in 1971, at a time when the unchecked excesses of modernism were cutting swathes through the nineteenth-century urban fabric, could still hail Glasgow as "the finest surviving example of a great Victorian city."[2]

Indeed, how many cities can boast of local architects of such renown as Alexander "Greek" Thomson, J. J. Burnet, and Charles Rennie Mackintosh? How many can emulate the limitless extent of the tenements, repetitive but never monotonous, or the regenerative vitality of the theme of the formal terrace? Who has not been astonished when unexpectedly viewing from afar Sir George Gilbert Scott's university buildings on Gilmorehill, the largest architectural commission after the Houses of Parliament; who has not gazed in wonderment from a distant height at the quartet of Italianate and Gothic towers, seemingly belonging to a cathedral of indefinable size and date, spanning Woodlands Hill where the outer terraces are a coronet of stone above the bosky groves of Kelvingrove Park?

That Glasgow is a sculptural city is evident not only in the massing of the buildings but in the huge quantity of the still underrated civic and corporate sculpture such as the heroic religiosity of Saint Mungo, patron saint of the city who, with hand raised in blessing beneath the porch of the art gallery, looks across the narrow valley of the river Kelvin to gardens below the university where granite plinths bear Lord Lister and Lord Kelvin, the one the discoverer of antiseptic surgery, the other the physicist who superintended the laying of the first transatlantic telegraph cable. There is allegory in the Kibble Palace, that unique conservatory, where beneath the translucent mother-of-pearl dome marble figures of Eve, the sisters of Bethany and a Nubian slave peep coyly

5. Kibble Palace, botanic gardens, J. Cousland

from foreign flora. (5) Educational but suggestive, too, in the algae-stained curves, of other thoughts, which prompted a councilor, when the Kibble Fine Art Palace was offered to the city, to proclaim "the exhibition of the statuary as immoral."[3] Often the best sculpture is associated in large masses with the city's major buildings. It is impossible to comprehend James Sellars's St. Andrew's Halls without John Mossman's muscular atlantes carrying the entrance porch or the caryatids on the end pavilions. Not so distant is the crescent of Charing Cross Mansions (6), where J. J. Burnet incorporated

6. Charing Cross Mansions, J. J. Burnet

THE MUNICIPAL BUILDINGS.
Visit of Our Special Commissioner.

Michelangelo figures and the city's motto—"Let Glasgow Flourish"—around a *grande horloge*. (7) Burnet's love of plastic forms, inspired by his French training, was fully displayed on the Clyde Trust building where Europa and her bull are among the personifications of the continents defying Neptune enthroned in ancient majesty above the tympanum where figures crouch as in a dripping sea cave. No building, however, is more expressive of Glasgow's role and of Britain's rule in the world during the third quarter of the nineteenth century than the City Chambers. Leeds and Birmingham had classical town halls in the 1850s and '70s; Manchester's Gothic triangular pile, which cost a million pounds, though begun in the 1850s was not completed until 1877. The Manchester town hall competition was the model for Glasgow's, which saw William Young of London emerge as the final prizeman.[4] Though not a local man, that surely can be forgiven since he gave Glasgow the most sumptuous civic palace on mainland Britain (8), with many a marbled staircase leading to a mahogany council chamber, a satinwood saloon, and a painted banqueting hall with dripping brass chandeliers spattered with Vaseline glass shades only partially obscuring the newfangled electric lightbulbs. Outside an enthroned Queen Victoria is surrounded by the peoples of the greatest empire on earth.

Despite its nineteenth-century appearance, Glasgow is a medieval town having grown around the most westerly ford on the river Clyde. On a hill above the alluvial plain stands the cathedral. (9) Though smaller than its major English counterparts, Glasgow Cathedral has its own interest with a two-storyed eastern arm, unique in Britain, and with the upper and lower churches rising to 148 feet so that the buttresses in the lower church continue through the eastern wall providing necessary additional stability.

Throughout the nineteenth century the cathedral was the subject of much antiquarian and architectural interest. Sir George Gilbert Scott much admired the lower church,[5] with its intricate configuration of saint's tomb, lady chapel, and devotional chapels, which may have been the inspiration for his own undercroft at the university; and John Honeyman,

7. Charing Cross Mansions, J. J. Burnet (*opposite*)

8. The City Chambers, William Young, *The Bailie* (*top*)

9. Glasgow Cathedral (*bottom*)

Mackintosh's mentor and the cathedral's superintending architect, carried out a long program of repair and adornment with new stalls, a communion table, and a reredos perhaps with the assistance of Mackintosh.[6] Whether or not the latter was a member of the Cathedral Sketching Club[7] is unknown although some of his earliest sketches are of mural monuments in the graveyard and his first large surviving watercolor shows the double-storyed east end of the cathedral silhouetted against the tangerine glow of a setting sun. Mackintosh drew details, too, of the university set midway down the High Street.[8] Founded in 1451, it was housed in the largest complex of seventeenth-century architecture in Scotland, which in the 1850s was being demolished to make way for a railway mineral and goods yard. Long before the deed of sale in 1865 the railway companies had had their eyes on the one open site in the heart of the old town. For their part the university authorities were eager to sell since the neighborhood had degenerated, becoming "one of the most densely populated, and wretched districts of the city, where the very poorest inhabitants, and a sprinkling of criminals found shelter."[9]

The loss of the university buildings and the abandonment of the Tontine Coffee Room by the cross in favor of the new Royal Exchange to the west as the city's place of commerce "changed the whole aspect of the central portion of the city ... for the upper and lower middle classes ... abandoned their old residence for more fashionable localities."[10] Yet so great was the need by the poorer classes for accommodation in the historic core that "Houses are found tenanted by separate families in every apartment, and they appear to teem with inhabitants. The ash-pit and other conveniences are altogether insufficient ... and the water supply is very defective and in many cases none is provided."[11] As a result infectious diseases were the scourge of all classes, with cholera epidemics in the 1830s and in the three following decades and with the worst outbreaks of typhus in 1864 and '65 followed by the City Improvement Scheme with the aim of eradicating the worst of the slums that so horrified contemporaries. "The squalor, destitution, alcoholism and prostitution of the Glasgow slums seem near incredible"; Nathaniel Hawthorne recorded: "The High-street, and still more the Saltmarket, now swarm with the lower orders, to a degree which I never witnessed elsewhere; ... Some of the gray houses appear to have been stately and handsome in their day, and have their high gable-ends notched at the edges."[12] Before all that was old was swept away many of the tenements were recorded by the photographer Thomas Annan. (10)

A hundred years before, Glasgow had accrued much wealth by importing tobacco from the new world. The imports grew from just over £7,000,000 in 1728 to the highest recorded figure of £47,268,873 almost half a century later. By then Glasgow's merchants were bringing in two-thirds of the tobacco exports from America.[13] The reasons for such success were many. The sea route from New York to Glasgow was shorter than that to the southern English ports where there was also the ever present risk of a vessel's seizure by the French in times of war, although even then the French remained substantial customers in the reexport trade from Glasgow to continental Europe. Such was the dominance of the tobacco trade that in the years between 1771 and 1775 it represented 38 percent of all Scottish imports and 80 percent of all reexports,[14] which included rum, sugar, cotton, and mahogany from the West Indies and rice, oil, potash, and timber from the Americas and wines and fruits from the Mediterranean. In return for the shipments to Europe there came naval stores and timber.[15] It was, however, the trade with North America that was the flywheel for much of Glasgow's and the west of Scotland's economy since the outward-bound ships carried cloth, metal utensils, and tools as well as the luxury goods then not available in the east coast colonial territories.

Inevitably, the outbreak of war with the colonies and its outcome affected Glasgow's trading status. "Well do I remember," noted one Glaswegian, "the melancholy and dejected countenance of every person in our city at the sad news of the loss of America." It was, he continued, "a deathblow to the old tobacco aristocracy ... for the capital lost and locked up in America was almost overwhelming to the city."[16] While it is true, as another citizen records, that "the American War was a dreadful stroke to Glasgow," there was,

even then, an undercurrent of change as a result of "their industry being more especially directed than before to the prosecution of manufactures"[17] so that within a generation one commentator could note complacently that "The staple manufacture is that of cotton," which was exported as "muslins, calicoes, shawls, handkerchiefs, threads and hose."[18] Then there were 15,000 looms employing 135,000 persons,[19] and soon it would be recorded that of the 134 cotton factories in Scotland, a hundred of these were in and around Glasgow,[20] where the mild, damp climate was as favorable to cotton manufacturing as in Lancashire. Although the textile industry in Glasgow would decline, because of European competition and the American Civil War, from 37.56 percent of industrial employment in 1841 to 20.75 percent half

10. Close, 65 High Street, photographed by Thomas Annan

a century later it was still a larger employer of labor than the engineering trades that gave Glasgow its renown but which accounted for 14.17 percent of employment.[21] A by-product of the bleaching of cloth was the growth of a chemical industry. By the 1840s Charles Tennant, the discoverer of chemical bleach, was producing vitriol, soda, and other compounds in the east end in the largest chemical works in Europe,[22] which were dominated by a chimney, Tennant's Stalk, that a German traveler likened to "the minster spire over Strasbourg, rising over the city and its fog." So noxious were the fumes that the botanic gardens had had to be removed to the west end.[23]

It was not until the second half of the nineteenth century that Gasgow became the world's emporium associated with heavy engineering derived from the coal and iron ore deposits from the city's southern hinterland. So spectacular was the diversity of Glasgow's manufactures it could be claimed that in the century after 1845 almost every article made elsewhere in the world was also produced in and around Glasgow.[24] Initially, there was pig iron. In the 1830s Scotland's tonnage increased a hundredfold to 400,000 tons per annum[25] with the number of furnaces quadrupling from twenty-five. With the "hotblast" ironstone selling at 15 percent to 20 percent cheaper than in England[26] the price advantage allowed the tonnage to rise throughout the remainder of the century. Already by 1859 a third of the British output came from Scotland, where the tonnage passed the million figure by the middle of the following decade.[27]

As local firms gained worldwide reputations their names became synonymous with that of Glasgow. In the east end William Beardmore had the Parkhead Forge, which covered forty-five acres and employed three thousand men, and had acquired elsewhere in the city an engineering works and a shipyard.[28] In the north of the city the North British Locomotive Works was foremost in Europe with two-thirds of its production going overseas.[29] It was a frequent sight even until recent times to see a huge steam locomotive destined for the Americas or some distant part of the empire being maneuvered through narrow streets to the dockside

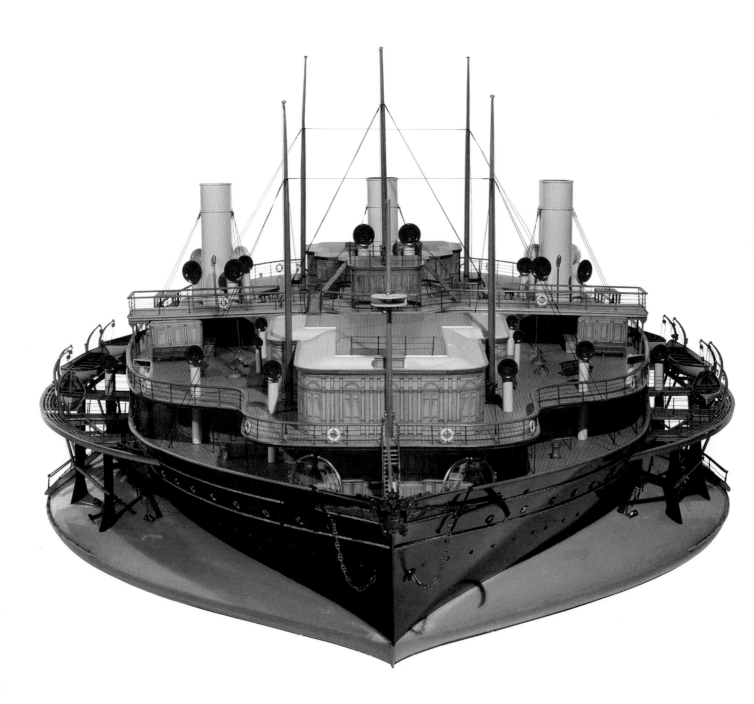

11. Model of the Russian imperial yacht, *Livadia*

to be hoisted by the Finnieston Crane onto a moored vessel. Also in the north was Walter Macfarlane's Saracen Ironworks. The firm's catalogues show the extensive range of products from roof gutters and ornamental lamp standards to fountains and bandstands that were dispatched around the globe.

The industry that made the name of Glasgow a byword in the greater world was shipbuilding, although it had been of little significance until after the cessation of hostilities between Britain and America in 1783 since "The building of vessels was formerly little attended to, all the large vessels belonging to Clyde being built in America."[30] As with so many other local enterprises talented and energetic individuals, in the next century, wrought such a transformation that by the early twentieth century a third of Britain's tonnage was being launched from the banks of the river Clyde.[31]

The new era was inaugurated with the *Comet*, the world's first seagoing paddle steamer, which at its trials in 1812 beat its course downstream from Glasgow to Gourock in three and a half hours. The *Comet*'s boiler had been supplied by David Napier whose later innovations included constructing an iron vessel in 1827. By then his cousin Robert Napier had taken over the family engineering business in the industrial east end of the city, appointing David Elder, a millwright, as manager. Then in 1836 Robert Napier acquired his cousin's shipyard and for the next forty years turned out such original ships, including the first four Cunarders, that he gained the soubriquet Father of the Clyde.[32]

David Elder's son John joined the engineering firm of Randolph Elliot and Company in 1852, which became Randolph Elder and Company. He was then twenty-eight years old. Within two years he had developed the first satisfactory compound engine using 30 percent less coal.[33] A new engine works was begun in 1858 on the south bank of the river not far from the city's commercial center. A single-story rectangle of deeply coursed stone with pylonlike window openings and an interior of iron and brick, it could be compared with the more renowned 1909 AEG Turbine Factory in Berlin by Peter Behrens.

In 1864 Randolph Elder and Co. moved downstream to the flat fields of the Fairfield farm at Govan where a new shipyard was laid out. In 1869, a year after becoming sole partner, John Elder died, leaving his widow as his main beneficiary.[34] Her wealth was used to good purpose. She gave Govan's people the open ground before the shipyard as a park. "It has been laid out into walks, drives and terraces by Mr. John Honeyman."[35] Mrs. Elder ran the shipyard, then the world's largest private shipyard employing four thousand men, for over a year when a new partnership was created. In 1888 the company was restructured becoming the Fairfield Shipbuilding and Engineering Co. Ltd. with an extensive and richly decorated range of offices by John Keppie.

By then, with well over two dozen shipbuilding and repair yards on the upper Clyde, marine engineering had become one of the city's largest employers of labor, which included the fitting-out trades—the joiners, cabinetmakers, painters, and upholsterers whose standards of work were such that for passenger liners the term "Clyde built" was synonymous with quality and luxury. The most luxurious and certainly the oddest-looking craft was the *Livadia*, the turbot-shaped imperial yacht built at Fairfields in 1880 for the czar of Russia. (11) In addition to the private apartments for the imperial family it had marble floors, a main saloon with a rose garden and illuminated fountains, and racks for ten thousand bottles of wine. Sadly, the *Livadia* ended a short seagoing life as a coal hulk.[36]

With its many sea lochs penetrating deeply into the land mass of the western highlands, the Clyde estuary had the most intensive steamship traffic in British waters. In 1819 the *Comet* was plying the first regular steamship service from Glasgow to the west highlands. Soon the dominant shipping family would be the sons and other relatives of the Rev. Dr. John Burns, much of whose ministry of seventy-two years was passed within the cathedral. His two younger sons founded G. and J. Burns, which ran an early steamship service between Glasgow and Liverpool with a connection by rail from there to London. Sir George Burns, in partnership with Samuel Cunard of Nova Scotia, founded the Cunard Line for conveying the royal mail between Liverpool and Halifax and Boston and, within two years, the Cunarder *Britannia* on her maiden voyage from Liverpool in 1840 reached Boston in a record breaking fourteen days and eight hours.[37] A relation of the Burns family was David MacBrayne who developed the carrying trade to the west highlands with such success that a wit reordered the opening verses of psalm 24.

> The earth belongs unto the Lord,
> and all that it contains;
> Except the western highland piers
> For they are all MacBrayne's

The design, technical, and craft skills, an openness of mind to the latest engineering innovations, and contacts with the wider world, all of which were inherent in the shipbuilding and shipping industries, permeated the day-to-day activities of Glasgow whether it was the output and costs in the iron and steel trades or the prosperity of the decorative and furniture trades. Certainly, the role of the owners of yards and of shipping lines in the public and artistic life of the city was not inconsiderable. Thus, James C. Burns acted as a governor of the Glasgow School of Art. At a meeting in 1882 to discuss '"he promotion of Artistic Design . . . Mr. J. C. Burns pointed out the scope there was for artistic decoration of vessels"[38] with two of the richest examples being the interiors of the *Livadia* by William Leiper and of the *Lusitania* in 1907, designed by James Miller, with a double-height, galleried first-class dining saloon over which a dome was painted with evanescent Boucher-like panels.[39]

Despite the size of its population and the scale of its industries, Glasgow was remarkably compact being no more than four and a half miles from east to west and six miles from north to south. Within that compass much of the topography was dominated by drumlins, a succession of low hills on the western edge, overlaid by a street grid. Always open to external influences Glasgow had imported the grid as a planning tool as early as the third quarter of the eighteenth century, possibly from the eastern towns of the United States of America. From the riparian plain the grid extended to the north and west where, in the early decades of the nineteenth century, the lands of the Campbells of Blythswood were laid out as Glasgow's first new town around Blythswood Hill, on the summit of which was an ornamental garden surrounded on four sides by a residential square from the outer edges of which more terraces lined the descending slopes, creating limitless vistas to the river, or else terminated by a public building filling a square as became the Glasgow custom.

For a hundred years the grid remained Glasgow's most characteristic urban form, often laid down in conjunction with the ubiquitous tenement block. Good examples of both are in Woodlands, a residential lower-middle-class development. Set at right angles between two parallel thoroughfares are cream and red sandstone tenements, four storys high and arranged as hollow rectangles with grass courts for children's recreation, the drying of washing, and the collection of refuse. Between opposing frontages there may be a tree-lined grassy space and at the rear a service lane bisecting the back courts. Shops, with flats or apartments above, line the ground floor of the short ends of the blocks on the main routes along which tramcars gave cheap and speedy access to the town center and other districts. There is a neighborhood school as well as a distinguished parish church by J. J. Burnet on one boundary and St. Mary's Episcopal cathedral on the other.

In the United States of America the word "tenement" has a pejorative meaning; in Scotland, as in many other European countries, it has an ancient and distinguished pedigree as being economical in both land use and servicing. The Glasgow tenement invariably retains a human scale with the basic layout enhanced by a lively classical tradition that allowed for variations on the street front in fenestration, including the introduction of bay windows, in moldings, string courses, and, here and there, sculpture even if it is only a pair of palmettes at the base of a chimney stack.

The tenement was acceptable to all social classes yet for those at the lowest end of the scale it was the universal dwelling type. Indeed, it has been stated that one half of the population lived in one- or two-room flats with parents and babies in one room and older children in the other.[40] If many of the rows of such housing were anonymous architecturally, others had a distinguished public face. The longest and undoubtedly one of the grandest examples was Queen's Park Terrace (1857), designed by "Greek" Thomson. As usual the ground story was a line of shops interrupted by a close or entry to the flats above each of which were a kitchen with a bed recess, a bedroom, and a parlor. A communal water closet would be used by the households on each landing. If the planning was ordinary it was what Thomson did with the front facade that was so extraordinary. With each first-floor window framed by a projecting aedicule there was created an endless colonnade above which horizontality took over with a molded band linking the second-floor windows while on the final story dwarf columns drew attention to the stone planes between the windows. Finally, a parapet is transformed into a classical cornice. Incised patterns and paterae added detail but could not detract from the supremacy of the solids over the voids or from the subtlety of the vertical recession of the wall planes and the diminution of window sizes.[41]

By the end of the nineteenth century architects were manipulating the standard architectural forms of the tenement no less than with other building types. How scintillating and provocative, therefore, is James Miller's Caledonian Mansions (1897) set over an unbroken line of shops (12) so that access to the flats is from a rear balcony reached by a staircase housed within a tall sandstone porch at either end of the block (13). Within the habitual upper three storys there are maisonettes as well as flats. At the end of the century the elevational treatment could be classed loosely as Jacobean with peaked gables and stretched chimney stacks responding to the chunky corner tourelles. That so many dominant design elements present a harmonious not to say unified composition on all four elevations says much for the design sophistication attained by talented

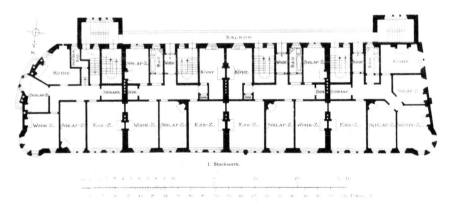

12, 13. Caledonian Mansions and plan, James Miller, *Die Englische Baukunst der Gegenwart*

local architects working within the tenement tradition, and it is testimony to the building's distinction that it was one of three Glasgow buildings listed by Hermann Muthesius in his survey of British architecture.[42] Equally distinguished, if quirkier, is the Anderston Cross savings bank (14), which combines the subtlety of exquisite carving with representations of Scotland's history (15) while skillfully utilizing continental decorative motifs. (16)

Another innovative and contemporary example is St. George's Mansions at Charing Cross (17) where strong modeling, French historical forms, and three facades outlining an important road junction produce a symmetrical center with hinged-back asymmetrical wings.[43] The hinges are formed with the contemporary leitmotif of tourelles between which a trio of mighty pilasters frames stacked bay windows topped by a gazebo or glazed loggia girded with a delicate iron balcony with more ironwork, giving a filigree flourish to the mansard roof. Tourelles, segmental pediments, and mansards all make obeisance to the opposing Charing Cross Mansions (1891) where J. J. Burnet's French training shows in the *grande horloge* with its encompassing sculpture and in the open gallery, reminiscent of the Paris Hôtel de Ville, of which a commentator remarked, "Won't those balconies on the Charing Cross Mansions command a splendid view of any royal pageant or other procession?"[44]

With its provision merchants, tearooms, jewelers, art and antiques shops, and dressmakers supplying the carriage trade, Charing Cross was a microcosm of the prosperity of the merchants, ship owners, and professional men who lived above on Woodlands Hill.

During the 1830s the southern flanks had been lined with terraces with the first of these, Woodlands Crescent (1831), setting two precedents with a curved frontage, trailing the rising contour of the hill, punctuated by Greek Doric porches. These were the city's introduction to a style that was to exercise a hold on Glasgow architects until the next century. In common with most of the other quite new streets in the western part of Glasgow, in which individual dwellings are vertical units within the whole, "the general heights of the

14, 15. Glasgow Savings Bank, Anderston Cross, James Salmon

houses are two and third stories; added sunk or half sunk stories being also frequent. The lower front storey is often rusticated, and the fronts generally are of smooth freestone, or, as it is commonly called, polished ashlar. Ornamental door and window cases are not uncommon ... a handsome iron palisade frequently occurs in lengthened line."[45]

After Woodlands was purchased by the town council in 1852 Charles Wilson drew up and eventually supervised the implementation of his own master plan, which included Kelvingrove Park and which was laid out, with Sir Joseph Paxton as a consultant, as the second public park (as opposed to the royal parks) in Britain. It was, therefore, only on Woodlands Hill that municipal patronage allowed one man's vision to be imposed and by and large fulfilled. From its beginning Woodlands was an enclave for the well-to-do. Here there were no shopkeepers, no tradespeople—"who are quite inconsistent with Paradise."[46] Public buildings were restricted to a Gothic parish church and Wilson's Free Church College and, on the southern edge of the hill, his Queen's Rooms as a place of assembly and musical events. An early Renaissance temple, its outline is enlivened by Alberti-like cadences of round arches, reflected in diminuendo on the attached tenement and by a figurative frieze in which the architect is portrayed carrying a roll of drawings followed by a staggering apprentice bearing a model.[47]

At the center of Wilson's layout was a unique double circus, which may have originated from a similar, though unrealized, concept by John Nash for Regent's Park. For the inner ring, however, with two entries in axis and a third aligned on the northern segment, one has to look to the earlier Ainslie Place in Edinburgh. Or had Wilson been studying the *grandes places* of Paris? Certainly the outer ring has French motifs, for the first time in Glasgow, with the taller intermediate pavilions crowned with mansard roofs and iron cresting, all to be read from afar, whereas the inner Park Circus is a contained ellipse without so much as a bay window to break the rhythm of the curved planes.

The internal layout of the individual houses was more or less standard. In the entrance hall a pair of marble columns

16. Glasgow Savings Bank, Anderston Cross, James Salmon (*top*)

17. St. George's Mansions, Burnet, Son and Campbell (*bottom*)

marked the transition to the staircase, often taking a third of the available volume. The dining room was to the front on the ground floor with a morning room for everyday family use at the rear. Above the dining room was the drawing room, usually L-shaped, and filling the full width of the front of the house. Behind was the master bedroom suite. A concealed secondary staircase led to a bedroom floor and garrets for the servants. The kitchen and other offices were in the basement, which was reached from a sunken front area. At the rear the stables and coach house, with lodgings above, gave onto a service lane. It has been stated the the cost of such a house was £5,000 or more, "enough to have provided one- or two-room houses of the tenement type for forty families."[48]

18. Park Circus, Charles Wilson,
looking towards Walter Macfarlane's house

Today three-quarters of the houses will be occupied as commercial premises. The home of the ironmaster Walter Macfarlane, which was a family residence for fifty years until 1932, was perhaps the most lavishly decorated. (18) The entrance hall, set out as an arcade of domed bays carried on marbled columns (19), leads to a white marble staircase and up to a galleried hall with an iron and glass dome carried on gilded pendentives. (20) The metalwork is from Macfarlane's Saracen Works as is the ornate conservatory and smoking room. Around the corner in Park Terrace the home of the city's leading magistrate was deemed grand enough to receive the czar of Russia. And was it the nearby home of the MacBrayne family that prompted a British ambassador to make a comparison with the interiors of Hitler's Berchtesgaden in the Bavarian Alps?

For the well-to-do the move to the west could be prompted by quick access to the city center, expansive hilltop views, leafy surroundings, including the Botanic Gardens, and the beneficent westerly winds overcoming the malodorous industrial and chemical fumes belching from the stacks to the east of the medieval city. The west end had the advantage, too, of being connected to the pure water supply piped from Loch Katrine in the Trossachs to defeat the recurrent outbreaks of cholera and typhus. It is not surprising that Glasgow's prominent citizens moved from the overcrowded, infested, and polluted historic core with its stew of social and immigrant mixes to the open countryside "being now entirely changed, and the locality at present forming the urban places of residence of our rich and fashionable folks, whose elegant mansions are rearing up their heads there on every side with magical rapidity."[49]

In the west end, where the two large estates of Kelvinside and Gartnavel had been consolidated in 1845, the owners began setting out feus along Great Western Road, the main exit from the old town,[50] which would become "this fashionable boulevard—the only one we have in Glasgow."[51] From the start it was intended that the west end would be a high amenity area with the feu charters imposing stringent conditions for planting, pavements, and the type of street gas

19. Walter Macfarlane's house, entrance hall, James Boucher

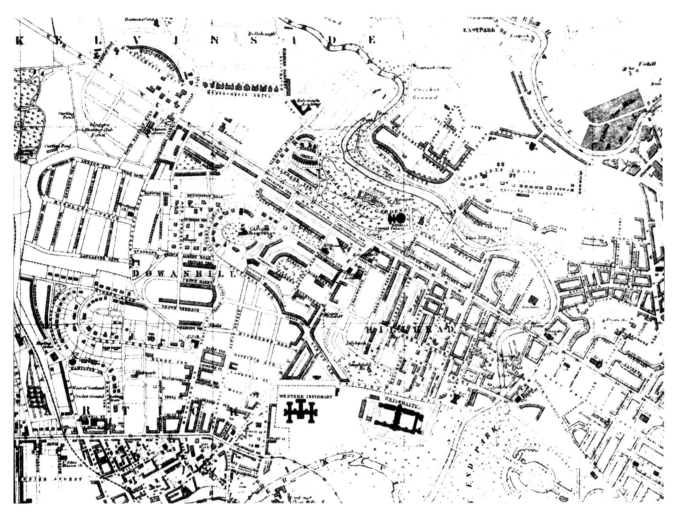

lamps.[52] Most unusually the estate proprietors had a London designer, Decimus Burton, prepare a master plan with terraces fronting Great Western Road and villas disposed on the higher ground.[53] Though the villas would be replaced by the more lucrative terraces there were villas aplenty to the south of Great Western Road. The ordnance survey map of 1861 (21) shows some twenty villas randomly disposed in Hillhead, with Gilmorehill House and Lilybank House having the most extensive policies, and with almost the same number placed formally around Dowanhill to the west.[54]

Within a quarter of a century Cleveden, on the extreme western edge of the city, would have villas lining Great Western Road and on the slopes above. None, though, could have been as grand as Northpark House. Facing into Botanic Gardens, this palazzo with shell-headed pediments and an expansive Venetian window over the porch was a showcase for the wares of a ceramic manufacturer. Begun in 1869 by J. T. Rochead and finished by John Honeyman, it was part of an Italian vogue among the very rich who generally employed James Boucher, as at Redlands House and the

21. Plan of the west end, 1880

20. Walter Macfarlane's house, the gallery, James Boucher

22, 23. Carlston, entrance hall and drawing room, James Boucher

nearby palatial Carlston (22, 23), a villa, complete with lateral service wings, for James Marshall, a partner of Walter Macfarlane in the Saracen Works.[55]

The first of the west end terraces was Charles Wilson's Kirklee Terrace, begun in 1845, with a pleasure ground falling down to Great Western Road (24) and private access to the Botanic Gardens. The orthogonal projection of the central and end pavilions and the heavily consoled balconies was not to be repeated so boldly again. Indeed, Grosvenor Terrace (1856) has an almost unbroken linearity (25) devoid as it is of ornamentation save for the necessary classical syntax providing a support system for the huge plate-glass windows. A modern writer of the most instructive fictional account of Victorian Glasgow has described Grosvenor Terrace as "A Victorian row 'commanding a beautiful view of the brilliant parterres of the Botanic Gardens with the umbrageous woods of the Kelvinside beyond," set back from the placid, easy-going traffic of a Great Western Road, where once in a while a green car rattled past on its way to and from Kirklee; where handsome equipages with their freights of silks and parasols glittered by on fine afternoons; the solemn, liveried flunkies, sitting high above the sparkling horses as they flew past brave, new terraces, built of the famous Giffnock stone—cream-coloured, and not yet blackened by the smoke of the encroaching city."[56]

The physical expansion of Glasgow juddered to a halt with the collapse in 1878 of the City of Glasgow Bank, with debts of £12 million, which ruined many citizens and disturbed Glasgow's confidence in itself. Thus, for many years "Greek" Thomson's Great Western Terrace marked the city's western limit. (26)

Though Thomson adhered to the tradition of a central pavilion he brought the terminal pavilions inward so that the lateral line continued through and beyond them. That could have resulted in a weak termination of the elevation although this was avoided by the careful matching and playing of one design element against another. In this late work Thomson dispensed with surface embellishments, possibly because of the northerly aspect, relying for effect on unadorned wall

24. Kirklee (formerly Windsor) Terrace, Charles Wilson (*top*)

25. Grosvenor Terrace, J. T. Rochead (*center*)

26. Great Western Terrace, Alexander Thomson (*bottom*)

panels punctuated by deeply sunk windows and tetrastyle porches, which, in the pavilions, are extended with antae.

In time many of Glasgow's most prominent citizenry settled in the west end—architects like Mackintosh, who removed from Blythswood, John Keppie, J. J. Burnet, and James Miller as well as artists, such as Francis Newbery, and many of the professional and mercantile classes. An example is the Blackies, members of the publishing house, founded in 1809 in the Townhead near the cathedral, one of whom would eventually commission Mackintosh to design The Hill House. By the early 1870s four heads of the family were living within walking distance of one another including the founder, John Blackie, who had begun his working life in the tobacco trade.[57]

By 1857 his eldest son, John (27), was residing at Lilybank House on the summit of Hillhead and facing south down to Gilmorehill where Scott's new university would arise. Lilybank House had been a modest villa but it was doubled in size by John Blackie who had "Greek" Thomson design a finely detailed porch and two large public rooms to meet the needs of a public figure. Having been a town councilor since 1857, John Blackie became Lord Provost in 1863. He used his new position to initiate the City Improvement Scheme,[58] a pioneering venture since it was not until after 1872, with the passing of the Artisans' Dwelling Act, that national legislation allowed specified town councils to acquire by compulsory purchase insanitary property for demolition and rebuilding. Birmingham, for example, voted to spend £1,310,000 to acquire forty-three acres.[59] In Glasgow, Blackie had earlier proposed that the city should acquire eighty-eight acres in Townhead, adjacent to the Blackie works, for £1,250,000. That was seen as too costly and at an election in 1866 Blackie was defeated, losing his seat on the town council.[60] One of his strongest supporters had been Thomson.[61]

In the late nineteenth century commentators looked on Birmingham as "the best governed city in the world," notable for "first, the intellectual calibre and social status of the councillors, second, the quality of the municipal civil service."[62] The same could have been said of Glasgow where, with "a

model municipal government,"[63] John Blackie Jr. was but one of many prosperous citizens whose Christian conscience prompted them to strive for the betterment of the lot of others. Thus, John Blackie brought forward the concept of free libraries, was one of the originators of model lodging houses, and was the main promoter of the Free Church College.[64]

John Blackie had left the established Church of Scotland at the Disruption in 1843 and adhered to the Free Church. With William Collins, printer of the Bible, he was involved in erecting twenty new churches in Glasgow besides taking a personal interest in Kelvinside Free Church, the first of some half dozen Presbyterian churches in the west end called for by "the extension of Dwelling-houses and consequent rapid growth of population ... this progress is likely to continue with undiminished activity for some time to come."

27. John Blackie

The promotional circular issued in 1857 noted that "a respectable and, for the most part, a church-going class of the community is settling in the neighbourhood" although hitherto "no steps have yet been taken to secure the erection of a church adjacent to the District," where a congregation it could be assumed would be "persons of some social status, influence and wealth." John Blackie, as chairman of the subscribers,[65] laid the foundation stone and in time would pay off the building debt.[66] The design was by J. J. Stevenson, "the first architect to plan the interior rooms of great ocean liners."[67]

The residence of John Blackie was the most westerly house in Kew Terrace, flanking Great Western Road and overlooking no. 1 Belhaven Terrace, the home of his second son, Dr. Walter G. Blackie, who beside his business concerns became principal of St. Mungo's College and one of the promoters in 1878 of Kelvinside Academy, one of the two private schools for boys in the west end. Designed in the Thomson idiom by James Sellars it has an elevated tetrastyle porch on the main front.

The third son was Robert Blackie (28), who became the first occupant of no. 7 Great Western Terrace, which had been begun in 1870 although Robert did not gain possession until 1872, a delay caused perhaps by the time taken to decorate the hall and staircase. "We have had a very tedious and bothersome business with Robert Blackie's house in Great Western Terrace," wrote Alexander Thomson. "Rodger and he are working at cross purposes and I don't know how matters will be settled. We are now getting on with the painting of it with the Brothers Orr in the usual pernickitty way." Later, Thomson's first biographer praised the iron balustrading of the hall staircase as one of the architect's finest works.[68]

Robert Blackie's interests were in the arts. Indeed, "he received a thorough training from the late W. L. Leitch, for many years drawing Master to Her Majesty and the royal family. Owing to his special tastes and qualifications the artistic department of the firm naturally fell under his charge."[69] Thus, it may have been he who appointed Talwin Morris in 1893 as the firm's book designer. The latter in turn

would recommend Mackintosh to W. W. Blackie to design The Hill House.

In 1871 Robert Blackie followed his brother John as a governor of the Glasgow School of Art, an office he was to hold for more than twenty years enabling him to offer commissions from the family firm to the most promising of the students. Given his long service Robert Blackie was ensured a prominent role in the affairs of the School of Art. It was he, together with Walter Macfarlane and James C. Burns, who offered Francis Newbery the headship in 1885 with all that the appointment would mean ten years on for Mackintosh and his friends.[70]

The firm of Blackie and Son having continued to expand the decision was taken to combine the publishing office

28. Robert Blackie

with the printing works in Townhead where a gap site in Stanhope Street was infilled in 1870 by "Greek" Thomson.[71] The choice of architect may have been Robert Blackie's since he admired Greek architecture for its "intellectual and abstract beauty of form and ornament."[72] As a mature work the Stanhope Street premises (29) had such distinctive Thomsonian motifs as banded masonry and a colonnade of pilasters, although the oversized and off-center doorway was an oddity.

After Thomson's death in 1875 Robert Blackie was one of the trustees of the Alexander Thomson Travelling Studentship. Mackintosh was awarded the second scholarship in 1890, which allowed him to travel through Italy for three months.[73] Another, albeit more tenuous link with Mackin-

29. Blackie's publishing works, Stanhope Street, with a centerpiece by Alexander Thomson

tosh was that Robert Blackie and his son and nephew were members of the Westbourne Free Church, standing immediately behind Great Western Terrace.[74] Designed by John Honeyman in 1878, it was the first classical church in the west end. The facade is an erudite rendering of early Renaissance motifs with a double-layered portico repeated in the facades of the attached terrace, a linkage used by Thomson in his two great city churches at St. Vincent Street and Caledonia Road.

It is difficult now to conceive the impact that Thomson's buildings made on the citizens of Glasgow in the late 1850s. To some the churches must have seemed as outlandish as did Mackintosh's School of Art half a century on. The first of the three great churches was at Caledonia Road. It is, despite the simplicity of the individual parts, the most eclectic and the most derivative in its sources. Not that they are all that obvious. Perhaps they are three. The hexastyle temple atop the entrance porch can be derived from the lodges at Thomas Hamilton's Royal High School in Edinburgh (which Thomson admired) or, to reach back to the ultimate source, the fifth-century BC Temple of Nike Apteros, sited for scenic effect on the precipitous bluff of the Athenian Acropolis. In the game of hunting the source it may be that the oddity (to some perhaps the solecism) of a tower alongside a temple front could be justified by the illustrations in early-nineteenth-century treatises on the remains of classical Greek architecture that include towers.[75] It is, of course, the adroitness with which Thomson adapts the Greek formulae without compromise to nineteenth-century requirements that is so convincing. Yet in his personal search for the truthfulness of form, Thomson recognized, as did others using the same chosen style, the clash between the Greeks' emphasis on the solid and the requirement in a northern country for daylight. So far as possible, therefore, the window was suppressed. Thus the elevated temple front obscures the fact that there is downlight into the porch and backlight for the rear gallery, and with the side lights set back from the stone face the upper wall reads as a continuous colonnade as in Schinkel's Schauspielhaus in Berlin.

In the St. Vincent Street and Queen's Park churches the historical analogies are more elusive as the personal language becomes more idiosyncratic in the search for the control of mass. Unfortunately, of the three churches only St. Vincent Street (30) survives intact. Mackintosh may have known its interior since his first married home was only a quarter of a mile up the hill. What would have been his impressions? Possibly the structural rationalism and stern logic of foliated cast-iron columns carrying entablatures of wood and stone, of the clear light from plate-glass windows, their fixings concealed within the masonry, of red and blue coloring (probably darker than what is seen now) playing over Thomson's favored yellow pine embossed with mahogany frets of discs, paterae, and anthemions. (31) Despite the mélange of historical sources their use is symbolic rather than archaeological.

It has been said that Thomson left no followers.[76] That is not so. The force of Thomson's creations can be demonstrated most notably with the St. Andrew's Halls by James Sellars (32), where there is a concentration on massing with a high basement, pseudo-isodomic masonry, and a decastyle colonnade copied from Schinkel's Altes Museum in Berlin.

Although St. Andrew's Halls can be criticized for lacking a central crowning feature, one is not required since the site constrictions mean that the facade can be viewed only obliquely. (33) Thomsonesque details were carried over into other works by Sellars, including Kelvinside Academy, of the same date as the nearby St. Luke's Cathedral, as it presently is named, which was commenced in 1877, five years before Sellars had made his first journey to France. He made good use of what he saw. Thus St. Luke's is a reminder of the Gothic of the Île-de-France with the slightly earlier church of Belmont and Hillhead modeled on the Sainte-Chapelle, a choice dictated in part by the intended congregation which decreed that there should be no pillars to obscure the sight lines. The aisleless space is also unusual among the churches of the west end in having no galleries for worshippers.

30. St. Vincent Street Church, Alexander Thomson

31. St. Vincent Street Church, interior, Alexander Thomson

The links between the Glasgow architects and Mackintosh begin to come into focus with Sellars and his design for the first of Glasgow's International Exhibitions in Kelvingrove Park in 1888. The anticipated profits would be applied to funding a new city art gallery and museum and a purpose-built art school,[77] an ambition prompted by the founding of London's South Kensington as an educational enclave, with the Victoria and Albert Museum as the centerpiece, using the profits generated by the Great Exhibition of 1851. Sellars's winning competition entry was in a loose Moorish style with domes and minarets chosen "not only from its suitability to the purpose," as Sellars explained vaguely, "but because it lends itself readily to execution in wood," which was painted cream and maroon. "The selection of the Oriental style of architecture as one which naturally lends itself to gay and festive treatment" (34) was acceptable to one critic, though, "At the same time the facility with which its forms can be imitated in wood is a snare which has been only too readily fallen into to the sacrifice of constructional beauty and truth in design." In the dome of the main exhibition hall the spandrels displayed allegories of industry, agriculture, science, and art by artists from the "Glasgow Boys," who thus received their first public recognition. Although the exhibition was devoted to the display of industrial goods, particularly local ones, so that on their stand Fairfield and Co. had a model of the *Livadia*, there were ten galleries devoted to art; seven of these were allocated for British and foreign paintings with examples in the loan section by Whistler, Burne-Jones, Watts, Rossetti, Monticelli, and Millet. Other painters were attacked in print for "cheap sentiment ... sentimentality ... hideous unreal realism ... meretricious prettiness." The sculpture gallery was arranged by Fra Newbery, and off that were two smaller rooms for photography by J. Craig Annan and architectural drawings. John Honeyman wrote: "The collection is perhaps the best of the kind that has ever been brought together," mentioning "two by Mr. Alexr. McGibbon of parts of Glasgow Cathedral ... that one magnificent work of art." Yet exhibitions of architectural drawings are not usually crowd pullers so that in his account of the "General Indifference to Modern Architecture" the architect G. Washington Browne opined that "the lack of interest taken in architecture ... is due in large measure to the absence of any personal identity of the architect with the art work he preaches. The personal identity of the artist with his work is a special characteristic of modern life and thought."[78]

With fine weather, an attendance of well over half a million, and no financial deficit, Glasgow's exhibition, dubbed by

32, 33. St. Andrew's Halls, James Sellars

Glaswegians as Baghdad by Kelvinside, was a success. One visitor was Charles Rennie Mackintosh, then twenty years old and just completing his architectural apprenticeship, who sketched (35) a minaret.[79] He was friendly with George McKenzie (36), a junior clerk of works for the exhibition and an architectural apprentice for the previous two years, possibly in Sellars's firm, since he was a friend of John Keppie, who had been assisting Sellars.

In the following summer McKenzie, Keppie, and another companion, Hugh McNab, traveled to the continent partly on holiday and partly to cast a knowing eye over the Paris exhibition and be dazzled by M. Eiffel's tower illuminated by gas. Thomas Cook had been advertising locally in the spring

34. *Glasgow Exhibition, 1888*, Sir John Lavery

offering to make "Travelling Arrangements with or without Hotel Accommodation, Carriage Drives, Sight-Seeing, Admission Fees." A month later the same journal reported on the "difficulty of finding hotel accommodation ... and the exorbitant charges" and the hundred francs for a season ticket.[80] Fortunately, McKenzie kept a diary,[81] hitherto unknown, which is not only informative but makes an illuminating comparison with the places and sights observed by Mackintosh on his Italian journey in 1891.

The three young men sailed from Queen's Dock in Glasgow on Sunday, August 4, on the *William Connal* although "the whole appearance of the good ship Wm. Connal was not calculated to inspire a great deal of confidence in one ... this ship has foundered three times." With time on their hands "John [Keppie] and I made colour sketches of the after deck of our ship." Before sailing they had laid in "some lemons, biscuits and a bottle of brandy," a wise move as "the food is wretched" and so much so that when the vessel called in at Newport, "We have decided to take in a small private store as we cannot face up to the greasy looking stuff put down to us." At Cardiff they purchased "some biscuits, lemons, sardines, a lobster and a couple of tins of tongue."

From Le Havre the voyage continued up the Seine to Rouen, which McKenzie and Keppie had seen before and where all three disembarked. After a brief visit to Evreux they stopped at Dreux for one night only "on account of the very primitive sanitary arrangements," then moved on to Chartres "and were met on our arrival by our old friend Andrew Prentice who had been travelling in Italy on the Soane scholarship and had come to France to join us in our proposed tour through the Loire district." Before setting off "we visited the Cathedral. No wonder Ruskin goes into raptures over it! ... The choir is superb. A most elaborately carved marble screen surrounds it and in some of the designs I recognised the originals of some plaster casts we have in the office and in the School of Art." In the town he "made some sketches of old iron work door handles etc." Next it was on to Orléans, which "we were quite agreeably surprised to find interesting as we had been told it was not worth visiting ... but in Orléans Cathedral

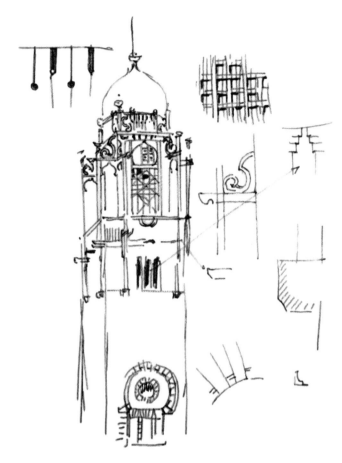

evening at a Caffe Chantant and most curiously sat down beside an Englishman who afterwards more curiously still turned out to be Briggs the Soane medalionist of four years ago. We made friends at once and Briggs decided to go on with us ... now in practice for himself in London."

In Paris, at last, their hotel was "moderate considering the high prices that are being in Paris just now and we are indebted to John Keppie's influence with Madame Pirie in getting such comfortable lodgings at something like our figure." At the "Grand Exposition ... we wandered over the grounds all beautifully illuminated with electric, Chinese and other lamps ... There are incredible numbers being admitted to the Exposition every day—as many in a day in fact as we got in a good week in the Glasgow Exhibition. The Eifel [sic] Tower is a wonder. The construction is a perfect marvel of lightness and we were quite pleased to find it is a graceful structure. We had heard so much and read so much about its being a foolish undertaking and a blot in the beautiful city ... Were very interested in Edison's Phonograph ... and were very much struck by the grand proportions and simple construction of the Gallerie de Machines." On the following day McKenzie was in Lucerne en route to Italy. Keppie returned to Glasgow to the office of John Honeyman where, at the age of twenty-seven, he had been taken on as a partner with Mackintosh as a draughtsman. ▪▪

for me was for the first time quite made clear the full meaning of a Gothic Cathedral." From there it was on to the château of Blois "to study details only as they will come in very useful and as we intend buying some photographs as our time is too precious to make a finished sketch." At Blois "we had to say good-bye to McNab who was going on to Paris as his holiday was limited to three weeks." At the château "Andrew is measuring the whole of the court facade and John is confining himself to making water colours." At Chambord they admired the dormers "from a closer inspection which our ascending to the roof allowed of," and at the château of Chaumont "we came upon a most interesting rustic bridge made of cement in imitation ... of fir roughly hewn." At Tours they "spent the

35. A minaret, Glasgow Exhibition, 1888,
sketch by Charles Rennie Mackintosh

36. A group photograph showing George McKenzie
on the left and Charles Rennie Mackintosh on the right

2 ░ "NEW ART"

The Harvest Moon, Charles Rennie Mackintosh

It may be justly said that when Mackintosh entered his chosen profession the heroic period that was Glasgow's in the nineteenth century was past. Thomson had died in 1875; Sellars, too, had died, having contracted blood poisoning from standing on a nail at the Glasgow exhibition; Honeyman's best work was behind him; and William Leiper was about to retire from the city, leaving behind the quirky polychromatic Templeton's carpet factory looking, to misquote a famous wit, as if the Doge's Palace had pupped in Glasgow. There would be an outburst of building in the Edwardian period, with more tenements infilling the city's edges and exotic, steel-framed, multi-storyed office blocks thrusting through the city center's grid like the temples of Angkor. For the time being, however, the city had its Gothic churches and commercial palazzi held with a classical matrix that was still vigorous in interpretation as in the great church of St. George's-in-the-Fields (1886) where, in the tympanum of a freestanding portico, a majestic Christ blessing the children is one of Glasgow's finest sculptural compositions.

Yet the city's two most prestigious architectural commissions, the University on Gilmorehill and the City Chambers, had gone to London architects. What had happened to Glasgow's confidence in its own men? And young men from well-to-do backgrounds no longer served an apprenticeship in a city office. Like the Americans H. H. Richardson and Louis Sullivan, and led by J. J. Burnet, John Campbell, John Keppie, and A. N. Paterson all spent time in Paris at the École des Beaux-Arts and in the atelier of Jean-Louis Pascal, the most distinguished of the patrons, thereby subtly changing in years to come the physiognomy of Glasgow.

On reentering his father's firm in 1877, J. J. Burnet won the competition for the Fine Art Institute in Sauchiehall Street where the facade, though not without some local mannerisms, was enriched by a surface plasticity enhanced by the use of lavish sculpture. Burnet is a telling representative of his age for, not being a devotee of any style, and certainly not of art nouveau, he could employ all—and do so well. Thus, the Barony Church, Queen Margaret Union, and Charing

Cross Mansions range from Scottish Gothic of the thirteenth century to Tudor collegiate and then on to a firecracker display of the French Renaissance from the Loire valley.

The most powerful purveyors of the rapid dissemination of ideas and fancies, and particularly, so far as Scotland was concerned, of the spread of such an English style as the Free Renaissance, were the journals. The oldest was the *Builder*, which covered all aspects of building and construction, whereas the twice yearly *Academy Architecture*, begun by Alexander Koch, the German architect, in 1888 and "popular in all architects' offices in Glasgow,"[1] was illustrative of new works in London, Paris, and America with a fair showing of Glasgow's output—though elsewhere in Scotland was largely ignored—with the selection of Glasgow firms indicative of their standing. In the years from 1893 the firm of John Honeyman and Keppie, which becomes Honeyman, Keppie and Mackintosh in 1903, is cited annually, except in 1905, until 1909, after which, significantly, there is nothing. "Charles R. Mackintosh" appears in his own right in 1901 along with "Margaret Macdonald, R.S.W." as the artists of the sketch panels for *The Wassail* and *The May Queen* "for Miss Cranston's Tea Rooms, Ingram Street, Glasgow."

In 1897 *Deutsche Kunst und Dekoration* and *Dekorative Kunst* were launched in Germany. In the next year furniture by Mackintosh was shown in the latter with further articles in 1899 and 1902. Of more practical use to Mackintosh and his confrères was *The Studio*. The first volume in 1893 included an appreciation of the extended Glasgow Art Club "from the designs of Mr. John Keppie" with mention made of "the decorations of the various rooms and large gallery" for which the decorations had been prepared by Mackintosh, although that was not said.[2] In the same issue there was praise for Aubrey Beardsley's illustrations with their erotic undertones since "he has not been carried back into the fifteenth century or succumbed to the limitations of Japan; he has recognised that he is living in the last decade of the nineteenth century"[3]; there was an interview with C. F. A. Voysey, who complained, "The danger today lies in over-decoration; we lack simplicity and have forgotten repose"[4]; and Walter

Crane opined that "design has more analogy to poetry: unless the motive is real and organic; unless the thought and the form have something distinctive and individual in them; unless the feeling is true, the work fails to interest us." Later came the thought, "That to imitate a bygone period in a dull and lifeless manner is hardly worth serious consideration; but to adopt just so much of the old style as is worth reviving, and infuse into it the qualities modern taste deems essential, is in its way a new creation."[5] That was from "A New Treatment of Bas-Reliefs on Coloured Plaster," which was succeeded by "Stencilling as an Art."

Mackintosh would seem to have perused closely successive issues of *The Studio*. For example, a piece on "flower studies of Apricot Blossom and Azaleas as shown by Japanese Artists"[6] must have been a point of departure for Mackintosh's layout and analysis of plant forms. Other sources may perhaps be less obvious. In 1894 a book cover design of rose trees and thorns (37) by Gleeson White[7] can be compared with Mackintosh's Buchanan Street tearoom frieze where briars encircle etiolated females. Associated with these may be the notice on "The Art of Utamaro," by Samuel Bing, who observed that the Japanese artist never portrays men, only women, as on the whole did Mackintosh and his circle, in which "elegance ... represented an end, an ideal, that restricted both choice and treatment of subjects, and to which all other considerations must be subordinated ... By concentrating his efforts upon the elaboration of the silhouette he frequently destroys the individuality of the lineaments."[8]

Commentators have always perceived a Japanese influence in Mackintosh's spatial dispositions and in design details. How did he receive that influence? That question has another strand in the architect's links with the Glasgow Boys, that group of painters who brought the artistic reputation of Glasgow to preeminence in the 1880s and '90s and the forefront of European painting with works hung in Paris and exhibitions in America and Europe where "Venice, Copenhagen, Stockholm, Dresden, Hamburg, Prague, Berlin and Munich are all anxious to secure good Glasgow pictures."[9] In Munich in 1894, where the exhibitors included J. Reid Murray, Fra Newbery, Stuart Park, and Grosvenor Thomas, the show was highly rated while "the Gallery of the Secessionists is also more than ordinarily attractive, Glasgow men largely predominating."[10] Most of the Glasgow Boys were a decade or more older than Mackintosh, although some, such as J. Reid Murray (1861–1906) and David Gauld (1865–1936), were contemporaries.[11]

The rage for Japonisme was confined neither to painting nor to Glasgow. Gilbert and Sullivan's *The Mikado* was first staged in 1885. Also smitten was James McNeill Whistler, who filled his London studio with Japanese prints and blue and white porcelain, commissioned the Butterfly cabinet, and signed the portrait of Thomas Carlyle with a mom. It was this work that the Glasgow Boys persuaded the city corporation to acquire in 1891, "making Glasgow the first city in Britain to recognise Whistler's work."[12]

37. Design for a book cover, Gleeson White, *The Studio*

Twenty years previously, William Leiper had decorated the drawing room of Cairndhu in Helensburgh with chrysanthemums and bamboo shoots. Indeed, for anyone interested in the arts of Japan, Glasgow, in the 1880s, was a storehouse. In response to the welcome accorded to the Japanese engineers who had come to the city to observe shipbuilding techniques on the Clyde the imperial government presented to the city in 1878 an important ethnographical collection. In 1882, to coincide with an exhibition of oriental art, Christopher Dresser, "who is a native of this city," lectured on Japanese artwork while the decorators J. and W. Guthrie had Japanese hangings on view.[13] The renowned Glasgow picture dealer Alexander Reid, famous as a sitter for van Gogh, was selling Japanese prints in his gallery.[14] In 1889 a sale advertisement listed "785 Japanese Draught Screens and Fire Screens" along with ivories "and a whole list of fancy articles and vases suitable for Drawing and Dining-Room Decorations."[15] Grosvenor Thomas, one of the Glasgow Boys, was dealing in Japanese curios, which in 1888 included sword guards in which "differences result from the use of family badges and symbols varying as widely as names. Emblems, in which Japanese art is so rich, play a prominent part."[16] In 1893 the gallery of Thomas and Paterson was showing a collection of Japanese prints, "the inspiration of Whistler and much of the stuff that has influenced the Glasgow School."[17] In the following year Thomas presented a series of Japanese prints to the Glasgow Art Club where they hang on the staircase to this day,[18] and a pair of prints were on show on the drawing room mantelpiece in the Mackintoshs' first married home.

Two who had direct experience of Japan were the painters George Henry and E. A. Hornel. Spurred on by Reid they traveled to Japan where they stayed for almost two years in "the land of lotus and almond,"[19] although Henry complained at one point because "We have not as yet got our noses out of doors with the rain. It is infernal! The tobacco is running out."[20] After their return in 1894 they were much in demand as speakers. "You have no idea," Henry complained to Hornel, "how I have been pestered by deputations from all the Philosophical Societies and Library Institutes in the country,"[21] and he was quite put out on hearing that Hornel had agreed to speak in public[22] although when Hornel was to lecture in the city art galleries he pleaded an indisposition so that his text was delivered by his friend John Keppie. Doubtless Mackintosh was present and if so he would have listened with more than polite interest to Hornel's "clever and entertaining lecture,"[23] in which he discussed "Japanese art ... the influence of which is now fortunately being felt in all the new movements in Europe." Within that art lay a reverence for nature that "finds its truest expression in their passion for flowers ... Nature ... is symbolism itself ... A few flowers, one or two twigs, quaintly put together in a beautiful vase, and these tiny parts of nature express a thought, a story, or a tradition." Later in his text Hornel wrote of the recent collapse of the power of the ruling feudal lords "who were true patrons of Art ... At that period no dividing line existed between arts and crafts ... nothing being too commonplace to form the basis of some work of art ... in which all useless details are laid aside ... I know of no art which for directness or im-

pressiveness can surpass the past achievements of the Japanese ... We in this country ... in striving to realise Truth have forgotten the Spirit."[24] When Hornel exhibited his Japanese paintings they sold well. "Nothing like them has ever been seen in the city. They are extraordinary, magnificent, sublime. Hornel has arrived!"[25]

Hornel and Keppie were members of the Glasgow Art Club, a fraternity that included the leaders of the city's artistic community, such as Fra Newbery, Alexander Reid, and many of the "Boys." Keppie remained a member until his death in 1945. By then he was "King John." Mackintosh was never a member. It is said that Keppie would have blackballed his application. Why do that to your partner? Perhaps the truth may be that for the willful Mackintosh the artist and architect members were those who conformed.

In their latter years Hornel and Keppie would bring in the new year at Broughton House in the High Street of Kirkcudbright on the Solway Firth. The eighteenth-century town house of a local landed family was purchased by Hornel in 1901. At the rear he laid out in homage to Japan a garden "where miniature lakes and waterfalls with quaint bridges, tiny landscapes with dwarf pines and shrubs relieved with stone lanterns, take you into fairyland ... "[26] Hornel's financial acumen as an artist and as a property investor allowed him to commission Keppie to add a picture gallery and a double-height studio.[27] It is not surprising that Keppie owned one of Hornel's Japanese paintings.[28]

If only because of the proximity of age and their common association with Keppie, Mackintosh and his immediate circle must have been acquainted with Hornel, although to what degree remains unknown. Others of the Boys who were Mackintosh's friends included Alexander Roche and David Gauld, for whom on his marriage in 1893 Mackintosh designed a suite of bedroom furniture.[29]

Given such friendships it is interesting to note that in the homes of Mackintosh and his wife what was displayed were

their works only. Nothing by another artist was to be seen. Nor indeed is there a record of them owning works by others. That was as true of Herbert and Frances McNair as photographs of their home in Liverpool prove. Yet after their return to Glasgow in 1908 their home may have been more conventional as they owned paintings by some of the second generation of Glasgow Boys such as J. Reid Murray (38) and James Mc-Goldrick, who had been an evening student at the Glasgow School of Art along with McNair. The latter owned Hornel's *The Brook*, which he paid for from a win in a prize draw at the Glasgow Institute of the Fine Arts.[30]

The institute's annual show was a highlight in Glasgow's social calendar so that after one conversazione, with the benches crowded with the well-to-do (39), it was noted that "Art [is] fashionable nowadays ... Consequently Hillhead and Kelvinside, not to mention Pollokshields and far-off Dennistoun, turned out in full force. Claw-hammer garb was the order of the night."[31] The institute's policy was, as it still is, to be a showcase for local artists while inviting loan works from national names including, in 1888, Burne-Jones's *The Tower*

39. The Glasgow Institute of the Fine Arts

38. *Calmpthout, Border of Holland*, J. Reid Murray

of *Brass* (40) and Whistler's portrait of his mother.[32] A few years later Beardsley's *Madame Réjane* (41) was in show.[33] An earlier exhibitor was William Stott of Oldham, a friend of Whistler, whose paintings with their extended horizontality and prevalence of blue and green shades were attractive to the Boys.[34] Along with Stott's admired naturalism there was latent symbolism, as in *The Ferry*, in which the composition is two verticals, a young girl, and behind her a silver birch tree, its trunk breaking into foliage as it disappears beyond the upper edge of the canvas. Later the symbolism is explicit, as in *The Nymph* (42), which was reproduced in the *Scottish Art Review* in 1888.[35] The nymph lies on the ground in a wooded glade with, in the foreground, roses and stems confining her body. It was an image that Mackintosh may have utilized, although unconsciously, when designing the frieze in the Buchanan Street tearoom.

Among the Boys who exhibited regularly at the institute's shows was E. A. Walton, the older brother of Mackintosh's contemporary and professional colleague George Walton. His brother's views of Helensburgh, the hilly seaside town to the west of Glasgow, depict horse-drawn carriages bowling along broad tree-fringed streets or unpretentious shops and houses, with a gable here and there, lining the seafront (43)—a microcosm of the comfortable bourgeois life that would be Mr. and Mrs. Blackie's after they commissioned The Hill House at the top of the town. Another regular exhibitor was Stuart Park, who became well known for his cascades of roses spilling from translucent glass vases against milky or sable backgrounds, which presage Mackintosh's stylized rose images.

And what was the hidden message in *The Brook* (44), his "little picture,"[36] that prompted McNair to acquire it? Was it the division between the umbers and russet and the contorted green watercourse, or the girls who with averted countenances gaze into the far distance, into a time and space that man will never know? Some of the same effects of nature had already been seen in George Henry's *A Galloway Landscape* (45), in which the acid tones are riven by a meandering stream. In the next year, 1890, Henry and Hornel collaborated on *The Druids* (46), which, when it

was hung in the Grosvenor Gallery in London later that year, was rated as "the most impressive work" in a show where "a large part of its interest and conspicuous merit is the Glasgow contribution."[37] *The Druids* was an essay on Celtic mythology, in which the triangular grouping of the figures, heightened by gold layering and religious symbols, is marked off by tree trunks, thick rooted like spectral lifeforms. In T. Millie Dow's *At the Edge of the Wood* (1886) and Hornel's *Pigs in a Wood* (1887) it is the trees, by the power of their life force, which take over the composition. Sometimes there are only trees, as in Arthur Melville's *Autumn—Loch Lomond* (1893) with its spindly silver birches (47),

41. *Madame Réjane*, Aubrey Beardsley, *The Studio*

40. *Danae* or *The Tower of Brass*, Sir Edward Burne-Jones

42. *The Nymph,* William Stott, *Scottish Art Review* (*top*)   43. *At Helensburgh,* E. A. Walton (*bottom*)

44. *The Brook*, E. A. Hornel (*top*)   45. *A Galloway Landscape*, George Henry (*bottom*)

46. *The Druids: Bringing in the Mistletoe*, E. A. Hornel and George Henry

which may be the starting point for Mackintosh's *Tree of Influence* and the evocation of the forest in his plaster frieze in the Willow tearoom. However, in Henry's *Noon* (1885), a tree and a young girl are a union, as in the Norse legends, with fibrous roots clutching the soil while spreading across the top of the canvas is a canopy of foliage, like the leafy pendants in the library of the Glasgow School of Art. The allegory of growth and womanhood is epitomized in Millie Dow's *Spring* where a girl, a virginal goddess, is embowered in blossom, a portent of Margaret Macdonald's imaginings.

On occasion the symbolism could jolt nastily. In *The Brownie of Blednock* by Hornel (1889) the hobgoblin, whose beard matches the frondlike tendrils of the passing stream, could fit into the Spook School, where Mackintosh may be included more by association; thus one may ask if Mackintosh's watercolor *The Tree of Influence* (48) might not be a leg-pull, as was surely his *Cabbages in an Orchard* (49), with accompanying text that must be a parody of the Boys' many renderings of cabbages, beginning with Melville's in 1887, although what comes closest to Mackintosh's squib must

47. *Autumn—Loch Lomond*, Arthur Melville

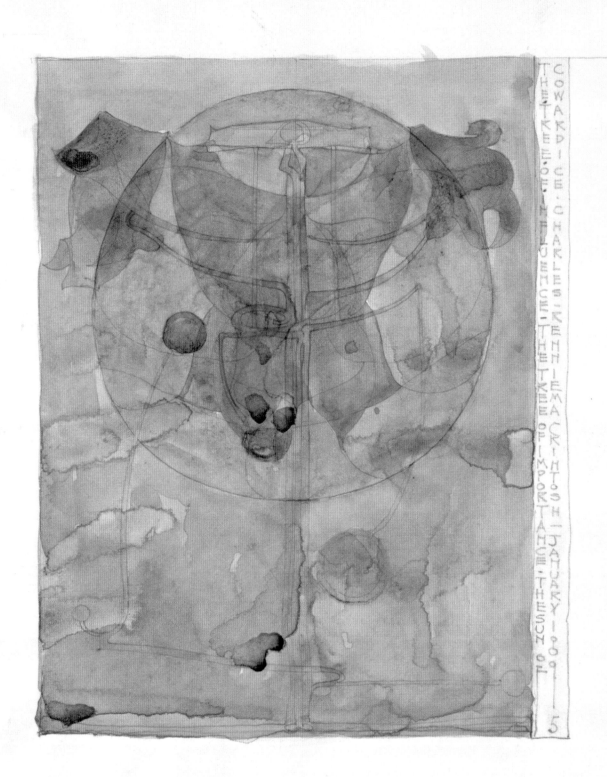

THE · TREE · OF · INFLUENCE · THE · TREE · OF · IMPORTANCE · THE · SUN · OF · COWARDICE · CHARLES · RENNIE · MACKINTOSH — JANUARY · 1909 — 5

surely be Henry's *A Cottar's Garden* (1885) where blowsy cabbages on angular white stocks crowd the foreground.

The opportunity of exhibiting in the institute's galleries was also sought by The Four and their circle.[38] John Keppie, for instance, first entered, in 1888, a street scene in Sienna and, in the following year, using the office address of John Honeyman and Keppie, a design for a memorial to James Sellars. Thereafter, in almost every year until 1943, two years before his death, Keppie showed watercolors, often of scenes in Spain and Egypt; after 1920 there is a preponderance of Scottish scenes frequently of the locality around Kirkcudbright. In 1894 he had painted the rose-red ruins of Sweetheart Abbey to which he returned in 1916 with his sister Jessie, whose institute entry in that year was *The Pond, New Abbey*. Her specialty was flower studies, beginning with *Broom* in 1892 and closing with *Ayrshire Roses* in 1950. One can only speculate about her influence on Mackintosh as a flower painter.

Frances Macdonald's entries were few. *Cornflowers* was shown in 1893, when her sister first exhibited, and four years later *The Star of Bethlehem* and *The Annunciation*, a relief done with Margaret Macdonald, whose name disappears from the catalogues after 1913, as does her husband's. In 1901 they exhibited separate preparatory studies, *The May Queen* and *The Wassail*, for Miss Cranston's Ingram Street tearooms. Apart from some Italian *veduti* in 1892 and '93, the mysterious *Harvest Moon* in the next year and *"Princess Ess" Fairy Tale* five years later, Mackintosh's hung work was architectural, beginning in 1891 with a competition design for a science and art museum, as was that of Herbert McNair. He began exhibiting in 1894 with *Night* and *Design for an English Church*. Then his address was the office of John Honeyman and Keppie; by the next year, however, when he had on the institute walls a *Proposed Cottage at Sea-Coast Town*, he was setting up his own design studio.

It is now claimed that Mackintosh saw himself primarily as an artist.[39] Can that be so? Among Mackintosh's early institute entries *The Harvest Moon* (50) is unique, although as Mackintosh had given it in 1892 to Keppie perhaps it was he who entered it. Certainly it must be telling that none of Mackintosh's flower studies or other nonarchitectural works were put on display, which perhaps reinforces the belief that for Mackintosh, in the early years at least, painting was a hobby, a relaxation while on holiday or when not engaged in the hurly-burly of making architecture.[40] That he preferred to exhibit as an architect certainly saved him from some of the obloquy heaped on his closest associates. "As for the 'ghoul-like' designs of the

49. *Cabbages in an Orchard*, Charles Rennie Mackintosh

48. *The Tree of Influence*, Charles Rennie Mackintosh

Misses Macdonald," wrote one reviewer in 1894, "they were simply hideous and the less said about them the better."[41]

Nothing of such controversies stirs the sedate reporting of the institute's committee meetings, which are concerned with receiving dates for entries in Glasgow, Edinburgh, and London, the provision "that Musical Promenades should be held on Saturday afternoons," and the need "to have Workmen's tickets from the beginning of the Exhibition."[42]

Less ephemeral and more benevolent was the mention by Neil Munro's fictional character Erchie, who, on receipt of two tickets from his minister, took his friend Duffy to the institute show in 1904 for " 'Ye have nae idea o' the fascination Art has for the people o' Gleska . . . There used to be hardly any picture-penters in Gleska; it was a' ship-buildin' and ca-

50. *The Harvest Moon*, Charles Rennie Mackintosh

landerin', witiver that is, and chemical works that needed big lums.' " Their attention was caught by Margaret Macdonald's *The Sleeper*, priced at £45, "a rather peculiar drawing with a lady artist's name attached to it . . . 'That's whit they ca' New Art.' " In the ensuing conversation Erchie explained about lady artists. " 'They bash brass, hack wood and draw pictures.'

" 'An can they mak' a living at that?'

" 'Whiles. And whiles their paw helps.' "[43]

Yet despite, or because of, the public criticism in 1894, it must have been a cause of no small satisfaction when McNair and the Macdonald sisters were asked to produce the institute's poster advertising the 1895 annual exhibition (51) although that, too, aroused passions in one reviewer. "Downstairs there are the posters. Some say they're naughty. See them! but, this caution: study the Poster not according to the gospel of St. Mungo, but according to the creed of St. Lautrec."[44] How the commission came to the three is difficult to say since the institute's committee meeting minutes reveal nothing, although friends and acquaintances, such as Newbery, Keppie, Gauld, Roche, and Millie Dow, were among those who attended annual general meetings.[45] In 1896 Mackintosh was asked to design a poster for *The Scottish Musical Review*. Then fair prospects must have beckoned. McNair and the Macdonald sisters now had their own studios and Mackintosh had won the competition for the new building for the Glasgow School of Art.

In the last decade of the nineteenth century Glasgow must have been brimming with ideas as young men and women argued and debated among themselves, traveled, read the art and architectural journals—and all at a time when the city was at the pinnacle of greatness and prosperity as witnessed in its heavy industries, its outward expansion, and its reflection of its own image in the grandiose public buildings. As one commentator observed: "Glasgow and the west of Scotland, owing to progress in wealth and population, afford a constant field for building operations."[46] There may have been no other city in Britain at the time that could have given Mackintosh what he needed as he entered his chosen profession. ▪▪

51. Poster for the Glasgow Institute of the Fine Arts, Margaret Macdonald, Frances Macdonald, J. Herbert McNair

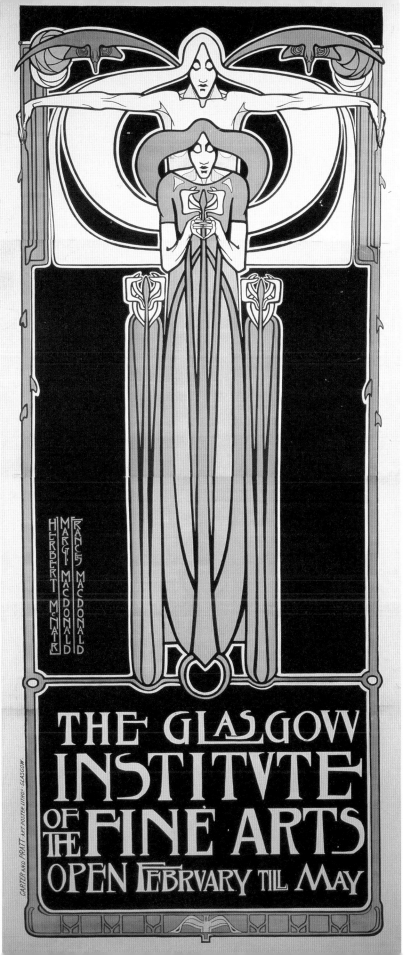

HERBERT McNAIR MARGT MACDONALD FRANCES MACDONALD

CARTER and PRATT ART POSTER LITHO· GLASGOW·

THE GLASGOW
INSTITVTE
OF THE FINE ARTS
OPEN FEBRVARY TILL MAY

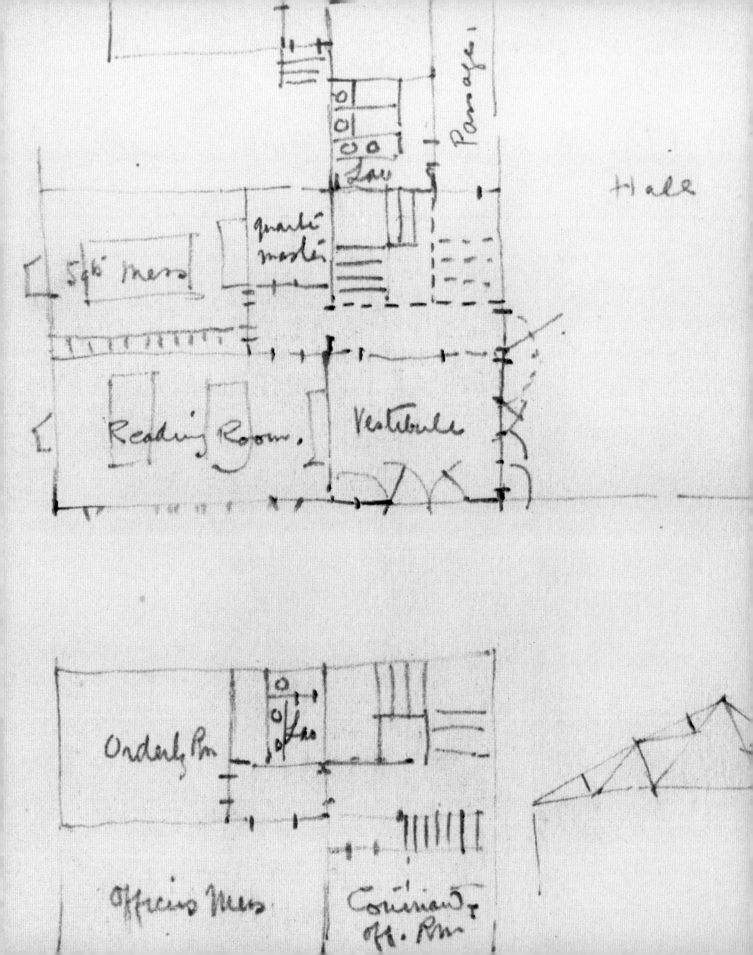

Passage

Hall

Sgts Mess

quarter
master

Lav

Reading Room.

Vestibule

Orderly Rm

Officers Mess

Commandt
Offi Rm

3 ⠿ THE MENTORS

Sketch, Charles Rennie Mackintosh

Once Mackintosh entered the office of John Honeyman he encountered three men who would most affect his professional and personal life. They were John Honeyman (1831–1914), John Keppie (1862–1945), and James Herbert McNair (1868–1955).

Honeyman (52) was the third son of a prosperous Glasgow merchant whose home in Carlton Place, a Regency double terrace in the city center on the south bank of the river Clyde, was upstream from the crowded wharves and noisome shipping traffic. Having served an architectural apprenticeship, John Honeyman could afford the luxury of travel to London and the continent, "studying ecclesiastical architecture in all the cathedral towns of England and in many abroad," before returning to Glasgow where, in his early twenties, he set up his own practice.[1]

Honeyman's first choice of career had been the church but he changed his mind and, as he put it, "lived to edify the church in another way." And, indeed, throughout his long life, Honeyman maintained an interest in all things ecclesiastical, which often matched his antiquarian studies. While still in his early twenties Honeyman was writing on the age of the cathedral,[2] and, more than forty years later, he was a major contributor to *The Book of Glasgow Cathedral*. Was it through Honeyman that Talwin Morris, then the art director of Blackie and Son, received the independent commission for the design of the cover? (53)

When the Aberdeen Ecclesiological Society, of which Honeyman was a member, visited Glasgow in 1894 it was "to meet the members of the newly formed Glasgow Ecclesiological Society, to inspect the Cathedral and the new Barony Parish Church" by J. J. Burnet. Honeyman, as "the Consulting Architect … guided the company" through the cathedral,[3] speaking perhaps of his reordering of the choir and the furbishment of the chancel with a stone reredos before which stood a communion table deeply carved with a representation of the Last Supper.[4]

One senses that Honeyman's love for the Gothic edifice, in his day the largest structure in Glasgow, rubbed off on Mackintosh, whose home lay just over the hill to the east. Al-

ready, during his apprenticeship, he had been sketching the cathedral and its environs. Also among his earliest watercolors are details from Elgin Cathedral, Morayshire, of the remains of the late medieval window tracery with curves, which, with hindsight, could be seen as proto–art nouveau.[5] But why was Mackintosh in Elgin? To collect details for the firm's portfolio? On an antiquarian holiday? Mackintosh's first large watercolor is a rendering of Glasgow cathedral from the east with its unique double story blocked against a tangerine sunset.[6] In Glasgow of the teeming shipyards and hosts of smokestacks, is a medieval cathedral not an unlikely subject for an alert young architect?

Like others of his wealth and standing, when confronted with the dire effects of rapid urban expansion, Honeyman

52. John Honeyman, *The Bailie*

was much exercised by those prime concerns of Victorian urban living: sanitation and ventilation. A paper on "The Drainage of Glasgow and the Purification of the River Clyde, with special reference to the Ventilation of Drains" led to the invention of his much imitated ventilating drain trap. He wrote, too, on housing for the poor, the need for open spaces in towns, as well as on "Trade Unionism, the Blight on British Industry and Commerce." As a leader in his profession, Honeyman was a founder in 1868, along with Thomson and John Burnet, of the Glasgow Architectural Society, of which he became president, as he was of the Glasgow Archaeological Society, of which he had been the first secretary.[7]

Not surprisingly, Honeyman gained numerous church commissions with some forty designs for all denominations issuing from the office prior to the partnership with Keppie. For what he hoped would be his first commission, the spire of the Free Church in the spa town of Moffat in the south of Scotland, Honeyman in 1852, at the age of twenty-one, displays that mix of antiquarianism and technical knowledge that was to serve him so well. The specification, which runs to ten pages, was for the "best freestone from Lockerbriggs quarry, free from all shakes, vents and other imperfections ... The Bosses at ends of label mouldings to be carved in an artist like good style ... Ten courses at top to be of cube through which the iron rod or Vane is to pass." An accompanying letter from 21 Carlton Place, doubtless his parents' home, states: "I submitted the plans to a first rate tradesman ... and his estimate amounts to £180."[8]

The first commission in Glasgow, which was won against other architects, was Lansdowne Church (54), begun in 1862, "when eleven gentlemen met and formed themselves into a Committee for the purpose of founding a church in the locality."[9] For a young architect seeking to make a name in the mid-Victorian Presbyterian city nothing could have attracted greater attention. The dramatic site was the east bank of the river Kelvin just where Great Western Road traverses the gorge to enter the west end. The disposition of the building's components displays Honeyman's innate sense of theater and an understanding of the principles of

church design as espoused by A. W. Pugin and the English Tractarians. Thus the plan is cruciform, the first in Glasgow since the Middle Ages. Honeyman's chosen style was Early English, doubtless dictated by his interest in the cathedral and supported by Ruskin's ringing declaration, "I have now no doubt that the only style proper for modern Northern work, is the Northern Gothic of the thirteenth century."[10] For Scott that was "the native architecture of our own country and that of our forefathers ... as indigenous to our country as are our wild flowers, our family names, as our customs, or our political constitution."[11] The more mundane Charles Eastlake, at almost the same time, was carping about new churches. "But of how many can it be said that

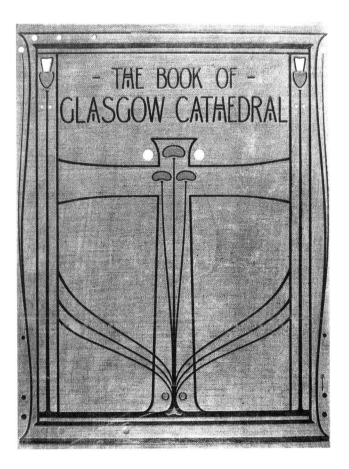

53. Cover for *The Book of Glasgow Cathedral*, Talwin Morris

they are the work of an artist's hands?"[12] At Lansdowne the answer must be in the affirmative since the parts are scholarly, elegant, and well placed in relation to the overall massing, with the more elaborate west elevation looking across fields toward the new residential suburbs. The church proclaims its emblematic status with a spire of 72 meters (218 feet), the most slender in the city, positioned unusually at the east end on the axes of the converging streets. Seating a congregation of one thousand, the church cost £12,400 but the opening collection, "one of the largest then on record,"

54. Lansdowne Church, John Honeyman

recouped a tenth of that,[13] which is perhaps not surprising given that "the erection of the Church and the undertaking generally, which had been so successfully managed," had been directed by merchants, iron founders, a shipowner, and "Callenderer," who together, and uncommonly for the period, sanctioned "a design for a stained glass window . . . prepared by Mr. Hughes of London . . . for the large west window" and "a design for the wooden screen" at the pulpit from Honeyman, whose final account was paid in October 1865 with thanks "for his services during the conduct of the work."[14] Lansdowne has been described justly as the most original of Glasgow's rich inheritance of Victorian churches.[15] However, in his late years, Honeyman could not "regard it with unmixed satisfaction."[16]

Although Honeyman was as much governed by the past as any of his contemporaries, his own output is distinguished by a discernible refinement and a sense of theater, as at Paisley Museum (1868)[17] where the Greek Ionic portico has grace and suppleness ranking it with the more acclaimed essays by Thomson. Honeyman's dramatic representational skill is most manifest at the Barony North Church (1878),[18] just to the south of the cathedral, where a campanile and the four evangels, borne aloft by Corinthian pilasters, soar skyward, with the theatricality softened by the apse, which should house a high altar but here contains a staircase.

Similar public effects are achieved at Westbourne Church. (55) As Thomson had done a quarter of a century before, Honeyman tied his facade into the adjacent terrace by replicating the order. The church was long in the making. In 1875 the Free Church Building Society had sought to establish a church on the western edge of Glasgow. A temporary iron structure was put up for a congregation of thirty-nine, including Michael Honeyman,[19] the architect's brother, who was present when early in 1878 it was resolved that "Mr. Honeyman Architect should be employed as Architect when a new church came to be built." By late October he had prepared drawings "after classical and Gothic designs . . . The classic plans were selected . . . as the most suitable." How-

cvcr, because of the collapse of the City of Glasgow Bank only three weeks before, "in the present gloomy state of business it would be unwise to proceed at once to build a permanent church," although there would be a meeting with the architect "to have carefully prepared estimates of the cost of erecting a Church after the style of the second classic design submitted." A year passed when, despite objections because only one architect had been approached and

despite the city's recession, it was agreed to build using "a classic design as being best suited to the site and more likely to secure internal comfort and good acoustics" because of the galleried hall plan. Although the completed building at £9,698 was a third over the estimate[20] more than half the expenditure was repaid within six months of the opening by the congregation, which included some of Glasgow's wealthier citizens such as Collins, the printer, as well as three

55. Westbourne Church, John Honeyman

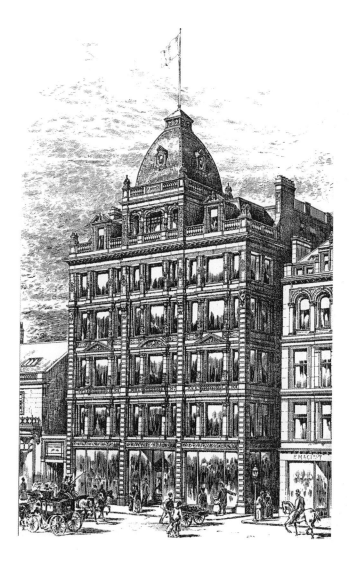

members of the Blackie family, including Robert Blackie at 7 Great western Terrace.[21] That there were wealthy folk, too, among the Lansdowne congregation had prompted an oft repeated ditty.

> This Church is not for the poor and needy
> But for the rich and Dr. Eadie.
> The rich step in and take their seat
> But the poor walk down to Cambridge Street.

56. Wylie Hill's warehouse, John Hutchison, *British Architect*

Yet both congregations were engaged in what today would be termed outreach programs in poorer neighborhoods. "Missionary operations are carried on with zeal and success" by a missionary and a "Bible-Woman." Lansdowne also supported a day school with some four hundred children. "A forenoon meeting of poor children ... under the auspices of the Foundry Boys Society" had an attendance of between two and three hundred with the same number filling a "Sabbath evening School."[22] An even more developed social program organized from Westbourne Church led to the foundation in 1898 of the Ruchill Mission hall designed by Mackintosh.

When Mackintosh began working for Honeyman he would have looked with interest at the firm's output and perhaps especially at the Ca' d'Oro warehouse in the heart of the city's commercial district and a street away from a warehouse (56) on the design and construction of which Mackintosh would have worked at the close of his apprenticeship with John Hutchison. Its style was described as Italian Renaissance; the facade with its wide window spans was "treated so as to give as much light as possible to the interior ... The entire building is fireproof construction ... The iron beams and columns are covered with titancrete, a new fireproof material."[23] Hutchison's office was in St. Vincent Street at the back of a furniture shop owned by his brother. Here Mackintosh was under the tutelage of Andrew Black. Mackintosh made an early impression in the office with his drawings of Ionic capitals, which were different from the copybook examples then common and which he would use later on in the *Glasgow Herald* building.[24]

When the Egyptian Halls were nearing completion "Greek" Thomson had written to his brother in the late summer of 1872: "Mr. Robertson is still unwilling to subdivide the upper floors ... The Smiths in Clyde Street were the only parties who made any serious proposals but they would not give the rent asked and as they bought the property between Union Street and Melville Lane including Thomas Hamble's shop and have pulled down the whole concern and began to build from plans by Mr. Honeyman."[25] As the Smiths were furniture warehousemen, the Egyptian Halls with deep floor plans and a single frontage of low ranges of windows deepset behind chunky stone columns were not for them. Their requirements for a strong yet well-illuminated structure were provided on the adjacent corner by a right-angled ferro-vitreous arcade on a stone base.

That Glasgow has a collection, unsurpassed in Britain, of cast-iron edifices should be no surprise given the city's pioneering achievements in engineering technology. As the majority were erected in the 1850s, the Ca' d'Oro (57) closes the sequence, which, given its provenance, is appropriate. In 1864, for the head office down by the river of the shipping magnates G. and J. Burns, Honeyman, in his first commercial building, integrated visible iron construction with classical details filched from seafaring Venice.[26] At the Ca' d'Oro, however, the historical detailing of the late medieval prototype was effaced in favor of decoration allied to construction (58), proclaiming allegiance to Ruskinian dogma with the double-height basement and the resolution of the vertical ascent within open-ended figures of eight (59), predating Louis Sullivan's Guaranty Building by a decade.

The 1870s were Honeyman's most prolific decade. With ninety-six entries in the job books he could afford to have a second home and a yacht at Skelmorlie on the Clyde coast.[27] These were to prove an investment since the slackening commercial and ecclesiastical commissions were compensated for in part by a succession of marine mansions around the Clyde estuary. Two of these have a relevance for Mackintosh.

The first was Skipness House, begun in 1880, in the shelter of the northeast corner at the head of the Kintyre penin-

sula in Argyll and commanding spectacular views down the Kilbrannan Sound to the island of Arran and the Ayrshire coast beyond. The site would have aroused Honeyman's enthusiasm since it contained the medieval Skipness Castle with its curtain wall embracing a sea gate and protecting a sixteenth-century tower house.[28] Here was inspiration for Honeyman's archaeological zeal. "Nothing," he wrote, "more distinctly national in its way is to be found in any country than the ancient castellated architecture of Scotland.

"The central feature out of which this Scottish so-called baronial style developed was the square tower or keep which in itself often rose to a great height ... by degrees became grafted the charming turrets, the gables and the other

57. Ca' d'Oro, John Honeyman

decorative accessories which add a grace and dignity to the square sombre masses that form the central feature of medieval Scottish mansions."[29] With a client keen on preserving the authentic medieval remains his architect could justifiably rededicate the forms of a baronial past, make obeisance to Scotland's unique inheritance of the tower house, and visibly connect past and present by using gray schist for walling with red sandstone dressings as in the prototype from which came, too, dimensions, scale, gables, chim-

ney stacks, and corner turrets. For Honeyman other architectural formulae in that setting would have been as unacceptable as the displaced Georgian harled mansion.

The layout of Skipness House (60) conformed to what had been developed throughout the century in response to the Picturesque.[30] A tall, narrow entrance front obscured family rooms strung along two floors on the seaward side (61), which were equaled in extent by the domestic offices arranged as subsidiary elements around the service yard and given con-

58, 59. Ca' d'Oro, John Honeyman

60, 61. Skipness House, John Honeyman (*opposite*)

AUCHAMORE HOUSE, GIGHA
JOHN HONEYMAN, R.S.A. ARCHITECT

delft tiles in the fireplace. The staircase, passing below stained-glass windows, ascended to an open gallery communicating with the withdrawing room, library, and family bedrooms with guest rooms stacked in the tower. The hall, as the heart of the household, used for family prayers, parties, and gatherings of tenants, was given an external identity by its horizontality and Tudor lights abutting the tower. Refined and scholarly, Skipness House had none of the bombast and overdecoration that made much Scottish baronialism a parody of itself.

The authenticity of Honeyman's handling of the tower-house theme at Skipness was diminished at Auchamore House (62) on the island of Gigha lying off the west coast of the Kintyre peninsula and therefore only a few geographical miles over the hills from Skipness. At the latter the use of a softer stone for the dressings and the disposition of the windows to match internal space makes the tower read true whereas at the larger Auchamore the conjunction of bay windows with design borrowings from Castle Menzies, Perthshire, and Fyvie Castle, Aberdeenshire, unbalance the historical equation. When Auchamore was on the job books of Honeyman and Keppie in 1896 and '97,[31] was it the younger

formity to the overall style with crow-stepped gables and a red sandstone trim delineating the laundry, kitchen, and butler's domain, each of which dominated its own range.

The family entrance, at the base of the tower, led into a double-height hall darkly paneled and with blue and white

partner who had control?[32] Did Mackintosh visit the site? Did he wonder at the spread of the domestic offices? (63) Did he ponder on harled walls with turrets and dormers dancing between the crow-stepped gables like so many phantasmagoric beasties? Were these the thoughts that

62, 63. Auchamore House and plan, John Honeyman and Keppie, *Academy Architecture*

would become the plan of The Hill House or the south view of the Glasgow School of Art?

One senses, one does not know, an empathy between Honeyman and the talented young draughtsman. For someone, too, with a professed love of his native architecture there could have been no better teacher than the fastidious, erudite Honeyman who would have taken in Mackintosh, freed from his apprenticeship, on merit rather than as a marriage of convenience, as was the case perhaps with Keppie. But when did Mackintosh begin his employment with

KEPPIE

1922

15. Dec. 11-15 p.m.

64. John Keppie by James Salmon

Honeyman? The accepted date is 1889 and that he followed Keppie. However, in his application in 1906 for fellowship of the Royal Institute of British Architects,[33] with Keppie as the proposer and J. J. Burnet as a supporter, Mackintosh stated: "Apprenticeship started August 1883. Draughtsman with Messrs. Honeyman and Keppie from 1888 till being assumed a partner." Keppie, on his part, states that his acquaintanceship with Mackintosh "commenced in the year 1881"—and that raises further questions! Was it Mackintosh who eased the path to Honeyman's office door for Keppie? Or was it because Keppie's family had Ayrshire connections with their house in Prestrwick? There was the death of Sellars[34] and the opportunity for Keppie to bring to Honeyman's practice the outstanding work from Sellars's portfolio at a time when Honeyman's workload and, therefore, income was diminishing.[35] Yet perhaps the simple facts are that Keppie, with his up-to-date knowledge of advanced French design and the success of the much acclaimed exhibition of 1888, was seen as a rising star. Even so, was Mackintosh the more favored of the new entrants? Was he, the younger professional, more open to Honeyman's guidance whereas for Keppie, having been the pupil and assistant of Sellars, "this association was the principal formative influence in Keppie's architectural life."[36]

In later years there were many who would not speak (if speak they did) kindly of Mackintosh. But of Keppie (64) nobody speaks with warmth or affection. Yet this was the man who was lauded in the weekly magazine *Quiz* in 1893 as "One of the most popular of our younger Glasgow architects."[37] Throughout his long life he remained on good terms with his contemporaries among the younger Glasgow Boys. His particular friend was E. A. Hornel, whose oil paintings of apple-cheeked girls in dappled bluebell woods or by the Solway shore provided a handsome income. In *Five Red Herrings*, from 1931, Dorothy L. Sayers depicts a thinly disguised Hornel as "well known and well liked, in spite of his small vanities and somewhat overbearing manner. He was wealthy, kept a good house, with an English butler and housekeeper, and owned two cars, with a chauffeur to drive them when required."[38] Was it the same man who in 1893 at a show in the Glasgow Art Club stuck a blue cow and "an abnormal moon" with wafers onto one of Henry's paintings?[39]

When Hornel wished to add to his eighteenth-century town house in Kirkcudbright's High Street in 1909 he turned to Keppie to provide first a double—height studio and then, between it and the house, a top-lit gallery or salon.[40] It was here that Keppie would come (65) with his sister and others "bringing in the New Year as usual," as he wrote once to Mackintosh,[41] although in 1930 the photographer Annan did "not feel well enough to come to Kirkcudbright so that I am afraid your party will be smaller than usual."[42]

Keppie was a son of a prosperous tobacco merchant and snuff manufacturer in Glasgow, which allowed him to study in Paris at the atelier of Jean Louis Pascal for eighteen months.[43] A French Beaux-Arts training and tutelage under Sellars fixed in him a love of surface plasticity in architecture, which found expression in the union of Renaissance idioms with integral sculpture as on Anderson's Medical College. As another

65. John Keppie, E. A. Hornel, [unidentified], and Hornel's sister Elizabeth, the gallery, Broughton House

Glasgow man noted, it was "a style that has powerfully influenced modern work."[44]

In the opening minute of the college's board of governors in May 1887[45] a building committee was appointed "to look out for a suitable site for the erection of buildings." By late summer James Sellars was advising about a site to the south of the university "and he is to submit sketch plans of the principal floors shewing the kind and extent of accommodation which can be obtained on the ground at the cost indicated viz: £5,000." Although the site was changed to one adjacent to the Western Infirmary after a site visit by the committee "with several of the professors of the Medical Faculty" and Sellars not all the ground would "be necessary for a building containing accommodation similar to that shewn on the sketch plan marked B." In March 1888 the governors had before them "plans of the proposed ground, first and second floors of the new School lithographed copies of which had previously been sent to the Governors and Elevation Sketch all prepared by Mr. James Sellars, Architect" (66), to cost £6,500. With a "new elevation plan" (67) a month later it was agreed to seek estimates that, with the 10 percent for fees, clerk of works, contingencies, and fitting out, totaled close on £8,500. Sellars, "along with the Medical Faculty, had visited the Edinburgh Medical School, after which the plans had been reconsidered for increased accommodation." Then on 9 October 1888 intimation was given of "the death that morning of the architect, Mr. James Sellars." A month later the building committee learned that "the existing plans and drawings are, under the superintendence of Mr. Sellars, prepared by Mr. John Keppie, Architect, who, however, has since Mr. Sellar's [sic] death, left the firm of Messrs. Campbell Douglas and Sellars, and joined Mr. John Honeyman, Architect, in partnership." Three years later the college opened its doors to students.

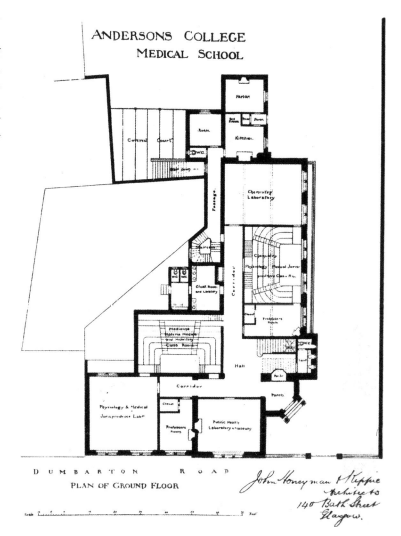

66. Anderson College Medical School, ground-floor plan, John Honeyman and Keppie

Keppie's interest in sculpture was reinforced by his friendship with the sculptor J. Pittendrigh Macgillivray. Thus, at a council meeting of the Royal Glasgow Institute of the Fine Arts in December 1891, "It was arranged that Mr. John Keppie act with Mr. MacGillivray in selecting and arranging sculpture."[46] At the medical college Macgillivray executed a life-size figurative group in which Dr. Peter Lowe, the founder of the teaching of medicine in the university, takes

a patient's pulse. The next commission was a pair of free-standing figures of a shipwright and an engineer on prows by the entrance to the offices of the Fairfield Shipbuilding and Engineering Company (68), established after the early death of John Elder. As a commentator had noted in his lifetime: "Messrs. John Elder's is fast becoming quite a show place. A distinguished visitor is always taken there first, and thereafter he is usually trotted down to Dixon's Blazes.

"Some how or other no one seems to think of taking him to St. Rollox Chemical Works. And yet a bigger or more evil smelling work no city can boast of."[47]

Given the patronage extended to Honeyman by the Elder family it can only have been expected that his firm would be

engaged, immediately the new company came into being, "and laid upon the table the proposed plans thereof, five in number ... the estimated cost of the proposed erection is between £10,500 and £11,000." Unfortunately, when "all the measurements had been received" three years later the costs exceeded the estimate by a third. "Mr. Honeyman's account for £820 for Professional Services was laid on the table. After an expression of opinion on the work done by Mr. Honeyman and especially in regard to the want of ventilation in the offices," the fee was reduced to £600, which the architect disputed.[48]

Although the Fairfield commission had come to his practice through Honeyman the stylistic evidence points to Kep-

67. Anderson College Medical School, John Honeyman and Keppie

68. Fairfield's Offices, John Honeyman and Keppie

still a young man, McNair could afford to pay £30 for Hornel's *The Brook*, one of several works that he acquired from the Glasgow Boys. Doubtless, Mackintosh was not in a position to afford such expenditure.

Of the early years of Mackintosh and McNair in the office of John Honeyman and Keppie one cannot speak. Doubtless, they would answer to one or other partner and do what was asked of them. However, when work was slack, McNair, as he told Howarth, "used to take illustrated objects ... chairs for example," and there were many, especially French boudoir pieces with sinuous curves, in the architectural journals of the day, "place tracing paper over them and try to improve on the original design, or better still, to evolve entirely new forms of his own invention."[60] Thus, when Howarth came to consider the two men's early artistic works he was of the opinion that "It is thus probable that he, and not Mackintosh, was the first of the Glasgow group to break new ground." A paper frieze by McNair of mermaids, the family crest, and a frieze of cats, his clan crest, by Mackintosh led Howarth to conclude that "the two friends were experimenting with original forms by 1890 at least."[61]

Five minutes away from the office was the art school, housed in the McLellan Galleries, where both men attended evening classes. The official records show that in 1891 McNair was examined in shading from models and painting the human figure and animals from casts. In the following year he won a book prize for a design for a village library and was drawing from the antique. In his next year in design and architectural design he attained second class and in 1894 in architectural and building construction he prepared a measured drawing and original designs, both of which were unpremiated. Unfortunately, nothing of McNair's student work survives.

Mackintosh first enrolled in the art school in 1883 and his last record as a student is in 1893. Between these years he won a handful of prizes[62] and in 1889 entered for the Alexander Thomson Travelling Studentship, possibly at the instigation of John Honeyman who had been an early trustee.

With the death in 1875 of Thomson, "an architect of genius, and an amiable and honourable man," as Keppie wrote, "Glas-gow and Scotland lost one of the greatest practitioners of Architecture which it ever possessed."[63] The Glasgow Institute of Architects initiated a memorial "and having invited the co-operation of Mr. Thomson's non-professional friends" opened a subscription list. Donations came solely from the west of Scotland. Honeyman gave £5, John Burnet double that, which was matched by Campbell Douglas and Sellars, and by Robert Blackie, a trustee, and by his fellow trustee the sculptor John Mossman. Other sums came from Thomson family members, iron founders, such as Walter Macfarlane, the photographers T. and R. Annan, and from tradesmen, including Andrew

73. Fairfield's board room, John Honeyman and Keppie

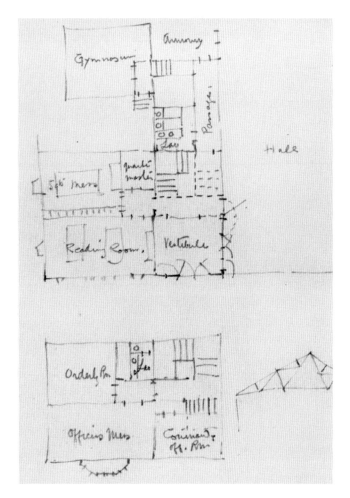

was the Geilston Hall (69), an assortment of offices for the local Volunteers, which required only an architectural mask to the roadway. (70) Just the job to hand to an eager recruit, as his first office assignment (71), who scribbled down his thoughts, probably at a site visit, in his pocket notebook.[50]

As Keppie was formerly the assistant to Sellars, once he was a partner of Honeyman who was Keppie's assistant? Office staff changed from year to year but a photograph (72) shows the junior staff perhaps in 1889 who include Alexander McGibbon, Mackintosh, McNair, and Charles Whitelaw, another who had studied at the Pascal atelier.[51] At the Fairfield offices, hiding from public view the myriads of grim, toiling men swarming over the ribs and flesh of ships, who was it then who drew out the capitals, scaled the pediment, detailed the board room (73), and in so doing gave the door handles a novel twist? Was it Mackintosh, newly re-

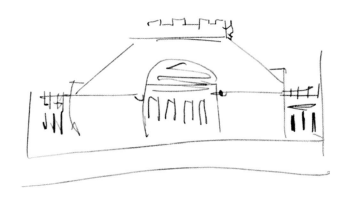

pie as the designer. He had learned much from his stay in France and doubtless, too, from his recent trip to the Paris exhibition. Yet why would Honeyman hand such a prestigious job to Keppie? That he was a young partner of promise and that Honeyman was now sixty would seem reasons enough. Perhaps, too, Honeyman was adapting to a supervisory role within the firm and limiting himself to design problems of particular interest such as the reordering of the cathedral chancel with new stalls and marble flooring or the massing of Craigrownie Church, Cove, with a liturgical division of nave, chancel, and transepts.[49] On the same littoral

69. Sketch, Charles Rennie Mackintosh

70. Sketch, Charles Rennie Mackintosh

was with Sir John Moore at the fatal Battle of Corunna and became a Knight of Hanover.[56] Greenfield was notable for its coal mines, which in 1779 were worth £4,000 to £5,000 annually possibly because they were the first with a steam engine to pump water from the pits.[57] In 1823 the output of coal from Greenfield was 20,000 cartloads.[58] However, as the nineteenth century wore on, the seams became exhausted and there were closures.[59]

Although the family fortune was in decline, and Herbert McNair was the younger son of a younger son, he was not without family means. Important, too, must have been his family background. What, for instance, did the eighteenth-century mansion of Greenfield contain in the way of pictures and furnishings? What was in his father's house at Skelmorlie? Surely a wealthy and, one assumes, a cultured and cosmopolitan background gave him the confidence and assurance to be attractive to Honeyman and to Keppie. Mackintosh, reared in artisan Dennistoun, would have had a more limited outlook. It is significant, for example, that in 1890, when

leased from his apprenticeship, whose design for the Science and Art Museum[52] relates to the Fairfield facade? Or was it James Herbert McNair who, according to Howarth, would resist and eventually, rebelling against Keppie's pedantry, quit the firm in 1895?[53]

McNair would have been a protégé of Honeyman. His father lived at Birchbank, Skelmorlie, and his name is entered in the firm's job books as a client in the early 1870s.[54] McNair's father wanted his son to be an engineer but eventually allowed him to spend a year in Rouen studying watercolor painting.[55] In 1889 Herbert McNair first appears in the art school records as an "Apprentice Architect" living in Buckingham Street around the corner from Fra Newbery. The McNairs were a landed, armigerous family whose coat of arms is emblazoned on a window in the cathedral sacristy.

The initial family fortune was made from sugar refining, which allowed for the purchase of a clutch of estates on the eastern edge of Glasgow. In 1759 McNair's great-grandfather purchased the lands of Greenfield (74), to the east of the city, to which he added neighboring Shettleston three years later. The next laird was an officer in the Peninsular campaign, who

71. Geilston Hall, Cardross,
John Honeyman and Keppie

72. The office staff of Honeyman and Keppie.
J. Herbert McNair (center), Charles Rennie Mackintosh (right);
bottom row Alexander McGibbon (center), Charles Whitelaw (right)

still a young man, McNair could afford to pay £30 for Hornel's *The Brook*, one of several works that he acquired from the Glasgow Boys. Doubtless, Mackintosh was not in a position to afford such expenditure.

Of the early years of Mackintosh and McNair in the office of John Honeyman and Keppie one cannot speak. Doubtless, they would answer to one or other partner and do what was asked of them. However, when work was slack, McNair, as he told Howarth, "used to take illustrated objects ... chairs for example," and there were many, especially French boudoir pieces with sinuous curves, in the architectural journals of the day, "place tracing paper over them and try to improve on the original design, or better still, to evolve entirely new forms of his own invention."[60] Thus, when Howarth came to consider the two men's early artistic works he was of the opinion that "It is thus probable that he, and not Mackintosh, was the first of the Glasgow group to break new ground." A paper frieze by McNair of mermaids, the family crest, and a frieze of cats, his clan crest, by Mackintosh led Howarth to conclude that "the two friends were experimenting with original forms by 1890 at least."[61]

Five minutes away from the office was the art school, housed in the McLellan Galleries, where both men attended evening classes. The official records show that in 1891 McNair was examined in shading from models and painting the human figure and animals from casts. In the following year he won a book prize for a design for a village library and was drawing from the antique. In his next year in design and architectural design he attained second class and in 1894 in architectural and building construction he prepared a measured drawing and original designs, both of which were unpremiated. Unfortunately, nothing of McNair's student work survives.

Mackintosh first enrolled in the art school in 1883 and his last record as a student is in 1893. Between these years he won a handful of prizes[62] and in 1889 entered for the Alexander Thomson Travelling Studentship, possibly at the instigation of John Honeyman who had been an early trustee.

With the death in 1875 of Thomson, "an architect of genius, and an amiable and honourable man," as Keppie wrote, "Glasgow and Scotland lost one of the greatest practitioners of Architecture which it ever possessed."[63] The Glasgow Institute of Architects initiated a memorial "and having invited the co-operation of Mr. Thomson's non-professional friends" opened a subscription list. Donations came solely from the west of Scotland. Honeyman gave £5, John Burnet double that, which was matched by Campbell Douglas and Sellars, and by Robert Blackie, a trustee, and by his fellow trustee the sculptor John Mossman. Other sums came from Thomson family members, iron founders, such as Walter Macfarlane, the photographers T. and R. Annan, and from tradesmen, including Andrew

73. Fairfield's board room, John Honeyman and Keppie

Wells. Nearly £800 was raised. A bust of Thomson was commissioned from Mossman with the interest on the remaining capital, providing a triennial traveling studentship for those between eighteen and twenty-five years.[64] Given that Thomson himself had never been abroad it was a curious decision.

After the first award in 1887 the second was to be made in 1890, with a prize of £60 to be paid in two equal installments "when the student has made arrangements to travel satisfactory to the Trustees" and after the receipt of drawings and notes as evidence of the student "having made the

improvements of his travels during at least three months." In November 1889 the subject was announced as "an original design for a public hall to accommodate 1,000 persons (seated) with suitable committee rooms and the design to be in the early Classic style, and for an isolated site." Between eight and ten drawings, of 40 inches by 27 inches, would include plans, elevation, sections, a perspective and services. "Details showing carving or sculpture are desirable." Five hundred copies of the conditions would be printed and advertisements placed in the *Architect*, *British Architect*, *Builder*, and *Building News*.

In September 1890 the five entries were put on public display in the corporation galleries,[65] which prompted the observation in the local weekly journal *The Bailie*, "It is to be hoped that the Trustees will this time in sending the successful competitor abroad to study have some regard for the genius of Thomson, and direct him to the consideration of some other style than that debased and meretricious Italian which was to Thomson an abomination."[66] On the following day the trustees assembled, and "after lengthy examination" of the entries they voted and "the sealed envelope bearing the motto attached to the drawings being opened it was found that the successful competitor is Mr. Chas. R. McIntosh, 2 Firpark Terrace, Dennistoun," which

news was duly reported to the architectural press.[67] Not only had Mackintosh selected the Ionic order, Thomson's preferred order, but he had composed his elevation and indeed his plan with numerous Thomson idioms, repeated by Sellars in the St. Andrew's Halls, such as pseudo-isodomic masonry construction in the basement and life-size figurative sculptured groups above. A few weeks later Newbery requested the loan of the drawings to be dispatched with other work from the art school to South Kensington, where they won a gold medal[68] despite the criticism that the design "loses something of effect from the placing of large statues above smaller ones."[69]

In the spring of 1891 two of the trustees and the secretary met with "Mr. Chas. R. McIntosh, the young gentleman to whom the prize had been awarded on 18 Sept. 1890." Mackintosh submitted his proposed tour on a map that he had prepared and asked, as he intended to be abroad for nine months, if he could receive the second installment of the prize money "when he had spent three months in Italy." That having been agreed, "The first half (£30) of the prize money was then paid to Mr. McIntosh and the Committee united in offering to him their best wishes for a successful tour and safe return."[70] Like Honeyman, Keppie, and McNair, Mackintosh would go abroad. ▪▪

74. Greenfield (demolished)

4 ⠿ ITALY

Sant' Apollinare Nuovo, Charles Rennie Mackintosh

he late Professor Howarth wrote that John Ruskin (1819–1900) was one of Mackintosh's favourite authors.[1] Though Howarth does not substantiate the remark, his text has sufficient references to Ruskin to imply that the noted art critic exercised an influence on the thinking and appreciative understanding of his Glasgow disciple. On the other hand another commentator, writing in 1968, on the centenary of the architect's birth, declared that "Mackintosh, as might be expected, was opposed to Ruskin's theory and methods,"[2] a contention that might be supported when one considers a review of the fourth edition of Ruskin's *The Stones of Venice* published in *The Builder* in August 1888 and which Mackintosh, at some time, transcribed in part.

What prompted Mackintosh's extensive notes? Were they to be private observations, a commentary derived from careful reading and judicious weighing up of the contents of the three volumes that constituted Ruskin's treatise on the architecture of Venice? That hardly seems likely. One has the impression that Mackintosh's careful copying from *The Builder*'s text was intended for a public in much the same way as his later lectures. Indeed, is it only coincidence that his copied text should have been retained by him along with his notes for his public lectures?

Like most architects in practice Mackintosh had neither the time nor the inclination to write about the profession of an architect. Perhaps, therefore, Mackintosh's curtailed copy of the review, since the text stops abruptly and is shorter than any of his surviving public lectures, was intended for a student seminar or debate. The barbed wit and heavy sarcasm of the reviewer would have gone down well with students versed in Ruskinian dogma. Perhaps just such an occasion was when Douglas Penman, a contemporary of Mackintosh, read a paper on *The Stones of Venice* to the Glasgow Architectural Association in the autumn of 1891,[3] when Mackintosh was fresh from his time in Italy. On the other hand it may be significant if the review was copied prior to his departure although that seems less likely.

John Ruskin was the most famous and most influential art critic of the Victorian age. At the age of eighteen he began publishing in 1837 and 1838 a series of articles on the "Poetry of Architecture." The title is significant in the context of Mackintosh for Ruskin's concern was the analysis, the understanding of architecture, an emotional penetration through the medium of words. Because he was a superlative writer, with an almost lyrical note in his compositions, his influence was vast especially after the publication in 1849 of *The Seven Lamps of Architecture*, "a book which was," according to Lord Clark, "in the history of taste, perhaps the most influential ever published."[4] In 1851 the first volume of *The Stones of Venice* appeared; volumes two and three were published two years later. Numerous subsequent editions of both works followed with the second edition of *The Seven Lamps of Architecture* in 1855 containing the famous preface as the summation of Ruskin's architectural philosophy.

In matters of architectural style Ruskin was prepared only to admit four categories as worthy of consideration. These were Pisan Romanesque, Florentine work prior to the Renaissance, Venetian Gothic, and English Decorated.[5] In essence, Ruskin preferred these as being superior in construction to Greek and Roman.[6] Although for Pugin honesty

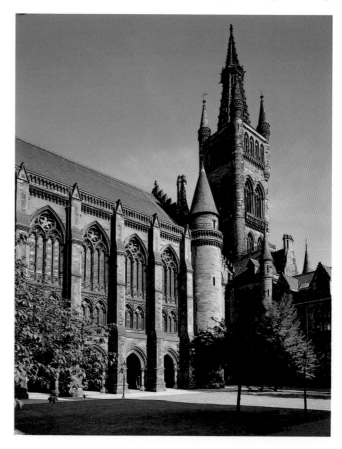

75. University of Glasgow,
Sir George Gilbert Scott and J. Oldrid Scott

of revealed construction was the indelible truth of architecture, for Ruskin it was ornament that was the principal part of construction and ornament should be visible, natural, and thoughtful.[7] In short, Gothic architecture, an alliance of construction and ornament, was what should be chiefly built. The teachings of Pugin and of Ruskin differed also in that for the latter sound construction was building since "All architecture proposes an effect on the human mind, not merely a service to the human frame,"[8] so that in 1855 he could write: "The fact is, there are only two fine arts possible to the human race, sculpture and painting. What we call architecture is only the association of these in noble masses, or the placing of them in fit places. All architecture other than this is, in fact, mere building."[9] And, he declared, "The forms of architecture already known are good enough for us, and for far better than any of us."[10] Yet Ruskin, despite his shortcomings, despite his distrust of structure, despite his appreciation of surface rather than of form, saw clearly the need for a morally sound architecture as a regenerative force eschewing imitation or copying. Not all, however, were convinced, for "professional architects, as a rule, regarded him in the light of a vain and misinformed enthusiast."[11] That was Eastlake in 1872, the year of the Ca' d'Oro, which is the very model of Ruskinian doctrine in that the window tracery supports the building.[12]

Another Ruskinian exemplar was Sir George Gilbert Scott's new buildings for the University of Glasgow. Composed in Ruskin's Northern Gothic the broad style was Anglo-French larded with features from Scotland's past and specifically from the university's former home, the old college in the High Street, details of which were sketched by the young Mackintosh prior to its demolition. Certainly Mackintosh would have agreed with Scott's sentiment that "we aim not at dead antiquarian revival, but at developing upon the basis of the indigenous architecture of our country, a style which will be pre-eminently of our own age,"[13] although he would not have accepted Scott's attack on "the wretched routine of our vernacular architecture."[14]

In the new university buildings (75), in use since 1870, there would have been much to interest Mackintosh, including the

iron columns, with foliated capitals, and iron-ornamented beams in the examination rooms (76) demonstrating Scott's professed belief, "Metallic construction is the great development of our age."[15] Another Ruskinian commitment to the alliance of construction and decoration was the vegetative stone carvings supporting iron balusters on the principal staircase.

It is, of course, ironic, given Thomson's well-known bias against the faults and failings of classical Roman architecture, that when Mackintosh won the Thomson Travelling Studentship he elected to travel to Italy. Perhaps, however, Mackintosh had been enchanted by Ruskin. Certainly, Mackintosh's travel diary—at the front of which he had inscribed his name and full address, like a schoolboy with a clean jotter at the start of the school session and from which came

76. University of Glasgow, Sir George Gilbert Scott

the essay for the Thomson trustees, along with the water-colors and sketches he was under an obligation to pro-duce—shows how imbued Mackintosh was by Ruskinian dogma. He was not alone. George McKenzie, on his journey around Italy two years previously, having viewed Titian's *Assumption of the Virgin* in the Bologna Academy, noted, "It is very fine although Ruskin runs it down most unmercifully."[16]

It was almost in a laconic vein that Mackintosh began his Italian diary. "I left Glasgow in February and after spending some days in London, sailed for Naples,"[17] where he arrived on the morning of Sunday, April 5, and in the afternoon made an excursion to Pompeii where he would later spend two days sketching. The main attraction in Naples was the museum housing the former royal collections including the numerous antique remains and sculptures inherited from the Farnese family. With such celebrated works as the Far-nese Hercules and the Farnese Bull the collection rivaled those in the Vatican and Capitoline museums in Rome. On his first visit Mackintosh "started to sketch but was turned out at four o'clock." This was to become a familiar plaint es-pecially as "Some churches are open from 10 till 12 and some from 3 till 5 find it a great nuisance going to a church and finding it shut."[18] As a northern Presbyterian Mackintosh must have been somewhat astounded when confronted for the first time with the exotic panoply of Catholicism and the zealotry of southern Italian baroque so that in his first church "the decoration surpassed anything I had seen be-fore." Other churches were shut, the duomo was under scaffolding, but Santa Maria del Carmine did have a "very good tower of which I took a sketch." (77) Toward the end of his stay in Naples the weather broke so he "wrote letters to Herbert McNair and Geo. Murray,"[19] abandoned a pro-jected visit to Paestum with its Greek temples, and set off in-stead for Sicily enduring a rough passage on a vessel "Just like a Clyde tug boat."[20]

At Palermo, which he found to be a "very much finer town than Naples," the weather was, if anything, worse so that often the cold and the rain forced him to abandon sketching. Another hazard was the curiosity of the Italians.

He had inspected the important collection of Romanesque churches, the cathedral being "all most miserable classic,"[21] and was drawing the finest surviving example of Norman-Saracenic architecture, the campanile of the church of the Martorana, when he was surrounded by "about 50 people looking at me as if I was a wild beast. Got very angry then

77. Santa Maria del Carmine, Charles Rennie Mackintosh

thought I would try the effect of laughing. Laughed at the crowd. They just looked at me as if I was mad."[22] What most entranced Mackintosh were the mosaic decorations. "Here was something I have never seen, never even dreamt of."[23] When visiting the royal palace, "Almost fainted on the spot with the magnificence of the interior of this chapel."[24] Its sparse geometry, defined by a nave arcade of reused Roman columns and capitals, was clothed with Byzantine mosaics as was the contemporary cathedral of Monreale. Founded in the late twelfth century and possibly the most notable monument of the Middle Ages in Italy, Monreale exhibits mosaics depicting episodes from the Testaments with the whole dominated by the portrait of Christ in the central apse. "Fairly took away my breath."[25]

In Rome Mackintosh "got letter from Geo Murray and one from Herbert and a paper from Father." He would stay for over a fortnight in the city. On his first Sunday "went to Presbyterian church where Professor Blackie from Edinburgh was preaching enjoyed service immensely. Wrote letters to Maggie, Billy and Mr. Keppie in afternoon." And he did likewise on the following Sunday.[26] It was in Rome that the subliminal influence of Ruskin becomes most apparent. Of course, one could not be in Rome and not visit the ruins of the Forum, still to be cleared and fully exposed by Mussolini only a few decades later. In one afternoon Mackintosh made a colored sketch of the Arch of Titus, the Colosseum, and the Golden House of Nero where "there are some very nice fresco decorations," which had been useful design material for architects from the eighteenth century onward. That Mackintosh was not in awe of the Caesars is evident from his note after drawing the Arch of Constantine: "Had a stroll through ruins of 'forum' before going for dinner."[27] He noted later: "I may add that the road from the Capitol to the Colosseum taking in the forum Romanum and the Campo Vacino bears a very striking resemblance to some parts of the east end of Glasgow assuming about two thirds of the population to be dead of cholera."[28] Nor was he much in awe of the masters of the Baroque. Bernini and Borromini were ignored while of the sixteenth-century twin-towered church of

Trinità dei Monti, set atop the Spanish Steps and closing one of the longest of the axial vistas, his sole comment was that "there isn't much to see."[29] Were there no flower sellers, no lounging foreigners thronging the steps, which swoop down to the piazza and the half sunk bark sculpted by Bernini? It would have been impossible also to have ignored the majestic series of the four early Christian basilicas. McKenzie had "visited the magnificent new church of St. Paolo in Fuori," then being restored after an earthquake. "It is the finest basilica I have seen."[30] Mackintosh, staying within the city center, admired Santa Maria Maggiore both outside and inside although without any mention of the mosaics. Surprisingly Mackintosh did praise the double-storeyed loggia of San Giovanni in Laterano by Fuga whereas the main elevation of St. Peter's by Maderna was rated a "very, very poor front."[31] Nor was McKenzie impressed. "When one enters the porch of the church everything seems common."[32] Mackintosh paid five visits in total to St. Peter's and to the Vatican Museum although after his first afternoon there he recorded sourly, "Didn't get half through. Go again. Closes at 3 awful fraud."[33]

It was in the north that Mackintosh encountered those architectural styles that were Ruskin's lodestars. Significantly, there is no mention in Florence of the early Renaissance Foundling Hospital or of the Pazzi Chapel, although Mackintosh sketched the adjoining Gothic Church of Santa Croce, "the Westminster of Florence," as McKenzie described it,[34] on three successive days as well as some of the palazzi. "Great bold projections," McKenzie had enthused, "and immense giant like proportions which give the palaces of Florence and Central Italy generally a dignity that one never sees now a days in the two feet thick walled buildings of the nineteenth century."[35]

There was the same selectivity of approach by Mackintosh in Milan, seen by McKenzie as "a Glasgow in Italy,"[36] at the end of his stay in late June, where he dismissed the churches, wrongly, as "being mostly late of a very inferior quality."[37] Mackintosh's first encounter with a Ruskinian exemplar began at Orvieto in the heart of Umbria between

ORVIETO.

CRM
1891.

Sienna and Rome and on the rail route north. The principal monument was the early-fourteenth-century cathedral by Maitani. Mackintosh was captivated by the cathedral's tall, paper-thin facade with a triple portal set beneath molded arches. (78) "Built of white marble with bands of red, purple blue black brown yellow marble, beautiful twisted columns."[38] The appreciation of smooth, time-worn surfaces and of constructional polychromy shows how well the lessons of Ruskin had been assimilated.

At Sienna, "Yes! it is like Edinburgh," McKenzie had exclaimed;[39] when Mackintosh went down to dinner in his pensione he "found Paxton and a fellow Dods sitting there," who would accompany Mackintosh to Verona where they separated.[40] After Orvieto the cathedral at Sienna, also by Maitani, seems to have been a disappointment, although in the travel diary the analysis is the longest for any building. Where the cathedral failed was because the desire for the expression of structural truth was subordinated to an appreciation of the beauty of materials and of ornament. Thus, "to begin with the front is a fraud it gives no indication of the interior ... Then when you examine the design you find that is almost 'not there' ... Then the sides, well they take the cake. There are no windows in the aisles ... but it wasn't good enough for the Sienisi. No, they must have windows, so they painted windows along the wall."[41] It is a reminder of McKenzie's jibe about Milan Cathedral and "the general jim crack effect of the interior."[42] Perhaps both young men remembered a sentence by Sir George Gilbert Scott: "We have repudiated shams, and can have nothing to say to them."[43] At Pisa also Mackintosh criticized the exterior of the duomo as "all arcade and no design."[44] Elsewhere, possibly because of his own inheritance of a stone building tradition in Scotland, Mackintosh found it difficult to come to terms with brickwork even when unadorned so that he had little to say about San Petronio (he called it S. Pietra) in Bologna, where the unfinished brick front is a fragment of what was intended to be the world's largest church. Likewise in Ravenna he rated the early brick churches of Sant' Apollinare in Classe and Sant' Apollinare Nuovo as "very

uninteresting outside" but with "some ripping mosaic work in both."[45] However, he did take time to produce a watercolor of the mosaic processional saints in the nave of Sant' Apollinare Nuovo (79), which were perhaps the germ of the idea for the decorations in the Buchanan Street tearoom.

Apart from his portfolio of drawings and watercolors, what intellectual baggage did Mackintosh bring from Italy and how does it correspond with *The Stones of Venice*? That his stay in Venice was short may have been because his money or time, perhaps both, was running out. Apart from dutifully praising the Gothic palaces and the mosaics in San Marco, he has little to say about Venice. Perhaps Ruskin had said it all for him—and at length. Having looked upon the frescoes by Tintoretto in the Scuola di San Rocco in Venice,

79. *Sant' Apollinare Nuovo*, Charles Rennie Mackintosh

78. *Orvieto Cathedral,* south transept, Charles Rennie Mackintosh

McKenzie had noted, "Ruskin has written a book of 450 pages on these frescoes as many as 50 pages being devoted in one case to the praising of the painting of a single tree. How absurd even great men are sometimes!"[46]

Undoubtedly Mackintosh looked at Italy through the eyes of Ruskin, displaying no real interest in work outside the Middle Ages even to the extent of shrugging his shoulders when confronted by the celebrated ferro-vitreous Galleria Vittorio Emmanuele in Milan, which he compared unfavorably with the one in Naples. Yet to look at Mackintosh's own subsequent architecture is to realize how much he had assimilated, consciously or unconsciously, from reading Ruskin's treatises. Central to all Ruskin's ideas was the need for honesty and therefore the avoidance of all falsity. "Never," he wrote in *The Seven Lamps of Architecture*, "imitate anything but natural forms."[47] There was, too, his emphasis on craftsmanship so that "the architect who was not a sculptor or a painter, was nothing but a frame-maker on a large scale."[48] And Ruskin must have struck a chord with his appreciation of stonecraft where "we should not lose the dignity of it by smoothing surfaces and fitting joints."[49] Even when Ruskin seemed to be most pedantic, as when lauding his favored northern Gothic, there was much for a young architect to ponder. "And it is one of the chief virtues of the Gothic builders, that they never suffered ideas of outside symmetries and consistencies to interfere with the real use and value of what they did. If they wanted a window, they opened one; a room, they added one; a buttress, they built one; utterly regardless of any established conventionalities of external appearance."[50] Although by the close of the nineteenth century many of the teachings in *The Stones of Venice* and other texts by Ruskin had become common parlance in architecture, Ruskin was still sufficient of a giant that a smart architect could read what he had to say and find profit for his own designs.

In the same month that he returned to Glasgow Mackintosh waited upon the Thomson trustees who, with Leiper in the chair, "then proceeded to examine the drawings and sketches ... the chairman having read the manuscript sketch of the tour which Mr. McIntosh had prepared," John Keppie moved that the second installment of the prize money be paid, doubtless to the benefit of his colleague's pocket. There was, however, a caveat in that in the future the condition requiring the study of ancient classical architecture should be adhered to.[51]

In its syllabus for 1891–92 the Glasgow Architectural Association announced for January 5, 1892, a "paper 'An Italian Tour' by Mr. Chas. R. McIntosh."[52] For some unknown reason, possibly pressure of work in the office, the talk was delivered only in the autumn "in a very racy manner."[53] The association had its own rooms, which were the setting for monthly lectures on historical subjects and what today would be called continuing professional development in which the firm of Honeyman and Keppie was to the fore. Keppie had lectured in 1890 on "The Accessories of Architecture," which began with "sculptor work (figured and ornamental) ... bronze casting, hammer work in all materials."[54] At the end of that year Honeyman spoke to the architectural section of the Philosophical Society on the recent changes in the cathedral.[55] Newbery lectured on "Impressionism in Architecture" and "the imitation of a suggestion from nature" in that "sculpture and painting ... have again and again had recourse to nature, and so preserved vitality."[56] At the close of that same winter Mackintosh spoke on "Scotch Baronial," a bold choice since David MacGibbon, a coauthor of the definitive five volumes on Scotland's castellated architecture, had lectured two years before on that subject, praising the style's adaptability and picturesque effect,[57] to which Mackintosh added "national association." Following MacGibbon Mackintosh divided his subject into five periods using "pencil drawings, water-colours and photographs, not a few the work of his own hands."[58]

But what of the office? Some jobs were still on the go since before his departure. Glasgow Cathedral was one. Fittings in the choir had been provided in 1854 by William Burn, the famous Edinburgh architect who had successfully established himself in London, "but Mr. Burn was not especially recognised as an authority on Gothic architecture

even as understood at that time." So thought a later generation, which turned to Honeyman whose interests in liturgy and antiquarianism found scope in providing "the new pulpit and communion table with the sedilia and screen behind" that was to have bronze statuettes with lesser ones of oxidized silver. By the time of Mackintosh's return to Glasgow all was in place save for the screen "for want of funds." With the promise of these in 1892 there was to be a reredos of Caen stone with shafts of alabaster. (80) "The dado is solid, just high enough to give a horizontal line above the chair at the communion table," but then "light and open so as not to obstruct the view of the building." Statues of Saint Ninian and of Saint Mungo adorned the corners. In the assured and strong draughtsmanship of a pricked tracing of the design does one not sense Mackintosh's hand?[59]

Also on the go was the protracted issue of an art gallery for Glasgow. At a meeting of the town council early in 1890 the Lord Provost had called on "our merchant princes, ship-builders, ship-owners, iron and coal merchants, iron founders, engineers, turkey red and other dyers, chemical, textile and other manufacturers, and to the large and wealthy owners of land in and around Glasgow" to subscribe the £150,000 needed in addition to the £50,000 profit from the 1888 exhibition.[60] The question for Glasgow was "whether we wish to be considered the second cultural city of the Empire or not?" What Liverpool, Manchester, Leeds, and other smaller cities already possessed[61] Glasgow must also have, "being now within sight of the accomplishment of the extension of Glasgow to her natural boundaries … in population, in wealth and in intelligence."[62] Glasgow saw itself "taking a position of importance in the Art world, second only to that of London, … "[63]

And there matters lay until the spring of 1891 when the city's curator of art outlined the "Requirements of an Art Museum." While he would not be drawn on any specific style he did advise that the building "should be capable of being indefinitely added to, without structural alterations in a simple, symmetrical and orderly manner," with the picture galleries on the upper floor "removed from direct communication with the external air," which, given the city's atmospheric pollution, was almost a necessity. "The incandescent electric light" was recommended as being "practically free from every objection which could be urged against any artificial system of lighting."[64]

By early summer, with the site of the 1888 exhibition in Kelvingrove Park having been set aside, "Arrangements are now in progress for the commencement of the City Art Gallery."[65] The cost was set at £120,000 and architects were invited to submit sketch designs for "a central hall, art

80. Reredos (demolished), Glasgow Cathedral, John Honeyman and Keppie

galleries, museum-hall and galleries, a school of art, refreshment rooms, etc." The closing date was December 1, after which the assessor, Alfred Waterhouse, would select six schemes with a premium of a hundred guineas for each.[66] Of the sixty-two schemes received nos. 40 and 48 by Honeyman and Keppie were placed among the six finalists. "Of Messrs. Honeyman and Keppie's designs, one is a free adaptation of early French Renaissance, the other being severely Classic; in both the large hall occupies a central place, the museum being erected to the east, and the school of art and picture-galleries to the west." In no. 40 top-lit corridors were "intended for the display of sculpture."[67]

In the story of Mackintosh the art galleries' competition has been overlooked yet it has a bearing when considering affairs to come. However, one immediate question has to be asked. Why would a firm submit two entries, "one being by Mr. Honeyman and the other by Mr. Keppie"?[68] Does that say something about internal politics and ambitions within the firm? But there is more. Of the two submissions one can assume that the classical version was by Keppie. But the other, who designed the other? Was it Honeyman? Or did he give only overall guidance? One asks since it was not stylistically a Honeyman scheme. The planning, maybe, but not the twin towers, not the vegetative ornament, not the draughting, not the lettering—these are by Mackintosh.

Although critics profess that there was little Italian influence on Mackintosh, surely that is not a substantive view.[69] There is the Italian pictorialism in the works immediately after the Italian sojourn, and there were longer-term consequences culminating perhaps in the desire after quitting Glasgow to return to the Mediterranean.

A first indication of the potency of Italy occurred with his success in the national competition of schools of art. Of the 50,311 works sent for examination, 3,217 were selected for the competition with the prizewinning entries to be exhibited at South Kensington, London, in the summer of 1892. Architectural design was one of many categories. Another was measured drawing with a silver medal going to Archibald Knox, from Douglas, Isle of Man, the future designer for Liberty,

ELEVATION.

"for set of drawings illustrating chapels and other historic remains, of Celtic crosses and their ornament." Other categories were mosaics and wallpapers, although the "Designs for decoration of rooms are very inferior," as well as carpets, cretonnes, pottery, ironwork, illustrations, and stained glass.

81. Chapter house design, Charles Rennie Mackintosh. *British Architect*

Among the schools of art, "Canterbury is to be congratulated on the number of students that have taken gold and bronze medals for designs—all lady students."[70]

Of the eight gold medals only one was awarded for architecture—to Mackintosh for his design for a chapter house which he had submitted, using the motto "Griffin" for the RIBA's Soane Medallion Prize in the previous year. The subject was a chapter house located on the east side of cathedral cloisters. (81) The competition was rated as "decidedly above the average in quality" although there were only nine entries among which "Gothic takes the palm, the clever Renaissance of 'Griffin' notwithstanding." At the same time Mackintosh had put in for the Pugin traveling scholarship, which was won by Detmar Blow, then working for Philip Webb, against Mackintosh's watercolors of a doorway of the Certosa in Pavia and of Santa Croce, Florence, as well as others of Palermo and Venice, together with pencil sketches of subjects in Elgin, Glasgow, and Linlithgow.[71] The last would have been the church of St. Michael (82), which Honeyman had been engaged to restore to its medieval layout.[72]

Reporting in the summer of 1892 on the South Kensington exhibition *The Building News* commented on Mackintosh's chapter house "of the Italian Renaissance character. The drawings treated exhibit considerable skill, and the details commendable,"[73] which was not to be wondered at as Mackintosh had drawn on some of Italy's finest monuments. It is, of course, impossible to fathom Mackintosh's creative process. Nevertheless, the published drawings imply that the basic concept was the mausoleum of Halicarnassus. This gave a high windowless base that allowed for canopied wooden stalls, examples of which had impressed Mackintosh throughout his Italian journey particularly in the baptistery at Pisa, which was the model for the upper stage of Mackintosh's design exercise although for one critic, "The attenuated form of the sculptured dormers round the dome ... very much detracts from the effect, though in some ways the design is very skilfully worked out."[74] The octagonal ground plan with a porch probably

derived from the baptistery at Cremona.[65] It is not, however, evident from the drawings how the circle of the dome would meet the octangle. Dome, narthex, cloisters, mosaics, and frescoes—all show just how far Mackintosh had traveled intellectually since leaving Presbyterian Glasgow for Italy.

In the art gallery schemes perhaps one should be looking for foreignness or what *The Builder*, in its summation of the premiated schemes, considered "a certain trickiness" marring Mackintosh's handling of the elevations. The two Honeyman and Keppie schemes had "a family likeness" but "a lack of directness in planning, doubtless increased by the

82. *St. Michael's Church, Linlithgow*, Charles Rennie Mackintosh

83. Glasgow Art Gallery, competition designs, John Honeyman and Keppie, *Academy Architecture*

mistaken exigencies of accommodating the art school." Of the two schemes, Keppie's elevations were the finer but the planning was deficient, with "a most commonplace concert hall ... and an ugly ceiling." Mackintosh had shown more skill in combining the central hall, "in spite of its railway-station roof," as a concourse and venue for music and its relationship with the adjoining zones. (83) The elevations were "a most curious medley of architecture"[76] reconciling the twin-towered facade of the Romanesque Sant' Abbondio at Como (84) with the triple porch of San Marco, Venice, and with low baptisteries crowning the corner pavilions. But the ornament—what is its origin? And that question raises another. Why, on returning from Italy, did Mackintosh divert from Paris to Brussels and then to Antwerp? Hornel and Reid Murray had both worked with the painter Verlat in Antwerp.[77] That may have been a reason for being in Antwerp. But why visit Brussels? Was it from there that Mackintosh imported the vegetative carving? And what about relations within the office of Honeyman and Keppie? How was the criticism of Keppie's scheme and the praise for Mackintosh's received?

For the latter the art gallery competition had been an opportunity to compose a complex scheme within a limited time scale, an experience that would be useful when the School of Art competition came along. In the meantime there was the Soane Medallion competition for 1893 for a railway station terminus. With fifteen contenders, Arthur Bolton, the future curator of the Soane Museum, London, was the winner.[78] Mackintosh's design was published by *The British Architect* (85) as possessing "much more architectural merit than that which was selected for the first prize in the competition." And there was further praise. "Mr. McIntosh has shown equal ability in his former essays and classic designs."[79] Here was a man to watch!

In the design of railway termini there was an inherent dichotomy between the administrative block and the engine shed. Only at King's Cross, London (1850), was the problem resolved by bringing the shed forward to become the facade and turning the offices off to the side. Mackintosh opted for

84. *Sant' Abbondio, Como*, Charles Rennie Mackintosh (*top*)

85. Design for a railway terminus, *British Architect*, Charles Rennie Mackintosh (*bottom*)

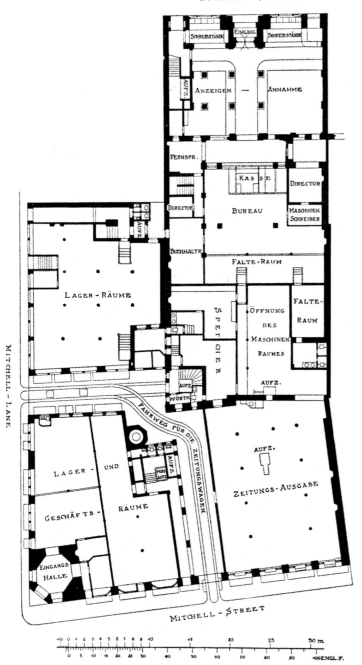

86. *Glasgow Herald*, ground-floor plan, John Honeyman and Keppie, *Die Englische Bankunst der Gegenwart*

the traditional approach, which had been in use since the first railway terminus at Lime Street, Liverpool (1836) which set down the formula of porte cochere, booking hall, platforms, and engines. What was unusual was Mackintosh's choice of Gothic—four center arches, turrets, decorated tracery, lofty towers—not Venetian as in the art galleries scheme but like them possessing decorative ornament that intrigues. The galleries had swirling foliage, writhing figures, and at the apex a female figure embowered in foliage, which grows up the station towers. How thrilling especially when set against the ponderous classicism of Keppie. And yet what is the source? What had Mackintosh seen in Brussels?

Mackintosh's interest in towers continued when the firm was commissioned to extend the premises of the *Glasgow Herald* newspaper. With a classical facade in Buchanan Street by James Sellars[80] there was a justification for calling upon Keppie for an extension to the rear. (86) He, in turn, handed over the design to Mackintosh. Why? Did he accept that the younger man was the more gifted designer? Or were his interests outside the office consuming time? Mackintosh's input is to be found in two sketches at the back of his Italian sketchbook (87), which show him feeling his way to the design solution.[81] *The British Architect* noted: 'It is erected on a corner site ... The streets unfortunately are very narrow, and this has been kept prominently in view, the vertical spaces being kept as simple as possible, and not broken up more than is necessary by bands or mouldings ... The tower at the corner is utilized as a watertower; a water tank containing 8,000 gallons of water being placed on the top at such a height that the whole building can be flushed and sprinkled with water at will."[82]

Mackintosh explored the design problem through the tower. Italy aside, his task was made easier as Glasgow's commercial district was studded with corner towers, many of them domed and many "in the fashionable red stone."[83] Having fixed on a design for the summit of his tower Mackintosh then had to decide on his side elevations. But in what style? At first he toyed with a classical system. He then moved on to something more grandiose, and indeed even American, with a high notional basement supported on a giant order and carrying, above the neighboring roofs, a multigabled skyline. (88)

When completed the building was hailed as "one of the most noticeable modern buildings in Glasgow, a building which may fairly claim to be a genuinely modern development." What was admired was "a quality of proportion and emphasis is such as makes architecture a thing independent of mere style."[84] Today the spectator will see proto—art nouveau in the organic swelling of the tower (89)—like a gigantic seedhead borne aloft on a multitude of stalks. And the gables—and their lesser kin—are they the flourish atop the old Scottish castles, but modern? Only if one accepts the fireproof construction, the internal use of iron, the red sandstone, and the lower stages with deep-set apertures devoid of ornament, perhaps even of grace, except on the ground floor with inverted Ionic capitals. Here then is the Free Style, but a style in which eroticism ravishes the gables.

Although the offices of the *Glasgow Herald* have long since been gutted by a horde of barbarian newspaper proprietors, one early set of Mackintosh interiors does survive more or less intact in the Glasgow Art Club, which was founded in 1867 in a tearoom above a baker's shop. After a series of moves the decision was made that the members would purchase property in order to establish a permanent home for the club. In November 1891 the club's council minutes record, "The lease of the Club house expires on Whitsunday 1893—eighteen months hence and it will be the duty of the Council elected for the ensuing year to make such arrangements for the renewal of the lease, or the taking of other premises as may be deemed expedient."[85] A Special Committee of four members, one of whom was John Keppie,[86] recommended that "the Club acquire property of their own."[87] After a search "two excellent lodgings" in Bath Street were purchased[88] with Keppie appointed as the architect for their conversion to a clubhouse.[89] That was a sensible choice as John Honeyman,

87. Sketch for the *Glasgow Herald*, Charles Rennie Mackintosh

88, 89. *Glasgow Herald*

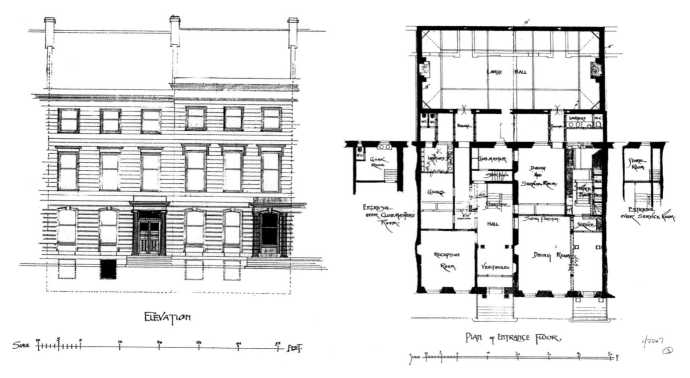

ELEVATION

SCALE

PLAN of ENTRANCE FLOOR.

1/2067

also a club member, had been the architect a quarter of a century before for the extension of the Western Club, the city's most distinguished clubhouse.

The Glasgow Art Club's acquisition was two adjacent town houses in a late Regency style terrace. (90) The eastern house was to be left intact; its neighbor was to be converted to a dining-room on the ground floor with a billiard room above. (91) A smoking room or gallery would be erected over the rear gardens of both houses. When "the rough estimate given by the Architect" showed a shortfall "the proposed Stone Mantlepieces" for the gallery (92) were replaced with designs in wood,[90] which, when the clubhouse opened in June 1893, were described as being "in Italian Renaissance style, freely treated and have a splendid effect."[91] All in all the introduction of "several new features suggested by the improvements in the latest constructed London West-end Clubs

90, 91, 92. Glasgow Art Club

reflects great credit upon the architect."[92] Even the newly founded *The Studio* reported favorably on the new clubhouse, where "the architectural alterations, decorations, and in fact all the details, have been carried out from the designs of Mr. John Keppie, I.A., and display much artistic taste."[93] That was a week after the *Bailie* had published a

CROSS SECTION.

SCALE

page of details (93) in which Keppie is credited as the architect but Mackintosh, in larger lettering, signs himself as the designer of all the ornamental details down to the bell push for the front door![94] This raises a number of issues.

What, for example, was Mackintosh's relationship with the Art Club? He may have given a lecture to its members in February 1893 since his paper on architecture was delivered to "an audience chiefly composed of pecture [sic] painters" who were informed that "old architecture lived because it had a purpose. Modern architecture, to be real, must not be a mere envelope without contents," which allowed Mackintosh to attack Glasgow's propensity for replicating Greek temples and to ask "whether the dignity is retained if we reduplicate the design and make it into a small black marble clock and put it on a black marble chimneypiece as is so often done." For Mackintosh buildings of such classical derivation were "as could [sic] and lifeless as the cheek of a dead chinaman" so that he foresaw the new men "freeing themselves from correct antiquarian detail and who go straight to nature. We must clothe modern ideas, with modern dress—adorn our designs with living fancy." He set forth his belief that "To get true architecture the architect must be one of a body of artists possessing an intimate knowledge of the crafts, and no less on the other hand the painter and sculptor and other craftsmen must be in direct touch and sympathy with architecture."[95]

That Mackintosh was never a member of the Art Club has always been a matter for speculation and the more so as the younger generation of the Glasgow Boys were. George Henry was admitted in 1884; Hornel two years later. David Gauld was a member as were J. Reid Murray and Stuart Park. Other members associated with Mackintosh included Newbery, the photographer J. Craig Annan, the architect James Salmon, and the decorator James Guthrie.

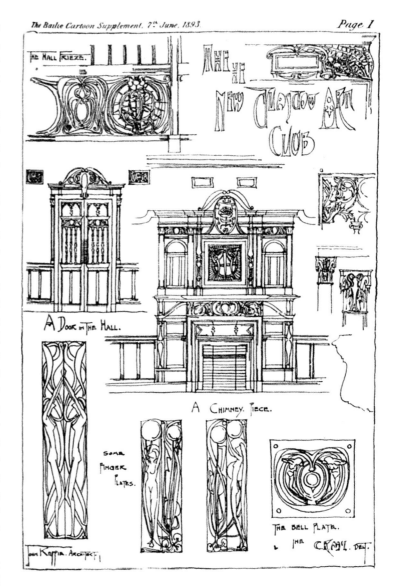

Keppie was admitted in 1888.[96] Club anecdote has it that if Mackintosh had applied for membership Keppie would have blackballed him, ostensibly because Mackintosh had jilted Keppie's sister, Jessie, for Margaret Macdonald. Perhaps there is some truth in that. On the other hand, it can now be shown that Mackintosh did apply for membership in 1899,

93. Sketch designs for the Glasgow Art Club, *The Bailie*

put up by the architect David Barclay and by David Gauld.[97] That Mackintosh's application was turned down need not cause surprise, however, since the club's records show that a second application was usually successful. Why then did Mackintosh not reapply? Was there enmity from Keppie? Was Mackintosh held to be a cad? It may be significant that McNair never deemed it worthwhile to apply and he was, by any standards, a gentleman. Perhaps, when it came down to it, The Four saw themselves as apart from their artistic brethren.

There is no mention of the Glasgow Art Club by Mackintosh's biographers, not even by the late Professor Thomas Howarth who, living in the city from 1939 to 1947, had contact with many of those who had known Mackintosh, although Keppie refused to meet him.[98] That the clubhouse was not open to the public may in part explain the lack of comment on Mackintosh's contribution, which is important as his first recorded scheme of interior decoration. The job books of Honeyman and Keppie contain an entry, hitherto uncited, for "Alterations in Bath St. for Glasgow Art Club," which lists the various trades and their costs including "Grosvenor Thomas and Paterson—Turkey carpets in hall" at £50:8:0, with the main supplier of the furnishings and carpets being Wylie and Lochhead. The gallery chimney pieces cost £134:0:0.[99]

Why were details by an unknown twenty-five-year-old designer published? Was Mackintosh rebutting claims that Keppie was the designer of the ornamental work? To judge by the errors in the wording on the published page the details would have been hurriedly set down. Or was an editor quick to grasp that here was a new style? In 1893 McNair produced *The Lovers*, Frances Macdonald *Ill Omen* (94), and Margaret Macdonald *At Home* for the School of Art Club (95)—each of which has a stylistic, thematic, and symbolist affinity with Mackintosh's details. Yet the gallery chimney pieces were designed by December 1892 "in Italian Renaissance style freely treated." Mackintosh's surviving Italian sketchbook includes tombs, monuments, doorways, and chimney pieces, which have a familial resemblance to details in the Art Club. But the brass fingerplates? Although much worn by assiduous polishing, the waving fronds and etiolated females are surely the first manifestation of the Glasgow style while defeating Mackintosh's own declared intent that "we must have a symbolism immediately comprehensible by the great majority of spectators."[100]

Mackintosh had drawn out for the gallery a design for a stenciled frieze, which was then a popular motif because of its "directness, simplicity and truth" and for the past thirty years "one of the commonplaces of decoration ... But the Japanese ... have once more opened our eyes ... to produce those broad and bold effects which are indispensable to the decoration of the walls of a room." The same issue of *The*

94. *Ill Omen*, Frances Macdonald

Studio in 1894 also reported, "A frieze looks best between good wide plain surfaces. If in a room, the wall from floor to frieze should be in a delicate tint."[101]

An entry in the job books records a payment for painter work to J. and W. Guthrie. By the 1890s they had a London showroom and were advertising themselves as "House and church decorators and artists in stained glass (domestic and ecclesiastical), plain and ornamental glaziers, art furnishers, dealers in antique furniture," and from about 1894 they would be associated with Mackintosh, stenciling patterns for Miss Cranston's tearooms and The Hill House.[102] One can fairly assume that their employment in the Art Club meant that ornamental work was to be done. That can be confirmed by a report in a local newspaper that, referring to the gallery, states, "The wall-painting etc. is all in quiet tones—cream and delicate greens predominating."[103] The accompanying illustration shows that the gallery frieze was indeed executed. As Mackintosh would have intended, the background color

95. *At Home*, Margaret Macdonald

96. Glasgow Art Club, the gallery, *Evening Times*

would have been pale cream and the thistle roundel sage-green, with touches of rose pink and mauve for the flower heads. The gallery, when finished, was not only Mackintosh's first interior scheme (96) but must now be seen as the first manifestation of the Glasgow Style, which in the Glasgow Art Club owed much to Italy.

Dipping into the Italian sketchbook one can guess that San Zenone, Verona, was a model for the campanili in the art galleries' competition, along with Sant' Abbondio, Como, which gave not only the frontispiece but perhaps the double aisle plan. The starting point for the tower of the *Glasgow Herald* building may have been the tower of Santa Maria in Organo, Verona, whose ribbed cupola has a resemblance to the dome on Mackintosh's chapter house competition entry while, on a smaller scale, the reredos in Glasgow Cathedral seem to have originated from a sarcophagus in Brescia Cathedral. Yet when all is said and done such searches are but games that art historians play. It is more realistic to consider that, for Mackintosh, Italy was a country of the mind in which he could wander at will in the years ahead. ▓

When Mackintosh, at the age of twenty-three, traveled to Italy, he was almost at the end of his pupilage as a trainee architect. He had entered the Glasgow School of Art in 1883 and would be a student there until 1893. In late 1895 his firm won the competition for a new, purpose-built school. By 1904 he was a school examiner in design and decorative art, joining Keppie who was an examiner in architecture and modeling along with W. F. Salmon, J. J. Burnet, and David Barclay.[1] By 1906 the second phase of the school building program had begun, and in 1910 the office of Honeyman, Keppie and Mackintosh prepared a set of drawings that are the truest record of the school as first completed. Mackintosh, therefore, had an involvement with the school for more than twenty-five years. Not only was the school central to Mackintosh's development as an architect but it was there that he formed his most lasting personal attachments and social friendships.

By chance or, more probably, by intention Mackintosh had been a pupil at Allan Glen's School in the Townhead. If Mackintosh was so disposed it was within walking distance of the Mackintosh home in Dennistoun so that each day he would pass the canal basin, crowded with barges, the cathedral, the gas-lit teeming tenements, and the industries, including Blackie's, to reach the school buildings in Cathedral Street. Though described by one biographer as "a private school for the children of tradesmen and artisans which specialized in practical subjects,"[2] that was not the whole story. Allan Glen's was not narrowly based socially. Founded in 1853 it was one of a clutch of private schools offering an alternative to the pedagogic instruction of the city's ancient high school. Moreover, Allan Glen's was unique in Glasgow in providing a scientific and technical curriculum until the school was abolished by a socialist town council in the 1960s. Having attended Allan Glen's Mackintosh would have found his introduction to the architectural course at the School of Art easier than did his fellows coming from a classical system of education. At Allan Glen's "a daily lesson is given in Drawing" to be followed in the next year when "Drawing is continued ... both freehand and with the use of

instruments." Then, "In Classes IV and V ... each pupil inclines mainly either to Chemistry or to Engineering." Even more innovatively, "Regular work in the workshop—first in wood then in iron—should begin in Class III, for some two or three hours a week ... to prepare both hand and eye for the difficult mechanical drawing in Classes IV and V."[3] No other would-be architect in Glasgow had such an early training in materials.

To become an architect one was apprenticed to a firm, worked a full week, and attended evening classes. It was a routine, now abandoned, that was arduous and required determination if one was to succeed in gaining a professional qualification. McNair, on the other hand, after a spell painting in Rouen, was privileged in that he is listed in the School of Art records as an "Apprentice Architect" from 1889–96 but with a gap in 1894. Did his father pay a premium to Honeyman to take on his son?

Although the first surviving architectural syllabus in the School of Art archives dates from 1893–94, by which time Alexander McGibbon was on the staff and Keppie was an examiner,[4] the nature of architectural instruction is such that one can make assumptions about the education that Mackintosh and McNair would have received. These assumptions can be supported by Newbery's thought on the training of architectural students in which he was guided by Ruskin's dictum "Drawing may be taught by tutors, but design only by Heaven," and accepted, too, Ruskin's premise that building is for use whereas "Architecture is the art which so disposes and adorns the edifices raised by man, for whatever uses, that the sight of them contributes to his mental health, power and pleasure." Newbery held to the view that "An art student ... should become the artist not in spite of but because of his education. Let the architectural student do the same." Indeed, he could see no reason why the latter "should be treated differently from an ordinary art student" since "the architectural student has this in common with all other art students, namely, that his education, like theirs, should be of a kind that should develop two great innate qualities, namely, the power of the hand to draw a line, and the power of the eye to rightly compose or apportion its length." Therefore, "I would have him draw with pencil, pen and sepia from fillet to temple and from Gothic leaf to cathedral, not as studies merely to enable him to have a command over his pencil, but, under instruction, seeking out and comparing their hidden beauties and subtle boundaries, till he realises what is meant by the power of a line," while the understanding of mass "can best be obtained by as does the sculptor, namely, by going through a course of modelling."[5]

For entry to the architectural course there was, in addition to other qualifications, an examination in drawing of "Ornament shaded from the Cast; a study of a plant or a flower from Nature." The professional subjects to be pursued included "mathematics; mechanics; physics; chemistry; perspective; stereotomy; and strength and nature of materials—the whole leading to construction." In addition the "course provides also for the study of Nature and from the life."[6] An essential component was architectural history with McGibbon teaching the Gothic period and W. J. Anderson undertaking the Italian Renaissance up to the end of the sixteenth century followed by "The Decline of the Renaissance," which would explain Mackintosh's limited perspective when in Italy. It is interesting, too, to note the recommended texts.

For the classical era these were Stuart and Revett's *The Antiquities of Athens*, the first primer on Greek architecture, which appeared from 1772 onward, and Sir William Chambers's *Civil Architecture*, published in 1759 and thereafter the definitive text on Roman classicism, along with W. H. Leeds's *The Orders and their Aesthetic Principles* of 1848. The set texts for Gothic were by Thomas Rickman, the Quaker chemist, who in 1817 introduced the divisions of Early English, Decorated, and Perpendicular. An edition was published in 1881 that coincided with George Gilbert Scott's *Lectures on the Rise and Development of Medieval Architecture*,[7] much of which would have appealed to a thoughtful student since Scott saw Early English not only as "the native architecture of our own country, and that of our own forefathers"[8] but as "the architecture of the modern as distinguished from the ancient world."[9] That being so "we

should cause it to take root, to spring forth, to germinate and to ramify."[10] In its details one could admire "foliated sculpture . . . founded on natural principles, yet not imitated from nature."[11] There was praise also for Glasgow Cathedral, "that noble temple yet preserved unruined,"[12] with its molded or unfoliated nave capitals. For the advanced course there were designated titles on building construction and the science of building along with "Viollet le Duc's Lectures and Dictionary." The latter featured in a booklist, compiled by Mackintosh, of titles in Glasgow's main reference library, a list that included Anderson's *Architecture of France and Italy* and MacGibbon and Ross's *Castellated and Domestic Architecture of Scotland*,[13] the many volumes of which, with their plans, sections, and elevations, would have been especially useful as "students should, in the vacation and at other times, measure existing mediaeval buildings and parts thereof and make drawings to scale. They should also practise sketching buildings in perspective."[14] And there were visits to sites of historic interest. A list in 1904 of past excursions includes Melrose, Stirling, and Culross,[15] each featuring in Mackintosh's sketchbooks.

From the school records it is clear that Mackintosh was the outstanding student of his generation. However, the records also show that others were catching at his coattails. John Keppie had been a prizewinner in 1883, for a "Design for a Fireplace and Overmantel," and in 1884. In the next year Mackintosh's name appears for the first time and then in 1887, for "Painting Ornament from the Cast, in Sepia," followed by George McKenzie and Helen Keppie, who received a commendation. An *annus mirabilis* occurred in 1888 when almost everyone in Mackintosh's circle was named, including Helen Keppie, Jessie Rowat (who would marry Newbery), and the painter John Pringle. The architectural ranks included Andrew Prentice (who would meet up with McNab, McKenzie, and John Keppie in France) and James Paxton (whom Mackintosh would encounter in Italy). Mackintosh's nearest rival at this time was L. D. Penman, which would support the notion of a friendly rivalry when they came to lecture on Ruskin. In 1888 Penman is named for the "best set of lectures on perspective" as against Mackintosh's notes on building construction, although the latter did, in addition, win £2:10:0 for a set of measured drawings of the city's Royal Exchange.

In the 1889 report they were again trailing each other with both winning a bronze medal, the one for a mountain chapel, the other for measured drawings of the St. Vincent Street Church. The governors' report carried in full extracts from *Building News*. "A very clever design for a mountain chapel, by Chas. R. McIntosh, Glasgow ... The plan is simple and well grouped. A low tiled roofed tower forms the vestry, attached to a vestibule and porch. A single span tiled roof, hipped at end, covers the church, the walling is of a bluish grey 'rag' making a pleasant contrast with the red-tiles." Mackintosh also pocketed a free scholarship, waiving future fees, and several local prizes, the most prestigious being the Haldane Medal. His office colleague Charles White-law was also mentioned.[16]

In 1890 Jessie Keppie was awarded a national silver medal for a "Design for a Persian Carpet" which was rather appropriate given that Glasgow's reputation as a major manufacturing center for carpets was led by James Templeton and Co. who were among the school's subscribers. The examiners, who included Walter Crane and William Morris,[17] thought that "the student has succeeded well with his [*sic*] borders, both colour and design are pleasing, but the forms are not worked with sufficient precision." Jessie Rowat also gained a bronze medal for a stained-glass panel, "Tempestas." The examiners were of the opinion that Mackintosh's design for a Presbyterian church, "with projecting roofs, is well suited for a rainy climate," and *Building News* categorized it as "somewhat American in style." Another book prize went to George McKenzie for an "Early English gable ... well drawn with large octagon turrets at the angles crowned by spirelets." McKenzie and Mackintosh were both prizewinners for architectural design. Whitelaw's name also occurs. However, it is Mackintosh who scoops the pool with first-class honors and a bronze medal for building construction. The names of Jessie Keppie and Whitelaw are in the report for 1891, along with a notice of Mackintosh's

success in gaining the Thomson scholarship "and also in having his works accepted for the Royal Institution Scholarship in Architecture. Being the sole competitor in the kingdom the Scholarship was withheld." However, he did win a silver medal for his designs for the public hall and the science and art museum and the gold medal in 1893 for the chapter house design.

By then the names of Herbert McNair and Margaret and Frances Macdonald emerge. McNair designed a village library and Frances Macdonald a majolica plate, winning a bronze medal, although, as the examiners reported, "The award would have been higher but for the poor execution and very disagreeable colour." Her sister was a more consistent prizewoman in anatomy, freehand drawing, and in the local competitions in 1895, with a design for stained glass, which followed on a design by Frances for hangings.[18] It was from the constellation of talent in the School of Art that what is known as the Glasgow Style emerged. But how, when, and from whom?

Mackintosh, McNair, and their like were "evening students and all mostly trade apprentices."[19] The day classes, on the other hand, contained a large percentage of female students so that in the 1893–94 prize list, for example, women outnumbered men two to one. The women were from the well-to-do, which resolved one problem. As an advertisement put it: " 'What to do with our girls' Send them to Learn Shorthand and Typing."[20] One of the few alternatives was attendance at the School of Art where "after attaining a sufficient proficiency in Drawing, Still Life Painting, Modelling, and a Knowledge of Ornament and the Figure" they could "obtain special technical knowledge in design for Textiles, Wall Papers, Metal Work, Pottery, Stained Glass, Wood and Stone Carving, Book Illustration,"[21] all of which took place in the cramped studios allotted in the McLellan Galleries.

There were times, of course, when the opposite sexes could meet. Architectural students "to develop the artistic side of the Architects' profession" were encouraged "to study Elementary Modelling, Ornament from the cast in outline, and Light and Shade, Monochrome Painting in schemes of Colour, and

will be given from the pictures in the Corporation Galleries."[23] Another possibility for social encounters was the Glasgow School of Art Club for past and present students "under the direction of the Head Master," Francis Newbery, which could be recommended for keeping the males "out of public-houses and music-halls, and away from football matches!"[24] In the 1893–94 session one of the treasurers was Jessie Keppie. Then, "No one who sees the nightmare work in the Glasgow School of Art Club's Exhibition can fail to be impressed by its cleverness, its imagination, and its drawing and colouring. But, at the same time, to the untutored, and even to the tutored mind, it suggests a gruesome practical joke ... Two of the chief perpetrators are sisters [The Misses Frances and Katherine (*sic*) Macdonald]."[25]

That the club had "A Vacation Sketching Scheme"[26] may explain the group holidays and the accompanying photographs of Mackintosh and his immediate circle. (97)

One wonders about Mackintosh's vacations. That he should visit York as a treasury of medieval architecture or the more distant Exeter is understandable but unusual, too, in that he kept away from industrial towns. Perhaps he had enough of grime, clangor, and crowds in Glasgow. Mackintosh probably never took a holiday as such. Time away from the office was an opportunity to seek out and to experience other architectural forms. That he was examining specific themes is revealed in his sketchbooks.[27]

Thus, on his first sketching tour in England in 1894 he traveled to Broadway, the surrounding hamlets, and Chipping Campden in the Cotswolds. But why? The area had not yet become associated with the Arts and Crafts movement. Was it because the painter E. A. Walton had lived in Broadway for some years?[28]

Drawing from the Antique and Life" as well as attend lectures on "Principles of Ornament, Historic Ornament, Figure Composition and Anatomy."[22] There was, too, the outdoor sketching class "for the study of landscape, animals and the figure," although "on wet days lessons in Landscape Composition

97. Sketching party. Charles Rennie Mackintosh (standing), Jessie Keppie (seated)

In June 1895 Mackintosh toured the south coast of Hampshire and Dorset before turning north into Somerset. He almost filled one sketchbook with a sequence of forty-nine drawings, storing up material that would reappear in Queen's Cross Church and the Glasgow School of Art competition entry at the close of that same year. That Mackintosh had been enchanted by what he had seen in the early summer is revealed in his sole excursion into print when, in the autumn, he responded to correspondence in *The British Architect* with two short accounts of his tour. In Dorset at Abbotsbury, "seven or eight miles from Dorchester, and is reached by train ... all the beauties of the place are arrayed in front of you in such a way as to raise in any architectural enthusiast burning desires of ambition and endeavour,"[29] while Wareham was remembered as "the most complete and beautiful old-world village, it has ever been my pleasure to see."[30] Very different, indeed, from the industrial heartland of the west of Scotland.

Apart from the purple prose what were the architectural gains for Mackintosh? They were twofold. In Broadway and Chipping Campden, "where I was the year before this,"[31] as in Dorset in 1895 he encountered villages grown rich on the medieval wool trade where "the streets are lined on either side with quaint and picturesque houses and inns,"[32] soft in outline, organic in growth, with one age overlaying another. It was a palimpsest such as Scotland could not yield. And dominating all else were the churches, each "an emblem of help and strength."[33] And what treasures they contained—paneled bench ends, carved choir stalls, cusped window heads—and all in that easy, luxuriant Perpendicular style to which Mackintosh came as a stranger. And there were fat, bulging towers, ribbed with fleshy buttresses and garlanded with pinnacles, like tiaras, especially in Somerset, "the tower county *par excellence*."[34]

"We made many careful examinations of St. Martin's while we were in Wareham," where "we stayed" at the Red Lion Inn.[35] Who was Mackintosh's traveling companion? One can probably assume that he was an architect. So was he McNair? And at Bridport did they stay with Newbery whose

hometown it was? And was it Newbery who suggested the journey to Suffolk in August 1897 when Mackintosh paid his first visit to Southwold and the inland churches? It seems that Mackintosh had attached himself to a students' sketching party. As a contemporary recollected: "He usually went out along with his sketch book and worked on screens, interior wood work etc. and returned in the evening frequently worse for drink," on one occasion being threatened with eviction by the landlord. "James Salmon and Gillespie often went with him on these occasions—great friends."[36]

Nearer home, with easy links by rail and by steamer, the Clyde resorts were popular destinations for all manner of Glasgow folk. Thus in 1895 Mackintosh was in the small hamlet of Corrie on the ducal island of Arran in the Firth of Clyde. With its hillside setting giving expansive views of the Clyde estuary, Corrie was an attraction for Glasgow's artists and, indeed, so much so that in 1888, "During the month of September no fewer than forty-eight artists were established in Corrie."[37] One wonders where they found sleeping quarters. It may have been in Corrie that the designer E. A. Taylor, the future husband of Jessie M. King, came across Mackintosh "at the edge of a pine wood ... in the island of Arran ... I was young then and full of enthusiasm for anyone who could draw and paint, and a man who planned buildings as well was a wonderful person. To recall that day is to visualise a large patch of vivid green grass out of which there rose tall, dark-boled, branchless pine trees against a sky of brilliant blue. I watched him draw those trunks with a thin nervous living line and colour them with black ink, and the grass a pure unshadowed green. How simple it seemed ... "[38]

According to Howarth, "When competition designs were being prepared Mackintosh was often invited to Keppie's house at Ayr, where they could work in more congenial surroundings. Herbert McNair, who was also at the office, frequently went along too."[39] The Keppie house was actually in the coastal village of Prestwick immediately to the north of Ayr. Within spitting distance of Prestwick Cross, it was a gray, nondescript semidetached villa looking down to the railway station and across to the golf course, one of the championship courses of Scotland and a challenge to Keppie's well-known golfing skills.[40] The villa had been purchased by Keppie's father in the name of Keppie's three sisters.[41] Howarth continues: "At week-ends the Macdonalds and other students from the School of Art sometimes joined them, and to house his guests on such occasions Keppie rented two bungalows christened 'The Roaring Camp' at Dunure,"[42] a coastal hamlet made picturesque by a harbor and ruined castle overhanging the sea. Doubtless, Dunure, situated away from Prestwick, offered more privacy for the parties of young men and women who called themselves The Immortals.

The name the Roaring Camp was borrowed from "The Luck of Roaring Camp," a short story by the popular American poet and author Bret Harte.[43] He had been the American consul in Glasgow. His initial response to the city in 1880 would not change throughout his five years' residency. "As to Glasgow. It's a big city—about as big as New York—very smoky, very damp they say." In his tales it became "St. Kentigern" and its denizens "the righteous St. Kentigerners of the tribe of Tubal-Cain, great artificers in steel and iron, and a mighty race of engineers before the Lord." Even his club held little attraction since the members spoke of steamships, iron, and wool.[44] He should have joined the Art Club!

"The Luck of Roaring Camp" is a sentimental tale of an illegitimate baby brought up by gold prospectors before being drowned by a winter flood. The story was disapproved of because of its reference to prostitution and the introduction of a swear word.[45] What was the attraction for The Immortals? Probably the bohemian lifestyle of the prospectors in a summer season of "pastoral happiness" with the infant's bower decked with flowers and sweet-smelling shrubs.[46] Yet perhaps the oversentimental and slightly fey composition and the sudden death of the child and the loss of dreams was a clouding of the glass-encased lives of "The Immortals."

During "the golden summer of Roaring Camp"[47] there would have been excursions. One is recorded in a Mackintosh sketchbook—a day passed among castles and ruins. In Maybole Mackintosh sketched the castle (98), the "town house" of the former earls of Cassilis.[48] Mackintosh chose his views carefully—in one omitting the later subsidiary structures that detracted from the verticality and in the other selecting an elevation not shown in the pages of MacGibbon and Ross but, rather conveniently perhaps, directly opposite a public house. The nearby castle of Baltersan was once "a stately fyne house, with gardens, orchards, parks and woods about it."[49] All had vanished and the broken turrets and diminished walls stood abandoned in a cornfield.

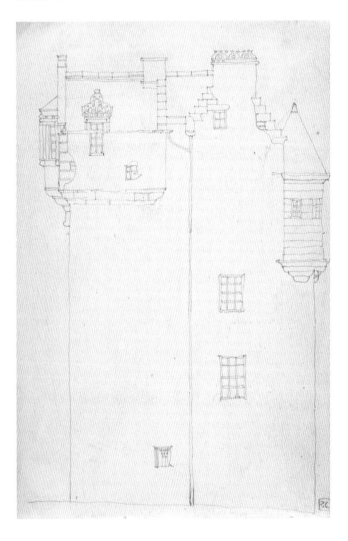

98. *Maybole Castle*, Charles Rennie Mackintosh

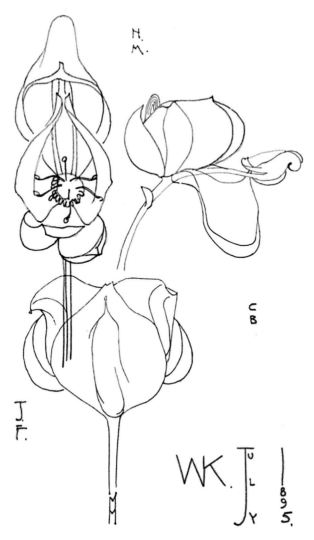

When Mackintosh was in West Kilbride farther up the coast it was not buildings that he sketched but flowers, delicate line drawings in which assured draughtsmanship conveys without accident, error, or change detailed botanical information without restraining the life force of stem, bud, and flower. In 1894 flower drawings are, for the first time, recorded in some number from Corrie, on the island of Arran, from Ascog, on the island of Bute, and from Glasgow.[50]

99. Flower drawing, Charles Rennie Mackintosh

Why? As the designer E. A. Taylor later recollected: "Flowers, too, and fruit, made a strong appeal to his imagination, not from their realistic colour, and form alone as much as the abstract lines and forms they would suggest ... Flowers had always for him a special attraction in a derivative way."[51] But what accounts for Mackintosh's expressed interest in 1894? Was it the notice in *The Studio* of Japanese flower studies?[52] In 1895 at West Kilbride Mackintosh put together in one sketchbook a plant collection. And a strange one it is for the drawings are not presented as conventional botanical specimens, although each flower is botanically correct in structure and form but without habitat, color, perspective, and little shading save for some strokes at the calyx of an antirrhinum. The drawings are formal, like medieval stiff-leaf foliage, and flat, like his architectural subjects, and almost one-dimensional for it is the line that tells all, an unbroken line composing without hesitation each bloom. Some spill across several pages, a precursor of those on posters and wall decorations. One (99) is initialed NM, JF, and CB (all unknown) and, within the stem of the lily, MM (for Margaret Macdonald). Thus begins Mackintosh's habit of incorporating the initials of his companions while betokening an awakening love for Margaret, which ended Jessie Keppie's hopes.[53] Whether she and Mackintosh were ever formally affianced has long been matter for speculation. That Mackintosh gave her a brass-bound jewel casket, made by himself, is evidence of something more than affection. Perhaps, since the casket was illustrated in Gleeson White's article in 1897, the sundering of the relationship occurred thereafter.[54]

From what McNair told Howarth it was Newbery who, recognizing a similarity in their work, brought The Four into contact with one another, whereupon they decided to become collaborators and, in time, to marry.[55] However, no hint of amorous passion is shown in a small collection of photographs that Jessie Keppie retained and that lay undisturbed in an envelope until many years after her death.[56] All of them, bar one of a sketching party including Mackintosh and Jessie Keppie, shows The Immortals skylarking in the countryside at Dunure. (100) John Keppie is there. Was he the photographer who, having set up the camera, hurriedly rushed into the group? Jessie Keppie and Margaret Macdonald are conversing in the most natural way. Mackintosh and McNair are barely distinguishable from each other except that in one photograph it is evident that Mackintosh's right leg is shorter than the left one.[57] He wears trousers whereas McNair has donned fashionable plus fours with all the panache bestowed by the comfort of old wealth.

After West Kilbride it would be true to say that The Four replaced The Immortals. If The Four are credited with evolving the Glasgow Style, who, within them, was the progenitor? Mackintosh, one might have thought. But is that the case? Perhaps it was McNair who, if he is considered today, would be seen as Mackintosh's alter ego.

When McNair was doodling designs in idle moments in the office "not a line was drawn without a purpose, and rarely was a single motive employed that had not some allegorical meaning. The whole design was contrived to embody 'the poetry of the idea,' " as McNair explained to Howarth,[58] who accepted that McNair, "and not Mackintosh, was the first of the Glasgow group to break new ground."[59] If that was so then the neglect of McNair is curious. Mackintosh's most recent biographer says nothing of import about McNair and neither does the biographer of the Macdonald sisters. While one can accept the verdict of Hermann Muthesius in 1905 that Mackintosh was the "driving force of the Scottish movement"[60] that does not mean he was the pioneer. McNair's early role is difficult to assess given a fire in his studio, as reported by Gleeson White in *The Studio* in 1897, with the loss of many works, including stained-glass cartoons,[61] the later sale and dispersal of numerous items, and the destruction by McNair of his own and his wife's archive after her death.

In 1895 McNair had left the office of Honeyman and Keppie to open his own design studio at 227 West George Street, on the fringe of the city's artistic milieu, as "architect and designer." The Macdonalds had their studio around the corner in Hope Street. In nearby studios at 160 Bath Street there were at different times Lavery, Roche, E. A. Walton, and others. Previously, Walton and Roche had been at 134 Bath Street, and the sculptor Macgillivray was in the same street. Guthrie, Henry, James Paterson, Crawhall—all were in the vicinity.[62]

Is it true, as Howarth said, that McNair "always restless and mercurial, had not taken kindly to the rigours of practice under John Keppie"?[63] That McNair, scion of a rich family, could strike out on his own has been seen as his escape from an unpleasant situation. From another point of view one can ask why McNair should not wish to emulate the commercial success of George Walton, the onetime bank clerk, who with much less in the way of financial security had established himself in an independent practice. Indeed, would Mackintosh have opened a design studio if he had possessed the financial wherewithal? Lacking that, he had to stick to the routine and, let it be said, the discipline of architectural practice.

100. The Immortals at Dunure. Frances Macdonald (rear), Margaret Macdonald (left), Jessie Keppie (right) next to John Keppie, J. Herbert McNair (front left), Charles Rennie Mackintosh (front right)

Success must have seemed within McNair's grasp. In 1896 The Four were invited to exhibit at the London Arts and Crafts Exhibition Society, one outcome of which was the decision by Gleeson White to travel to Glasgow and, subsequently, to publish a series of articles on The Four, Jessie Newbery, and Talwin Morris as well Oscar Paterson, George Walton, and J. and W. Guthrie who, although seen as slightly apart, were included within "the Glasgow Arts and Crafts movement," in which the éminence grise was Francis Newbery, "sympathetic, tactful, and peculiarly capable."[64]

Having been a teacher at the South Kensington schools in London and an admirer of William Morris, Newbery was in touch with the English Arts and Crafts movement and "was probably the catalyst in the development of the Glasgow Style."[65] From 1884 Morris was lecturing at the Glasgow School of Art, as was Walter Crane. In 1893 technical art studies, including metalwork, needlework, book binding, stained glass, and ceramic decoration were introduced into the syllabus of the school, after which came mosaics and enameling in the 1894–95 session followed by gesso work, furniture, and other crafts.[66]

Such changes would have emanated, in some part, from the lead given by the London-based Arts and Crafts Exhibition Society. Its first exhibition in 1888 was followed by another in 1889 when the sole Glasgow exhibitor was "Guthrie, Messrs John and William, 231 Oxford St., W.," which was their London showroom.[67] When the society's council met in mid-November 1889 it considered a proposal to transfer the exhibition to Glasgow. The details were gone over a fortnight later when "Mr. Paton, representing the Museum and Galleries Committee ... agreed to take for sale at one penny 1,000 copies of the essays printed with the catalogue."[68] Did The Four buy copies when the exhibition opened in mid-January 1890 in the McLellan Galleries? If so, they might have perused with some interest the essay on the domestic use of stucco and gesso.

Alongside pieces by Crane and Morris, "a number of examples of local products in artistic textiles, furniture and glasss were shown."[69] The exhibition had been arranged by Newbery and Kellock Brown, who was himself an exhibitor with "some capital specimens of hammered copper and brass ... and a large sculptured panel."[70] In the galleries' annual report it was "noted that the exhibition had proved of special interest to the students at the School of Art, by whom it was largely taken advantage of."[71] Others were not so impressed. "Now while I don't believe that society is likely to be elevated and the masses redeemed by the contemplation of aesthetic gas brackets, etc., etc., still I do think that a vast deal of national enjoyment might be added to life by more of this kind of thing."[72]

At the third of the society's London exhibitions in the autumn of 1890 exhibitors included George Walton and Kellock Brown whose entries included some of the pieces shown in Glasgow.[73] At the fourth exhibition in 1893 Kellock Brown was again featured but in association with Jessie Newbery as the designer. And John Guthrie showed a gesso panel, *The Annunciation*.[74]

It was at the fifth exhibition in 1896 that the Glasgow School was most widely represented alongside such national figures as Crane, Lethaby, de Morgan, Ashbee, and Voysey—indeed anyone who mattered in the arts and crafts. Margaret and Frances Macdonald had submitted jointly a "Clock in Beaten Silver with beaten brass weights and aluminium pendulum" and a brass and iron "Muffin Stand," along with *The Annunciation* and *The Star of Bethlehem* beaten on panels of aluminium, then a new and modish material. A hall settle, designed by Mackintosh, was made and exhibited by the Guthries. And Jessie Keppie had made *Vanity*, to Mackintosh's design, in brass, which he exhibited along with one designed and made by Lucy Raeburn. Mackintosh's own pieces included a brass panel, *Art and Literature seeking the Inspiration of the Tree of Knowledge and Beauty*, together with the panel *Part Seen, Imagined Part*. Also from Glasgow there were book covers by Talwin Morris for Blackie and Son and a *Book of Emblems* by Jessie Newbery.[75]

All the chosen items had been before a selection committee, which, for one exhibitor, posed a difficulty as he wished to show "a Cup with Cloisonne Enam[el] Lid. However, the

Queen has just purchased it and although we should still like to send it and think we may be able to borrow it for the exhibition, we dare hardly propose it unless it cd. be assured in passing the Committee of Selection. It is only a small cup 6 ins. High." There was, too, a royal foundation trowel and "in this again we prefer not to run the risk of rejection."[76]

During the exhibition run the purchasers included "G. F. White" and Talwin Morris, who bought *Part seen, imagined part* for three guineas and the hall settle for ten. The silver clock was acquired by the Countess of Lovelace.[77] It is significant that the buyers were personal friends—a question worth asking when confronted by the criticism, as expressed in *The Studio*, of the Macdonalds, and by implication of McNair, for their posters for which "the spooky school [the first use of the term] is a nickname not wholly unmerited. Can it be that the bogiest of bogie books by Hokusai has influenced their weird travesties of humanity?" Mackintosh "is obviously under the same influence, which is still more clearly noticeable in a panel entitled 'Part seen and part imagined.' " Yet it was admitted that "these new combinations of lines ... crowned by faces of weird import" constituted "a style of decoration which owes absolutely nothing to the past." Even so, "Probably nothing in the gallery has provoked more decided censure than these various exhibits."[78] That would seem to be confirmed by Muthesius.[79] However, Talwin Morris, who, one presumes, had been in London, says only that the Macdonalds' altar panels "attracted very considerable interest and comment," although he does add that "Maeterlinck insists that a positive hatred of the beautiful has ever been almost universal."[80] According to Muthesius, admittedly writing after the event, "at the next exhibition in 1899 ... their pieces were refused,"[81] a statement that has been accepted subsequently and become integral to the myth of Mackintosh as the rejected prophet. Yet the 1899 catalogue lists oak chairs by Mackintosh, a "Lacquer panel" by Margaret Macdonald, and works by Jessie Newbery, including a pulpit fall, Oscar Paterson, and Kellock Brown and James Salmon's "Electric table

Lamp."[82] The truth may be that the Glasgow folk no longer felt the need for exposure in London.

In 1895 a second Arts and Crafts exhibition was held in Glasgow. The convener of the selection and hanging committee was "Mr. F. H. Newbery who has a proper enthusiasm for Ruskin and Walter Crane," assisted by George Walton, a designer of the exhibition, John Keppie, and Craig Annan, among others.[83] The Queen's Rooms had become "a bazaar in a southern Spanish town ... Around the walls underneath the galleries on the principal floor the stalls have been arranged ... divided from one another merely by uprights ... with a decorative shield ... designed and painted by students of the School of Art ... by far the greater proportion of the exhibitors, especially in the non-professional section, are ladies." First-time exhibitors included Mackintosh, although more to the fore was McNair, whose cabinets were "notable for design" and whose threefold screen, entitled *The Birth and Death of the Winds*, was embellished with panels designed and beaten by the Macdonalds. Mackintosh's seven wallpaper designs attracted the comment, "Distinctly unconventional in treatment, they, however, contain little suggestion of that eccentricity which marks much of Mr. McIntosh's work."[84]

Others, too, were coming to the fore. At the close of 1896 "a little exhibition of industrial art work by Mr. J. Edward Charles Carr and Mr. J. Tyler Stewart ... is undoubtedly the beginning of a new art movement in Glasgow ... During the last few days a number of local artists, architects and others have paid a visit to the studios ... To architects, in particular, the exhibits have been a revelation in industrial art ... The exhibits include mosaics, metal work, gesso, glass staining, general decorative, and general art furnishing. An interesting section ... is that of metal work, and the artistic effect that can be got out of metals ... a very fine draught screen ... in yellow pine, it is stained and ornamented with modelled copper, brass and irridescent venetian glass ... and brass worked finger plates are on view, showing how great an artistic effect the ordinary furnishings of a household may possess when so treated. The gesso work is quite an

101. Smoker's cabinet, J. Herbert McNair

artistic novelty, the Composite used being a secret of their own. There is a beautiful peacock panel, an elegant portion of a frieze."[85]

A cornucopia of similar material was to be found in the early volumes of *The Studio* which, as for so many others, was a veritable vade mecum for The Four. Volume one had opened with the motto "Artists as Craftsmen" and although architecture was not its concern design premises were. Thus, in a discussion about "Artistic Houses," it was set down that "There is no reason why all art workers should not combine to produce the many things that are necessary to complement a really artistic house."[86] That practical aim could be allied to the proposition that "Romance ... is in the air. The old glamour, banned by realists and actualists, is once again upon us ... What would seem to be once again coming to the fore is the allegory."[87]

In that Gleeson White found The Four in accord, but in the outsiders' perception of their standing relative to one another McNair emerges "in sympathy with the other artists ... and has also found his own individuality of expression.

"In his work there is more conscious symbolism ... than is apparent in the work of his neighbour ... naturally it is absent from the furniture," as in the smoker's cabinet (101), which White admired as "distinctly novel ... The pleasant curves of its design owe nothing to precedent in furniture ... it is rarely one finds so much actual novelty with so little applied decoration."[88]

Whereas Mackintosh's pieces of the same period are plain and substantial, the smoker's cabinet has rose-bearing wings enfolding a chalice from which flow drops of blood, making the cabinet the most distinctive and significant piece in the development of the Glasgow Style and one, too, that introduces the most durable motif of the "Unfolding pungent rose, the glowing bath / Of ecstasy and dear forgetfulness."[89] What White, "a mere matter of fact Southerner,"[90] failed to see in the cabinet was more obvious in McNair's two-dimensional work. (102) "His bookplates will convey a hint of the symbolic manner Mr. McNair adopts in his paintings. Not a line in them is without intention, the poetry of the idea

(as their author explains it ...) it were best perhaps not to vulgarise by any attempt to supply an explanation."[91]

McNair's ranking among The Four can be assessed by turning to the albums of "The Magazine," a compilation by Lucy Raeburn between 1893 and 1896 of offerings by The Immortals with the exception of McNair.[92] One wonders why. In the first album there is "A Fairy Tale" by Jessie Keppie about a good and spotless princess who, with the aid of fairies, overcomes the wiles of "two wicked old witches" to separate the princess from her "noble lover." That the tale has been construed as an allegory for Jessie's despair at losing Mackintosh to Margaret Macdonald[93] seems mistaken as her relationship does not appear to have waned until two years later and, even then, there must have been companionship as shown in the similarity of Jessie Keppie's and Mackintosh's flower studies, in which there are identical vertical alignments of signatures and dates. However, Jessie Keppie's "simple and charming studies of flowers, pansies, sweet peas and wild flowers" in the scrapbooks pale against the offerings of "the brilliant sisters Macdonald," such as *Despair*, by Frances, a stained-glass design of "two figures whose sorrow has worn them to shadows, and whose tears have watered their eyelashes, and made them grow to rather an alarming extent"[94]; or Margaret's *Summer*, a stained-glass design similar to the stained-glass mermaids in the bookcase belonging to McNair. The close working partnership is also demonstrated with McNair's *For God So Humbled Himself* (103) of 1896 in which the Holy Ghost as a descending dove hovers over the Virgin Mary cradling the Christ Child and which belongs to the episodes of the birth of Christ also worked in gold and silver by the sisters, of which Talwin Morris remarked, "The treatment of the most subtle allegories, and mysteries of religion is everywhere impressive."[95]

Alongside the bats, owls, and elves in The Magazine there is the consanguinity of the contributions by the Macdonalds, by Mackintosh, and, in his absence, by McNair and the impossibility, after more than a century, of fathoming their meaning. All have the same characteristics—usually a symmetrical composition in acid greens and yellows, harsh blues

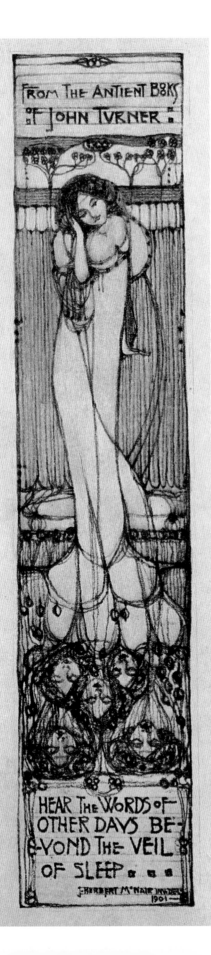

FROM THE ANTIENT BOOKS
OF JOHN TURNER

HEAR THE WORDS OF
OTHER DAYS BE-
YOND THE VEIL
OF SLEEP ...

J HERBERT McNAIR INVDEL
1901

FOR GOD SO
HUMBLED HIM-
SELF THAT
MAN SHOULD
BE GLORIFIED

J HERBERT McNAIR
INV - DEL - 1896

and violets and purples depict morbid subjects whether it is the satanic grins of the swollen tadpoles in *A Pond* by Frances Macdonald or *Nov. 5* by Margaret, both of which have undertones of the explicit eroticism in McNair's *The Lovers*. In tone, form, and construction Mackintosh's earlier *The Harvest Moon* is more subdued, better executed, and more consciously thoughtful and more akin to McNair's bookplates. Yet perhaps one should not take the mock heroic productions in a student magazine too seriously. There is Mackintosh's rather heavy-handed humor when explaining his portrayal of *Cabbages in an Orchard* and attempting "to satisfy the ordinary ignorant reader." The Immortals would have understood and appreciated that he was sending up the Glasgow Boys when rhapsodizing over "the rich variety of colour, the beautiful subtlety of proportion and infinity of exquisite forms" of his cabbages in an orchard where "the trees are old trees, very old trees, they are far away from any other trees, and I think they have forgotten what trees should be like." But then they are depicted by "the artist who is no common landscape painter, but is one who paints so much above the comprehension of the ordinary ignorant public,"[96] who remain bemused to this day by *The Tree of Influence*, which is more spare, more abstract than any other contemporary work by The Four.[97] Although Mackintosh did on occasion succumb to romanticism, as in *The Fairies*, he avoided McNair's sentimentality, as in the latter's bookplate of 1910 (104), and the ghoulish conceits of McNair's *The Well of Youth* of 1905. (105) Also by confining his entries in public exhibitions to architectural studies Mackintosh escaped public obloquy. "As to the weird designs" in the School of Art Club exhibition in 1894, "to the making of which went impossible forms, lurid colours and symbolism, that requires many footnotes of explanation, the less said, perhaps, the better. Blake ... and Beardsley ... are not always safe guides for the young to follow,"[98] although, as Talwin Morris observed, "The somewhat sombre realism of their work ... is not entirely for the crowd."[99] Yet to Gleeson White The Four were part of a pan-European movement. "The fact remains that in Scotland as in England, in Germany no less than in Belgium, and in many

104. Bookplate, J. Herbert McNair

102. Bookmark, J. Herbert McNair (*left*)

103. *For God So Humbled Himself*, J. Herbert McNair (*right*)

other places, there is a return to mysticism, and to superstition and legendary fancies."[100]

The notoriety that The Four attracted could become an asset for others whose business was self-promotion. A skillful practitioner was Joseph Wright of the Glasgow Umbrella Factory, who not only advertised his wares frequently and extensively in the local press but developed stunts including sending his "Drooko" (the Scots for drench) umbrellas to every member of the cabinet and claiming that his product

105. *The Well of Youth*, J. Herbert McNair

"shelters more crowned heads than any other umbrella known." Hardly surprising then that the astute Mr. Wright should show that "in aesthetic matters the firm is still on the move"[101] by commissioning the Macdonalds to design a poster that was almost a mirror image of Mackintosh's poster for the Glasgow Institute of Fine Arts in 1895. In both a female figure, clad in Beardsley-like costume, grasps a flower stem. In the first it opens at the top like an umbrella; in the other a hand caresses a lily stem encapsulating male genitalia, and more explicitly so than in Beardsley's *Toilet of Salome*. Although the institute had previously commissioned poster designs from artists, such as Stephen Adam's "very large artistic poster" in 1893,[102] there was a departure in 1895 when it was announced that "An exhibition of 'posters' and designs for posters will be made in the entrance hall and vestibule of the Institute," with the forthcoming show "advertised in the streets of Glasgow by means of two specially designed posters full of originality and suggestion."[103] That was certainly true of Mackintosh's poster—some nine feet long—although a wag likened it to "a map of the new subway with the down lines red, and up lines black."[104] It was followed by one for the *Scottish Musical Review* in tones of drab blue and purple balanced by green highlights (106), the design of which corresponded to the metal discs atop the Glasgow School of Art frontage and to the torso in *The Tree of Influence*. Mackintosh is cross-dressing his motifs. The second poster for the institute by the other members of The Four—with their names vertically aligned—features a male figure covering a female. His raised arms and outstretched hands imitate a pose adopted by Frances in one of the Dunure photographs.

Despite, or possibly because of, the criticisms at the 1896 Arts and Crafts Society exhibition in London, Gleeson White traveled to Glasgow to meet The Four and their associates. He had his reservations, particularly about Mackintosh's posters. While accepting that they should indeed attract notice he did opine that "Mr. Macintosh's posters may be somewhat trying to the average person," while having the insight to perceive that Mackintosh's decorations for the Buchanan Street tearooms

THE SCOTTISH
MUSICAL REVIEW

PUBLISHED ON THE 1ST OF EACH MONTH
PRICE TWO PENCE

"appear to be the first examples of permanent mural decoration evolved through the poster."[105]

White accepted the unity of purpose among The Four, whom Talwin Morris referred to as "this little group of Glasgow workers,"[106] but he did distinguish between Mackintosh and his fellows. Mackintosh was an architect and that was what set him apart. The Macdonalds and McNair remained within a semimystical symbiosis of thought, working with the private, small-scale, and two-dimensional while Mackintosh was practicing a public three-dimensional art. Was it because McNair could not compete that he would make the decision to leave Glasgow? It is one view. On the other hand, he had an exhibition in London in 1898 of pastels hailed as "the work of a dreamer in love with the land of faery,"[107] and the showing of *Ysighlu* and *The Dew* in Liverpool "attracted the warm comment and encouragement of very competent critics."[108]

Also in 1898 McNair was offered and accepted a post in Liverpool as an instructor in decorative design at the School of Architecture and Applied Art, which was noted for its allegiance to the arts and crafts. It was a prestigious job, "an obvious great success," Muthesius called it,[109] and it guaranteed a regular salary, which meant that at the close of the academic year he could afford to marry Frances Macdonald at St. Augustine's Episcopal Church in Dumbarton on 14 June 1899. The witnesses included George Best McNair and Charles Macdonald, who also witnessed the marriage of "Charles Rennie MacKintosh, Bachelor, age 31" to "Margaret Macdonald Spinster, age 35" in the same church on 22 August 1900, when Mackintosh gave his address as "120 Mains Street, Glasgow." The sisters were married from Dunglass Castle, to the west of Dumbarton, the home of their brother Charles Macdonald, a Glasgow lawyer, who took over the property in 1899 from Talwin Morris who had acquired it in 1893 when he came to Glasgow. After their marriage Herbert and Frances set up house at 54 Oxford Street, Liverpool, and Charles and Margaret in the first-floor corner flat in the Blythswood new town. Inevitably, therefore, the close association of The Four dissolved. ▪▪

106. Poster for the *Scottish Musical Review*,
Charles Rennie Mackintosh

Along with his crib of the review of Ruskin's *Stones of Venice* Mackintosh left six sets of lecture notes,[1] all of which, apart from "Seemliness" of 1902, belong to the early 1890s when Mackintosh was in his early twenties. To whom was he lecturing? That is not always known although one audience was "a literary society" in Glasgow, judging by the allusions, and another, "chiefly composed of pecture [*sic*] painters," may have been the members of the Glasgow Art Club. Such audiences would account for the discursive nature of the papers, giving, too, an assurance that he could extract and use as his own, without being challenged, whole passages from Ruskin or from a text as recent as W. R. Lethaby's *Architecture, Mysticism and Myth* of 1891. The remaining papers, more specific in subject matter, were for professionals. The narration of the Italian sojourn was read to the Glasgow Architectural Association in the autumn of 1892 some eighteen months after the paper on "Scotch Baronial." But the didactic "Elizabethan Architecture"? An extraordinary subject for one subsequently hailed as a pioneer of modernism.

And why in a short space of time should Mackintosh be called upon so often to lecture? That the two partners of Honeyman and Keppie frequently addressed fellow professionals as well as the Philosophical Society of Glasgow, within which there was an architectural section, may have provided a rostrum for Mackintosh and perhaps, too, for Charles Whitelaw, another assistant, who lectured to the Architectural Association on "Early Irish Architecture" when Alexander McGibbon was in the chair.[2] Who was behind the invitations given to Mackintosh? Was he Honeyman's protégé? Was he an up-and-coming name? Or was he a compulsive self-publicist nourished by the numerous press reports of his student progress and his design projects?

That he chafed at the professional restraints that governed the accreditation of design work to the partners is evident in *The Bailie* and his defiant claim to authorship at the foot of the page of drawings of the Art Club details. That was as far as he could go publicly. Even so the episode must have been the talk of the town. Privately, however, he gave vent to his pent-up feelings to his new friend Hermann Muthesius in 1898. "You must understand that for the time being I am under a cloud—as it were—although the building [the *Glasgow Herald*] in Mitchell Street here was designed by me the architects are or were Messrs. Honeyman and Keppie—who employ me as an *assistant*. So if you reproduce any photographs of the building you must give the architect's name not mine. You will see that this is very unfortunate for me, but I hope when brighter days come, I shall be able to work for myself entirely and claim my work as mine."[3] And one can but sympathize when, at the opening ceremony for the first phase of the Art School building, Mackintosh jostled with the crowd in the street while Keppie presided above with the platform party.

Like hens in a dung yard scholars have picked over Mackintosh's lectures. Yet it is doubtful if the texts would have been published[4] three-quarters a century after his death if their author had not become an idol of the chattering classes. The lectures bear evidence of being the hastily gathered thoughts of a young man who rather disingenuously claimed that his "knowledge of books is only that of the general reader"[5] when his cited sources ranged from the theoretical *Discourses on Art* by Sir Joshua Reynolds to Charles Eastlake's *Hints on Household Taste* and the award of the RIBA gold medal of the Royal Institute of British Architects to the French proponent of symbolism César Daly in 1892. In his acceptance speech, which was extensively quoted in the architectural press, Daly called for architecture to be "not only a useful building matter, but a poetical form of life."[6]

In the first untitled paper Mackintosh, despite his reservations because Ruskin was "unprofessional,"[7] nails his colors to the mast by espousing allegiance to Ruskin. "Let me state here that I shall refer frequently to Ruskin throughout the paper—not that I consider him by any means the Architectural critic, but as one whose writings are more practical and captivating to the ordinary listener, than the dryer but more truthful treatment of other Architectural critics and historians."[8] Was it for this paper that he so sedulously cribbed the review of *The Stones of Venice*? "Few books can be more eloquent more enthusiastic or more beautifully illustrated than his Stones of Venice or Seven Lamps of Architecture,"[9] and he continued with "one of Ruskin's aphorisms which is as good a definition as I am acquainted with 'All Architecture proposes an effect on the human mind not merely a service to the human frame,"[10] which leads him to endorse Ruskin's criticism of the Crystal Palace where "the want of appearance of stability is fatal to the introduction of such a style for either domestic, civil or ecclisiastical [sic] buildings."[11]

The other author whom Mackintosh leans upon, often without due acknowledgment, is Sir George Gilbert Scott, who is, however, quoted directly when arguing that architecture unlike the sister arts of sculpture and painting is unique in that "apart from practical necessity or utility it arises from the necessity and then from the desire to clothe the result with beauty."[12] One can almost hear Scott when Mackintosh writes later: "Here let me note in parenthesis, one of these curiosities of popular criticism so often encountered, namely, that Gothic as opposed to Classic is quite unsuitable for present day requirements,"[13] leading him to assert that "we should be a little less cosmopolitan and rather more national in our Archi[tecture],"[14] which allowed him to admire Scott's St. Mary's Episcopal Cathedral in Edinburgh (1873–79) where "he yet took the ornaments peculiarly Scotch as seen at Holyrood, Kelso etc. as his models."[15] Odd that Mackintosh did not select as his chosen model for approval the new buildings of the University of Glasgow, the embodiment of all that he wished to convey.

It is, however, when speaking to the "pecture [sic] painters" that Mackintosh reveals a more directed polity derived, however, from Lethaby's musings. One can hear, too, the voice of experience for "there should come of regular apprenticeship and long practice in any art or craft a certain instinct of insight not possesed by mere outsiders although never so learned."[16] Even so the practice of architecture is not exclusive, being "the synthesis of the fine arts, the commune of all the crafts,"[17] and he sets down a text which, though first expressed by Lethaby, has come to be one of Mackintosh's own mission statements. "Old architecture lived because it had a purpose. Modern architecture, to be real, must not be a mere envelope without contents."[18] Then comes the great rallying call. "We must clothe modern ideas, with modern dress—adorn our designs with living fancy. We shall have designs by living men for living men."[19] Noble sentiments robed in borrowed words. But how to implement them? There was the rub.

Mackintosh would have considered with a keen eye Scott's University of Glasgow buildings then rising anew over the bosky groves of the Kelvingrove Park in the city's west end for the edifice was witness to Scott's moralizing on "nature as the great guide"[20] and the uses of "the three great features" of a Gothic building: "the pointed arch, the mullioned window and the high-pitched roof"[21] in unison with the "triumph of metallic construction."[22] Yet this, as the undergarment beneath French, Scottish, and English habiliments, would not have offended Mackintosh's aesthetic sensibilities, since, "These two comparatively modern materials iron and glass though eminently suitable for many purposes will never worthily take the place of stone, because of this defect the want of mass."[23]

To a young professional the university buildings must have supplied many an idea and not least because Scott was that rare phenomenon in Glasgow, a southern architect and one who was equally celebrated as an expositor. Thus, when Mackintosh was composing his paper on "Scotch Baronial Architecture," he introduced into the text not only Scott's thoughts but his very words so that Scotland's architecture was "as indigenous to our country as our wild flowers, our family names, our customs, or our political constitution."[24] That the true author was not acknowledged—that is not uncommon with those who must be composing in a hurry. Mackintosh saw his country's architecture as offering "that irrisistable [sic] attraction which compels many of the members of this association to visit the various castles and policies in this country, not only under the balmy influences of summer, but along muddy roads and snowy path, and with glowing heart but shivering hand to sketch the humble cottage, the more pretentious mansion, or the mutilated though venerable castle with feelings of the most indescribable delight."[25] And he praised, albeit with Scott's words, "the extraordinary facility of our style in decorating, constructing, and in converting structural and useful features into elements of beauty … many examples of which still remaining show how all the arts were united in one building."[26] Scott had railed because "the equally monstrous practice of castle building is, unhappily, not yet extinct,"[27] but Mackintosh in his time accepted that, "from some recent buildings which have been erected it is clearly evident that this style is coming to life again."[28] Why was that? Some of the answer was encapsulated in the record of Mackintosh's papers in which he considered style. "The Elizabethan may be more properly called Transitional Architecture,"[29] which permitted the inclusion of George Heriot's Hospital, Edinburgh (begun in 1628), "so escentially [sic] in the Transitional style,"[30] as well as the old college in Glasgow. It was a style in which "Features originally admired for defence were clung to with that instinctive affection which springs from use and tradition … The great English mansions thus came to assume that air of mingled dignity and homeliness, which has ever been considered their most pleasing characteristic."[31] For Mackintosh they were the epitome of "the comfort and refinement of English home life,"[32] words that could have been penned by Muthesius when he came to write *Das Englische Haus.*

Mackintosh was in no doubt as to who had effected what came to be known as the Free Style. "And I am glad to think that now there are men such as Norman Shaw, John Bentley, John Belcher, Mr. Bodley, Leonard Stokes and the late John D. Sedding … men who more and more are freeing themselves from correct antiquarian detail and who go straight to nature."[33] Mackintosh had contended earlier that, "If we trace the artistic form of things made by man to their origin, we find a direct inspiration from if not a direct imitation of nature."[34] If nature was the guide, "What then," asked Lethaby, "will this art of the future be? The message will still be of nature and man, of order and beauty; but all will be sweetness, simplicity, freedom, confidence and light."[35] Even ten years later, when burdened with the responsibilities, tensions, and worries of architectural partnership, Mackintosh could still proclaim his credo, echoing

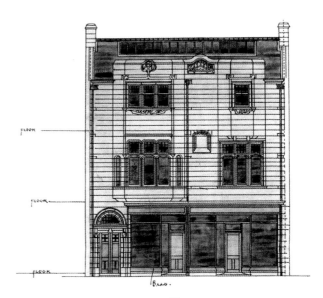

FRONT ELEVATION

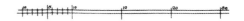

Ruskin: "Art is the flower—Life is the green leaf … you must offer the flowers of the art that is in you."[36] Fine, albeit borrowed, words but difficult to put into effect. A first forced and literal attempt was the Conservative Club at Helensburgh,[37] where Mackintosh introduced his enthusiasm for Elizabethan architecture (107) with "the mullioned windows and projections common in Elizabethan work serving to redeem the front from flatness and insipidity."[38] The major bay is framed, as in the oriel window at Maybole Castle, by moldings dropping from a tree to carved heads.

While Mackintosh was struggling to evolve his architectural philosophy and compromise his aestheticism he was living out his daily life in the Second City. Its contrasts are summarized in one short entry in *The Bailie* in 1896. "Great Western Road, the noblest thoroughfare in Glasgow, has its drawbacks. Not long after passing Botanic Gardens you have a palace of 'doul' and sorrow [Gartnavel Asylum] to the left of you, pits to the right of you, and if you go straight ahead,

107. Design for the Conservative Club, Helensburgh, John Honeyman and Keppie

you stumble against the iron works of Knightswood, and the miner's houses of Scatrig.... The very sensitive Glaswegian should never go west of Kelvinside."[39]

Across the city 'the heavy, ugly, and provincial side of Glasgow cannot be well ignored ... where work-people ... must make their dwelling-place and spend their lives ... fifty to one common stair."[40] In 1890 the city's medical officer of health reported that "354,000 of the population of Glasgow lived, or rather tried to exist, in houses of one or two rooms."[41] In that same year the Dean of Guild Court, which had jurisdiction over building control, at one sitting granted permits for building starts totaling "1,270 in all, of which 54 were for houses, 19 for churches and halls, 103 for warehouses and stores, and 94 for alterations and additions. The number of apartments in each class of house was—230 of one room, 905 of two rooms, 274 of three rooms, 83 of four rooms, 36 of five rooms, and 17 of six rooms."[42] So when Mackintosh and his bride set up home in a rented flat, as was usual, of six rooms, one of which was for a maid, how was it affordable on a draughtsman's salary?

And Glasgow was expanding with "the crazy work-shops straggling over acres of outskirts, the gaunt, blind barns that hide the smelting, forging and casting ... From the flats above the canal at Port-Dundas, you examine the whole topography of the city ... the fashionable suburb in the distance is seen to be hedged in by a district of mills and factories that draw nearer on either side, and at your feet the gables of tenements gape at you, with the hearths already provided for un-born people."[43] Of this same area it was reported in the summer of 1895: "No wonder the building trade is flourishing when no fewer than 2,200 houses have been added to the city since May last. These have been erected mainly in the north-western district"[44] of Maryhill, which lay below Port Dundas, an inland port serviced from the Forth and Clyde Canal that, even by the mid-century, "is now covered with factories, colour works, chemical works, dye works, grinding mills, mills for log-wood, dye and bread stuffs, founderies, machine shops, potteries and soap works, etc.—presenting within the area of a few acres, a view of manufacturing and curious industry unparalleled in any other city in the world."[45] It was to the open ground to the north that there came Macfarlane's Saracen Iron Works and the North British Locomotive Works, sucking in huge numbers of workers in whose wake came women and children. All needed social, religious, and philanthropic programs such as those provided by the Canal Boatmen's Institute. (108)

"Fully a year ago," it was reported in June 1893, "an appeal was made for subscriptions to build and furnish a mission hall, refreshment and reading rooms at Port Dundas, for the benefit especially of the canal boatmen and their families ... The institute, designed by Messrs. Honeyman and Kepppie, is the most attractive building in the district."[46] One benefit was that "it will have a drying-room where the men in such a condition may have their clothes dried. Hitherto, they have been wont to see one or other of the public houses which cluster in a most extraordinary way round this

108. Canal Boatmen's Institute, John Honeyman and Keppie, *Academy Architecture*

district."[47] The drying room in the basement was "fitted up with hot-water pipes, the temperature will be so high that boatmen coming in from their work drenched to the skin will have their clothing dried without loss of time ... The number of boatmen travelling to and from Port Dundas is about 800, and in addition to these there are a great many labourers working at the wharves." There was a coffee room with "a service-window in the vestibule, which will enable a carter who is anxious to snatch a hasty refreshment to do so, and at the same time keep a watchful eye on his horse." With its savings bank and reading room the Institute would surely be a beacon for "the social and spiritual good of the district."[48]

As is usual with an architectural commission there was a long gestation beginning in 1891 when Honeyman and Keppie "received letter from Mr. King accepting our letter to do work at 5p/c not charging for preliminary sketches etc. Oct. 20. At Committee meeting held in Major Allan's office today ... received instructions to accept the following offers," which included mason work at £1941:7:6 with a reduction of £20 if the red sandstone from the Locharbriggs quarry in the south of Scotland was selected.[49] With the costs established there was an appeal for funds, which may have continued into 1896, three years after work had started, when, as the press announced, "The Boatmen's Institute ought to be well patronised on Saturday evening, as a very select party from the West-end have organised a concert for that evening. Among other attractive items on the programme is a whistling solo by a lady who is well known in fashionable circles."[50] One donor was Major Allan who "presented the building with a handsome turret clock. There is no other public clock in the vicinity ... It really supplies a long felt want ... The clock is lighted at night."[51] Its design of intertwined nude females was considered by *The British Architect* to be "so original and clever" that it was reproduced alongside a perspective of the building, inviting comparison with the clock dial in the gallery of the Glasgow Art Club and thus suggesting the hand of Mackintosh, although, given the dating, the genesis of the design should be credited to Keppie with the style best described as transitional. The

massing, on a steeply sloping corner site, was robust and held together as a composition by the sturdy clock tower crowned by a lead-covered wooden belfry, which was praised as "a Scottish type, examples of which may still be seen in Fife, Stirling and Dumfries. It is now the only tower of this kind in Glasgow since the fine one which existed at the old college buildings has been demolished."[52] If that was the model can one assume that the institute tower was detailed by Mackintosh?

The early 1890s were busy years for the practice of Honeyman and Keppie, with a mixture of work that must at times have demanded all the energies of the staff so that one cannot always define that this or that building is by Mackintosh. As in any established practice old clients would return. So perhaps the shipping agent who was Major Allan at the Canal Boatmen's Institute was the son of Allan the shipowner at Lansdowne Church of thirty years before. The job books are an indication of the number and range of the firm's commissions. Alongside the schools and the larger commercial works, such as the Fairfield offices, the *Glasgow Herald*, and the Glasgow Art Club there were the churches, which were a staple of the firm.

Prestwick Free Church required a tower and spire and East Kilbride Church a "Communion Table" and a "Platform Chair." A chapel was mooted for Loretto School, a new Free Church at Kirkcudbright, and works at churches in Skelmorlie, Rhu, and elsewhere. Around the Clyde estuary there were mansions such as Dunloe at Wemyss Bay and Moreland in nearby Skelmorlie where, following on a site visit by Keppie and the approval of plans, "Submitted working drawings in pencil. These approved and instructed to proceed inking them in and make necessary scale drawings." In 1893 "Mr. H[oneyman] visited Castlemilk and got instructions with regard to additions." Castlemilk, to the south of Glasgow, was a sixteenth-century tower with eighteenth- and early-nineteenth-century additions and was grand enough to warrant a site visit by the firm's principal as did Camis Eskan, a marine villa on the north shore of the Clyde estuary. A week after Honeyman's visit "MacIntosh and Stoddart went to Craigendorran and measured house."[54] Perhaps they sailed downriver from Glasgow to the pier at Craigendorran, a day out, which would have been a break from the routine of the office where estimates for the Queen Margaret College medical wing were lying. That the firm was masterminding that project doubtless owed as much to the personal recommendation of Mrs. Elder as to the success of the Anderson Medical College. And it would have been of interest to one of the firm's partners that the first intake of students in 1884 had included Elizabeth and Jane Keppie.[55]

Queen Margaret College, "now become part of the University and is its Department for Women," was founded by local philanthropy but in this case led by wealthy, intelligent, and forceful women, headed by Mrs. Elder, who in 1883 "bought for the use of the College North Park House, a large handsome building in the west end of Glasgow adjoining the Botanic Gardens, and about ten minutes walk from the University . . . erected in 1870–72 by Mr. John Bell with the object of utilising it partly as a picture gallery and museum of curios and partly as a dwelling-house. The College is built in the Renaissance style. Its architect was the late Mr. J. T. Rochead, Glasgow, and on his retirement from business on account of severe illness before the building was completed, his designs were carried out by Mr. John Honeyman, Glasgow."[56] Mrs. Elder was prepared to forgo a rent and pledged that the title deeds would be handed over once an endowment fund of £20,000 had been raised,[57] for which Mrs. Campbell [of Tullichewan] having by drawing rooms held in Glasgow and different parts of the surrounding country and by other means and at the expense to herself of much time and trouble during the last year and a half succeeded in awakening the interest of Glasgow and the west of Scotland."[58] When almost all the requisite capital had been ingathered "a sum of £2,000 has been gifted to the College by Mrs. Elder . . . to meet several expenses of the Medical Classes which have now been established,"[59] as by the close of 1891, "The Laboratory accommodation now available would be entirely inadequate and insanitary in case of an increase in the number of students in a further session."[60]

So it was that in October 1892 a Grand Bazaar to raise £10,000 was to be held in St. Andrew's Halls over five days. Sideshows would include "Concerts, Shadow Pantomime, Bicycle Races, Grand Variety Palace, Palmistry, Marionettes, Theatricals, Banjo Bands, Aunt Sally, Sketches by Boz." In the raffle of paintings a volume of sketches by "Her Imperial Majesty the Empress Frederick of Germany shows very considerable power and dexterity. James McNeill Whistler has been gracious enough to send a most exquisite etching. It is a view of a flat country and in the horizon a host of windmills . . . Mr. John Lavery has a delicate watercolour of a morocco dancing girl . . . among the gems of the collection are examples of R. Macaulay Stevenson, David Gauld . . . Miss Constance Walton, Francis Newbery, Alex. N. Paterson, Grosvenor Thomas." As individuals, such as the chemical manufacturer Campbell White, who subscribed £500,[61] gave generously the sum raised totaled £11,973 less expenses of £1,303.[62]

When the medical extension (109) was opened in November 1895 the interior (110), long since gutted, was commended for "its compactness, its complete equipment and the very artistic nature of the woodwork and painting . . . while the cool greens and whites are so pleasing to the eye. . . . The central hall is square and lofty with a gallery on the second floor which, reached by a turret staircase gives entrance to a small laboratory for work in connection with the museum, the microscope room and the gallery of the museum. The museum itself is on the right hand of the entrance . . . On the left one finds a cloakroom furnished in green woodwork . . . one of the brightest and prettiest features of the College. Beyond it is the lecture room with tiers of raised seats . . . the south wall is covered with cement, which gives a white surface for the projection of lantern pictures. Parallel to the theatre is the dissecting room, lit by three ranges of windows arranged like a modern factory roof."[63]

However, not everyone was so enthusiastic and even before the completion there was much criticism in the press. "What is this hideous fire-brick monster that is raising its ungainly form and assuming such alarming proportions in the grounds of Queen Margaret College? . . . This intruder is an

eyesore and an outrage to anyone with even a slight trace of the artistic in their composition." Two days later there were more specific criticisms. "The two large openings in the east wall look like places for running a bogie railway for supplying material for the crematorium, and the two small dungeon windows, I have no doubt are meant to shed a little light on the 'New Woman,' who may have grown refractory, and required a little solitary confinement." Another likened the building to "a Russian country jail" while another saw in "the sickly, yellow wall" the influence of Beardsley. Attention was drawn to the "plans of the building which may be seen in the Fine Art Institute."[64] And that prompts a question. Who was the designer? Perhaps it was a question that was being asked when the building opened since a paragraph in the *Glasgow Herald* recorded the indebtedness of the lecturer in anatomy "to Professor Thomson, of Oxford, whose model anatomical department he and Mr. Keppie were permitted to examine ... a feature which characterised the building throughout, and which made it unique among its kind—viz. The simplicity, but variety and artistic quality of the detail."[65] Forty years after the opening Mackintosh was recollected as "a young apprentice with Mr. Keppie who designed the building. A good deal of the detail, of the decoration was by Mackintosh."[66]

That is the division of labor between a principal and an assistant that one would expect in a busy architectural practice. Yet still one raises the question. Who determined the overall style which was so at variance with the florid detailing of the attached palazzo, whereas the college's medical wing was a Scottish tower—with a turret staircase and the overall mass pierced by less than a handful of small windows—reminiscent of the Ayrshire castles

sketched in 1895? But Keppie was one of that party. Was he not out and about sketching? The three large upper windows with their tongued lintels reappear in Keppie's work. Yet it was Mackintosh who drew the perspective (111)—an image of the Pre-Raphaelite *hortus conclusus* where two damsels walk in an enclosed scene in which the college's addition stands

110, 111. Queen Margaret College, laboratory and perspective,
John Honeyman and Keppie, *Academy Architecture*

109. Queen Margaret College,
John Honeyman and Keppie

isolated within a grove. Here there is no hint of the factories, forges, quays, and mills crowding the slopes less than a mile to the north where a teeming populace, lodged in tenements crowding every newly mapped street, stabbed the conscience of the well-to-do living to the south across the gorge of the river Kelvin.

Since its inception the congregation of Westbourne Church had subscribed to and organized in Maryhill a social welfare program, which was headed by "a most conscientious Bible Woman ... visiting families who had no Church connections," and receiving, after the Sunday evening meetings, reports "of blessing received and comfort derived from the addresses given there by the various speakers." Tracts were distributed. "These often form the subject of remark during the week when the Bible Woman is visiting, thus giving her excellent opportunities of bringing home the truth." In 1893 the Sunday school had a roll of 213. The practicalities of daily life were provided for by a kitchen meeting, a girls' sewing class, a penny savings bank, and a library of 480 books. The drawback to further endeavor was "the inadequacy of the Mission premises," although the hope was expressed in 1894 that "a building worthy of our congregation may soon be built and occupied."[67]

Four years later "a letter from Messrs. Montgomerie and Flemings [the owners of the Kelvinside estate] offered land for a church and mission hall," with John Honeyman consulted about a site. In January 1899 sketch plans were submitted for "the proposed Mission building together with a house for the officer," but omitting the church, at a cost of £2,500. By the end of that year the Ruchill Halls were ready after "various small deviations from original plans had been made ... in consultation with Mr. Keppie."[68]

A mile to the east another mission was supplied by the congregation of St. Matthew's Free Church, which "sprang ... out of the revival movement associated with the name of Mrs. Moody which swept over the city in 1874."[69] At first there were rented premises "above a large spirit shop," which were replaced by "model mission premises" in 1886.[70] A decade later "there set in an extraordinary extension of house-building in the vicinity, in consequence of which the population has so increased that the call for a new church seems to be imperative"; with generous benefactions from two members of the congregation of St. Matthew's "the new buildings are now in course of preparation."[71]

When a decision had been made in November 1896 to upgrade St. Matthew's mission into an independent charge and "the name of a competent architect" having been submitted, "Mr. Keppie accordingly prepared a sketch which had been under the consideration of the committee showing the proposed church" whereupon the committee advised that "it would be desirable to obtain an additional sketch as applicable to the western site" of the steading, an indication of its once rural nature. In March 1897 "the plan lying in the Church Hall which had been inspected by members was the one which the Committee proposed to accept." A year later concerns were expressed about the slow rate of building. Another year on and it was reported that it was "not possible to open the Church for worship sooner than six months from this date," although "the Architect is of opinion that the actual expenditure will not exceed the estimates." Yet when the building was handed to the client, the estimate had risen by £2,000 over the previous one of £7,000.[72]

As Mackintosh's only built essay in Gothic, Queen's Cross Church must be an aberration to those who would see him as a twentieth-century modernist. When considering Mackintosh as just that Pevsner omits the church from the canon of architecture, and Howarth, though setting down a factual account, gives no stylistic classification. However, Charles Marriott, writing some thirty years before Howarth, ascribes originality to Queen's Cross albeit "modern ecclesiastical architecture has a certain air of unreality, a lack of conviction."[73] Half a century previously, Eastlake had hit upon the dilemma. "Architects must learn to sacrifice something of their antiquarian tendencies: the Public must learn to sacrifice something of their conventional taste."[74] Such changes in architectural perception and consciousness were eased because, as Marriott noted, "It was observed that the latest phase of the Gothic Revival was closely associated with the Arts and Crafts movement. This association produced a definite school of church architects careful of colour, texture and surface, and enthusiastic in decorative detail,"[75] which just about sums up the achievement at Queen's Cross where in larger respects Mackintosh fails. A design had to be produced to secure the commission; if that meant using the Gothic style then so be it, even if the impression left is of a rushed job, of a lack of commitment so that the finished product is like the curate's egg.

The massing of Queen's Cross Church (112) may be compared to Honeyman's Trinity Congregational Church, Glasgow (1863–64), that is, with a tower at the intersection of two streets and a main elevation with groups of paired lancets, although in rearranging these Mackintosh fractured his composition. Marriott recognized that "only the flavour of Gothic" was retained at Queen's Cross[76] where the flat unarticulated planes of English Decorated and Perpendicular are combined

112. Queen's Cross Church

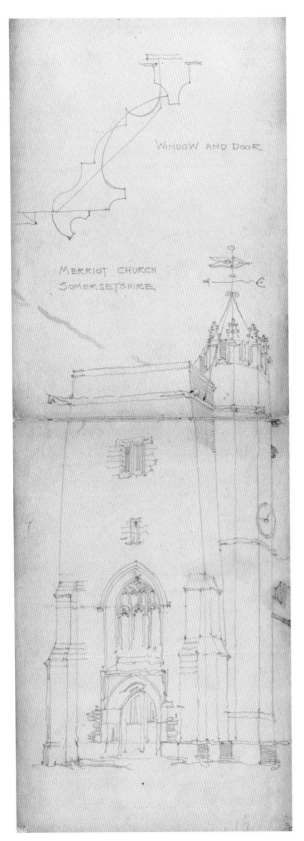

WINDOW AND DOOR

MERRIOT CHURCH
SOMERSETSHIRE

113. Merriott Church tower, Somerset,
sketch by Charles Rennie Mackintosh

with the Picturesque principles of projection and recession and variety in height and fenestration.

It has long been known that the tower is a pastiche of an 1895 summer sketch by Mackintosh of the unfinished tower of Merriott Church, Somerset, and illustrated in *The British Architect*. (113) Why use that model? Given Mackintosh's avowal of the architecture of his own land why not cull the volumes of Scottish church architecture published by MacGibbon and Ross from 1896 on? Or was there novelty in using a source that defied antiquarianism with battered walls, slit windows, and no spire, the omission of which was a saving, avoiding the potential embarrassment of never being affordable.

The pair of linked bays to the east of the tower has low windows (to light an aisle) with larger Decorated-style windows above (to light a gallery). The succeeding recessed bays are locked in place by a double-height porch (114), an unusual feature in Scotland but derived perhaps from St. Nicholas Church, Abbotsbury. The Queen's Cross porch is topped not with pinnacles but with miniature square turrets as at another Abbotsbury church—St. Catherine's, notable for "a pointed tunnel vault so closely panelled that it looks like twenty-four hoops across ... one thinks of Scotland rather than England or of the Continent."[77] Or of the closely boarded vault of Queen's Cross?

And what of the plan? That has puzzled commentators who have looked to contemporary English works by men for whom Mackintosh had expressed admiration. Mackintosh, however, seems to have laid his own audit trail—one that has been overlooked—with the drawings that he retained and published of yet another Dorset church, St. Martin's, Wareham (115), with Decorated windows, two south doors, and an aisle carried on square bases, featuring a chancel and once a western gallery—the justification perhaps for a feature at Queen's Cross not seen to accord with current liturgical usage. Thus it leads to a consideration of Queen's Cross as an exemplar of advanced liturgical thinking so that one marvels that the adherents of perceived strict Presbyterian thinking accepted a layout and ritualistic arrangements (116) not so far removed from those commonly found

114. Queen's Cross Church

in more Catholic denominations, a hint of which was expressed when the *Glasgow Herald* reported, "The church is somewhat novel in plan; the whole of the nave being roofed over without obstruction," and remarking too on the "one transept" illuminating the south gallery.[79] But there was more. For Mackintosh to take a Saxon church as his model avoided any taint of medieval Catholicism while permitting the introduction of a stepped sanctuary, a piscina, and an arched and parclosed chancel with a traceried east window set high to catch the light filtering between the enclosing tenements. To further emphasize the sacramental nature of worship the pulpit lost its central position by being placed, as was once traditional, on the north side of the chancel. (117) Such changes, preceded as they were by those in Glasgow Cathedral, were no doubt indicative of the High Church leanings of Honeyman. He would have been interested in Govan Old Parish (by Rowand Anderson) of 1884 and Burnet's Barony Church of 1886 as well as Sedding's Holy Trin-

ity, Sloane Street, London, of 1888, all of which dispensed with structural compartmentation. At Queen's Cross gone were arches, triforium, clerestory, and arcades, leaving narrow passage aisles on the north and on the south where it passes below a gallery with dropped panels, preceding those in the library of the School of Art. (118)

And what of the decoration necessarily restricted in scope and form by the tenets of Presbyterianism? According to Lethaby, "What we now call 'ornament' and 'decoration' once had a purpose and meaning."[80] That was not upheld by Mackintosh's colleague Alexander McGibbon, who had delivered a paper to the Glasgow Ecclesiological Society on "Symbolism in Architecture" in which he contended that "In thus stripping the church fabric of symbolism, I trust few will think that architecture loses anything of real worth. Symbolism is only good in so far as it is understood by those whom it is intended to impress, and the evidence that is submitted to prove that this alleged symbolism was at one time currently accepted is quite inadequate . . . To maintain that the function of Mediaeval Church Architecture was to set forth Christianity is to misunderstand a noble art, and to disservice alike theology and ecclesiology." At the conclusion of the meeting "the opinions expressed were in opposition to the views of many members of the Society,"[81] among whom Mackintosh could have been numbered since the published perspective of Queen's Cross[82] indicates a brotherhood of stained glass and statuary (119), very little of which was executed although the Holy Ghost as the dove does descend over the pulpit. And the carved stems, fronds, and seed heads around the chancel—will they fall "into good ground and bring forth fruit," according to the parable of the sower in the Gospel of St. Matthew, where it is enjoined, "Who hath ears to hear, let him hear," an injunction particularly relevant to the founding of Queen's Cross by St. Matthew's Free Church, where the sermon would have been predominant in the service.

If one wishes to assess the subtleties that lift Queen's Cross from the mainstream of conventional church architecture one need look only to the firm's other large ecclesiastical

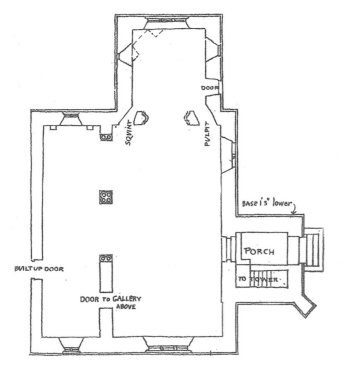

115. Wareham Church, plan, *British Architect*

116. Queen's Cross Church

117, 118. Queen's Cross Church, pulpit and south aisle

A meeting took place in Brechin, Angus, in the late summer of 1897 "for the purpose of considering the plans of the restoration of the Parish Church prepared sometime ago by Mr. Honeyman, Architect" at the behest of the late minister.[84] An awakening interest in restoring the cathedral to something like its medieval form meant undoing the reparations made at the beginning of the century[85] by "taking down 4 stone stairs to Galleries" and "the ruble work filling opening between Nave and Choir"[86] as well as the necessity of considering the "girth of mouldings"[87] and "the cost of responds, pillar and arches."[88] The perspective (121) issued to boost the appeal fund's income, though rendered dramatic with swirling clouds and grainy shadows,[89] had none of the fancy of imagination of the Queen's Cross perspective. Brechin was a study in antiquarianism. Honeyman attended meetings though beginning to lose his sight, so that, as he reported in the winter of 1899, he had "been laid up for about six months with inflammation in one of my eyes,"[90] and by the start of the new century he was sending "Mr. T. Taylor on Saturday by the early train"[91] possibly because Keppie "is now abroad."[92] Although David Gauld was engaged to provide stained glass and Kellock Brown executed statues of St. Matthew and of St. Paul in silvered bronze for the pulpit,[93] there is no indication at Brechin of Mackintosh's hand, which is so unmistakeable in even the most mundane of commissions for the local school board.

Such boards had come into existence to enact national legislation in 1872 ordaining compulsory education for all children between the ages of five and thirteen years. In Glasgow board schools were rising just as "the Improvement Trust is busy in its endeavour to remove from Glasgow the stigma which has fallen upon it, in having such an exceptionally high death-rate, by demolishing whole districts of unhealthy dilapidated dwellings and thus indirectly causing the erection of numbers of new

commissions, such as the proposed restorations of Iona Abbey and of Brechin Cathedral, both of which in scale, antiquarian interest, and national significance were the particular concerns of Honeyman. Although a perspective of Iona in 1891 (120) showed a restored choir, transepts, and crossing tower,[83] ten years would elapse before all came to fruition.

119. Perspective of Queen's Cross Church, *Academy Architecture* (*top*)

120. Perspective showing the proposed restoration of Iona Cathedral, *Academy Architecture* (*bottom*)

houses in the outer parts of the city," where the new schools "will be large and lofty, with spacious classrooms, ample ante-room, and lavatory accommodation, with efficient heating and ventilating apparatus ... there will be separate entrances and playgrounds, and even separate staircases, to enter the class-rooms, so that the boys and girls may never associate except when under actual instruction in the eye of the teacher."

The program of school building got under way in Glasgow in the mid-1870s, with designs sought from five local firms including John Honeyman's. At this time he would have had contact with the Glasgow School Board chairman, Alexander Whitelaw, member of Parliament, the father of Charles Whitelaw, the future architectural apprentice.

Of Honeyman's three commissions Henderson Street school "will be in the Gothic style, having a corbelled out, or bay window in the center of the façade, and a belfry ssurmounting the principal entrance"; for Tureen Street the chosen style was Italian; and Rockville School "will be in an effective style of architecture ... Perhaps the most noticeable feature in connection with this building, however, is the novel plan of the ventilation. The heating is by means of hot water-pipes, which are carried round the various rooms inside the

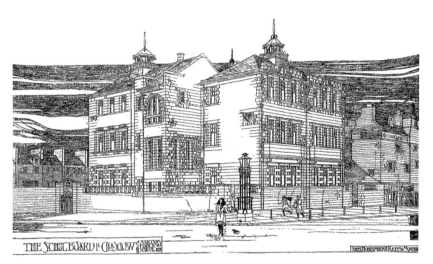

cornice, into which a supply of fresh air is also introduced by means of small gratings in the walls. Provision is thus made for a fresh current of hot air circulating constantly from the roofs of the various departments, while the foul air is drawn through gratings in the skirting, into flues placed under the respective floors, these flues again communicat-

ing with a central shaft reaching from basement to roof of the building."[94]

With the Martyrs School (122), and very much less so at the later Scotland Street, School Honeyman could only have exercised a supervisory role. With the sketch plans for Martyrs School having been approved early in 1895 the Scottish

121. Perspective showing the proposed restoration of Brechin Cathedral, *Academy Architecture* (top)

122. Perspective of the Martyrs School, *The Builder* (bottom)

Education Department sanctioned a loan of £11,700 to be repaid over fifty years.[95] The estimate for the contractual work was £10,000 plus architects' fees of £645 and fitting-out costs including "330 Boys and 330 Girls Desks and seats @ 10/− per child . . . 333 Infants @ 9/− per child."[96]

Toward the end of the building contract there was the usual urgency to meet the opening date so that "it will be necessary that you should have three or four additional plaisterers." And with the clearing away of the former mission school "it will be impossible that you can have a room in the new premises for your Savings Bank until the middle of August," after which permission was given to the neighboring churches to have "the use for Sabbath School purposes of the class rooms on the two upper floors."[97]

The layout was that of many another board school with the utilities in the basement, a drill and assembly hall flanked by classrooms, just inside the entrance, as well as two floors of classrooms and ancillary accommodation above ranged around a galleried light well illuminating the drill hall. (123)

123. Martyrs School (*top*)

124. Perspective of Scotland Street School, *Academy Architectur* (*bottom*)

Scotland Street School was very different. "The architects were Messrs. Honeyman, Keppie and Mackintosh, but it is clear that the last named has controlled the design."[98] Mackintosh's name in bold letters on the published perspective (124) was indicative of his status as a partner. Now he could be his own man, which allowed for the untrammeled originality of the design. Indeed, John Keppie would describe it as "a new type for the Glasgow Board having all the class rooms lighted from the south. All details have been carefully gone into and the result artistically and practically is excellent."[99]

With the lateral plan (125) set athwart the confined site there are only two prominent facades. The south is planar (126) with standard-size classroom windows and is without modeling save for the abstract reliefs on the ends and center of trees (127)—the armorial of the city of Glasgow—with branches and leaves enlivened by the low sun of the west of Scotland. (128) The north-facing entrance front (129) has little decoration save for foliated patterning on the circular towers flanking the entrance (130) and offset by bands of horizontal glazing. This facade had a pedigree as an adaptation by Mackintosh of his sketches (131) of the sixteenth-century Falkland Palace, Fife,[100] mediated by an office design of 1897 for the Paisley Technical School (132), where a central tower bears a frieze of marching figures[101]; it is modernistic, too, as a precursor of the Fagus Factory at Alfeld-on-the-Leine, Germany, where in 1911 Walter Gropius fulfilled what Frank Lloyd Wright called the "etherealization" of architecture by allowing the staircase to follow the curve of the glass perimeter.[102]

Scotland Street School was commissioned in August 1903 "at a fee of 3% on the cost of the building this fee to include the supplying of sketches of the proposed buildings as well as plans for the Scotch Education Department and for the Dean of Guild."[103] However, the genesis was to be painful.

Difficulties began in the next year. Modifications were asked for on the north elevation, and although "the architect strongly recommends that this should be built of white Dullatur stone" cheaper red sandstone from the Locharbriggs quarry in the south of Scotland was preferred "as scheduled."[104] A year later relations reached a breaking point when an exasperated client tried to rein in Mackintosh's ever expanding vision for the design finishes. (133) After one meeting with Mackintosh, who "was leaving town for some time," it was put to him in a letter of 1 November 1905 that "the light scheme of Tiling indicated in my letter of the 18th ultmo must be adhered to. The Board do not consider themselves responsible for the dark tiles which you have ordered and this will be a question of legal settlement ... the Stair Railing as shewn on the original Plans be adhered to ... in

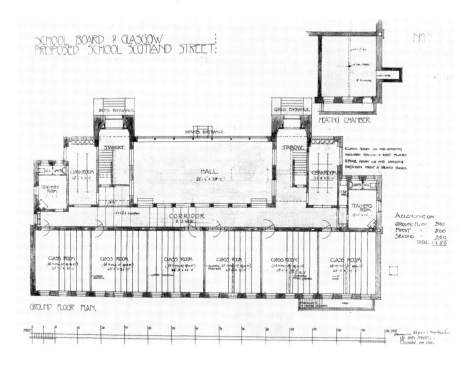

125. Scotland Street School, ground-floor plan

126. Scotland Street School, south elevation

127, 128. Scotland Street School

the matter of large windows in the Hall, and of the Class Room Doors you have departed from the Plans without the Board's sanction ...

"I am to add that the Board are very dissatisfied with several deviations which you have made without their knowledge." The row rumbled on. It seems that two sets of drawings had been issued. "This is the first instance in a long experience of school building in which an architect has considered himself at liberty to submit one set of plans to the Board and Scotch Education Department and to forward another to the Clerk of Works ... changes have been introduced which are absolutely objectionable from the point of view of school working ... in at least two important instances instructions were given to the Contractors directly."

The board's concerns were practical so that the substitution of the small panes of glass in corridors and class rooms was "not a matter of appearance but of cleanliness," which was a reason, too, for the desire to extend the staircase landings to the perimeter wall (134), although that did not happen. There were safety concerns because Mackintosh had conceived the separation of the raised corridor behind the drill hall as an open loggia, and externally (135) 'the gates

129, 130. Scotland Street School

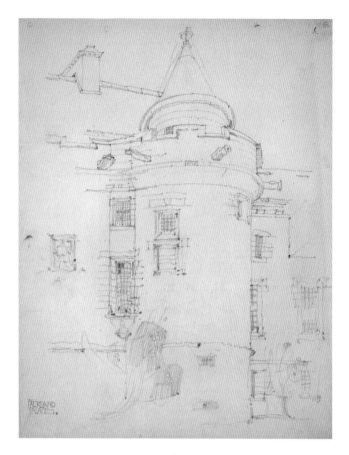

131. *Falkland Palace*, sketch by Charles Rennie Mackintosh (*top*)

132. Design for Paisley Technical College, *Academy Architecture* (*bottom*)

should be unclimbable and have no projecting stay, and also that the railings be unbendable.'[105]

It is surprising, therefore, that Mackintosh was allowed to invest his facades with so much stone carving, which was sketchy on the preparatory drawings, to evoke a series of designs, especially on the south front, which are unique in the European art of this time. Foliated embellishments had appeared on facades, such as the Majolica House, Vienna (1898), and the Innovation Store, Brussels (1901), where they bend, they swell, they curve. At Scotland Street School they are rectilinear; the sandstone arises like thickets of red twigs bearing the first green leaves of youthful spring so that it could have been of Mackintosh that Sullivan wrote: "His is a brotherhood with the trees . . . He knows that the young leaves love the dew; that the tendril reaches quietly for the twig it may cling to."[106]

More austere were the tree forms on the facades of the offices of the *Daily Record* newspaper. It may have been common practice to dress a secondary elevation in a light well or service lane with white glazed bricks, but nobody had thought such concealed facades worthy of embellishment. Yet here were tiers of bay windows and between and alongside them tree patterns of red and green stitched across the facades as three-dimensional pointillism. Unlike any other artist working in Britain, Mackintosh had achieved what Eastlake had sought to admire, namely, "Probably the most noble type of decorative sculpture is that wherein the forms of animal life and vegetation are found to be *suggested* rather than imitated."[107]

In less than a decade Mackintosh had abandoned the naturalistic decoration of the Helensburgh Conservative Club for geometric rationalism and in so doing fulfilled Lethaby's judgment that "The square when discovered became a rival, and more than a rival, of a circle in representing the functional conception of a building."[108] In his odyssey to fulfill the promise that "Art is the flower" Mackintosh would begin to understand and to demonstrate that "Art is more than shape and seeming: it is embodied soul, and can only be understood when seen against the psychological background."[109] ▪▪

133, 134, 135. Scotland Street School

ince 1869 the Glasgow School of Art (founded in 1840) had rented upper rooms in the McLellan Galleries from the city corporation. However, in a government report from the Science and Art Department at South Kensington in London in 1882 the accommodation was deemed "ill adapted for the purposes of a School of Art ... It is not too much to say that with the aggravation of the Grey dull atmosphere prevailing here for half the Year the Students labour under a positive disadvantage in Executing works for National Competition ... The Room for painting Still Life and other Groups is the Worst of the Series," with inadequate lighting and two bookcases "which are continually overhauled by the students." The modeling and lecture rooms were reached by seventy-two stairs, which were "inhumane and difficult for the Teachers. These two rooms are terribly Cold in winter and the reverse in Summer. Owing to the Heat the Lectures have to be broken off in April each year. In Winter they are afraid of introducing proper heating apparatus, in as much as being entirely constructed in Wood it would burn like tinder.'[1] What was to be done?

The remedy was a proposal "to erect a Museum, Art Gallery and School of Art on the Vacant plot of ground adjoining the Corporation Galleries"[2] for a cost of £25,000. At the close of the year sketch plans were exhibited in the Queen's Rooms.[3] The result? Nothing except for the resignation two and a half years later of a disappointed headmaster of the art school in the face of what he saw as apathy.[4]

Having advertised the post nationally and having written to "the Department ... asking as a favour if they could suggest a Suitable Successor"[5] a short leet of three names was drawn up in April 1885.[6] The front-runner was Francis Newbery (136) from the South Kensington School who, having been invited to Glasgow for an interview, was recommended as headmaster on May 19.[7] On taking up his post in September he addressed the students at the commencement of the new academic session. Coming from South Kensington as he had, it can hardly have been a surprise when Newbury stated the need "to bring manufacturers into direct communication with the school and students" to enable

Glasgow to produce 'a race of designers of her own creation, capable of supplying the manufacturers of Glasgow with workable designs, suitable for any manufacture on which the influence of art can be brought to bear,"[8] which reflected the message delivered in Glasgow some few years before by Thomas Armstrong, the art director at South Kensington, that "whereas formerly designs were mostly brought from France now they are almost entirely produced at home; some were even bought from the Art Schools in England by French manufacturers for their own use, English furniture was now largely sold in Paris in consequence of the excellence of its design," to which J. C. Burns the shipowner responded on "the scope there was for artistic decoration of vessels ... and Cabinet Work as a

136. Fra Newbery, *The Bailie*

greatly improving trade was pointed out as requiring every assistance to develop its most artistic forms."[9]

Newbery has become a legend in the annals of the Glasgow School of Art. Familiar with the teaching methodology espoused at South Kensington he had drive, was innovative, and had "a genius for teaching,"[10] so that when the new school was opened it was seen from afar as a place "where the studies of the whole school are directed by one who is himself an artist" and one who was noted for "his encouragement of original art,"[11] which had resulted some years before in praise for the students' work sent to the Liège Arts and Crafts Exhibition for "what has above all astonished us in your work is the great liberty left to the Pupils to follow their own individuality."[12]

Within weeks of assuming his post at the School of Art Newbery was requesting that potted plants be brought in from the Botanic Gardens or that "cuttings should now and again be given to draw from," and he sought and was given permission to purchase "2 Books on Design"; Leiper, J. J. Burnet, and H. E. Clifford consented "to act as a Visiting Committee to the Architecture Class" and were joined by James Thomson and James Sellars.[13] By the close of his first term in Glasgow Newbery had permission for "painting, repairing and removing a large Number of Valuable Casts from the Cellars where they were rapidly spoiling with dry rot," and an allowance was made "for a lad to assist the Janitor as Messenger and Jobbing hand and Librarian." The Glasgow Institute of Architects would put up prizes: "For the best Set of four drawings of Architectural Ornament drawn from Casts in the School of Art" as well as for measured drawings and "the best Set of lecture notes on building Construction." Newbery would lecture on anatomy and give public lectures, with the entrance money reserved as "a Nucleus of a fund for a New School of Art."[14]

Newbery also used his London contacts to invite Walter Crane to lecture, who returned in 1888 when he spoke on "Expression and Imitation in Art" with William Morris in the following year, drawing an audience for "Arts and Crafts"[15] having given notice that he "would for once try to eschew politics; and that all the more as I see something hopeful in the line that Crane and others are on; in a small way I mean."[16] In 1890 Newbery proposed that Alexander McGibbon from "Mr. Honeyman's office should be invited to act as a Visiting Master to the Architectural Class which was approved."[17] And always there was the quest for a purpose-built school "equal to any possessed by other cities,"[18] and although hope was engendered with the winding up of the 1888 exhibition and the disposal of the financial surplus the subsequent competition for an art gallery, museum, and school came to nought.[19]

In 1893 a deputation, which included Newbery and the architects W. Forrest Salmon, J. J. Burnet, and William Leiper, traveled to Manchester, Birmingham, and London to inspect schools of art "and their relationship to Technical instruction." Manchester had a school "erected fifteen years ago at a cost, land and buildings, of £28,000," where "Particular attention has been given to the development of the advanced stages of decoration and applied design"[20]; the Central School of Art in Birmingham was rated "one of the first and certainly the best equipped School in the three kingdoms."[21] In London Thomas Armstrong at South Kensington intimated that, given that schools of art were "to educate the designer in the art of design," the Glasgow School would receive encouragement "to promote instruction in such subjects as glass staining, wood carving, metalwork, pottery, bookbinding or any other industries of Glasgow and its neighbourhood in which Art is an important factor" while not allowing for the production of objects. What was not debatable, however, was that while student work in Glasgow was "equal to that done by the Art Schools of Manchester and Birmingham, it will be seen that we are far behind these Schools in matters both of accommodation and monetary aid."[22]

A year after the report was published an approach was made to the Bellahouston trustees for financial assistance "if a School for proper premises of a permanent character could be put in shape and presented to them," with Newbery, Salmon, Burnet, and Leiper being asked to measure the school's floor areas, to compute the space requirements in a new building, and to inquire as to the cost of vacant ground in nearby Renfrew Street.[23]

Negotiations dragged on until January 1895, when news came that the trustees "did not see their way to go beyond the sum of £10,000 by way of aid to the School of Art," which would permit the purchase of the ground at £6,000 with the balance of £4,000 to be handed over once the school had raised £6,000.[24] At an extraordinary meeting of the school governors in September the cost of a new school, including the land purchase, was given as £21,000, allowing for "a plain building affording accommodation equal to that at present in use."[25] In the following spring Newbery was "asked to prepare a block Plan showing how the whole Site might be utilized ... On this plan might also be indicated how much of this accommodation might be immediately constructed." That would be the basis for setting the conditions of an architectural competition for which "not more than eight Architects in Glasgow should be invited to compete" and that £14,000 "be given as the total cost of the building inclusive of lighting and heating and ventilating apparatus." If there was a 10 percent overrun on the costs a competitor would be disqualified.[26]

Although "the Conditions of the New School as prepared by the Head Master ... should be put in type,"[27] the competition brief was lost until a copy was discovered almost a century later. The submitted designs were to comprise "a plan of each floor, a longitudinal section, two cross sections, and three elevations, north, east and south." Perspectives were not allowed nor was shading "except that a flat tint of dark Indian ink may indicate the clear opening of doors and windows and a lighter tint the roofs and any recessed portions." Classrooms, some of which were "to be divisible by a moveable partition," were to have a north aspect with "windows free from mullions and small panes, and should be in the length of the room" and with the "Ornament Room ... contiguous to a corridor, or other place, where casts may be hung or stored." A flower painting room was to have a conservatory "with an exposure to the sun, in which plants and flowers, when not in use, may be kept." There were to

be studios for stained glass, china painting, metal work, wood carving, and needlework as well as a lecture theater, library, and museum, which "need not be a special room, but might be a feature in connection with the staircase." Each set of drawings "must be marked with a seal, sign, or motto," with a similarly marked envelope containing the architect's name and office address.[28]

The number of competing firms having been increased to twelve one dropped out. William Leiper wrote, "I don't think any Architect holding office as Governor or otherwise should enter the competition but that it should be left to some of the younger men whose names I have already mentioned to make designs,"[29] leaving them to lodge a complaint that the cost limitation could not provide the stipulated accommodation. "We suggest that the competing architects should be asked to state what portion of their design could be carried out within the limit of £14,000 and to give also the estimate of the completed Scheme." The signatories included J. J. Burnet, H. E. Clifford, John Honeyman and Keppie, A. McGibbon, A. N. Paterson, and James Salmon and Son. The response was that the conditions would not be altered as "it is but a plain building that is required."[30]

The architects agreed that the percentage penalty clause in the brief would "exclude any plan that can be submitted," not least because of the site, which with "its long frontage and steep gradients it is a costly one to build upon and necessarily involves a large amount of underbuilding." It was agreed, therefore, that the architects' drawings would be marked to show "Such portion of their design as can be carried out for the Sum."[31]

By December the assessors "had specially approved of one Set of Plans in particular." Notwithstanding, all the competition drawings were dispatched to South Kensington for perusal by "Mr. Thos. Armstrong, Director for Art and Major General E. R. Festing, F.R.S. of the Science Museum, S.K., who after careful inspection had selected the Same Set of Plans as best suited to the requirements of the New School." The assessors recommended "the design which bears as a distinguishing mark three Merrythoughts or

Crossed Bones," with the caveat that "instead of erecting at present the dark shaded Central Block ... the design should be so far modified as to begin the present building at Dalhousie Street and carrying it on westwards as far as the available funds will allow."[32] On Wednesday, January 13, 1897, "at 3.15 o'clock pm the Chairman ... opened the Envelope with the Motto of the Approved Plan and intimated that the name of the successful competitor was Messrs. John Honeyman and Keppie, 140 Bath St."[33]

And who were the governors who were present on that winter's afternoon? In the story of the Glasgow School of Art they are the forgotten men. Yet it was they who made the important decisions, they who were responsible, through the finance committee, for meeting the building costs, and they, through the building committee, who appointed architects, accepted prices, and supervised the progress of the works.

As with any board changes in membership occurred through the years, although continuity was maintained with nominated representatives from the town council, the university, medicine, the law, engineering, and shipbuilding as well as from the mercantile and trading communities. It was a roll call undoubtedly of the great and the good but at the end of the day they were men of substance, property, and achievement who gave Glasgow its place in the world. Not all who were asked to join the board did so. Among the few to decline were the engineer J. B. Mirrlees of "Redlands, Hillhead" and the shipbuilder William Denny of "Helenslea, Dumbarton," which had been designed by John Honeyman. Those who gave many years of voluntary service included the shipowner J. C. Burns, Robert Blackie, the sculptor John Mossman, and James Fleming of the Britannia Pottery who in time would become chairman and be knighted. Artists included Sir Francis Powell and James Guthrie, and as prominent in their field were the architects David Barclay, J. J. Burnet, W. F. Salmon, William Leiper, and John Keppie, many of whom would retire when the competition was under way.

The competitors had followed the conventional procedures, but as always there are elements of interest. Was it an oversight that a west elevation was not asked for in the brief? If so, it was an omission that was to allow Mackintosh his greatest triumph, although the firm's competition entry did include a west elevation but as a reflection of that on the east. There is the puzzle of whose hand guided the design drawings. Was there a recognition within his office that Mackintosh had the prime talent? Given the appearance of some personal design idiosyncrasies that would seem to be so. Yet the prestige and long-term job prospects would not allow a firm to leave such a competition entry entirely in the hands of a twenty-nine-year-old assistant. In the schedule of works the preamble refers to "the Authors of this design," and although that may have been a conventional nod to the position one has to note that a fortnight after the announcement of the competition result the building committee convened and "A Conference with Mr. Keppie was then held, when he received instructions to prepare the necessary finished drawings of the whole design."[34] And the canard that Newbery influenced the choice of Mackintosh's design? As it was he who had produced the competition brief it would have been strange if the competitors' drawings did not pass before him. And if Newbery was present on the winter's afternoon when the winner was declared he would have recognized Mackintosh's hand in the device of the three wishbones. Perhaps Newbery's influence or at least approval is seen in the overlayering of the initial competition concept as the design evolved.

The tenders amounted to £22,753:2:6, with a recommendation from the architects that if the construction be "from the eastern boundary and runs west to the western wall of the main entrance" that would be within the budget of £14,000, half of which was for excavations, brickwork, and masonry.[35] A foundation stone was laid on May 25, 1898, with "Cake and Wine to be served in the Corporation Gallery after the Ceremony,"[36] and the opening ceremony to inaugurate phase one took place eighteen months later with a procession of dignitaries, including John Honeyman, with Newbery's daughter Mary bearing a wrought-iron key on a white satin cushion for the unlocking of the main

THE GLASGOW
SCHOOL
OF ART
167

167

door. (137) In response to the vote of thanks to the architects John Keppie made a reply.[37] The school was opened for viewing and in the evening there were concerts and dancing with notice being taken of Margaret Macdonald, "whose auburn hair was well set off with her fawn frock."[38] The next day's issue of the *Glasgow Herald* gave some account of the school, "which has been designed by Mr. John Keppie."[39] He was, of course, the public face of the firm. An interesting footnote was "the presentation of 5 trees and suitable protection for them to be planted at the corner of the New School" as the gift of the draughtsmen in the office of Honeyman and Keppie.[40] But who put them up to it?

Mackintosh was on the platform at the annual public meeting of the school when reference was made "to the very complete character of the new buildings, and that, too, notwithstanding the criticisms that had been made on them."[41] Worse was to come when in September 1901 the contractors lodged their certified accounts when "the Architects were preparing a detailed statement of items in explanation of the large excess in the Accounts over the estimates." The chairman of the governing board made a loan to cover the shortfall until in the next year the debt was cleared with a further grant from the Bellahouston Trust.[42]

The schedule of contents accompanying the competition drawings[43] included the statement that the "building expresses the purpose for which it is intended by a frank acceptance of the requirements in which the useless expenditure of money on mere embellishments has played no part." By and large the competition brief was adhered to except that the library was to be on the ground floor as being "more available for all departments of the School"; a students' common room and an anatomical room, "an essential of a wholly equipped School of Art," were added; and on the upper floor a flower painting studio was to have a conservatory, which were some of the changes recorded in a set of drawings prepared in 1910 at the conclusion of works. (138–144)

The public faces of the building were to be of freestone, "built in square dressed rubble work with all the scuntions, corners and dressings tooled," leaving the rear elevation "to be rough cast with Portland cement" over brickwork, which would be used for all internal walls.

The basement floor was to be asphalted; the upper floors would be laid on wooden joists carried on rolled iron girders with rolled iron cased in plaster housed over the north studio windows. Colored mosaics would be laid in the concrete floor of the vestibule, perhaps after the fashion of the patterned floor in the cathedral chancel. The vestibule was over the heating chamber. "The system of Ventilating suggested on the plans is by drawing from the outer air by a Blackman or other Fan, a Current, which being cleansed by a washing screen, passes over a heating Coil" and thence by ducts, "delivering the fresh tempered air into the various apartments," from which extracted air was ducted to roof ventilators. In view of the claims made for the originality of the system[44] it is worth quoting from the schedule. "This system is almost too well known to require advocacy and has been applied with success to many well known buildings in Glasgow." Indeed, it had been in use in Scott's university buildings for several decades.[45]

At the tender stage "an arrangement has been come to ... which permitted the use of two stones viz: white spot and Giffnock at choice"; electricity was preferred to gas despite its higher cost; and a charge of £700 was accepted for laying foundations for the entire building "to secure present stability and future security for the building." Then late in the day the governors required the inclusion of two flats, "one for the Fireman and one for the Janitor."[46]

What, then, caused the overrun in costs? The devil was in the details as the drawings became three-dimensional reality.

The Studio, in almost the only national comment, reported on the new art school (145) as an educational institution, "which is in some ways unique," and gave a description of the new building in which the most telling observation was that "Embellishments have been carefully concentrated, and gain in value from their juxtaposition to plain surfaces."[47] Yet the correspondent had surely missed an inner significance. Perhaps it would have been significant if the niches flanking the studio entrances had each

137. Glasgow School of Art, north entrance

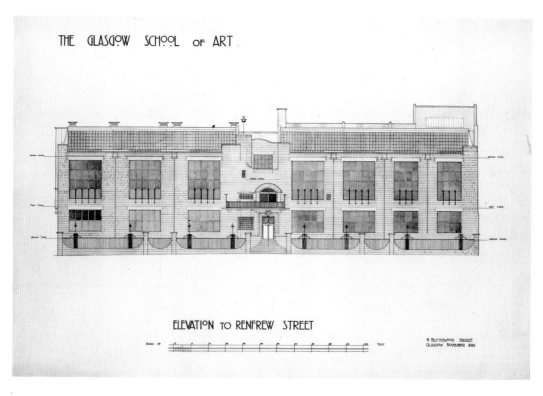

THE GLASGOW SCHOOL of ART

ELEVATION TO RENFREW STREET

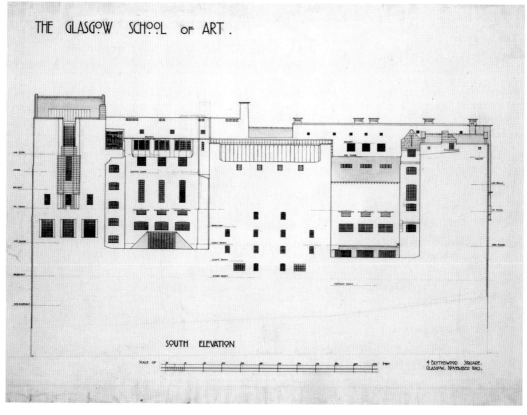

THE GLASGOW SCHOOL of ART.

SOUTH ELEVATION

138, 139. Glasgow School of Art, north elevation (*top*) and south elevation (*bottom*)

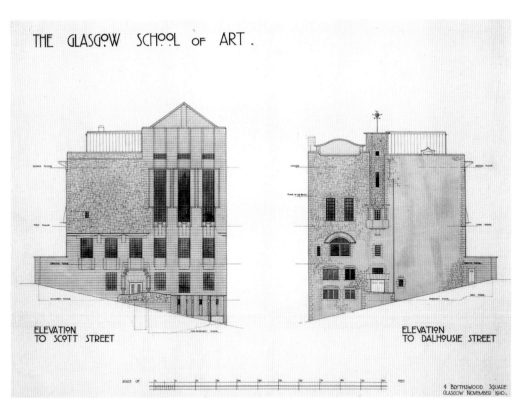

THE GLASGOW SCHOOL OF ART.

ELEVATION
TO SCOTT STREET

ELEVATION
TO DALHOUSIE STREET

4 BLYTHSWOOD SQUARE
GLASGOW NOVEMBER 1910.

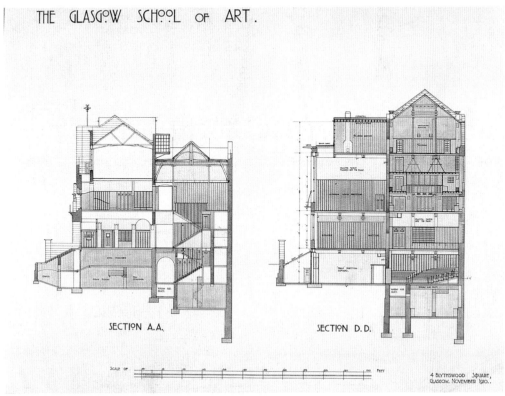

THE GLASGOW SCHOOL OF ART.

SECTION A.A.

SECTION D.D.

4 BLYTHSWOOD SQUARE,
GLASGOW. NOVEMBER 1910.

140, 141. Glasgow School of Art, west and east elevations (*top*) and two sections (*bottom*)

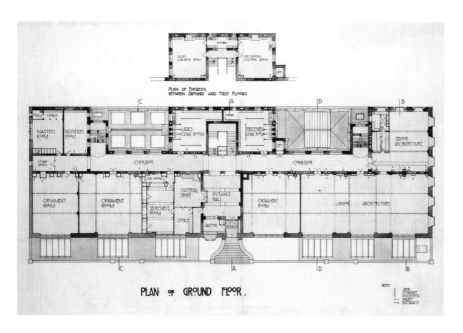

PLAN of GROUND FLOOR.

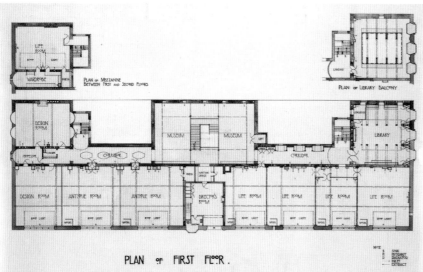

PLAN of FIRST FLOOR.

142, 143, 144. Glasgow School of Art,
ground-floor plan, first-floor plan,
and second-floor plan

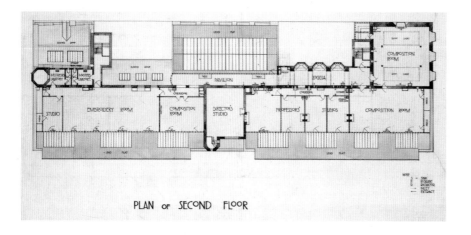

PLAN of SECOND FLOOR

145. Glasgow School of Art,
north elevation (*opposite*)

146. Glasgow School of Art, former board room

contained a fresh flower. Even so to pass between the dark, rose empaneled doors was to enter a grove of apple green wood and of gray heaped stones bleached by the sky and be confronted by ferrous skeins of thistledown, their stalks bent by the north winds against the pleached glass of the great windows. Or the once and former board room (146), white on white with each tonal shadow tinctured and shaded by tapering jambs set free from the door frames or by the curvature of the window recesses in which the rhythm of the boarding is heightened and narrowed. For here, as in the director's room, "White is the favourite colour, the great all-gathering original tone, all the chords of lesser colours rest softly like the tones of a harp."[48] There is the ironwork—the city's coat of arms—set like a seedhead on rooftops or as an abstracted panel over the stairwell, and sculpture, less than was wished for, but housed above the entrance as profiled females whose tresses fall into the stone jambs. (147)

147. Glasgow School of Art, north entrance

With no surviving working drawings one wonders how such works were instructed. For the female sculptures Mackintosh made a maquette in 1899.[49] In a studio he ordered the ends of girders to be split and rolled back, provoking a strike by the blacksmiths; plaster wall details, put up in his absence were later summarily torn down. What did all that cost? Were Mackintosh's wishes understood? Not by the governors with their mundane concerns. In May 1903, "The Secretary was instructed to write to Mr. Keppie regarding the Technical Studios ... as to rendering them more comfortable and rainproof";

in November, when students were working in the corridors and more accommodation was required for the antique class (148), "part of the Museum should be partitioned off."[50] Next spring, at a meeting when Mackintosh was in attendance, estimates for furnishing the director's room were accepted "and the style of furniture generally approved with some slight modification with a further meeting to be agreed upon to discuss the need for a secondary staircase."[51] In January 1906, "Mr. Keppie agreed to prepare a Sketch Plan with estimate of approximate Cost" of between £25,000 and £30,000 for the

148. Glasgow School of Art, the museum being used as a classroom

completion of the building,[52] with Honeyman and Keppie's acceptance a year later as "Architects of the new addition,"[53] ratified by the governors, ever mindful of the excess over the budget for phase one, only "on the understanding that they are not at liberty to instruct any Extra Work on any alterations on the plans or Specifications as endorsed by the Committee involving any addition to or modification of the Work without the Written Authority of the Building Committee."[54] Once the plans were before them the governors "agreed to ask the Architects to furnish Sections, plans also Elevations of Scott St. end of building,"[55] to which Mackintosh replied, "We think it undesirable to commit ourselves to any Elevational treatment until the general scheme of internal arrangement is approved by the Sub Committee."[56] The new work was under way in the autumn of 1907 but with the promise that the £1,000 for stone carving and the £400 for oak fittings in the library "should not be gone on with meantime."[57]

In the following February, when, as Honeyman and Keppie reported, "We are sorry to say Mr. Mackintosh is still confined to bed,"[58] there was the making of a serious dispute. The chairman of the building committee, "Referring to my informal conversation with your Mr. Keppie in the Art Club today," complained because "On leaving a meeting today, six of the Governors inspected a newly erected Sub-basement Porch and Entrance in Scott Street (149) and were surprised to find that this work was carried out in an extravagant manner and not in accordance with the plans and estimates which are now submitted and signed,"[59] which elicited by return "an admission by the Architect that he had misapprehended his position and hoped to make savings elsewhere,"[60] one of which was to substitute asphalt instead of lead for the

roof, prompting the governors to ask for "a Report on this new material Asphalt."[61]

As always with a contract there were opportunities for changes either in anticipation or with hindsight. In the spring of 1908 it was "agreed that the Conservatory now at the end of the 1st floor corridor be removed and meantime stored, to allow the building operations to proceed." A fire stair "if built would seriously destroy the lighting in the several rooms of

149. Glasgow School of Art, west entrance

the East Bay."[62] Mackintosh compromised. What had been external windows were left in place, giving a liveliness to the internal room from the shadows passing on the staircase. In the autumn, concern was expressed about "the present heating ventilators admitting the hot air into the rooms. These have never worked satisfactorily, they have always caused draughts and given colds, and with the Two Fans now running the discomfort is being more strongly felt. Students and models both complain particularly the models."[63]

Some days later the ceremonial drawing back of a curtain in the museum gave public access to the completed second phase. Mackintosh, now among the platform party, having become a partner in his firm, heard these words. " 'He had shown that it was possible to have a good building without plastering it over with the traditional, expensive and often, ugly ornament.' (Hear, Hear)."[64] As always there was a snagging list. Mackintosh had included a dovecote at the top of the east gable. "It was decided that no special permission in the shape of a house be built for these birds and that the Architect was requested to carry out the remit as regards the cementing of the ledges."[65] More of a worry for Mackintosh was the possible removal of the west balcony from the library (150), which, he insisted, "would to a great extent spoil the proportions and design of this room,"[66] although he would have been cheered at being asked for a design for nine clocks when "the cost estimated by the Architect for the dial proposed by him would not exceed 2/6 [25 pence] each." When a magazine rack for the library was asked for it was ingeniously slotted over an existing table.[67] Then he was criticized because the chairs "for the Students' Common Room are too weak and ill made for their purpose," to which Mackintosh replied indignantly on the same day, "Nothing but unnecessary maltreatment could account for the present condition of these chairs."[68] The staff, including Herbert and Frances McNair, petitioned unsuccessfully for a passenger lift to be inserted in the well of the main staircase,[69] and the architect's office supplied a complete set of drawings "of the Buildings as they have been carried out."[70] And that to all intents and purposes was the finish of Mackintosh's

most significant commission, which, because it had run for fifteen years, most fully reflects the maturing of his style.

Essentially the School of Art is a young man's building with the competition design continued into phase two, although by then the plan is no longer the generator of form. Mackintosh would have come to see that the almost painful honesty of translating the plan into the east elevation had made for hesitancy and irresolution in expressing the elevation. In phase one he would have agreed with Voysey who, when praising Gothic architecture, opined that "outside appearances are evolved from internal fundamental conditions, staircases and windows come from where most convenient for use. All openings are proportioned to the various parts to which they apply."[71] When these precepts conflicted with Mackintosh's later design vision, as on the library elevation, he abandoned them as he did historicism.

Perhaps it was foregone that the summer trips of 1895 to Ayrshire and to Somerset should stoke the design of the School of Art once the competition was set to. Maybole Castle is replicated on the east elevation, where Mackintosh made use of the most publicly visible elevation, one that had not been overlaid by the hand of the architectural improver. Montacute House gave not only the genesis of the overall plan of the School of Art but also the continuous glazed screen on the attic story, the dropped oriels on the west elevation, and perhaps their intended figure sculptures. There is, too, the copybook patterning from well-publicized London models with the street railings adapted from the Mary Ward Settlement and from Norman Shaw's New Zealand Chambers, a source perhaps for the asymmetric, almost unbalanced entrance composition, which, despite the sleight of hand in disposing the facade, is on the meridian line and which is continued internally in vaulted passageways that in early photographs have the bleak, spare geometry of Piranesi's *carceri*. Ahead is the staircase (151), washed by a cascade of light, its balusters crowding the perimeters with others in the center crowded like thickets of sedge pushing through still waters, imagery redolent of *The Pond* by Frances Macdonald. At the museum level (152) four posts,

150. Glasgow School of Art, library

reaching to the roof, are an open cage over the stairwell descending to primitive forms in the inchoate darkness of the basement so that "the arts of design, which, like the sap from the central stem, springing from connected and collective roots, out of a common ground, sustain and unite in one organic whole the living tree."[72] Lethaby was more succinct. "Great art was a sacred tree having very deep roots."[73]

Such analogies may be no more than the stuff of fancy. Indeed the staircase has a historical lineage in the Elizabethan example at Crewe Hall of which Mackintosh noted: "It is a newel stair built round a central well hole and is of oak ... it is easy and convenient, and occupies but little space."[74] Factuality, however, was never enough for Mackintosh, who would have concurred with César Daly's plea "to make architecture, not only a useful building, but a poetical form of life."[75] That the posts are not replicated in the corners of the museum, though caps are attached to the roof timbers, is surely an indication that their prime role is not structural.

For Lethaby "all architecture ... is one vast symbolism: symbolism controlled by and expressive of structure might be the definition of architecture in the higher sense."[76] If that is so then the School of Art is the vessel for a program of symbolism originating in Egypt as outlined by Lethaby—a program that begins with the exterior where the leaf-embowered railings, "associated with sacred trees," guard a staircase made holy by a sanctuary lamp over which are "the four branches of the great tree world and typify the four cardinal points."[77] Gazing down are the imperturbable female deities, "The goddesses of the south and north," commonly placed "on the underside of the lintels of the front doors," beyond which the inner staircase reaches the museum, which is the earth, "a flat and shallow place longer than its width; the sky ... held in place by four immense props or pillars."[78]

The library, approached from the museum, is entered side on. (153) Diagonally ahead is an avenue of oak posts disguising the metal hangers, which suspend the library, descending from cross beams in the floor above (now the furniture gallery). The oak posts stand free from the shadows of the enclosing aisles, rising to a coffered ceiling in which lightbulbs are fixed like stars. Below them hangs a

galaxy of black and silvered metal lamps, like miniature skyscrapers of the 1920s, with glass inserts of pink, mauve, and hyacinth as a tissue of evanescent color "as in temples of old"[79] above the magazine rack containing "the ever watchful eye" of the god Amun. That was a conceit, as Gleeson White noted in 1897, favored by more than one of "the Glasgow arts and crafts movement," which appeared to be most strongly influenced by Egypt, although in the studios he did not "see any casts, photographs, or other reproductions of Egyptian art."[80] None was needed, as the sources were literary, allowing the imagination to transform them into symbolist interpretations including the iconography of the tree.

In the museum the tree forms, stripped of decoration, are bleak and spare—sticks frozen in an icy pond. The library has a richer metaphor. The oak posts are apart and independent of the surrounding balconies (154), where the pendant panels are pierced by canopies of leaves filtering the western sun. Balusters, spanning from post to balcony, are notched and colored white, green, red, and blue. Do these not represent the seasons of the year, or the festivals of the Christian year? And the spindly chairs that once were eased beneath the tables are surely a coppiced undergrowth where leaves cut into the table legs.

Representations of trees appeared externally on the facades of the Majolika House and the Secession House, both in Vienna, in 1898, and the Samaritaine Department Store in Paris, in 1905, and in London on the Whitechapel Art Gallery in 1897. More influential than these exotic exercises may have been the Ladbroke Grove Free Library, London, of 1890 (155), where a Tree of Knowledge, which with shields and literary figures is more akin to a Tree of Jesse, has exposed roots, knotted trunk, and a foliate canopy spreading into the highest gable.

As with the Glasgow Boys so in the graphic work of The Four trees abound and most tellingly in designs for bookplates. One by Margaret Macdonald shows wisdom as a female tree spirit; with McNair art and poetry embrace the Tree of Knowledge, from above which dew falls as inspiration from a falcon's wings[81]; and, as has been noted, Mackintosh

151, 152. Glasgow School of Art,
main staircase and museum (*opposite*)

153, 154. Glasgow School of Art, library

exhibited in 1896 a beaten brass panel of "Art and Knowledge seeking Inspiration of the Tree of Knowledge and Beauty." All was derivative of the Norse myth of Yggdrasil, the mighty ash tree on which the cock "sits on the topmost bough"[82] as it does on Mackintosh's rooftop armorials. Other myths were explained by Sir James Frazer who, in his seminal study *The Golden Bough*, examined the oak worship of the Druids.[83] In the library of the School of Art Mackintosh converted the paper exercises of the other members of The Four into a grove of trees enclosing a space sacred to learning and radiated from above by holy light. Walter Crane sums up Mackintosh's achievement: "The designer, like the poet, rejoices in certain limitations, which, while they fix and control his form and treatment, leave him extraordinary freedom in dealing suggestively with themes difficult or impossible to be approached in purely naturalistic form."[84]

155. Ladbroke Grove Free Library, H. Wilson and T. Phillips Figgis

156. Glasgow School of Art, library

To safeguard the sacerdotal role of the library Mackintosh isolated it from the outside world, just as he had done with the museum staircase, by having voids separating the internal horizontal planes from the trio of lights to the west. (156) That separation explains why Mackintosh does not use the large panes of glass, as in the studios, preferring a multitude of small panes glittering like a carapace or in the western sun like a cloak of many colors pinned by the crossed lines of the glazing bars. Was Mackintosh making use of Tudor oriels as reinterpreted in the Bristol Reference Library of 1902 where, as the historian John Summerson noted, "The flattened gables and symmetrical disposition of the main front ... suggests in a remarkable way what Mackintosh was to do a year of two later in Glasgow." For Summerson, "This free Tudor" was "the most profoundly characteristic and most distinctly unifying architecture in Britain around 1900."[85] It is true that the Glasgow School of Art has an affinity with Tudor forms but that is no more than a distant cousinage. Was it necessary when recomposing the west front for Mackintosh to look further than

Scotland? The moldings, linking feature to feature, are indicative of the sixteenth-century Crathes Castle, Kincardineshire (157), and the oriels with the shouldered half rounds for statuary could have been adapted from the exterior of the great hall of Stirling Castle or from the stacked windows in the center of Fyvie Castle, Aberdeenshire, the show front of which has some resemblance to the south face of the School of Art. For the sculptor Pittendrigh Macgillivray, "Architecture is the necessary setting or background of sculpture. Sculpture inhabits architectural places; it is for the jewelling of cities."[86] Sadly, cost cutting meant no representations of, among others, Benvenuto Cellini and Saint Francis of Assisi (an incongruous pairing), which allowed the modernists to receive the western elevation of the School of Art as their own so that it could appear on the front cover of Pevsner's *Pioneers of Modern Design* alongside the Eiffel Tower, Paris (1889), Olbrich's Wedding Tower, Darmstadt (1907), and the Factory at the Werkbund Exhibition, Cologne (1914), by Gropius and Meyer.

Put aside doubts as to whether or not the Glasgow School of Art should be in such company and there is the comforting assurance that the school, or at least the west elevation, is one of the twentieth century's iconic architectural statements. Yet that should not blind one to the inherent design faults. Nobody can look at the meeting of the east and north facades and not wince. And the composition around the entrance—is it not clumsy? And the ants, the bees, and the roses in colored glass—is the moralizing not overdone and is that why it is omitted in phase two? One can carp. But just as between the Martyrs School and the Scotland Street School so it is that in the School of Art the curve, the circle, the figurative, and the naturalistic give way to the straight line, the square, the abstract, and formalism. Hence it was that in 1936 Pevsner described Mackintosh as an "abstract artist," seeing the library as "an overwhelmingly full polyphony of abstract form" while maintaining of the school as a whole that "not a single feature here is derived from period styles."[87] It was a line of thought followed by Howarth in his biography of Mackintosh in 1952. For both Pevsner and Howarth the erasure by Mackintosh of the cornice and the

pilasters by the entrance was an initiation into twentieth-century modernism so that, in the library, "Uprights and horizontals, squares and oblongs determine the effect."[88] In accepting these limitations both Pevsner and Howarth accepted a wilful, indeed almost personal obfuscation of the past. History was skewed in denying, as Crane put it, that, 'In the region of poetic design symbolism must always hold its place.'[89] If the Glasgow School of Art is revealed as a place of pilgrimage in which the shrine is the library then one could agree with Lethaby's observation when viewing the past that "the greater buildings were not only for ritual purposes, but they themselves embodied magic,"[90] which was fulfilled uniquely in his own day amid the grime and sulfurous smoke of Glasgow, where Mackintosh invested the School of Art with "a meaning and a message; it was religious, magical, symbolic and cosmical."[91] ▓

157. Crathes Castle, Kincardineshire

In an architectural practice it is the bread-and-butter jobs that sustain a firm's finances. Mackintosh may be esteemed as an artistic designer par excellence, as at The Hill House with its inner meanings, yet such jobs can be loss leaders. It is more lucrative to be erecting commercial blocks using standard industrial components than engaging a myriad of craftsmen making one-off design pieces.

It must have been a client's satisfaction with the printing and dispatch offices at the *Glasgow Herald* building that brought the contract for a new building for the *Daily Record* newspaper to Honeyman and Keppie. Curiously, the job has been overlooked by commentators although as an industrial building it was one of the most significant in Mackintosh's oeuvre.

Drawings were prepared in 1900,[1] presumably when the newspaper's title was purchased by Lord Northcliffe. The landlocked site was narrow, squeezed as it was between two lanes. Lacking a presence on a main thoroughfare there was no need for a bombastic Renaissance show front. Mackintosh would have drawn on his previous experience of laying out a newspaper production line for the planning was efficient and economical. (158) As in the *Glasgow Herald* offices the basement was for storage and the printing presses, with a lift to allow for dispatch from the ground floor alongside the public entrance fronting a counting house, above which there were to be reporters, subeditors,

the editor, and wire clerks. Other floors were designated "warehouse."

It is the facades (159) that, if they had been studied and assessed, would put the building in the first rank of modernism and ahead of the later library wing of the Glasgow School of Art. They accord with Louis Sullivan's plea from Chicago for "that regular and equable spacing of windows, that general suggestion of business and business housing, which would be unmistakable."[2] Another of Sullivan's observations may be relevant. "Just so soon as your thoughts take on an organic quality, your buildings will begin to take on an organic quality."[3] So do the waves of blue tiles recall the sea battle off Cape St. Vincent after which the lane is named? And are the thin green verticals masts? Or do they represent the knowledge churned out daily by the printing presses? And are their mechanical forces represented externally by the staccato rhythms of mechanical bricks? Who knows. Almost alone in Glasgow—and possibly in Britain and in Europe—the *Daily Record* building conformed to Sullivan's dictum that "the tall office building should not, must not be made a field for the display of architectural knowledge in the encyclopaedic sense."[4] In 1896 when writing of "The Tall Office Building Artistically Considered" Sullivan posed the question, "What is the chief characteristic of the tall office building? And at once we answer, it is lofty. This loftiness is to the artist-nature its thrilling aspect ... It must be every inch a

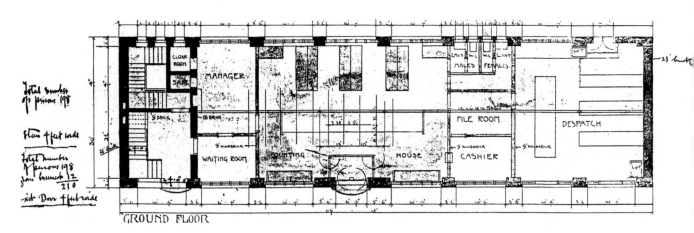

158. *Daily Record,* plan

SOUTH ELEVATION

EAST ELEVATION

John Honeyman Keppie
architect.
140 BATH STREET.
GLASGOW. APRIL. 1900.

proud and soaring thing, rising in sheer exultation that from bottom to top it is without a single dissenting line."[5]

That is the sum of the achievement at the *Daily Record* building, an achievement won despite and because of the constraints of the site. Mackintosh was certainly not the first in the city to make use of multicolored bricks (that had been done by William Leiper at Templeton's carpet factory some years before) or of the serial canted bays in which dark green mullions sprout like thickets of branches in the undergrowth of the sunless alleys below the sun-kissed carvings at the wallhead, the whole enlivened with the colored piers delineating, as Sullivan declared, "the simplest elemental rhythms

159. *Daily Record*, elevation

of Nature, to wit the rhythm of growth, of aspiration, of that which would rise into the air: which impulse we shall call the Rhythm of Life."[6]

In 1894 a competition design, possibly, to judge by the vegetative overlay, with some Mackintosh input, was got up for the Royal Insurance Company,[7] which had procured a corner site on the ultra smart Buchanan Street, allowing for a pair of shops that would yield a good rental. (160) The design overall was full-blown neo-Baroque with seaweed fronds, as if cast by a tide, swaying around the upper windows above which a domed tempietto finished off a polygonal corner tower, now an accoutrement for any public location. Some

years later Honeyman and Keppie would be among the subscribers to Belcher and Macartney's *Later Renaissance Architecture*, which championed such exoticism. "For public buildings it possesses just those qualities which answer to the requirements of modern times—less of the romantic and picturesque, no doubt but more of the practical and convenient, combined with a substantial measure of real beauty."[8] If the indulgences of the neo-Baroque were toned down later in the *Glasgow Herald* additions that may have been in part because of its less public exposure but because, too, Mackintosh, having perhaps a greater design input, had begun the reductive process that would culminate in the use of machine-made industrial materials at the *Daily Record* building.

Such materials may have been permissible only in back lanes and the anonymous production of newspapers. With

160. Design for the Royal Insurance Co. *British Architecture*

other commercial work it was Keppie who was the lead architect. The department store, a new concept demanding innovative technical and engineering solutions, of Pettigrew and Stephens is as useful an example as any of the development of retailing for which Glasgow became a byword. Pettigrew and Stephens, "now one of the largest undertakings of the kind in Scotland, and employs six hundred hands," began in 1890[9] with a shop and upper flat, which expanded to five storys in 1899, when, "As portions of the building must at once be handed over to the tradesmen the whole stock (including Thousands of Pounds worth of New Goods purchased for the Spring season) must at once be sold."[10] Yet within a decade, "the building was practically taken down and built up again," to be finished off with a gold-capped lantern and a dome (161), which was a recycled version of Mackintosh's competition entry for a chapter house, sheltering "a 'view tower' and camera obscura which will especially please the youngsters."[11]

The store's internal layout was "even more astonishing and attractive." To entice the leisured well-to-do in their new pastime of shopping, "Visitors ... are free to come and go over the vast establishment" using the passenger elevator, which had cost £350, to arrive at the "tea and luncheon rooms,"[12] illuminated by an "electrolier" and with decorations of sculpture and stained glass by Albert Hodge, Kellock Brown, and Stephen Adam.[13] And to promote the new store there was Mackintosh's trade stand at the exhibition in the west end park.

There was glamour and novelty, too, in Annan's photographic and fine art salon. Like his father, James Craig Annan had an enviable reputation as a pioneer in the art of photography. It was he who had introduced the photogravure process into Great Britain, having learned it while in Vienna in 1883 with his father. James Craig Annan corresponded regularly with Alfred Stieglitz of New York; at home fellow enthusiasts included the sculptor J. Pittendrigh Macgillivray[14] and John Keppie, who owned a collection of works by D. O. Hill and was himself an active photographer.[15] Annan was commissioned by Honeyman and Keppie to photograph the *Glasgow Herald* building in 1896 and, some years later, the

Daily Record offices.[16] His portraits of the Mackintosh circle included Anna Muthesius, when on a visit to Glasgow, and Margaret Macdonald Mackintosh in the drawing room of the Mains Street flat, and, earlier, the celebrated likeness of Mackintosh who was every inch the debonair bohemian with limp collar and billowing cravat.

When the firm removed to new premises in 1892 James Craig Annan used his friend George Walton as interior decorator. With wall tints of gray and green, "The scheme of decoration is admirable, being light, graceful and quite removed

161. Pettigrew and Stephens, *Academy Architecture*

from the commonplace,"[17] against which there were works "surrounded by a square, flat, broad frame, the whole carrying out the idea of a Dutch tile,"[18] a reminder perhaps of Annan's recent tour of North Holland with the etcher D. Y. Cameron. Success at the 1901 Glasgow exhibition, where Annan was "the convener of the photographic sub-committee of the art section,"[19] allowed the firm to move to custom-built premises at the west end of Sauchiehall Street, closer to the wealthy carriage trade. Now, as Walton had departed to England, it was Keppie who was handed the building commission.

But whose was the choice of a gabled Dutch facade in eye-catching red stone? (162) The novelty in Glasgow of Pont Street Dutch gave a restrained and dignified frontage which overcame the insignificance of the narrow feu, and with the Michelangelesque figures enthroned on corbels indicated that within these premises the productions of the dark rooms and laboratories were art.[20] The composition shows Keppie—for it was he—as a careful designer prepared to be inclusive of the new style with louche pediments. Beyond such a gesture he either could not or would not go for it was Mackintosh "whose handiwork is still visible in the pierced beams of the gallery and the wrought iron decorations of the lift and balustrades in the front shop."[21] Annan once again seemed to be separating architecture from decoration.

The townscape of central Glasgow was changing. The mannered terraces of the Regency and post-Regency eras were being ripped apart. "During the Edwardian period there was a marked boom in office building in central Glasgow."[22] The scarcity and hence the cost of building plots necessitated a maximum economic return by introducing ingenious plans incorporating internal light wells and by building ever higher, using new building techniques such as reinforced concrete, as at Salmon's Lion Chambers (1904), or, more generally, steel-framed construction, as at Salmon's St. Vincent Street Chambers (1898), which allowed the visible facade to be non-loadbearing and become a diaphanous membrane.[23] Although the *palme d'or* goes to Mackintosh the pace of change of office building may have been set by Salmon's nonhistorical elevations. The St. Vincent Street

162. Annan, *Academy Architecture*

Chambers' facade is a conjuring trick where elements appear and reappear at a bewildering series of levels (163, 164); the Lion Chambers are without classical allusions or ornamentation, relying on rather clumsy alliances of massing and volumes and abrupt changes in fenestration.

All these offices were serviced by elevators. Perhaps their first appearance in Glasgow was in J. J. Burnet's Athenaeum where an aedicule is suspended in vertical space like a motionless car. In 1890 it was reported that "Messrs Henderson and Co., coach-builders, are at present building a unique specimen of their craft. It is a vehicle for carrying the passengers in the lift of the new Athenaeum, and is constructed of the materials and in the style, of their justly famed carriages. It is from a design suggested by Mr. Burnett [*sic*]."[24]

That Honeyman and Keppie should construct two newspaper offices and printing houses demonstrated the value of contacts in specific areas of the life of the city. Sadly, as events would reveal, experience and contacts in other areas were to prove deficient as the twentieth century began its course and after Honeyman withdrew from the practice in 1904, making way for Mackintosh's promotion as a partner although he, unlike John Honeyman and John Keppie, was not a public figure and the completion of the Glasgow School of Art would be the sole significant commission thereafter. Also, despite the office boom, all was not well with Glasgow's economy so there was a dearth of new work. For other practices there was the clapping of brick stacks of water closets to insanitary tenements, or the speculative running up of new tenements although even these sources of income would peter out because of "the cyclical decline, post 1905, which brought a virtual cessation to house building and was so severe as to warrant a special report in the 1911 census."[25]

Although "Messrs. Honeyman and Keppie's designs are amongst the most noticeable and original in this country,"[26] they were unsuccessful in the limited competition for the Royal Insurance Company just as they were in 1898 in the run-up to Glasgow's second international exhibition, to be staged in 1901.

163. St. Vincent Street Chambers, James Salmon

164. St. Vincent Street Chambers, James Salmon

The intention to hold an exhibition was announced in October 1897 when financial guarantees were called for from among Scotland's nobility and the mercantile, industrial, and professional classes from the west of Scotland and beyond. It is evidence of his standing in the city that John Honeyman offered to put up £100. If £50,000 was subscribed then the city corporation would agree "as they did in 1888, to guarantee a sum of £5,000." For 1901, however, it was further agreed "to give the use of the new Art Galleries Building, and adjoining ground, as nearly as possible of the same extent as was given for the 1888 exhibition," together with "an ample number of tea rooms and temperance dining-rooms in the buildings and grounds." An executive council of the great and the good of the city included the architects John Honeyman, J. J. Burnet, and W. Forrest Salmon, the sculptor Pittendrigh Macgillivray, and the warehouseman William Pettigrew. Many of these names reappeared on the Building, Lighting and Grounds Committee, which on April 20, 1898, convened to discuss the procurement of the exhibition buildings, whereupon Honeyman submitted his resignation "on account of the possibility of his firm joining in the competition for designs," which was restricted so that "only those architects in business in Glasgow or its vicinity should be invited to compete."

The two main buildings would be an industrial hall and "a grand hall for musical entertainments, etc. . . . and capable of seating about 4,000 persons," to be constructed of steel, iron, and glass. "The buildings should present such architectural treatment in harmony with the design of the New Fine Art Galleries building at present in course of construction."[27]

The more innovative of Mackintosh's two surviving entries[28] was a circular hall with a shallow dome extending to encircling internal galleries (165) but with no specified materials, save for glass roof lights, or of supports apart from buttresses tied into the inner walling, perhaps, as with the eventual exhibition structures, to be of "prefabricated panels of plaster on a sacking base . . . Roofs were red, and cupolas felted and painted green to resemble copper."[29] Doubtless these are the same materials intended for the industrial hall, which, as in 1888 and again in 1901, was basilican with a low

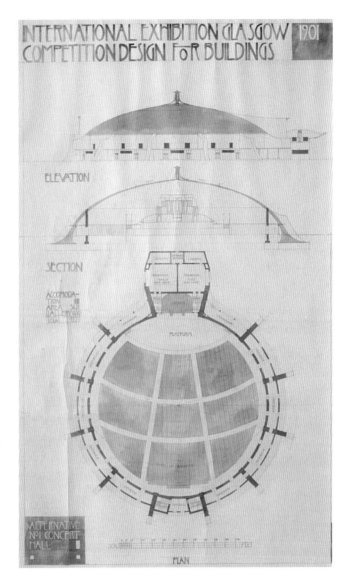

dome compressed by chunky piers rather as Joseph Olbrich would do with the Secession House then being designed in Vienna. The unadorned structural forms of Mackintosh's entries did not accord with the stylistic requirement whereas James Miller tapped into "the rich mine of Spanish Renaissance architecture, which, with its strongly marked traces of Moorish

165. Design for a concert hall, Charles Rennie Mackintosh

influence, seems to lend itself admirably to architectural pageantry in stucco." With his flamboyant Spanish extravaganza Miller had played the game and secured both commission and reputation, leaving Mackintosh with nothing more than a couple of exhibition stands "breaking away from the gingerbread show-case style of design."[30]

Competitions are costly in office time and resources. So why did the firm enter two sets of designs for the competition for a cathedral in Liverpool? Of one set nothing is known. The other was entered by Mackintosh under his own name. Why so? Was Mackintosh already so divergent from the consensual philosophy of the office?

The Liverpool Cathedral competition was announced in the autumn of 1901 and, like many another, became mired in controversy not least because of a previous competition fifteen years before. The initial restriction on the competitors in favor of Early English, as shown in "portfolios of ecclesiastical structures erected by them," was soon relaxed and the submission date was set for June 30, 1902.[31] As Mackintosh's drawings were matched to the intended site one assumes he visited and stayed with his in-laws. Like most of the competitors he opted for a loosely based Gothic, "which is not surprising considering the known proclivities of the Committee." From the more than one hundred entries, including some from the Continent and one by Cram, Goodhue and Ferguson from the United States, it was the twenty-three-year old Giles Gilbert Scott (grandson of George Gilbert Scott) who was the eventual winner.[32] Mackintosh's entry was commended. "In its generous proportions and details an effect of much dignity and richness is obtained in this remarkably able design."[33]

Howarth identified many details picked up from contemporary architects and cited Durham Cathedral as a source for the general massing[34]; he overlooked a source nearer home—namely, Glasgow Cathedral. But did Mackintosh's colleagues have no input? Would Honeyman not have been leaning over his shoulder? And Keppie as well, who had taken over the running of the Brechin Cathedral job?

In his travels Mackintosh did not head for cathedral cities. In Scotland where there were few working models one would turn to Glasgow's medieval cathedral, which was the one great church familiar to Mackintosh and with which the firm had had a long engagement and would have meant that the office library would hold a pattern book such as James Collie's survey of 1835. Almost inevitably therefore one sees much in the Liverpool competition entry (166) that is from Glasgow. The finlike buttresses replicate those Mackintosh depicted in his 1895 watercolor study of his own native cathedral with its soaring east end. A preliminary Liverpool study (167) shows the angularity of Glasgow's planning and the deep, pillared presbytery at the east end.[35] The internal nave elevation is reproduced from the choir of Glasgow. However, given the austerity of its Early English style, the overlay of decoration with which Mackintosh doodled is culled from his

166. Perspective of proposed design for Liverpool Cathedral, *British Architect*

Italian travels, with the processional figures in the choir triforium from Sant' Apollinare Nuovo in Ravenna and from Milan Cathedral the figured capitals in the nave.

Though competitions consume office time that has to be accepted because of the need for a possible lucrative award. For many reasons, therefore—prestige, a future commission and, with it, a cash flow over many years, possibly Honeyman's interest and passion for ecclesiology as well as Mackintosh's ambition—all meant that the firm had to be committed to the Liverpool Cathedral competition. How very different it seems was the entry in 1901 for the competition for a House for an Art Lover sponsored by the German magazine *Zeitschrift für Innendekoration*. How did Mackintosh hear of the competition? One imagines that there was an encouraging intermediary. If so, it could well have been Hermann Muthesius. He had taken up the post of cultural and technical attaché at the German embassy in London in 1896, enabling him to visit the Arts and Crafts exhibition where the Glasgow artists "suffered the ridicule that is always levelled at important artistic achievements. Few could make sense of the dream-like designs of the copper beaten panels, the strange tangle of lines in the figural compositions, the stark forms of the furniture."[36] What is one to make of his oft repeated statements about the rejection of the Scottish artists? Was that notion fed to him by Mackintosh? Muthesius would certainly read Gleeson White's encomia of the young Glasgow artists with more than passing interest since he would visit the city when compiling his survey of current British architecture as a handbook for the German architectural profession with the main thrust being the emergence of the Queen Anne style and the phenomenon of the independent middle-class dwelling as developed by

Norman Shaw together with a scattering of such public and commercial buildings as the Ladbroke Grove Library and the New Zealand Chambers with Glasgow being represented by Caledonian Mansions, the Athenaeum and the *Glasgow Herald* extension. It was the inclusion of the last which would have brought the author into contact with Mackintosh. The ensuing friendship must have grown quickly as in May 1898, when Mackintosh wrote about the entry in the German's guide, he felt free to vent his frustration at his lack of public recognition. After Honeyman, Muthesius was possibly the most important influence on Mackintosh's career. Given his official position others would listen to his views. It was Muthesius who could give Mackintosh star billing on the European exhibition circuit while he was yet a draughtsman in middle-class Glasgow.

The German connection began with a notice in the first number of the new magazine *Dekorative Kunst*. Was the anonymous text supplied by Muthesius? "Mackintosh, the two Misses Macdonalds, G. Walton and others have, within a short time, given Glasgow which was only known through

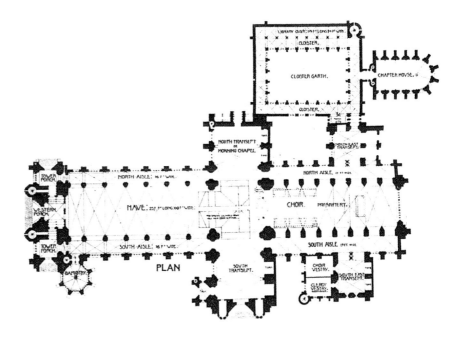

167. Plan of proposed design for Liverpool Cathedral, *British Architect*

the successes won in Munich by the dreamy Scottish painters, a new face in Germany,"[37] inspired, as reported in a subsequent issue, by "an almost overwhelming amount of new impulses," among which "spiritual inspiration has been important; lyric symbolism draws them away from nature."[38] Later came the assertion by Muthesius that "Anyone who wants to see new art has to go not to London but to Glasgow," where there was "the new decorative school in the center of which Charles Mackintosh and Margaret Macdonald Mackintosh stand."[39] When Muthesius travelled to Glasgow he found that "the newer, bigger buildings of Glasgow are conspicuous for their very striking, very personal architectural forms ... Maybe the most peculiar of these buildings is the new business house of the *Glasgow Herald* ... In the peculiar style of the building there seems to be the feeling of the young Glasgow artists' group, that has become conspicuous over the last years in the field of applied arts by its achievements."[40]

The House for an Art Lover competition attracted thirty-six entries but with no overall winner, although as the judges, who included Olbrich and van de Velde, reported, "Baillie Scott's design would have won first prize if he had not executed the exterior elevations of his house in a spirit opposed to the masterfully handled interiors, and more in a Modern spirit."[41] Half-timbering, Dutch gables and an entrance guarded by drum towers, like a medieval gatehouse, were not what was wanted!

Technically, Mackintosh had disqualified himself from the competition by failing to include interior perspectives, probably because of other demands on his time. Even so, his entry was deemed worthy of a special prize for its "novel and austere form, and the unified configuration of the interior and exterior" and he must have been more than gratified when his drawings (now with the interiors) and those of Baillie Scott and Leopold Bauer were issued as folios in 1902, adding piquancy to the remarks by the judges that "without the participation of foreigners, the results of the competition would have been very questionable indeed."[42] The reviewer in the influential *American Architect* reflected that "the most

interesting of the three" was the scheme by Mackintosh (168–171), and although the interior decoration was admired as "wholly non-architectural so far as historical precedent is concerned ... It is fanciful, capricious and not a little wierd."[43] Nevertheless, one wonders what thoughts were stirred in some readers by the accompanying elevations. (172)

An introductory essay by Muthesius, "Mackintosh's Art Principles," allowed him to assess the Scotsman's place in "the new English art movement" that had begun when "the Scottish designers" had first exhibited at "the Arts and Crafts Exhibition of 1896, when their appearance on the scene was very much that of strange guests, and the work they presented was emphatically regarded as a caprice." For Muthesius the Scottish artists, with Mackintosh "the leader of the little group," and their Continental counterparts surpassed the English by having "a wider conception of the aims of interior decoration ... Not one of the Arts and Crafts exhibitions so far has contained the representation of a completely furnished room."[44] What Muthesius would have had in mind was Mackintosh's exhibit at the Secession House in Vienna in the last months of 1900.

From its foundation in 1897 the Secession artists wished to broaden the concept of art in the city by introducing new talent especially from beyond the periphery of Austro-Hungary and by being more inclusive by admitting the decorative and applied arts.[45] In doing so they were following on the heels of similar breakaway movements in Berlin and in Munich that had early championed the Glasgow Boys.[46] After one of their shows in Munich it was reported back in Glasgow in 1894 that "No better show has been seen in the Bavarian capital since the schism which occurred two years ago."[47] The Glasgow artists had included J. Reid Murray, Stuart Park, Grosvenor Thomas, E. A. Walton, and others, many of whom would be invited to show by the Vienna Secessionists in 1898 and in 1899.

The eighth Secessionist exhibition was entrusted to the young Viennese architect Josef Hoffmann as vice president of the Secession. The exhibition was to be an international display of applied art. The largest collection came from La Maison

168, 169. House for an Art Lover, perspective of design and proposed ground-floor plan

C. R. MACKINTOSH. GLASGOW. HAUS EINES KUNST-FREUNDES.
VERLAGS-ANSTALT: ALEXANDER KOCH-DARMSTADT. — TAFEL V.

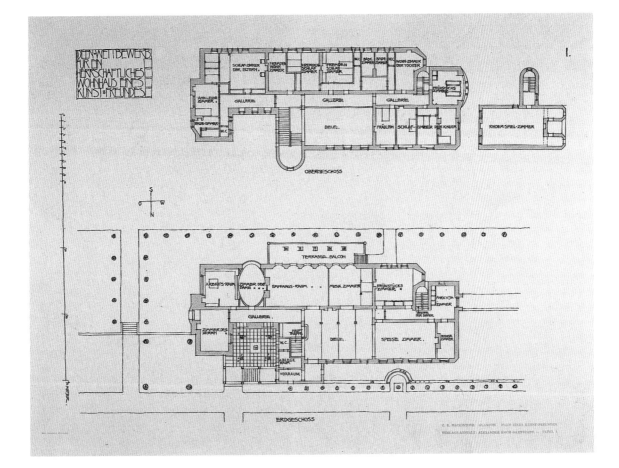

IDEEN·WETT BEWERB
FÜR EIN
HERRSCHAFTLICHES
WOHNHAUS EINES
KUNST·FREUNDES

OBERGESCHOSS

ERDGESCHOSS

C. R. MACKINTOSH. GLASGOW. HAUS EINES KUNST-FREUNDES.
VERLAGS-ANSTALT: ALEXANDER KOCH-DARMSTADT. — TAFEL I.

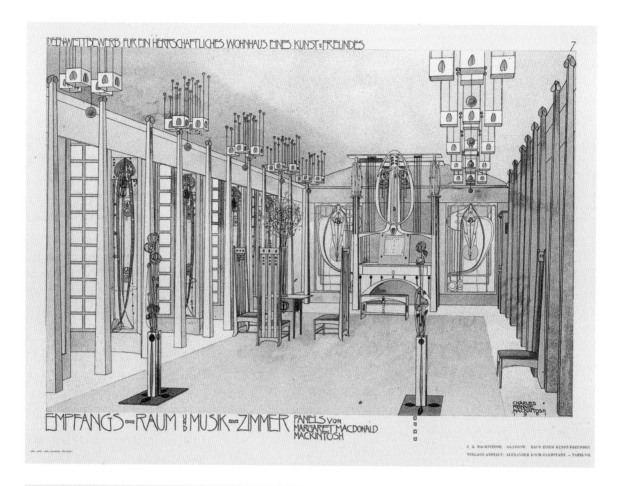

EMPFANGS---RAUM U.D MUSIK---ZIMMER PANELS VON MARGARET MACDONALD MACKINTOSH

C. R. MACKINTOSH: GLASGOW. HAUS EINES KUNST-FREUNDES.
VERLAGS-ANSTALT: ALEXANDER KOCH-DARMSTADT. – TAFEL VII.

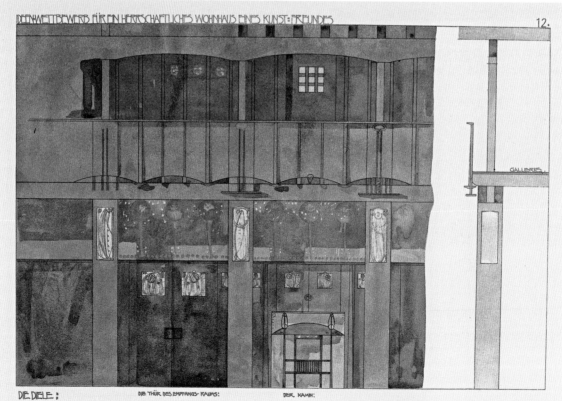

GALLERIE.

DIE DIELE: DIE THÜR DES EMPFANGS-RAUMS: DER KAMIN:

C. R. MACKINTOSH: GLASGOW. HAUS EINES KUNST-FREUNDES.
VERLAGS-ANSTALT: ALEXANDER KOCH-DARMSTADT. – TAFEL XII.

Moderne in Paris; the next was fifty-three items from C. R. Ashbee and his Guild of Handicraft in London. In April 1900 Hoffmann had written to a colleague asking him "to negotiate if possible with Aschbee [sic] with regard to the exhibition. To be able to show real English art and craft in Vienna would be worth the trouble."[48] A month later when the wealthy Anglophile textile industrialist Fritz Waerndorfer was planning to visit England he recollected in a letter to Hoffmann, "You have sent me to Glasgow."[49] Why? Doubtless because Waerndorfer, according to his wife, had been attracted to Mackintosh's work "through pictures in 'The Studio' "[50] and perhaps, too, he had visited the Munich Secession show of a year before. For Hoffmann, Mackintosh was a designer, not an architect.

When Waerndorfer would have reached Glasgow Mackintosh was preparing for his wedding and was setting up house in the Mains Street flat. Excitedly, he wrote to his friend Muthesius: "We have a very nice trip in prospect for October. We have been asked to send work to the Vienna Secession. We are to get a room to ourselves and are to go to Vienna and arrange our own exhibition. All the expenses of sending our exhibits and ourselves are being paid. We are going to make a great effort as it is a chance one seldom gets."[51] Given the short notice for the exhibition Mackintosh would have had to lay his hands on whatever objects were available, which meant that the newlyweds' home was robbed of much of its contents. The McNairs supplied the smoker's cabinet and illustrative items, which may have been on hand in Glasgow. And two recently completed and complementary gesso panels, *The Wassail* by Mackintosh and *The May Queen* by his wife, were also dispatched. One can but guess at the nervous energy and excitement in selecting and packing up the collection for its journey across Europe by steamer and by train. It was, however, a job lot. So whose was the idea of placing it within an enclosed setting (173), which, when it was installed, gave the pieces the beauty of flowers within a *hortus conclusus*, an effect repeated less tangibly in the drawing room of The Hill House, and prompting a Viennese reviewer to write, "The inner truth of these works ... has an overwhelming effect. The severity, purity, simplicity, and ardor of this construction allow us to see the opposition between a lively expression of atmosphere and the artificial boring flatness in products that for many years have pretended to be modern."[52]

Almost contemporaneous was the dining room commissioned in Munich by the proprietor of *Dekorative Kunst* and *Deutsche Kunst und Dekoration*, for whom Mackintosh supplied wall furnishings including cabinets with glazed doors, similar to a still surviving piece, which with its billing doves and McNair crest may have been a wedding present from Mackintosh to his in-laws. The Munich interior had a wall frieze of skeletal trees with some fronds of leaves, although the ensemble was overwhelmed by a clutter of ornaments and the mundane freestanding furniture.[53]

For the room for the Vienna Secession can one assume that full-scale drawings were forwarded from Glasgow, as was done later for the Waerndorfer music room? That must have been so since the Mackintoshes did not arrive in the Austrian capital until after the exhibition had opened, when enthusiastic students drew the Scottish couple in their carriage through the streets. Margaret attracted admiration as "a young lady with reddish hair, dressed elegantly in an unusual manner, Mrs. Margaret Macdonald Mackintosh, who next to her husband, the Scottish Secessionist Charles R. Mackintosh, is registered as exhibiting."[54] And what would have been Mackintosh's reaction on first seeing the Secession House, Olbrich's masterpiece, with its gilded foliage by the entrance and the "Golden Cabbage," the nickname for the pierced metal dome, softening the abstract silhouette?

Some twenty-four thousand spectators thronged the exhibition where Room X was a highlight—not just for the integrated display but for its harmony with the exhibits, whereas in the other display areas designers had to compete with Hoffmann's divisions of screens and grills. The Scottish work was most representative of the ideals of the arts and crafts as much had been made by The Four and not by hired craftsmen. And the taut lines and inexpensive materials were expressive

170, 171. House for an Art Lover, proposed design for a music room and design for the entrance hall

within the embryonic enclosing framework of squares and rectangles within which, however, there lurked dark forces as expressed by the ideograms within the gesso panels and other two-dimensional works. Although these with their swirls and curves accorded with the molten lines of Austrian art nouveau there was a deeper, darker disturbance with the sinuous arms of the dressing mirror reaching up to the central female figure in the panel above. The emotions aroused were mixed. One review is worth quoting. "One of the interiors ... lies quite beyond good and evil ... In the total [there is] a simplicity which appears to enjoy itself with virtuosity ... The artists hardly spend their family life in such rooms but perhaps they have a special ghost's room in the house, hobgoblin's closet or something like that, as other people have a guest room, and this is the way it looks."[55]

The understated observance by Muthesius was that "the works of the group have received a lively acknowledgment at the Secession exhibition in Vienna ... In Glasgow in the meantime a whole school has come into being,"[56] which was accorded national recognition and status in 1902 as the Scottish section at the first international exhibition of modern decorative art in Turin, where "nothing would be accepted but original work showing a decided effort at renovation of form."[57]

England was represented by the Arts and Crafts Exhibition Society, which sent out a flyer asking for items to sent in for evaluation by February 1902, with the insurance and carriage costs to be paid for by the Italian organizers. The society's president, Walter Crane, who would be the English assessor on the international design jury, accompanied by Anning Bell and the architect C. H. Townshend, left London on April 1, arriving in Turin the next day to find the progress on the exhibition venue "in rather a backward state, the walls of our gallery at the entrances and screens having to be finished and wanting a final coat of whitewash." Of the exhibits that had arrived the sole breakage was "one of Mr. De Morgan's pottery friezes," which was in half although as the break was clean a speedy repair was effected. A few days later the William Morris tapestry *The Four Seasons*, lent by

172. House for an Art Lover

flowers for the rooms. "They walked into the country, and Toshie culled from the hedges trailing twigs etc which he arranged to his satisfaction in his special way."[73] And it would have been Mackintosh who instructed, albeit indirectly, that "The lists in the Mackintosh room and the McNair room are to go on *Posts* and not on the walls."[74] Were they decorated by the "french painter who worked for Mr. Mackintosh" and was paid £30?[75] And why had Frances McNair in Liverpool ordered "35 yds. white linen burlap" or canvas?[76] Was this for the door panels, which would narrow the passageway in Turin? And if so, who did the stenciling? And did Margaret execute the panels known as *The White Rose and the Red Rose* and *The Heart of the Rose* especially for Turin or was there an earlier but now unknown purpose behind their creation? Placed within the return walls of the Rose Boudoir their meaning has been a puzzle. "The panels' enigmatic imagery may illustrate the theme of love—of passive love and awakened love symbolised by the personification of red and white roses."[77] Perhaps, however, the symbolism can be explained. Among his Italian newspaper cuttings of the exhibition Newbery inserted a poem, "White Moss Rosebud."

Draw thy veil o'er thy face, sweet bud
And on thy mossy pillow rest thee
Thou white mossbud, so pure and rare
. . .
Soft mother moss, which circles thee
Cries, "Nothing in myself am I;
I live thy guardian dear to be . . .
The roses red in lovely throngs
Keep "Hushie" lest thy sleep be broken . . .[78]

Walter Crane may have been derogatory about other national displays but with the English artifacts skied and cluttered one can appreciate why, in the Scottish section, "A feeling of quiet repose, of coolness and of freshness pervades the rooms."[79] If one accepts that there is an inner meaning within the Mackintosh room can one accept that the McNair room has not only an aesthetic disposition? The curtained and glazed settle, with its cushion of nesting birds, was set by the Tree of Knowledge, which stands on "a baby's crawling-rug on which the young mind creeps through art to a quaint knowledge of Natural History." Beyond this hung silver repoussé panels within which human figures were caught[80] "so meshed with half remembrance hard to free," in D. G. Rossetti's line

within the embryonic enclosing framework of squares and rectangles within which, however, there lurked dark forces as expressed by the ideograms within the gesso panels and other two-dimensional works. Although these with their swirls and curves accorded with the molten lines of Austrian art nouveau there was a deeper, darker disturbance with the sinuous arms of the dressing mirror reaching up to the central female figure in the panel above. The emotions aroused were mixed. One review is worth quoting. "One of the interiors ... lies quite beyond good and evil ... In the total [there is] a simplicity which appears to enjoy itself with virtuosity ... The artists hardly spend their family life in such rooms but perhaps they have a special ghost's room in the house, hobgoblin's closet or something like that, as other people have a guest room, and this is the way it looks."[55]

The understated observance by Muthesius was that "the works of the group have received a lively acknowledgment at the Secession exhibition in Vienna ... In Glasgow in the meantime a whole school has come into being,"[56] which was accorded national recognition and status in 1902 as the Scottish section at the first international exhibition of modern decorative art in Turin, where "nothing would be accepted but original work showing a decided effort at renovation of form."[57]

England was represented by the Arts and Crafts Exhibition Society, which sent out a flyer asking for items to sent in for evaluation by February 1902, with the insurance and carriage costs to be paid for by the Italian organizers. The society's president, Walter Crane, who would be the English assessor on the international design jury, accompanied by Anning Bell and the architect C. H. Townshend, left London on April 1, arriving in Turin the next day to find the progress on the exhibition venue "in rather a backward state, the walls of our gallery at the entrances and screens having to be finished and wanting a final coat of whitewash." Of the exhibits that had arrived the sole breakage was "one of Mr. De Morgan's pottery friezes," which was in half although as the break was clean a speedy repair was effected. A few days later the William Morris tapestry *The Four Seasons*, lent by

172. House for an Art Lover

within the embryonic enclosing framework of squares and rectangles within which, however, there lurked dark forces as expressed by the ideograms within the gesso panels and other two-dimensional works. Although these with their swirls and curves accorded with the molten lines of Austrian art nouveau there was a deeper, darker disturbance with the sinuous arms of the dressing mirror reaching up to the central female figure in the panel above. The emotions aroused were mixed. One review is worth quoting. "One of the interiors ... lies quite beyond good and evil ... In the total [there is] a simplicity which appears to enjoy itself with virtuosity ... The artists hardly spend their family life in such rooms but perhaps they have a special ghost's room in the house, hobgoblin's closet or something like that, as other people have a guest room, and this is the way it looks."[55]

The understated observance by Muthesius was that "the works of the group have received a lively acknowledgment at the Secession exhibition in Vienna ... In Glasgow in the meantime a whole school has come into being,"[56] which was accorded national recognition and status in 1902 as the Scottish section at the first international exhibition of modern decorative art in Turin, where "nothing would be accepted but original work showing a decided effort at renovation of form."[57]

England was represented by the Arts and Crafts Exhibition Society, which sent out a flyer asking for items to sent in for evaluation by February 1902, with the insurance and carriage costs to be paid for by the Italian organizers. The society's president, Walter Crane, who would be the English assessor on the international design jury, accompanied by Anning Bell and the architect C. H. Townshend, left London on April 1, arriving in Turin the next day to find the progress on the exhibition venue "in rather a backward state, the walls of our gallery at the entrances and screens having to be finished and wanting a final coat of whitewash." Of the exhibits that had arrived the sole breakage was "one of Mr. De Morgan's pottery friezes," which was in half although as the break was clean a speedy repair was effected. A few days later the William Morris tapestry *The Four Seasons*, lent by

172. House for an Art Lover

within the embryonic enclosing framework of squares and rectangles within which, however, there lurked dark forces as expressed by the ideograms within the gesso panels and other two-dimensional works. Although these with their swirls and curves accorded with the molten lines of Austrian art nouveau there was a deeper, darker disturbance with the sinuous arms of the dressing mirror reaching up to the central female figure in the panel above. The emotions aroused were mixed. One review is worth quoting. "One of the interiors ... lies quite beyond good and evil ... In the total [there is] a simplicity which appears to enjoy itself with virtuosity ... The artists hardly spend their family life in such rooms but perhaps they have a special ghost's room in the house, hobgoblin's closet or something like that, as other people have a guest room, and this is the way it looks."[55]

The understated observance by Muthesius was that "the works of the group have received a lively acknowledgment at the Secession exhibition in Vienna ... In Glasgow in the meantime a whole school has come into being,"[56] which was accorded national recognition and status in 1902 as the Scottish section at the first international exhibition of modern decorative art in Turin, where "nothing would be accepted but original work showing a decided effort at renovation of form."[57]

England was represented by the Arts and Crafts Exhibition Society, which sent out a flyer asking for items to sent in for evaluation by February 1902, with the insurance and carriage costs to be paid for by the Italian organizers. The society's president, Walter Crane, who would be the English assessor on the international design jury, accompanied by Anning Bell and the architect C. H. Townshend, left London on April 1, arriving in Turin the next day to find the progress on the exhibition venue "in rather a backward state, the walls of our gallery at the entrances and screens having to be finished and wanting a final coat of whitewash." Of the exhibits that had arrived the sole breakage was "one of Mr. De Morgan's pottery friezes," which was in half although as the break was clean a speedy repair was effected. A few days later the William Morris tapestry *The Four Seasons*, lent by

172. House for an Art Lover

the Victoria and Albert Museum, and some lesser material by Ford Madox Brown and Burne-Jones arrived.

With time running short the mounting of the display was incommoded by the whitewashing of walls and the cleaning of windows. There was a need for more hammers and ladders, and showcases had to be constructed for "the books, table glass, small objects and jewellery," and attendants had to be appointed. Anning Bell's knowledge of the Italian language must have been a godsend! When all was completed Walter Crane was pleased with "the various exhibits looking remarkably well upon the white walls, the black framed cartoons, the coloured plaster reliefs and tapestry and printed and woven hangings especially so, and the simplicity of the ensemble was in rather striking contrast to the elaborately ornate character of the decoration of some of the neighbouring galleries."[58]

In "Premières Impressions à l'Exposition de Turin" Alexander Koch wrote: "L'Ecosse est avantageusement représentée par ce couple d'artistes qui a nom M. et Mme. Mackintosh et par the Glasgow School of Art ... mais elle n'offre rien d'essentiellement différent de ce qu'elle montrait à la Sécession Viennoise en 1901."[59] While it is true that the Scottish section, from which Edinburgh as "the capital is conspicuous by its absence,"[60] was solely represented by Glasgow-trained designers their number had been considerably increased. John Ednie and E. A. Taylor sent furniture made up by the commercial cabinet makers Wylie and Lochhead and J. Gaff Gillespie's overelaborated electric fire in brass repoussé and "containing a glass mosaic panel of St. Anthony of Padua" would be one of the star items. Among the drawings there was John Ednie's highly finished *Design for Hall Interior* and George Logan's ethereal *The White Boudoir*. Women were represented in force by *The Secret of the Rose* and *The Dance of the White Rose* (owned by J. Craig Annan) by Jessie M. King, by the embroidery of Ann Macbeth and Jessie Keppie, and illustrations by Agnes Raeburn, among others. Fully half of the Scottish exhibits were by The Four. Mackintosh was the most prolific with forty-four pieces, McNair with half that number, and Margaret and Frances with eleven each.[61]

In Glasgow in March 1902 household furnishings were once more being removed from the Mains Street flat to be taken up the hill to the School of Art for forwarding to a railway station; in Liverpool McNair goods were packed up and transported across England for shipment to the Continent from the port of Grimsby.[62] Mackintosh's collection included drawings for the House for an Art Lover (although Koch would be selling the published portfolios in Turin), designs for *The Wassail* and *The May Queen*, for sale at ten guineas each, and a writing desk, with inset panels by his

173. Room at the Vienna Secession, *Dekorative Kunst*

wife, of which duplicates could be had for £50. McNair's selection included designs for bookplates, a revolving bookcase embodying the concept of the Tree of Knowledge, and a pair of iron and copper candle sconces (174) forged to resemble flowers, whose three-dimensional geometry placed them more in the European camp of art nouveau than the more rigid and abstract metal designs of Mackintosh.[63]

As Newbery had overall authority for the Scottish section it was presumably he who called upon his "friend Mr. Mackintosh"[64] to be the designer. After all, he "has had some experience in work of this nature."[65] And was it Newbery who allocated a room to be set aside as the Rose Boudoir (175) for the Mackintoshes and another as the Lady's Writing Room (176) for the McNairs, even though they were now long gone from Glasgow, with the remainder of the Glasgow contingent being lumped together? Drawings and measurements from Italy must have been to hand since Mackintosh made "stencilled curtains at doors" as well as "4 electric pendants, 4 electric brackets,"[66] and he indented for the postage of drawings, stencil paper, canvas, and colors.[67] McNair's four leaded-glass panels were intended "for a window shown on the plan. The absence of this window is the fault of the authorities."[68]

Newbery and Mackintosh traveled to Turin in April to mount their display and to meet up with and renew acquaintanceships with English and Continental colleagues, such as Fritz Waerndorfer,[69] so that as Olbrich wrote, "In the evening I got together the Misters Berlepsch, Walter Crane, Mackintosh, etc. for a fine meal at the Restaurant Cambio. Afterwards, we were joined at our table by the Grand Duke [of Hesse], and we chatted until a quarter to eleven."[70] One does not know but one can imagine that Mackintosh would have been shocked on seeing the exhibition buildings, which were in the florid style then in vogue for expressions of national identity. Indeed, the domes and statuary groups with their histrionic posturings were akin to what Glasgow had chosen for its exhibition in the previous year. How different from the spare, untrammeled lines of the Secession House.

174. Wall sconce, J. Herbert McNair

A seasoned observer noted that Mackintosh's experience in Vienna "has been turned to account in Turin . . . From the first, the architect decided that the rooms without any exhibits should be in themselves and for themselves matter for exhibition," whereas the German exhibition was not cohesive "but contains as many ideas as there are states in the German Empire" while the Belgian section was "the agglomeration of the work of several brains."

There are indices pointing to how Mackintosh wished his own settings to be viewed. Daylight was screened out; artificial light was forbidden. The lofty, barnlike gallery was whitewashed with its height cut down by a top rail above which nothing was to be hung. The softly enameled white framework was the stage set that divided and unified the compartments in which the progressive colors of the rooms—rose to gray to purple—were made iridescent with silver and gold before which inlaid ivory roses, purple silk coverings, beaten silver, and polished gesso panels, placed like altarpieces in side chapels, shimmered fleetingly like dragonflies in the reedy ponds of summer.[71] Mackintosh arranged bowls of wired blossoms for which one critic professed a dislike.[72] Earlier he had burst into a rage when Newbery suggested buying

flowers for the rooms. "They walked into the country, and Toshie culled from the hedges trailing twigs etc which he arranged to his satisfaction in his special way."[73] And it would have been Mackintosh who instructed, albeit indirectly, that "The lists in the Mackintosh room and the McNair room are to go on *Posts* and not on the walls."[74] Were they decorated by the "french painter who worked for Mr. Mackintosh" and was paid £30?[75] And why had Frances McNair in Liverpool ordered "35 yds. white linen burlap" or canvas?[76] Was this for the door panels, which would narrow the passageway in Turin? And if so, who did the stenciling? And did Margaret execute the panels known as *The White Rose and the Red Rose* and *The Heart of the Rose* especially for Turin or was there an earlier but now unknown purpose behind their creation? Placed within the return walls of the Rose Boudoir their meaning has been a puzzle. "The panels' enigmatic imagery may illustrate the theme of love—of passive love and awakened love symbolised by the personification of red and white roses."[77] Perhaps, however, the symbolism can be explained. Among his Italian newspaper cuttings of the exhibition Newbery inserted a poem, "White Moss Rosebud."

Draw thy veil o'er thy face, sweet bud
And on thy mossy pillow rest thee
Thou white mossbud, so pure and rare
. . .
Soft mother moss, which circles thee
Cries, "Nothing in myself am I;
I live thy guardian dear to be . . .
The roses red in lovely throngs
Keep "Hushie" lest thy sleep be broken . . . [78]

Walter Crane may have been derogatory about other national displays but with the English artifacts skied and cluttered one can appreciate why, in the Scottish section, "A feeling of quiet repose, of coolness and of freshness pervades the rooms."[79] If one accepts that there is an inner meaning within the Mackintosh room can one accept that the McNair room has not only an aesthetic disposition? The curtained and glazed settle, with its cushion of nesting birds, was set by the Tree of Knowledge, which stands on "a baby's crawling-rug on which the young mind creeps through art to a quaint knowledge of Natural History." Beyond this hung silver repoussé panels within which human figures were caught[80] "so meshed with half remembrance hard to free," in D. G. Rossetti's line

from *Willow Wood*, which one critic quoted when writing of "Mackintosh und Die Schule von Glasgow in Turin," where "one can hardly believe how much one appears to be among poets if one is in the Mackintoshes' rooms or looks at their dreaming sheets. Often one thinks that the dream is an end in itself here, as if the creators did not want to have an impact on the real life ... One wants to play pieces of Maeterlinck in these places; and one can as well imagine that the fateful fairies of this poet are in these rooms, sitting on these high-backed chairs, like sisters of the figures on the carpets ... but also one is in doubt whether human beings made from flesh and blood can work and rest and eat and laugh and bring up children there: sinuous strong-boned Scots with red-blonde hair, threatening brows and strong chins."[81]

Although the Scottish section attracted much attention and admiration[82] one commentator went so far as to rate the interiors by the artist couples "the most artful of the whole exhibition"[83]—it was, as a whole, written off by Newbery as a financial failure,[84] with too few visitors, especially in the hot months, so that sales were low.[85] Among the Scots Mackintosh's sales were the highest with three vases, a panel, and a chair, which totaled £33:11:6. Next came E. A. Taylor and Talwin Morris at half that, along with McNair,[86] whose sales included one of his two display cabinets to his father in Skelmorlie.[87] Unluckily, his "embroidered carpet" was lost in transit to Britain. As Mackintosh reported in January, as the exhibits returned from Turin, "The only item in this list which I have found among my things is ... Prints and Photographs by D. S. McColl. Besides this I have two coloured panels by Mr. and Mrs. McNair and several electric light reflectors by James Salmon." Presumably McNair's lost property turned up as later two panels and an "Art Carpet" were dispatched to Liverpool.[88] And what about the orders for Mackintosh's square vases? Would those ordered for Budapest be sent? Mackintosh's reply was curt: "No more square vases."[89]

Vienna and Turin—how did they profit Mackintosh? There would be other exhibitions. In Dresden in 1903 there was "an exhibition of over thirty fully-furnished rooms from designs by the artists, Baillie Scott, Behrens ... Mackintosh."[90] Another year on and he was showing a dining room in Berlin.[91] More immediate and more prestigious was the invitation to participate in an exhibition of "Architectural and Artistic Crafts of the New Style" promoted in Moscow by the Grand Duchess Elizabeth, the sister of the Grand Duke of Hesse, at the close of 1902 and the New Year of 1903.[92] As the Grand Duke's architect, Olbrich was in Moscow and made a pertinent comment when interviewed by a journalist. "Oh this foolish critic—this dumb lamb allowed himself in my presence, to make fun of Mackintosh's work." For some unknown reason the relationship between the Austrian and his Scottish counterpart cooled so that, in an undated letter, Olbrich writes: "Today I also thanked Mackintosh without great feeling, but politely."[93] What had gone wrong? Was it that for him as for a compatriot, writing from London, "The evil rumour about Mackintosh is corroborated for me in that he, like most Englishmen, is said to drink a lot but nevertheless could not be called a drunkard, and at present he is supposed to be entirely normal."[94]

As at Turin, the Moscow exhibition included installations of rooms together with furnishings by, among others, Olbrich, Mackintosh, and Fedor Shekhtel, who had supervised the design and construction at the Glasgow exhibition in 1901 of "the four splendid pavilions erected by the Russian Government," representing "Russian architecture of the 17th century ... In addition to the prevailing colours of red, blue and green, there are large expanses of gilding and silvering."[95] Yet Shekhtel was well informed about contemporary European architecture. During his sojourns in Glasgow did he seek out any of the local architects? And, if wandering the streets of Glasgow, what would have caught his eye? Who, one wonders, issued the invitation to Mackintosh to pack and send to the farthest extremity of Europe chairs, tables, lamps to be set down against rose-strewn stencils by Margaret Macdonald Mackintosh—all to be glimpsed through an archway guarded by the strongly modeled chairs (almost Egyptian in their abstraction of power) from Windyhill? That the designer couple did not travel to Moscow, "being too fearful of the Russian winter," perhaps spared them the criticism

175, 176. Turin Exhibition, rose boudoir, Charles and Margaret Mackintosh, and writing room, J. Herbert and Frances McNair, *The Studio*

of their white drawing room, which was likened to "an operating theatre, or a Moscow hairdressers. Staying in it was very wearisome and boring: everyone fled from it, from those dreadful straight lines, the lifelessness ... But I do not believe it is created without a precise symbolism: the white colour presumably speaks of desires that are out of our control."[96]

Yet despite the international renown, only one serious commission came to Mackintosh from the Continent—a music room (177) for Fritz Waerndorfer's villa on the outskirts of Vienna, where it would be set up alongside interiors by Hoffmann, making the Waerndorfers' home "a place of pilgrimage for lovers of art" among the bourgeoisie and cultural elite of Viennese society.[97]

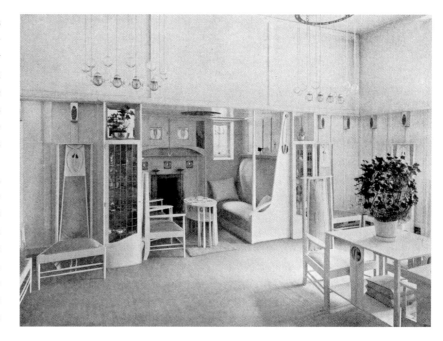

It seems that Mackintosh received the commission between the closing of the Secession exhibition in Vienna and the opening of the Turin extravaganza, for in the spring of 1902 Waerndorfer refers to Mackintosh's full-scale drawings.[98] At some time the Mackintoshes paid a second visit to Vienna "and spent six weeks in the city," perhaps returning in 1906 for the setting up of the gesso wall panels.[99] The room was of a piece with the exhibition spaces but with a more elaborate plan, featuring an inglenook and fireplace.

In the autumn of 1902 Mr. and Mrs. Waerndorfer traveled to Glasgow and took the opportunity (or were directed) to travel down the Clyde coast visiting the Rosneath peninsula, the domain of Princess Louise, where her architect "Luytchens [sic] is the creator of this very charming inn—saw today beautiful house by Bailey [sic] Scott, white, red roof, shall bring you photographs," as Waerndorfer wrote to Hoffmann.[100] While viewing The White House did the party climb the hill to where Helensburgh ceased and the moorland began to inspect the ongoing building progress at The Hill House? Could Muthesius and his wife have been of the party? They had

been urged by Mackintosh to lengthen a proposed visit to Glasgow for "the longer you stay the better we will be pleased. Yes, we know only too well how many people are against us, but I am very sorry to hear that any one condemns you for writing about our work. I will not have very much new work except the Vienna drawing-room—but you can be quite sure that I shall be only too glad to give you anything that I have. I am afraid there is little chance of us getting a grand prix at Torino, but when you say that we should have 'it' we feel that we have got something we value much more."[101]

At the same time Newbery's agent was sending news from Turin, where "The Jurymen are working very hard! ... I am doing my best for your section and I hope [you] will be satisfied.'" And indeed within a month he was conveying congratulations on the diplomas of honor "conferred from the Jury to you and Mr. and Mrs. Mackintosh."[102] Newbery was granted an audience by the King of Italy, "who is an accomplished English scholar. The King was so pleased with the explanation made by Mr. Newbery, as to the part taken by Scotland in the Exhibition, that he created him a Cava-

177. Music room for Fritz Waerndorfer, Vienna, *The Studio*

lier of one of the Italian orders."[103] The Turin exhibition had "represented the apogee of the Glasgow style and placed the work of the ex—students of the Glasgow School of Art at the forefront of artistic developments."[104]

Honors aside, how did the cultural interchange between Glasgow and Europe work to the advantage of either side? On a personal level there were the individual relationships. If it is true that in 1900 "the Scots, at this time, were the artistic leaders, while Hoffmann, Moser and the others were admiring followers,"[105] one can understand the warmth of Hoffmann's regard for Mackintosh, which continued to be expressed after the Secessionist exhibition was packed away. There was the post-exhibition stay by the Mackintoshes in Vienna to discuss and oversee the Waerndorfer music room, and in December 1902 Hoffmann could be gently chided, according to Waerndorfer, as Mackintosh "is furious because you were in Glasgow for two days only, and he is delighted by you more than ever; this indeed seems to be vice-versa."[106] In the following spring Mackintosh offered moral support for the formation of the Wiener Werkstatte and he sent a design for its signet declaring that "every object which you pass from your hand must carry an outspoken mark of individuality, beauty and the most exact execution. From the outset your aim must be that every object which you produce is made for a certain purpose and place. Later … you can emerge boldly into the full light of the world, attack the factory-trade on its own ground, and the greatest work that can be achieved in this century, you can achieve it: namely the production of objects of use in magnificent form and at such a price that they lie within the buying range of the poorest."[107]

But it was not to be. Mackintosh, alone of British designers, with the exception of Baillie Scott, awarded European status, admired by Muthesius, Waerndorfer, Hoffmann, and others, was in Glasgow on the northwestern periphery of Europe whereas his admirers dwelt in an imperial capital, the hub of a polyglot, multicultural empire with the stimuli of discourse and debate with colleagues and students.

As to Mackintosh's influence on the course of European decorative art some examples of that have been cited. Thus, at the Austrian exhibition in Paris in 1904, "In the mural decoration [by Hoffmann] there is perhaps somewhat too strong a suggestion of the familiar *motifs* of the Glasgow School."[108] Perhaps. Mackintosh had presented an alternative four years before in Vienna of rectilinearity within the simplicity of white painted furnishings without resorting to organic sinuosity. Had not Klimt skied his Beethoven frieze after the manner of the gesso panels, and were not Viennese architects using the grouped four squares?[109] One can argue about who used or who developed this and that motif but it is like engaging in a debate about the number of angels that can dance on a pinhead. In the larger sphere of architecture it may be, as Howarth claimed, that Mackintosh's entry for the House for an Art Lover competition was the inspiration for the evolution of the Palais Stoclet in Brussels,[110] except that the starting points were different—the one from the arts and crafts, the other from central European neoclassicism; the one symbolic, the other cerebral.

What did Mackintosh return from Europe with? When completing his Italian tour in 1891 and homeward bound for Glasgow he had traveled via Antwerp where he called in at the Decorative Arts Museum and sketched a mid-seventeenth-century oak bed, details from which became structural elements in the gallery doors of the Glasgow Art Club.[111] So from Vienna may have come, as has been noted before now, influences on the design program of the guest bedroom at 78 Derngate, Northampton.[112] But what about Hoffmann's polychromatic posts and screens in the Secession exhibition of 1900—do they not become the decorative balusters in the library of the School of Art? And the grouping of four lamps in the *Herrenzimmer* of Waerndorfer's villa—surely one sees them reappearing in Mackintosh's own interiors.[113] For the Mackintoshes, however, the abiding memory of their European adventures must have been their journey together, only a few months after their marriage, across Europe to the capital of the Hapsburg empire where the draughtsman's wares would be seen alongside those by the elite of Europe's designers. No wonder that for Mackintosh it was "the high point of his life!"[114] ▉

When Gleeson White, having viewed the Arts and Crafts exhibition in London in 1896, traveled to Glasgow to meet The Four and their like-minded colleagues, he found himself surprised. For a start, as another critic had found, Margaret and Frances Macdonald made an impression as "two laughing, comely girls, scarce out of their teens." That that was not quite true was part of their allure. Gleeson White was impressed when informed that their beaten brass candlesticks, bronze sconces and copper frames were "worked entirely by the two sisters." Then there was the imagery that suffused the works of McNair. And Mackintosh? Although he had his own output of furniture and graphics, what caught Gleeson White's fullest attention were his large mural decorations, "an opportunity rare at the present time," for "a large building to be known ... as Miss Cranstoun's [sic] Tea Rooms,"[1] which revealed an outsider's ignorance of the standing of the Cranston name, a byword in the city where tearooms were "among the newer features of Glasgow life."[2] Although there would be imitators it was the Cranstons who, with their sure sense of innovation in presentation and of self-publicity, would remain in the forefront, forging the link between the tearoom and "the New Art movement."[3]

Catherine Cranston's father and uncle had been earlier stalwarts of the catering trade in Glasgow. The latter, Robert Cranston, ran the Waverley Temperance Hotel in Buchanan Street, an early haunt of the members of the Glasgow Art Club. George Cranston, Catherine's father, was the proprietor of the Crown Hotel in George Square and in time would take his son, Stuart Cranston, into the business. In 1871 the latter began a new business for, having trained as a tea taster, "his success in infusing a cup of tea or coffee, and selling it at 2d, was nothing less than a foregone conclusion."[4] Such an enterprise, conforming to the Cranstons' temperance principles, met a need "for those who desired refreshment beyond the bar of the public house and the parlour of the restaurant."[5] Thus, there came about "Tea Rooms for Ladies shopping, and Gentlemen during business hours," which were not only modish but provided with "comfortable, well-ventilated lavatories."[6]

When a third Cranston tearoom, in the Argyle Arcade (178) next to Joseph Wright's umbrella shop, was opened in October 1889 *The Bailie* featured a profile of the proprietor as the pioneer of tearooms "not in Glasgow only but over the entire country," with London following Glasgow's lead. A succession of advertised and widely reported opening ceremonies began with a reception of invited guests, and afterward the public could inspect the premises, which, according to a full page advertisement, "are unequalled for Extent and Beauty, Lightness and Airiness, replete with every comfort which science and experience can suggest and comprise Ladies' Reading and Writing Room, Ladies' Tea Room, Gents' Tea Room, Smoking Room, Lavatories, etc. etc." It was announced, "The

178. Proposed new entrance to the Argyle Arcade, *The Bailie*

Scheme of Ventilation is unique. The fresh air, before being admitted to the Salons, is cleaned, deprived of all dust or smoke, heated in Winter by hot-water pipes, and cooled in Summer by blocks of ice; and all the air of the Rooms is expelled and replaced every twenty minutes by a continuous and imperceptible movement."

It seems that the hyperbole was justified. "This is ... the biggest set of rooms ... not only in Glasgow, or in Scotland, but in Britain, or, indeed, any where."[7] And was there a designer, as opposed to a supplier, of "the very fine stained glass" and of "the charming wall and ceiling decorations"?[8] And for what were Honeyman and Keppie paid a fee in 1889?[9] Certainly, there would have been an affinity between Honeyman and Stuart Cranston, who was a prominent churchman.

Glasgow has always had a black and white reputation. At the same time as it was "the drunkenest city in the Empire,"[10] by the time Stuart Cranston was opening up in the Argyle Arcade, "Tea-rooms have become an institution in the city. Not many years ago such places were practically unknown, now they abound,"[11] which prompted the question: "How do they all pay?"[12] Although Burns's tearooms in Ingram Street promised "a capital cup of the cheerful beverage,"[13] there could be the lure, as at Assafrey's "Chocolate and tea salon," of "artistically arranged luncheon salons"[14] often with a touch of novelty so that there was the Mikado Tea Room[15] and the Indian Tea Company, the windows of which displayed "a beautiful collection of Indian vases and other eastern works."[16] Not to be outdone Stuart Cranston offered "Japanese Goods ... Vases, Flower Pots, Tete-a-Tete Sets, Hanging Flower Vases, Salad Bowls, Spills, Beakers, etc. in the following wares: Cloisonne, Satsuma ... and Blue and White."[17] Tearooms had also to be technologically innovative. The premises of Nesbit and Company, "constructed and arranged to the designs of Mr. H. D. Walton, the architect" in 1893, were fitted with electric light,[18] as at Skinner's, equipped with telephone rooms "for Day Committee Meetings,"[19] where "the Baroness Kelvin turned on the electric light" in the presence of "a host of other West-end ladies and

gentelemen."[20] By the start of the twentieth century "Glasgow, in truth, is a very Tokio for tea-rooms."[21]

What might be called the tea ceremony occupied much space in the local journals. "I have no faith in scolding servants," ran one commentary, "besides, as a lady said to me the other day, 'it quite spoils the expression of one's face,' "[22] and hostesses were reminded that "Silver forks, or fruit knives and forks, ought to be provided at afternoon tea feasts, so that guests may prevent the spoiling of their gloves."[23] While there may have been a perception, beyond the drawing rooms of the west end, of "the Girl of the Tea-Room" as "this sweet votaress ... she has a pale and aesthetic appearance ... this angel of the tea-cups,"[24] the reality was that "In many of the city restaurants the poor unfortunate waitresses are kept at work from 7 am till 9 pm daily."[25] Miss Cranston, however, had a reputation as "a model employer" and "the hundreds of young women in her service are the subject of her unceasing care."[26]

If Stuart Cranston was the pioneer of tearooms it was his sister Catherine who, with her style and promotional skills, made her name a byword in Glasgow, giving rise to the expression "quite Kate Cranstonish." In 1878 she appears as a "restaurateur" at 114 Argyle Street, "thereby starting what may be called a beneficent revolution."[27] She was then living with her brother close to the center of town, but within a few years they would remove westward toward the more affluent Woodlands. In 1892, in the year of her marriage, Stuart Cranston quit the city for the western suburb of Bearsden and his sister set up home at Hous'hill near Barrhead, a township to the southeast where her husband, Major Cochrane, had his business.[28] By then Catherine Cranston had a second tearoom in Ingram Street where, in the autumn of 1888, she was preparing to open luncheon rooms with "electric light used throughout." (179) The exotic decorations would seem to have been rather at odds with an advertisement of a classically robed waitress alongside a fluted column.[29] The extension was opened in January 1889 when "Miss Cranston gave a House-heating and servant's dance," which was "carried on with great enthusiasm till an early hour in the morning." The hundred and more guests drank her health "while Mr. Cranston, senr., feelingly replied for the beneficiane."[30]

By 1896 Miss Cranston was in possession of a narrow three-bay feu at the southern end of Buchanan Street, Glasgow's smartest shopping thoroughfare, and, unusually and very ambitiously, rather than undertake a conversion she decided to seek increased accommodation in purpose-built premises using as her architect George Washington Browne.[31] Why? That is the first of many questions about Miss Cranston's choice of those whom she decided to employ. Washington Browne was a Glasgow man who lived and practiced

WILL OPEN ABOUT 11th SEPTEMBER

Miss Cranston has much pleasure in announcing the acquisition of Luncheon Rooms at 209 Ingram Street, when she hopes to receive an extension of the generous support already accorded her Tea Rooms.

· ELECTRIC LIGHT USED THROUGHOUT ·

179. Advertisement for the Ingram Street tearoom, *The Bailie*

in Edinburgh and his sole Glasgow commission had been a study and dining room in Westdel, the residence in Dowanhill of Robert Maclehose, a publisher and printer.[32] The new tearoom was in Pont Street Dutch (180)—eye-catchingly colorful with a red sandstone base lightened by cream striation above and topped by a multilayered gable. A wrought-iron balcony at the first floor was pierced with the initials of the proprietrix as in a royal monogram.

"The pretty little gabled front of some tearooms … charmingly detailed in a very refined manner" attracted wide coverage in the journals,[33] although Gleeson White, as a critic of some internal features, declined to name the architect while accepting that there was "knowledge, good taste, and a capacity for planning spaces that entitle him to very high praise."[34] Maybe, but that did not stop Miss Cranston from handing over the furnishing and decoration to younger men, beginning with George Walton, whom she had first patronized in 1888 in her Argyle Street tearoom thus enabling him to leave banking and set up his own decorating company,[35] which now executed the decorations on the lower floors; the three upper floors were designed by Mackintosh but realized by the firm of the Guthrie brothers. One wonders about the human drama of the personalities involved. Was there to be a team effort by the two mural designers? Or was Walton displaced and Mackintosh brought in by the strong-willed patroness? True, there had been a connection between Honeyman and Keppie and Stuart Cranston but his sister's name does not appear in the firm's job books until later. Can one assume that Miss Cranston made a personal approach to Mackintosh? Why? Was she aware of the scale and impact of the gallery frieze in the Art Club, which had been Mackintosh's sole experience in decorating? As Gleeson White saw it, "not a few of those who devoted special attention to the modern poster were interested far more in the influence it promised to exercise upon fresco and stencilled surface decoration."[36]

Undoubtedly Miss Cranston had caught a mood. "The renaissance of public mural decoration is now making notable progress,"[37] encouraged by Newbery "as interim secretary to the Committee on Artistic Art" promoting "the introduction of pictorial wall painting into the decoration of public buildings in this country."[38] The scope could be widened for as Newbery would write later: "Commercialism neither lays down a role nor demands the following of a tradition. All that is asked is that the productions of the artist should be comprehensible to the commercial mind ... And withal Art seems to flourish under the somewhat eccentric conditions that arise out of this companionship with commercialism."[39] That certainly was so in Glasgow for when it was announced that the decorating firms of J. and W. Guthrie and Andrew Wells would merge, their united catalogue of works included "the painting of the New Club, of Cairndhu House, Helensburgh, of St. Andrew's Church, of Hillhead Established Church, of the Ramshorn Church, of Mount Stuart, of the house of Sir William Arrol, Ayr, of Ardencaple Castle, of the house of Mr. Cross, M.P.,"[40] a proliferation suggesting that in the future "the richest work of the artist will be found in wall and screen painting."[41]

For Gleeson White, "The decorative movement in Great Britain today is showing many signs of vitality which promise well for the future."[42] However, he may have felt, having looked over the Buchanan Street tearooms, that Walton's contribution failed that test (181), which may explain why the promised account did not appear. Besides, Walton, as White saw it, did not sit easily alongside The Four.[43] It is true that Walton's somewhat bland and repetitive patterning struggled inadequately against the weight of Washington Browne's interiors with their elaborated pilasters, ornate chimney pieces, molded ceilings, and intrusive ventilation grills. Mackintosh's scheme was both simpler and more dramatic and adapted to a structure from which extraneous ornament had been stripped away.

One innovation was a galleried light well, which would recur in the Oak Room in the Ingram Sreet tearoom and again in the Willow tearoom. It was a device recently introduced into the larger retail stores, such as the nearby Wylie and Lochhead premises. Also the introduction into department stores of tearooms and ladies' restrooms would

180. Miss Cranston's Buchanan Street tearoom, G. Washington Browne, *The Builder*

not have gone unnoticed by the Cranstons. There was, too, a vogue for the Moorish style, as in Liberty's "Arab" tearoom in the mid-1880s, a precursor of the Cloister Room in Ingram Street.[44]

With a light well allowing both vertical and horizontal expression of movement Mackintosh could take his base colors from green to "a greyish-greenish yellow" up to blue[45] as a revelation of the cosmos in which, as Gleeson White had noted, "Because of the use of vertical lines and its archaic treatment of the figure, many people prefer to say that all the Glasgow work is based upon Egypt," although he personally considered "the debt to be but slight."[46]

Are there other pointers to the inspirational sources? Given the complexities of Mackintosh's creativity and cognitive thinking and the few scraps of illustrative evidence it is hazardous to guess, although as pointed out earlier there are indices from Japan, Italy, contemporary art, and, as always, *The Studio*, in which there was a discussion by Baillie Scott on wall decoration where 'the effect is that of trees set around the room under which is a meadow spangled with

181. Buchanan Street tearoom

flowers receding in the distance."[47] Conventional enough it may be, but not with Mackintosh who had half a dozen varieties of trees at one level while above others commingled with entangled female forms.

The Buchanan Street murals were the largest and most complex decorations produced by Mackintosh. Whereas Walton's wall scenery in the billiard room was pictorial, Mackintosh's had an evident depth of meaning. But how to unravel it? Is the attempt profitable? Or should one accept that when the tearooms opened in May 1897 there were mere novelties attracting "large crowds of visitors."[48] Yet if one has interpreted aright the earlier works there must be a suppressed meaning bearing in mind Joshua Reynolds's observation, quoted by Lethaby, that "Invention, strictly speaking, is little more than a new combination of those images, that have been previously gathered and deposited in the memory."[49]

Mackintosh treated his three levels as a unity so that the frieze of one is the base for the next. Rising through this cosmos there were stenciled trees evoking memories of the Norse myths, in which, "The axis of the three levels ... was the mighty ash tree, Yggdrasill ... Yggdrasill had three roots."[50] Folk myth had it that "the tree spirit is often conceived and represented as detached from the tree and clothed in human form, and even as embodied in living men and women."[51] Does that occur in the ladies' room? (182) Here perhaps Mackintosh's longings for the unattainable Margaret Macdonald are expressed in the imagery of the medieval poem *The Romance of the Rose*, "in which the whole art of love is contained" so that "I dreamed that it was May, the season of love and joy ... this is the time when the earth becomes so proud that it desires a new dress, and is able to make a dress so lovely that there are a hundred pairs of colours in it. The grass and the flowers . . . these are the dress that I am describing," while the woman's robe "which was white, signified that she who wore it was gentle and noble," although "the love that has ensnared you offers you carnal delight, so that you have no interest in anything else. That is why you want to have the rose, and dream of no other possession."[52] Such may be the allegory of the ladies' room.

Gleeson White did not attempt to explain Mackintosh's decorations although he was struck by the application of the paint, noting, "Whether owing to the surface or some clever manipulation, the effect is of flat but not even colour with a fine texture in that it imparts a surface not unlike that upon the 'self-colour' bottles of Chinese porcelain."[53] Was an interest in technique part of the desire to ensure that with

182. Buchanan Street tearoom

each new commission there would be no repetition of effect? And to what extent does that reflect collaboration between the executant firm and the proposer of the idea?

A further stage in the development of surface technique may have been the interest in gesso work, which was being promoted in the first volume of *The Studio*, where Walter Crane wrote: "Decorative design in gesso stands, it may be said, midway between painting and sculpture" to be employed "with all kinds of domestic furniture and adornment."[54] Other advantages were utilitarian. "For merely practical reasons, the comparatively slight harbourage it affords for dust, the greater facility for cleaning the surface, and its subordinate effect in interior decoration combine to render low relief better adapted for our climate and for our homes."[55] Given Glasgow's fog and sulfur-laden skies how practical was it to set up gesso panels in the Ingram Street tearoom?

The premises were acquired from 1888 onwards, which accounted for the piecemeal development that continued until 1912. That may explain in part the rather staid planning. There were screens and galleries to subdivide individual rooms. Nevertheless, it is true to say that Mackintosh never seems to have shown the degree of interest in planning that he gave to decoration. It may be that, with the exception of the library in the School of Art, he was more concerned with line, surface, and color than with form. If so, some would see him at one with Robert Adam, another Scottish architect whose name has become a household word in decoration.

That Mackintosh and his collaborators were the heirs of the Pre-Raphaelites in the use of esoteric, anticorporeal forms is shown in the gesso panels, by Mackintosh and Margaret Macdonald, *The Wassail* and *The May Queen*— titles that are beholden to folk myth.

How did it come about that Mackintosh and his wife indulged in such conjugal exercises? Were they inspired by the local Arts and Crafts exhibition of a few years earlier and, before that, by John Guthrie who had exhibited in London? And was Miss Cranston enamored by the novelty of the enterprise? As a pair the panels are interesting. What was the genesis? Where were they worked? In the Macdonalds' studio, one presumes. And whose was the idea of placing them high as friezes? "Just now," Mackintosh wrote to Muthesius in the summer of 1900, "we are working at two gesso panels for the frieze . . . Miss Margaret Macdonald is doing one and I am doing the other . . . We are working them together and that makes the work very pleasant. We have set ourselves a large task as we are slightly modelling and then colouring and setting the jewels of different colours."[56] More prosaically, the panels were "pinned with ordinary pins through the center of twine on the plaster ground work, in order to obtain required relief, and covered with gesso."[57]

In the flush of discovered love husband and wife worked side by side on the same project using the same materials of hessian, gesso, string, and colored glass—which makes the differences between *The Wassail* and *The May Queen* all the more telling, for the former is a tighter composition, more sophisticated, more compelling. At the time of the Secession exhibition in Vienna the works of The Four aroused in Muthesius thoughts about "the peculiar use of the human figure . . . the central source of criticism for many people of these works. The central question seems to be here whether it is permissible to stylise the human figure. Can we distort the human figure and change their proportions arbitrarily to fit in with an ornamental scheme of lines."[58] Was the douce, middle-class clientele of Glasgow disturbed or enlightened sitting beneath roses and garlands? Looking at the ladies' luncheon room (183) one has to remember that Mackintosh must have learned much from his earlier collaboration, if that is what it was, with Walton. Before the start of the Buchanan Street tearooms Walton had had ten years when he was designing

for the restaurant trade. Did Mackintosh borrow from that experience when creating an all-white interior with its dance of high- and medium-backed chairs?

Miss Cranston eventually had four sets of tearooms and Mackintosh was employed at each of them. At Buchanan Street, Ingram Street, and Argyle Street his role was different in each and his job was to effect compromise. Each room was a test bed for the culmination of his employment by Miss Cranston when she began custom-designed premises—the Willow Tea Room in Sauchiehall Street. After chopping and changing architects Miss Cranston seems to have found in Mackintosh the one person whose designs could match her aspirations for the perfection that outclassed that of her competitors and imitators.

An early patron of the Buchanan Street tearooms had been the English architect Edwin Lutyens who, in June 1897, when en route to Rosneath in connection with his works for Princess Louise, Duchess of Argyll, was taken by

183. Ingram Street tearoom, *The Studio*

James Guthrie, "a glass painter and decorator," who had worked at Ardencaple Castle, another Argyll property, "to a Miss Somebody's who is really a Mrs. Somebody else. She started a large Restaurant, all very elaborately simple on very new school High Art Lines. The result gorgeous! and a wee bit vulgar. She has nothing but green handled knives and all is curiously painted and coloured. Most delicious blue willow pattern sets of china ware she has and as a great favour she is going to make me up a basket." A year later and he was back again "to these queer, funny rooms and had a most excellent breakfast—tea, butter, jam, toasts, baps and buns—2 sausages, 2 eggs—speak it not in Gath— all for 1/1d! so clean. Most beautiful peonies on the breakfast table." That there were flowers in abundance may have been one of the bonds between Mackintosh and his patroness. "Miss C. is now Mrs. Cochrane, a dark, busy, fat, wee body with black sparky-luminous eyes, wears a bonnet garnished with roses, and has made a fortune by supplying cheap clean foods in surroundings prompted by the New Art Glasgow School."[59]

The most complete example of the style was the Willow Tea Room in Sauchiehall Street. It had been noted, "The throng that formerly after noon was wont to parade Buchanan Street only, seems now to some extent to have become attracted to Sauchiehall Street, and, more especially to the immediate neighbourhood of Copland and Lye's warehouse, and the Institute ... you will encounter the beauties of the West, and you will see that they are responsible for a large following of the opposite sex."[60] The response was another ambitious project by Miss Cranston, "convinced of the idea that tea and beauty are congenial to each other,"[61] involving, once again, building on a narrow feu but with the difference that both outside and in all was controlled, down to the production of ladies' hat hooks and flower containers, by Mackintosh. No longer was he acting in a private capacity; as a partner with a legal responsibility for a construction job the work was now itemized in his firm's job book. That he had accepted in the past commissions outside the firm must have riled at least one partner.

Tenders for building work were submitted in March 1903.[62] Site work commenced that spring with the trades following in sequence—joinery, plumbing, and then electrical installations in the early months of 1904. Although some of the prices would move upward or downward from the estimates the building cost was less than calculated. As with the main contractors so for the fitting out, many of the suppliers were firms associated with the practice. George Adam's wrought-iron work included the "2 lamps at Front" and "2 Hanging Signs" as well as the internal stair rail for which Cooper and Co. supplied five dozen green and blue glass beads as also the glass globes, glass drops, and clear and ruby beads for the chandeliers in the Ladies' Room, together with the expansive flower bowl, fitted with "23 Flower Tubes," which would be suspended within a wooden cross frame in the front salon. All was ready by November. "Hitherto Miss Cranston has been famous for the daintily artistic character of her several establishments. However, her new establishment fairly outshines all her others in the matters of arrangement and colours. The furnishing, besides, is of the richest and most luxurious character ... Her 'Salon de Luxe' is simply a marvel of the art of the upholsterer and decorator."[63]

The Willow Tea Room was the most complete of all Mackintosh's artworks. And yet it is as a decorator that he best succeeds, although one has to accept that by any standards the facade (184) is remarkable for its time whether in Britain or in Europe. But did anyone in Glasgow realize the significance of the planar front subtly differentiated in its parts? That could be done only with the smooth mono coloring, by a slight bowing in the eastern portion, the deeply recessed windows in the upper half, the angled glass entrance screen, and the line of squares marking off the limits of the design concept. Nothing could have been more distant artistically from the putti and pediments at Buchanan Street or the quirkiness of the barge boards at Argyle Street. Here instead was a work that was the very memory of Mackintosh's stay in Vienna.[64]

Deutsche Kunst was alone in recording and analyzing an undertaking that could have been formulated only in Glasgow,

184. Willow Tea Room, *Deutsche Kunst*

which, according to *The Studio*, "is not a city of tradition" but a place where there was "absolute independence of outlook, and disregard of formulas, and a vigorous mode of rendering their ideas that in many instances is almost aggressive in its modernity."[65] And it was these qualities that set apart the works of Mackintosh and his followers from their fellows on the Continent. "The 'modern style,' it has been said, 'is essentially a submarine style, because the only forms which appear really novel belong, as the submarine animals do, to the invertebrate class.' "[66] The quip may have applicable in Europe; not so in Glasgow.

The Willow Tea Room was the only one of Miss Cranston's establishments to have had a single theme. Whose idea was that? Miss Cranston, although "an eager art-lover,"[67] could not have made that imaginative leap although she would have heartily applauded the intention. Was it Mackintosh? Or was it Margaret Macdonald? After all, one of Mackintosh's studies for the intended plaster frieze has it smothered with banks of roses.[68]

Already in 1902 in *Deutsche Kunst und Dekoration* when discussing "Mackintosh and the Glasgow School in Turin" the opening paragraphs dealt almost exclusively with the influence of the Anglo-Italian poet Dante Gabriel Rossetti and in particular with his sonnet "Willowwood." "These verses are like a motto to the ornaments of Margaret Macdonald Mackintosh. Sounds that cannot be analysed seem to fade away in the distance and we always think we are to hear the song of yearning, the song of souls which wait in the dark apartments of death for the new day which does not come. There is hardly a panel or painting or symbol of the Mackintoshes that one could not connect with this motif."[69] Given the derivation from the Scots tongue of Sauchiehall Street as the house of willows (rather than "the alley of the willows," as commonly given) then it was inevitable that "Mackintosh chose the willow as the main pattern of the decorations of this house."[70]

Whereas Baillie Scott and Walton would have realized that intent using paint and embossed leather on the walls with the furnishings in a void, for Mackintosh all and everything

was conceived and designed to be within a unified and symbolical concept. Thus to look down from the staircase (185) into the front salon with the scene partially dissolved by a foliate screen of glass beads and bent ironwork into a forest clearing was to hear subconsciously the words of Voysey. "Go back into the woods, and feel once more the sublime breath and repose of a natural glade, or the fringe of a moor at sunset, when the lands unite with horizontal lines to soothe the weary eye and breathe repose with the troubled brain!"[71] More prosaically, here one could have "tea for a few pence" but one could also "dream of being in wonderland."[72]

Throughout the ground floor (186) the symbolism was restrained with the decoration elevated to the panels of the decorative frieze in which taut and sparse lines recede into a distance and in which there is neither time nor space. As the writer in *Dekorative Kunst* put it in 1905: "In the stylised decoration of the rooms, the willow pattern dominates the walls and pillars of the ground floor halls and the gallery. The arrangement, in rows, seems to point higher to an invisible yet near room,"[73] which was the upper Ladies' Room, soon to be immortalized as the Room de Luxe (187), a room

185, 186. Willow Tea Room, *Deutsche Kunst*

that inspired in Mackintosh his most subtle and brilliant interior decoration, although the allegory is now dimmed by the insertion of modern-day replica furnishings to allow its continued use as a tearoom. So it is that one has to think about and consider the allusions contained within this rectangle, this *hortus conclusus* when a hundred years ago Pettigrew and Stephens supplied lavender silk for the dado covering and Wylie and Lochhead the purple velvet for the silvered chairs. Today's replicas are thickly coated with aluminum paint. For Mackintosh that would have been too crude, too opaque for his gossamer boudoir. Outside there was "the rich, rough city of Glasgow,"[74] inside "the musical rhythms of Architecture and something of the universal spirit of Poetry."[75]

Mackintosh was thirty-five when he came to design the Willow Tea Room. It is a significant age for many an architect or designer. The long apprenticeship is over and with the first age of maturity comes a blossoming. So it is that the Willow Tea Room is Mackintosh's first complete symbolic creation before which the Vienna and Turin exhibits had been compromises, the House for an Art Lover a paper exercise, and the later library of the Glasgow School of Art a somber and thoughtful crescendo, whereas the Room de Luxe, despite the undertones of loss and sorrow, is effervescent with a life force.

The room is focused on Margaret Macdonald's gesso panel, not skied but placed at floor level to give reality to Rossetti's lines.

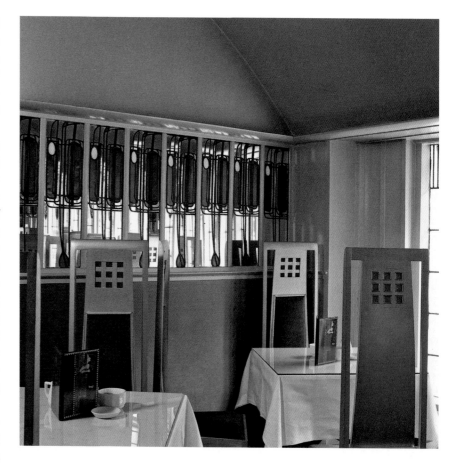

> O ye, all ye that walk in Willowwood
>   That walk with hollow faces burning bright

Other recollections are brought to mind.

> And I was made aware of a dumb throng
>   That stood aloof, one form by every tree,
>   All mournful forms, for each was I or she,
> The shades of those our days that had no tongue.

Given, as was noted in 1902, the significance of these lines for Margaret Macdonald perhaps one should probe deeper into the psychological mysteries of the Room de Luxe which in depth of meaning is unequaled in the European art of its time. Is it the "dumb throng" that is reflected in "the rich glass jewellery"[76] of the frieze over the lavender dado? (188) These "mirrored eyes" of the poet also reflect the chairs in their purple mourning dress. But they tell too of a future life in the broken silvered silhouettes—a grove of trees where the crimson-eyed squares are like the berries of fruitfulness and fertility.

Such analysis may seem overresponsive were it not for *The Claims of Decorative Art* in which Walter Crane enunciated, "We are bored to death by what is called realism."[77] As he pointed out: "The Briton can get his art cheap too—wholesale and retail. He can have cheap dadoes and coloured

187, 188. Willow Tea Room

glass thrown in here and there. If these are not enough he can fill his house with early (or latest) English furniture, 'surmounted by something Japanese,' as the comic poet saith."[78] For the creative designer "the problem of how to associate art with everyday life"[79] was compounded, because "The artist has become more and more specialised, and the unity of the arts has been broken up."[80]

Walton had designed tearoom interiors with a thought to uniting wall decorations and furnishings and Mackintosh, observing the effects, then took forward the ideas such as contrasting color effects—black in a white setting—of chairs of different height, of adapting vernacular styles and materials. Yet with Mackintosh the decorations are not just containers for the furnishings, for such is the unity of all the components that the totality is lifted onto another plane. As Crane had put it: "New art applied to furniture has the same, or rather a higher, power than time, for it can, by beauty of design and workmanship, invest a seat or cabinet or a fireplace with a poetry of its own, far more subtle, penetrating and suggestive than perhaps any form of art, because indissolubly associated

189. Argyle Street tearoom, the Dutch Kitchen, *The Studio*

with daily life and its drama," although such a goal could not be attained "under the ordinary conditions of trade."[81]

Whereas Walton would repeat his chair designs in different locations, with Mackintosh each commission demanded fresh designs often proportionate to specific situations.[82] Thus, in the Willow Tea Room chairs are no higher than the table tops—a device picked up from Walton—whereas around the perimeter tall ladderbacks preface the adjacent wall decorations just as in the Argyle Street luncheon room the slatted chair backs parallel Walton's decorations. Walton's chairs spoke of an ancestry from earlier times; those by Mackintosh are uncompromising in denying antecedents so that a fictional visitor to the Room de Luxe was made to expostulate that "The chairs is no' like ony other chairs ever I clapped eyes on."[83]

Having discovered Mackintosh Miss Cranston remained loyal to him, and if there could be no more Willow Tea Rooms at least he could be called upon when changes to the existing establishments were required. When the Ingram Street tearoom had opened in 1889 it was "gorgeously and sumptuously got up,"[84] but when in 1903 "a new ladies' room, billiard-room and general tearoom have been added by Mr. Macintosh [sic]" the tone was restrained, with the gesso panels and the large lead-encased fireplace highlighting a white interior. Later on there was the galleried Oak Room, for which long vaseline glass shades were made, and the Oval Room with the complex finished off in 1911 by the sharply colored Chinese Room and the Cloister Room.[85] Interesting as decorator's essays, they lacked the emblematic imagery of the Willow Tea Room. Gone were the days when a lamp design for a gentlemen's smoking room would be annotated "olive trees—the flower of peace—with pendant olive fruit of purple glass."[86]

Of greater import was the Dutch Kitchen (189) installed in 1905 in the basement of the Argyle Street tearoom.[87] As seen in old black-and-white photographs[88] the Dutch Kitchen, with the curved lines of the inglenook opposed by those of the plate rack and each set against the black-and-white checkerwork, was like a Mondrian painting. Yet even here Mackintosh seems to have lost the power or perhaps the will

to invest his designs with a deeper meaning, which would have a last flourish in the library of the School of Art. Perhaps, therefore, the Willow Tea Room is a watershed. There is the symbolical imagery but there is, too, much that comes from Vienna. While there are longueurs in the Room de Luxe, on the ground floor the frieze may be a reminder of Hoffmann's plaster frieze cut for the Secessionist Exhibition of 1902. And if a commentator at the Turin exhibition disparaged Mackintosh's exhibit because the "many blossoms . . . give to the whole area a feminine and unserious impression,"[89] then the Dutch Kitchen could be viewed as masculine despite the nod to an indefinable past age given by the inglenook, the plate rack, and the blue and white delft tiles. The overall expanse of black relieved by white squares may be in homage to Hoffmann's dining room in the Waerndorfer villa. And even when Mackintosh showed his designs for chairs to his patroness the presentation was stark—gray tones against an even paler gray background.[90] Romance it would seem had been overcome by the neoclassical rationalism of Vienna.

Walter Crane had written years before of architecture as an art. "I am taking the term architecture in the widest sense, considering it not only as an art in its effect upon other arts, but as the fundamental, comprehensive, and sustaining framework both of life and thought."[91] Perhaps as Mackintosh came to his middle years that effort was more difficult. If today the Willow Tea Room and especially the Room de Luxe can be seen as unique in European art then how much greater must have been its impact when first revealed to the Glasgow bourgeoisie, the stockholders of the roaring forges, the clangorous factories, the shipyards, and the commerce of the warehouse. The paradox was not lost on an aesthete such as Crane. "Modern life with all its hideous luxury and squalor; its huge, ever spreading, unwieldy, unlovely cities" posed the dilemma for the artist as to "how to assert the supremacy of Beauty."[92] That was Mackintosh's achievement in the Room de Luxe amid Glasgow's grime where, as a critic noted in 1905, "he raised the banner of beauty in this dense undergrowth of ugliness."[93]

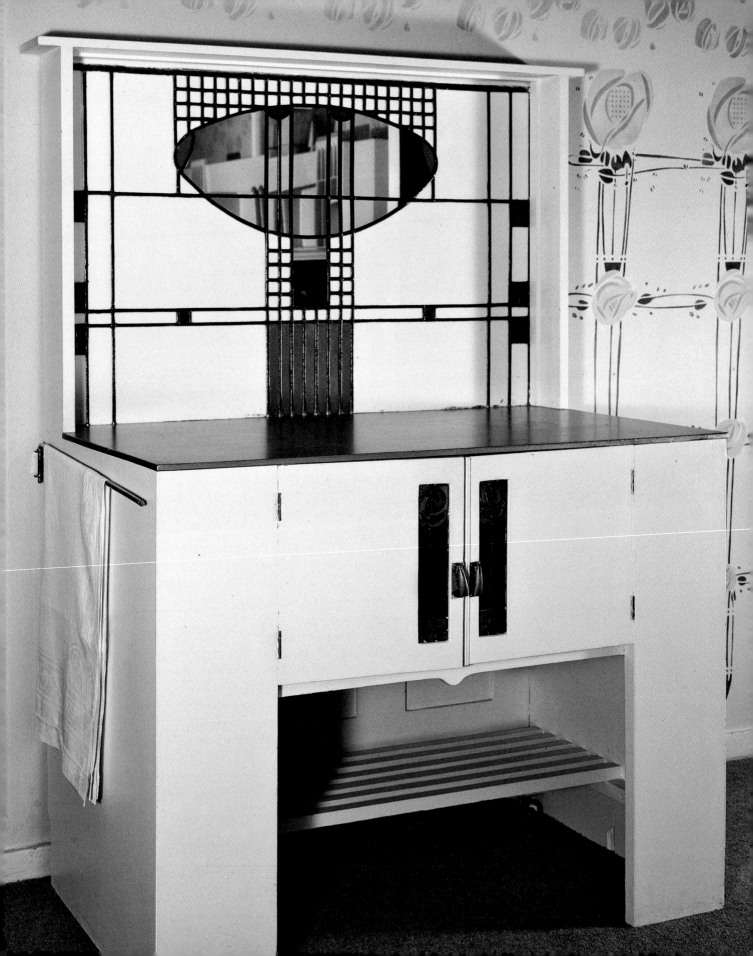

"The last century was chiefly remarkable for the numerous attempts to revive styles belonging to the past, most of which have failed in a greater or lesser degree owing to the fact that they have misrepresented modern conditions and modern requirements."[1] So wrote E. S. Prior in a prefatory note in a supplement issued in 1901 by *The Studio* in which "the progress made during the last few years in Domestic Architecture and Decoration may be prominently set forth at the commencement of the new century" by illustrating "the latest and best examples of these Arts by British designers."[2] The invited contributors included Ernest Newton, Oscar Paterson (the Glasgow stained-glass designer), E. S. Prior, Baillie Scott, E. A. Voysey, and George Walton (who cheated slightly by sending interior views of Miss Cranston's Ingram Street tearoom), together with The Four who, sticking to the remit, showed their own homes but omitting the modest urban exteriors, which would have looked out of place alongside the line drawings of the handsome featured country houses of the other contributors. The Four, alone among the contributors, demonstrated a commitment to the new century by refraining from displaying in their rooms antique furniture, studio oil paintings, and old china.

The Mackintosh home at 129 Mains Street was a six-roomed flat above shops in a sandstone tenement on a bustling corner of Sauchiehall Street and a stone's throw from the Willow Tea Room. Within his own home Mackintosh was untrammeled by the demands of office supervision or by a client's uninformed desires. Indeed, the sole constraint was the need to respect the fittings and inherent structure of a rented property and also, to some extent, of finance, since the photographs of 1901 reveal that not all the rooms were fully furnished although they were not without the appearance of modest wealth. That was evident, too, in the interiors at 54 Oxford Street, Liverpool, the residence of the McNairs, who both possessed some private money and an income from a salaried position. There was also coziness because of the smaller scale of the rooms, and comfort, too, for this was a family home with a baby whose toy kangaroo sat on the nursery mantelpiece, whereas the Mains Street interiors were settings for a refined lifestyle that overawed and thrilled some visitors.

"Meet, then, the occupants of this house of white and violet. A gentleman, thirty-five, years old, tall, dressed all in black, with long dark hair parted in the middle.

"A lady of fine Scottish build and carriage, with her supple lithe figure neatly and artistically clad in a simple dress. A massive head of tawny hair crowns a fresh coloured visage with strong features of a womanly kind. On the girdle that encircles her plain costume at the waist one sees again the violet and old silver motif of the Mackintoshes—this time in framed pebbles of amethyst colouring."[3]

In Liverpool the McNairs were seen by one colleague as "a delightful couple. They had a small Georgian house in a back street which for a time with its funny decoration was a center of much merriment and entertainment."[4] Another visitor was the artist Augustus John, who taught drawing alongside Herbert McNair. "We dined with two artistic people called MacNair, who between them have produced one baby and a multitude of spooks—their drawing room is very creepy and the dinner table was illuminated with two rows of night lights in a lantern of the 'MacNair' pattern ... However, the MacNairs have a homely way of conversing which immediately sets people at their ease."[5]

For the McNairs Liverpool would have presented many similarities to Glasgow as an international seaport and a regional commercial hub although as an artistic center it could be deemed provincial. Even so, for the McNairs there would have been advantages. Perhaps for both of them there had been a need to quit Glasgow, to strike out as independent artists and not to be in another's shadow. Admirable though it may have been in 1897 that "the Misses Macdonald are quite willing to have their work jointly attributed,"[6] that would no longer be the case when each had a husband. And Liverpool was not without its own artistic challenges. "Signs of excellent progress," reported *The Studio* in 1900, "in the students' work of the Liverpool School of Art were unmistakeable at the annual exhibition of prizes recently."[7] It would be the amalgamation of the School of Art "with the

that 'with the exception of certain assistance in joinery, all the objects here illustrated are their sole handiwork,"[12] which accorded with Talwin Morris's observation on Mackintosh. "In the bookcase and linen press, the beaten panel and other ornamental features, are his own execution. The leaded glass doors are a simpler example of a craft in which he has done much beautiful work," as did McNair.[13]

Unfortunately, in the 1901 photographs not all of the Oxford Street dining room (190) is shown. Can one assume that the mermaid cabinet (191) had a place here beneath the yellow and purple mermaid frieze? With its billing doves and McNair crest in the glass doors the cabinet would seem to have been Mackintosh's wedding pres-

School of Applied Art of Liverpool University"[8] in 1905 and the ensuing disappearance of McNair's teaching post at the latter, which would mean in time an enforced return to Glasgow. Before that humiliation, however, there were plaudits. An exhibition in 1900 at the Walker Art Gallery was worthy of praise. "In the decorative design under Mr. Herbert McNair" there were "some cleverly executed illustrations in pen and ink, theatre posters and stencil friezes."[9] Two years later *The Studio* had a notice of an exhibition of "painted silks, stained linens and stencilled hangings" when "Herbert and Frances McNair's silvered metal panels, dessert table-glass, silver ware and jewellery, all of original character in design, gained special attention."[10]

In looking at the photographs of the interiors of the Mackintosh and McNair homes[11] one is struck by the stylistic consanguinity. That there were common roots and mutual objectives in Glasgow is emphasized by the appearance in Liverpool of items that had been featured in *The Studio* in 1897 when it was noted approvingly of the Macdonald sisters

ent. The dining room walls were hung with brown paper, which Mackintosh used also in his own dining room (192). A jarring note in the Oxford Street interiors was the retention of the cornices in the public rooms, where the walls were divided horizontally by a flat plate lining up with the lintel of the doorway. In the nursery there was an incomplete frieze of daisies and children in green and white.

In general the effects had much in common with the interiors at Mains Street although there the larger volumes allowed for more dramatic interventions, such as coiling the ceiling gas pipes into circles. (193) Here, however, there were no stenciled friezes—all the decoration was confined below the prescribed height of the wall plate, with the wall planes segmented by white painted vertical strips offsetting pale gray canvas and a gray carpet, though one visitor spoke of it being violet. The larger items of furniture established a unified backdrop, leaving a few smaller pieces dotted in the foreground. That the only framed images were works by the artists themselves, save for the pair of Japanese woodcuts,

190. Oxford Street, Liverpool, the dining room, *The Studio*

hurried way, but done gradually as funds and time allow."[15] Such a prescription was printed some years after an account of the Japanese interiors worked by A. H. Mackmurdo, where the effect "depends for its attractions entirely upon its hand-made decorations—all machine-made ornaments being rigidly excluded ... a house, to be in the highest sense, an artistic house, should contain no decorations but those made by the hands of man, especially adapted to their surroundings."[16]

And there was practical advice, too, in these same pages. "Some stains for wood, manufactured by Mr. H. H. Stephens, whose ebony stain, intended for articles of furniture and the like, has become the most favourite fluid for ordinary drawings for reproduction, are distinctly good. The green is vivid, yet exactly the right colour to look well on oak or pine; the scarlet is also admirable ... [they] offer opportunities for that legitimate use of bright colour which is so valuable in our homes."[17] Then there were the illustrations. The seventeen reproductions of Japanese sword guards[18] may have been the starting point for the bracket ends on the studio windows of the Glasgow School of Art. And the illustrations of settles in 1894[19] were soon followed by a similar item exhibited by Mackintosh at the Arts and Crafts exhibition in 1896 and by a bench end in the library at Craigie Hall. (194)

A mansion set in extensive policies in the newly fashionable south side of Glasgow, Craigie Hall (195) seemingly deserves no more than a quick glance in the story of Mackintosh. Yet, for the tutored, it is, with its plantations and semirural setting, within the tradition of the *villa urbana*,

accorded with the program set out in *The Studio*, which was, in effect, the young designers' style guide. "Although the collection of pictures has ceased, of late years, to be a general fashion ... a convention has grown up that other, and perhaps better ways of adorning modern houses can be found than the old desire of covering the walls with a hetergeneous collection of different dates, and without any community of style."[14] The alternative was that "The walls may be covered with a plain canvas of a coarse texture, and the woodwork painted white ... In the decoration of the house generally, it is suggested that, finished at first without pattern of any kind, it should be gradually adorned with carefully disposed ornaments, not executed in the modern

191. Mermaid Cabinet (*opposite*)

192, 193. Mains Street, Glasgow, the dining room (*top*) and drawing room (*right*), *The Studio*

194. Craigie Hall, bench end

195. Craigie Hall, John Honeyman, extended by John Keppie.

which, originating in imperial Rome, revived in mercantilist Venice, and adopted with enthusiasm by the aristocratic cognoscenti in eighteenth-century Britain, is become the seat of a Glasgow merchant. The ancestral and hierarchical origins can be traced in the entrance elevation with its tripartite divisions, like the parts of a motet, underscored by channeled masonry, the differentiated fenestration-like staves, and the pillared porch trumpeting the baroque splendors of wood, glass, and stone within. All this was done in 1872 when Honeyman was at his most inventive.[20]

Two decades later there was a new owner, Thomas Mason, deacon convener of the city's ancient and worthy Trades House. He was a contractor whose profits from constructing the Glasgow City Chambers, railway lines, stations, and cotton mills[21] allowed for the extension and lavish decoration of the interiors of Craigie Hall. By now it was John Keppie, a member of that same Trades House, who was the partner in charge. Initially, it was his wish to put work in the way of George Henry.

The surviving correspondence between Henry and Hornel is also of interest in detailing an artist's travails. Henry had taken a studio in Glasgow "and for the last three weeks been nearly driven frantic with the unredeemed pledges of tradesmen etc."[22] On Christmas Day 1891 he complained because, "Weather here awful, cannot work for fog."[23] Next he solicits a review for the *Quiz* magazine from Hornel. "Also if you have Art News send them on, we are gasping for something to relieve Guthrie who is writing for 'Quiz' you know." Was it Guthrie, therefore, who, using "Megilp" as a byline, afforded posterity with invaluable anecdotage? Henry closed this letter, written on Glasgow Art Club writing paper, with a postscript. "Macaulay [Stevenson] and [Grosvenor] Thomas are in the billiard room, and desire to be remembered."[24]

Perhaps the possibility of a commission at Craigie Hall had been talked of for a while but "is not ready yet to go as the house is only building."[25] In the summer of 1892 the discussion was more focused. "Can you give me any advice," Henry asked Hornel. "In a decorative thing I may get to do ... Keppie is the middle man." What was in mind was the

196. Craigie Hall, music room (*opposite*)

197. Dunloe, Ayrshire, entrance hall,
Academy Architecture

decoration of the frieze in the ante-drawing room but with the caveat that "What the man wants are pictures so that if he sells the house etc. he could take them down and frame them as ordinary pictures." But the price? "John [Keppie] speaks of perhaps £400 ... Guthrie is strongly of opinion ... do them cheaply is to handicap yourself, and give the patron a benefit in the way of getting a collection of pictures cheaply." There was also the hope that Keppie's client might purchase Henry and Hornel's painting *The Star of the East*. "We must part with it cheaply—or not at all," although for the time being Henry was "submitting some sketches for four windows in his home."[26] From all such hypotheses there came nothing but dashed hopes.

If the client rejected one of Keppie's protégés what about the other—Mackintosh, for it must have been he who designed the library fittings that flow like dark chocolate and are the nearest that he ever came to continental art nouveau. And there was a music room (196) with an organ for which £38:5:0 was charged for the case,[27] which was the predecessor of the one thought of for the House for an Art Lover. Who opted for these outré fitments? The client, the architect, or the chief draughtsman? The detailing would not, one imagines, have met with the wholehearted approval of Keppie, whose preferences as indicated in "Accessories of Architecture" were for stone and marble and cast metals and "decoration (interior and exterior) embracing such things as papers, painting, frescos, mosaic work, glass, tiles, upholstery and cabinet work"[28]—the whole gallimaufry used, albeit with great skill and assurance at Dunloe (197), another of the

Skelmorlie commissions. The rich neo-Jacobean effects were exhibited in lavish and indeed dramatic drawings in 1891 (198) and in the national architectural press.[29] Dunloe was a commission to be proud of, an advertisement of the firm's standing.

If the apportionment of the design input at Craigie Hall and at Dunloe can be allocated to this individual or to that one, elsewhere there is doubt and confusion. Redlands (now Beauly) at Bridge of Weir (199) was under construction in

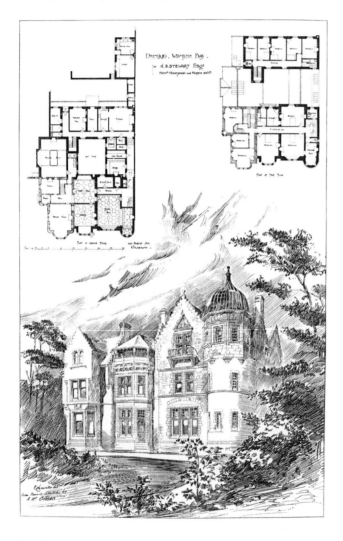

198. Dunloe, Ayrshire, *Building News*

1898 and finished in the following year using a familiar roll call of Honeyman and Keppie's building contractors,[30] with, for example, Guthrie and Wells on hand for painter work and leaded glass. Ostensibly, Redlands is a Keppie job, but the bull-nosed stair tower and its corona of leaded lights bespeaks Mackintosh's touch. Of course, once he became a partner there is clarity in the attributions so that in his fellowship application to the Royal Institute of British Architects he set down the domestic commissions over which he had control. "Dwelling Houses at Kilmacolm, Fairlie, Helensburgh, Whistlefield, Nitshill and Killearn all in Scotland"[31]— each indicative of the greater artistic freedom that came with being a partner. But there was, too, change in the air. For the more thoughtful architects there could no longer be a dutiful obeisance to historical precedents. The doubling in size of The Cliff,[32] a littoral neighbor of Dunloe, with a baronial tower, awkwardly crenellated, to which clung a spiky tourelle replicated by nearby lug turrets, would have been cause for derision. (200) Would Mackintosh have mocked it for it is undeniable that with the coming of the twentieth century there was to be a decisive change in his domestic architecture.

One reason perhaps was his involvement at Dunglass Castle (201), which was acquired in 1893 by Talwin Morris before passing in 1899 to Charles Macdonald, the brother of

199. Perspective of proposed design for Redlands, Renfrewshire, *Academy Architecture*

live."[35] Dunglass may not have had the exoticism of Dunloe nor the historical bombast of The Cliff but it was aglow with the patina of the centuries in the embrasured sea wall, a dovecote, an obelisk set up to honor the marine engineer Henry Bell, and a house protected by harled walls. As Mackintosh saw it, "In beauty of external outline, grouping of parts, boldness, freeness and variety of conception, very few styles approach it ... our style shapes itself to every accidental requirement: grapples with every difficulty and converts it into a source of beauty ... how it disdains all deception."[36] Given such qualities it should be possible to use Scotland's native style not to "copy its ancient examples" but "to make them conform to modern requirements."[37]

Margaret and Frances. Morris had trained as an architect but, with a slump in church building, he turned to illustrating and became the art director in the Blackie publishing house. After visiting the studio of the Macdonald sisters he became an influential member of their circle, where, fresh from London, he would have been a stimulating and novel influence.[33] Morris was interesting enough as a designer that Gleeson White, himself a designer of book covers, traveled downstream from Glasgow to call on him in "his own house, which is the habitable portion of an old Scottish castle, on a rocky mound far down the Clyde. The ruins of this castle still remain as a familiar landmark from the river; behind them, half-hidden, is a stone building with low rooms and windows set in walls of great thickness."[34]

At Dunglass Mackintosh came into close contact, for the first time, with a class of building that he had eulogized in his lecture on Scottish Baronial architecture. True he had made studies of castles but they were not "the very houses perhaps in which some of us

That was the challenge that Mackintosh set himself with the design of Windyhill. Not only was it a new generic type when compared to what had been produced hitherto by the practice but it stood unique in Great Britain and beyond.

200. The Cliff, Ayrshire, *Academy Architecture*

201. Dunglass Castle, Dunbartonshire

How did the commission come to Mackintosh? That is not known. The client was William Davidson, a Glasgow wholesale provision merchant with no previous connection with the firm although he had earlier commissioned some furnishings from Mackintosh. But did the commission for Windyhill begin with the firm? There is no mention in the archive. The surviving cash book has the occasional intriguing entry such as "Perspective of Conservative Club—4 gns," and two years later Alexander McGibbon was paid two guineas for a sketch of the *Glasgow Herald* building. And there is an occasional reference to Mackintosh. "1897 7 June Glasgow School of Art CRM outlays to London £6:10:0." Two years on and he claimed expenses for traveling across the country to St. Serf's Church in Dysart,[38] which was to be decorated, as he must have told Muthesius, with "the bird of peace, the tree of the knowledge of good and evil, and the trinity shown by the interwoven circles."[39]

Of Windyhill there is not a mention—no fee income, no travel expenses, no list of tradesmen's estimates. And the drawings of 1900 bear Mackintosh's name, not those of the firm's partners.[40] That this was initially a private commission may be confirmed by the retention by Mackintosh of the relevant paperwork in his personal archive. By the autumn of 1902 Mackintosh was authorizing final payments for the building works and associated trades, bringing the cumulative expenditure to £2,626:17:9.[41] What did the client get?

With a southern exposure on the Renfrewshire hills and a speedy train service to Glasgow, Kilmacolm was fast becoming a dormitory suburb for those who could afford to flee noxious Glasgow. Stockbrokers, lawyers, shipping magnates—all sought modish homes. An architect such as James Salmon could be self-indulgent with his own house, Rowantreehill, "as we are to call our House. Everyone else calls it Klondyke." It would soon be joined on the neighboring feu by Windyhill which was doubtless why "Charlie Mackintosh came down and stayed over Sunday" in the spring of 1899.[42] With its timbered black-and-white top hamper, Rowantreehill acknowledged Voysey's early work as evidenced in the 1891 design for an artist's cottage, which became in time the Forster House,

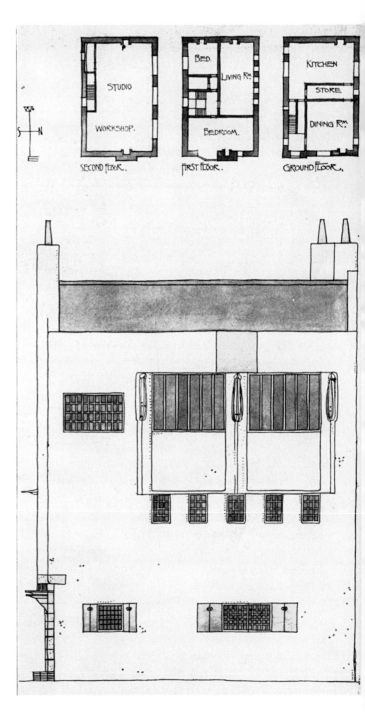

202. Design for an Artist's Town House, Charles Rennie Mackintosh

"perhaps the best known of all this artist's work."[43] And is the Forster House the starting point for Mackintosh's designs for a Country Cottage for an Artist and for a Town House for an Artist? (202) According to Muthesius in 1902, "The plans refer to the planning of a home of their own for the artist couple"[44] and, indeed, there may even have been a site in mind for the town house—perhaps an end one in a terrace. Conjugal offerings apart, the designs could have been prompted by *The Studio*'s competition in 1902 for designs for country cottages, costing no more than £750, and "not intended for occupation, at a remunerative rent by an artisan, a workman or farm-labourer . . . the building was to be of the nature of what have of recent years, near London and other cities, been known as 'week-end' cottages."[45] That Mackintosh's town house design had an upper studio and a full-height window may have been one borrowing. Other Voysey mannerisms were shutters pierced by hearts, low leaded windows, bracketed eaves, even a water butt. Yet what gives Windyhill (203) one of its unique qualities, and one not commented upon, was the use of harling, which on the Forster House was to be yellow-colored although in the illustrations the house was a white cube. As Muthesius noted of Voysey, "It may be due to him that rough cast has become the fashionable finish for exterior walls."[46] Although harling had long been traditional in Scotland it had not yet been picked up by Mackintosh's firm. So here is another puzzle.

In a Mackintosh sketchbook there is an undated sketch and plan of the sixteenth century Tankerness House in Kirkwall,[47] the capital of the Orkney Islands lying off the north coast of the Scottish mainland. to which Mackintosh traveled in 1903. Why go to Orkney? Was it "to get a brace up," as his wife wrote?[48] And did he view Melsetter House then newly

constructed to the designs of Lethaby?[49] And since it was not written up in the architectural press would he have known of it from his traveling to and contacts in London? Yet Melsetter, with its harled walls confined by the rigidities of stone margins at the angles and around the openings, may have been a disappointment whereas when sitting on the cathedral steps in Kirkwall and gazing at Tankerness House, Mackintosh may have become more aware of the possibility of abstract composition since planes, quoins, lintels, reveals—all could be coated with a membrane across which light could float and be reflected in a thousand scintillas like the dew on the morning grass. But it was not with the eye of poesy that Muthesius regarded Mackintosh's designs for artists' houses. "Severe and almost repellantly undecorated . . . the unstructured bodies remind one of the lonely greatness of Egyptian pyramids." Muthesius may not have seen the pyramids but he did see Windyhill "on a hill of rocky moorland that has a rough appearance and therefore the artist wanted to stick to the severe simplicity of the local style."[50]

Windyhill was the first work within the firm where Mackintosh exercised unfettered control. Yet it is fair to say that

203. Windyhill, Renfrewshire, *Dekorative Kunst*

dining room belying the hierarchic formality of the furniture's placing, all of which could have been a response to a contemporary injunction: "To make a thoroughly comfortable house, every apartment must be planned by itself, and for its own uses; and the designer will do well in all cases to take into account—in fact, to plot upon his paper plan—the disposition of his furniture,"[51] advice that Mackintosh would heed. He had written in June 1901 to his client: 'I have now got 3 estimates for your Hall and Bedroom furniture." That in the hall was to be stained green and varnished. "But to bedroom furniture must be added cost of painting say £10 and door and drawer handles say £3," to which would be added the "Special fee for stencils £7:7:0."[52] With no mention of the public rooms and no illustrations of complete settings it may be that they were not fully furnished. Even without a full complement of furniture, Windyhill was unique, its interiors more sophisticated than Voysey's, less tricky than those of Baillie Scott, although it was the latter, more than the former, who was Mackintosh's guide.

the end result, at least externally, was not an unqualified success for there are many gaucheries. The component dwelling units do not meld for there are awkward junctions and even in the first photographs of the house (204) there is water staining because of the lack of runoffs for the rainwater. Even so, the elevations, if not pleasing to Muthesius, betoken a determination to try to pin down the future.

With Mackintosh it was the plan (205) that generated the new forms even though the plan is very much of its time so that half of the ground floor is given over to the domestic offices—the power house that kept the house functioning according to the accepted regulations of household management. Within the offices there was division and subdivision of function. The pantry, for the storage of china, was adjacent to the dining room and beyond was the scullery, for the washing up, then the kitchen, large laundry, a coal house, for there were a dozen fireplaces, and, at the extremity of the plan, a shed for the hot ashes. Given such fissiparous zones it is surprising to find only two public rooms and, most unusually, alongside them is the nursery. These rooms were entered from the hall (206), which could do service as an informal

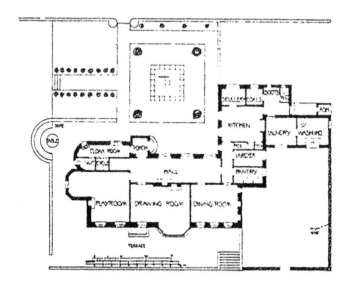

204, 205. Windyhill, Renfrewshire, and ground-floor plan, *Dekorative Kunst*

seminal series of articles to *The Studio* beginning with musings on "An Ideal Suburban House" for which "we shall demand, not only convenience of arrangement, but beauty of proportion and design," allowing him to dismiss "the doll's-house-like prettiness of the so-called Queen Anne bijou residence." Baillie Scott noted that "Of late years there has been a great revival of the hall as central feature in a house. The hall is to be a place where the family may assemble around the fire in the evening,"[55] without disturbance from servants or unwelcome visitors. "The solid constructive character of heavy timber beams and posts will also help to suggest the same homely simplicity ... with no arbitrary division between construction and decoraton,"[56] as Mackintosh intended

in the hall of the House for an Art Lover. Its double height, dark paneling, pillars carrying a gallery below which was to be a painted frieze of trees, and the sliding partition into the dining room with its mysterious congregation of male and female gesso panels—all suggested close study of Baillie Scott.[57] As he was against "pictures in rooms which are occupied from day to day"[58] he recommended in their upper register "a frieze of plain creamy plaster" or "a modelled frieze in white ... or a broad and simple stencil pattern."[59] The drawing room, "in the delicacy and daintiness of its treatment, presents a pleasing contrast to the broad and homely character of the hall ... conspicuously absent are the host of so-called decorative articles which make locomotion perilous in so many drawing rooms."[60] Baillie Scott concluded that the design of the interior should encompass all the furnishings even down to the door and window fastenings, with each item "specially designed for their special positions and not selected from the pattern-book of the manufacturer."[61] Such were some of the admonitions that Mackintosh heeded when he came to set out his most famous work, The Hill House at Helensburgh.

When the celebrated author and architect Robert Kerr wrote of the plan of the domestic interior in 1899 he noted, "In no other country have the amenities of home life been so well developed in respect of the plan of the dwelling as in the British islands ... in our middle class dwellings innumerable examples may be found in which domestic convenience is almost unanimously perfected, and the conditions of family enjoyment exquisitely fulfilled."[53] However, it was Muthesius who pointed out that the fashionable architects "took little or no part in the actual appointing of the house" whereas "Baillie Scott's concept of the house is already that of an organic whole to be designed consistently inside and out ... Baillie Scott is the first to have realised the new ideas of the interior as an autonomous work of art ... Scotland, however, started out in the new direction at the same time as the continent; though with the poetical and mystical colouring that ... always marks the Scottish work,"[54] by which Muthesius meant Mackintosh and his circle.

Muthesius was writing post hoc. Mackintosh, alone in his efforts to evolve a personal idiom, found guidance from Baillie Scott who, between 1894 and 1900, contributed a

206. Windyhill, Renfrewshire, entrance hall, *Dekorative Kunst*

Although Helensburgh was laid out by the local landowner in the fourth quarter of the eighteenth century, it owed its first period of expansion to the development of the steamship. Henry Bell used the *Comet* to bring in tourists who could enjoy the fashionable delights of his Bath Hotel, "with its hot and cold baths into which one may step all hours of the day, or night. There is also a large swimming-bath ... filled with fresh water from the sea every tide. Immediately above this there is an elegant greenhouse plus coffee and reading rooms, a library and ballroom."[62] By the 1820s Helensburgh was "a favourite retreat of the merchants and manufacturers of Glasgow, Greenock and Paisley during ... the sea-bathing season" because of its boasted advantages of "the salubrity of the air, the moderate distance from Glasgow, the excellence of the road, and the convenience of a daily post."[63] After the middle of the century the arrival of the railways confirmed Helensburgh as a desirable locale for the prosperous.

Although Honeyman's practice had built all down the Clyde estuary, the firm's input into Helensburgh was limited between 1858 and 1878 to one house, a church, and the modest municipal buildings. That a commission came from the local Conservative association in 1894 was almost an aberration since quality work was within the grasp of another Glasgow architect, William Leiper, who made his mark in Helensburgh with Cairndhu (207), a mighty evocation, complete with prospect tower, of the Loire valley plonked defiantly by the gray waters of the Clyde.[64] Of more moment perhaps were the Japanese decorations of sunflower and bamboo introduced by Daniel Cottier. In the autumn of 1887 members of the Glasgow Architectural Association visited Cairndhu. "Conducted by Mr. Leiper, the architect of the house, and past honorary president of the association, an interesting scrutiny was made of the rich decoration and artistic equipment of this well-known and often illustrated mansion, and much admiration expressed ... Thereafter some of the neighbouring houses of note were looked at—Dunholm House [probably Dalmore], an interesting type of old Scots architecture, and Aros, an equally good, half-timbered work, both designed by Mr. Leiper."[65]

Having settled in Helensburgh, doubtless on the strength of the commission for Cairndhu, Leiper had built himself a house, Terpersie, a promotional exercise hinting at the style of Norman Shaw who, according to Muthesius, "has been responsible for the best of the English country-houses built during the past thirty years,"[66] and to such effect that even "American suburban architecture has been largely influenced by the movement,"[67] which made much use of "materials which have been deemed hitherto of no importance."[68] These included red roof tiles, shingles, half-timbering, and distinctive barge boards—all in evidence at Leiper's Brantwoode (1895), its Englishness accentuated in its being named after Ruskin's home in the Lake District. It is, therefore, ironic that when an English architect, Baillie Scott, arrived in Helensburgh and designed The White House (1899) he eschewed all historical memorabilia leaving a smooth white exterior to enclose a double-height hall with a galleried upper corridor and below that a book-lined inglenook sheltering beneath a painted forest canopy,[69] whereas the interior of Leiper's Clarendon was the epitomy of high Victorian taste with a heavy modeled ceiling and frieze bearing down on brocaded walls and bought in furniture. Clarendon was illustrated in *Academy Architecture* in 1894 just when Baillie Scott was arguing, "The conception of an interior must necessarily include the furniture which is to be used in it, and this naturally leads to the conclusion that the architect should design the chairs and tables as well as the house itself."[70]

This was the program which would be enacted at The Hill House. The client was Walter W. Blackie, a grandson of the founder of the family publishing house, which, still based in Townhead, had become an international business, specializing in educational and children's books, with branches in the colonies and the dominions. One of Blackie's most popular and successful authors was the former war correspondent G. A. Henty whose historical tales "may be confidently recommended to every parent who is desirous to give his boy a Christmas present."[71] Titles such as *With Clive in India* dealt with the rise of the British empire although *With Buller*

207. Cairndhu, Helensburgh, and drawing room ceiling, William Leiper

in Natal was an up-to-the-minute retelling of "the eastern portion of the South African campaign."[72] By then the Blackie book covers were being designed by Talwin Morris who, having answered an advertisement in *The Times* in 1893 for an art director, was the chosen candidate. Given the early friendship of Morris with The Four it is of interest that an early notebook has a detail from Montacute House and on the opposite page Celtic crosses from the Nunnery on the island of Iona together with references in 1895 to designs by Owen Jones and Christopher Dresser, along with such aide-mémoires as "For Roses see Leighton, pl. 21" and "Ornamental Arts Japan."[73]

By 1900 Morris was recognized by *The Studio* as "the most typical and prolific of the Celtic school of design," and it was noted that "the formula which one may call the 'compressed heart' is a special favourite with the decorators of the present decade. We have it in our carpets, our wallpapers, our inlaid work, our beaten metal, in every form of wrought, woven, stamped, or printed ornament, and in the book-covers of Talwin Morris it greets us yet again."[74] A good example would be the initialed cover design for *The*

208. The Hill House, Helensburgh

Book of the Home, in six volumes, in which some colored frontispieces give food for thought as to Mackintosh's design sources for some of his furniture.

When Walter Blackie married he set up home in the small cathedral city of Dunblane, some thirty miles to the north of Glasgow. Some years later he decided in 1902, for the benefit of his daughters' education, to remove to Helensburgh, having obtained a feu of a potato field (208) near the crown of the town where the building line ceased and the moorland began.[75] In choosing an architect he sought the advice of Talwin Morris, who undertook that Mackintosh would call on his employer. "I told him," recalled Blackie of their first meeting, "that I disliked red-tiled roofs in the west of Scotland with its frequent murky sky; did not want to have a construction of brick and plaster and wooden beams; that, on the whole, I rather fancied grey roughcast for the walls, and slate for the roof, and that any architectural effect sought should be secured by the mass of the parts rather than by adventitious ornamentation." Clearly, client and architect were meant for each other. Mackintosh, having suggested that his putative client might inspect Windyhill, then called on Mr. and Mrs. Blackie at Dunblane to see what manner of folk they were. In the hallway stood a wardrobe purchased from Guthrie and Wells, which Mackintosh, while a student, had designed for "the trade." When the designs for The Hill House arrived they were for the inside only. (209) Once the layout was approved the elevations arrived, after which came, within a few days, another set, which was accepted.[76]

What kind of house did Blackie receive? Inevitably, it owed much to its predecessors—Windyhilll and the scheme for the House for an Art Lover—but without the clashing elevational idiosyncracies at the former or the internal decorative eccentricities of the latter, for The Hill House was a coming of age, a celebration of the architect's maturity, so that when he handed the house over to the client early in 1904 he would say: "Here is the house. It is not an Italian Villa, an English Mansion House, a Swiss Châlet, or a Scotch Castle. It is a Dwelling House."[77]

But what kind of dwelling house could it be if bereft of multihued pictorialism? As early as 1880 in the opening pages of *House Architecture* J. J. Stevenson had posed the dilemma. "A question which must be settled before commencing a house, is the style of architecture it is to be built in."[78] Stevenson reckoned that Ruskin's "practical influence on modern architecture has to some extent been mischievous,"[79] and nor could he accept unreservedly Sir George Gilbert Scott's advocacy of Gothic as "the question whether Gothic is the most suitable style of architecture for modern domestic use needs reconsideration."[80] The chosen way forward was both surprising and novel. "The old Scotch style," wrote Stevenson, a Scot from Glasgow, "is well fitted for modern houses," possessing as it did "a moderation which makes the buildings look sensible and quiet."[81]

For Mackintosh there was also a personal dilemma. Conscious that he was a man apart from his architectural confrères and that he could not conform meant that he trod a lonely furrow, especially in orthodox Glasgow. Such was the intellectual isolation that he had to have recourse to published texts, which are critical when assessing The Hill House.

Once pictorialism was jettisoned what was left? Subliminal associationism? That can be instanced at The Hill House where the compositional juxtapositioning of the horizontal wing against the domestic and children's quarters could be a transposition from the sixteenth-century Crathes Castle, where "ordinary sash windows could still be used" along with crowsteps and angle turrets to make Stevenson's exemplar of the "Scotch style."[82] And Crathes would have appealed too for being robed in harling by which "perhaps the more powerful means of effect is by shadow."[83]

As a practicing house architect of repute Stevenson's observations on the practical and social organization of a well-to-do middle class home could have been useful to an architect lacking perhaps an intimate knowledge of particular domestic requirements. Stevenson required that "the day-rooms called for by English middle-class habits are, at the least, three—a dining-room, a drawing-room, and a third room of smaller size, variously termed parlour, study, library, or breakfast-room."[84] For the first the positioning of the windows was to be a consideration so that "the master at the foot of the table may have light for carving."[85] The drawing room, given over to diverse uses, "should therefore have a number of separate centers, such as deep window recesses or a couple of fireplaces."[86] The hall was to be "of the old type ... the oak floor may be left exposed ... a few oak benches and tables are all that is required."[87] Upstairs, in the master bedroom, the bed should be placed "out of the way of the draughts between window, door and fireplace."[88] The nursery could be "shut off from the rest of the house; for, however interesting children may be, there are times when our appreciation of them is increased by their absence,"[89] just as "the perpetual practicing of scales on the school-room piano" was best consigned to a distance.[90]

209. The Hill House, plans, *Academy Architecture*

Many of these precepts were taken over by Robert Kerr in his chapter in *The Principles and Practice of Modern House Construction*, published in 1899 by Blackie and therefore, one assumes, of more than usual interest to Walter Blackie. Kerr accepted the necessity of three public rooms, to which could be added a billiard room, for the relaxation of the gentlemen, and "a subsidiary drawing-room called the 'morning-room,' " for the ladies' with 'a ready outlet to the lawn, perhaps by a casement window'—all of which was in the original plan for The Hill House.[91] In the dining room "the mistress of the house is properly seated with her back to the fireplace . . . and the master with his back to the sideboard . . . in touch with the butler and the wine."[92] Kerr set out plans in one of which the marital bed sits in a recess in the master bedroom for which "it is most essential that the furniture should be plotted on the drawing."[93] The servicing of the house was to be provided by "certain arterial lines of thoroughfare clearly distinguishable"[94] so that "the family department and the servants' department are distinctly separated . . . it is simply that the family desire to enjoy freedom from interruption, and the servants have the same objection to be unduly disturbed or overlooked."[95] So it was that "the front containing the entrance, secondly that containing the garden windows, and thirdly the offices, be so planned separately as leading features, that never on any account can they be confused together."[96]

As one cannot divine Mackintosh's creative processes, the matrices listed above may be no more than a hen's farmyard peckings. Nevertheless, there are enough coincidences within the published texts to allow the assumption that they informed Mackintosh's abilities, although these were not without deficiencies when devising the larger architectural elements at The Hill House where the juxtaposition of the horizontal wing, for the clients' accommodation, and the vertical layering of the domestic offices and children's and servants' quarters show a faltering in the certainties of scale. Still the intended drama is evident in the three perspectives published in *Deutsche Kunst* in 1905. Save for a glimpse of a distant yacht no concession is made to location or topography.

Here is a fortress of the imagination, the spell so binding that neither mortal creature nor moving shadow can cause disturbance. Confronted by an ethereal vision one recalls the sentiments of Burne-Jones. "I mean by a picture a beautiful romantic dream of something that never was, never will be—in light better than any light that ever shone—in a land no one can define, or remember, only desire."[97]

But The Hill House was a home to Mr. and Mrs. Blackie (210) and their children, "making it cheerful like a white bright birdcage,"[98] and also to the nanny, cook, table maid, and housemaid as well as the gardener and undergardener.[99] And with people came possessions. By the 1930s, the drawing room was stuffed with a "chesterfield settee in striped moquette," another settee, "3 ebonised armchairs,"

210. Mrs. Blackie in the drawing room of The Hill House

and a variety of others plus an assortment of tables, mostly ebonized, including a coffee table inlaid with mother-of-pearl, a two-tier table, worktable, card tables and a "Nest of 3 ebonised oblong tea-tables." There was a grand piano for entertainment, a "table gramophone in mahogany case, collection of about 100 records," and a "Murphy A.C. mains wireless receiving set, in walnut cabinet." Other diversions were the books with "65 volumes general literature, various bindings" by the window seat. And there were ornaments—thirty-six of them—and a "Mantel Clock with black and white painted dial, in wood cage," one of the pieces in the room designed by Mackintosh. [100]

How different was the house in 1905 when *Deutsche Kunst* commissioned the one and only article on The Hill House. Then the harled walls (211, 212) evoked surprise because of the immaculate freshness with which the house seemed to be washed from top to bottom, highlighted by "rhythmic chords" of light and shadow. The effect would have been even more impressive "if the house would have been completed in total agreement with the artist, following all his original plans"—a reference to the intended billiard room wing by the entrance.

As "the magnificent bedroom (213) and the hall (214) may be the best spaces in the house," it was those that the photographers, "who were here for quite a while," as Blackie recalled, illustrated fully, as the drawing room (215), "with its mysterious flowers," was not fully furnished and in the dining room the furniture had been brought from the Blackies' previous home.

If the interior of the house is a "poetic vision of a fact"[101] and as the vision was Mackintosh's what was the role of the clients? One asks since The Hill House is unique in Mackintosh's domestic oeuvre in having so much stenciled decoration. But is it that—decoration? Or is there a symbiotic relationship between the somber hall and the master bedroom to which a groom would carry his bride to lay her on the marriage bed set in an alcove, its walls drenched with roses so that "no man ever saw such joy or such delight as was in that garden."[102]

To complete the simile of the bower Mackintosh intended a screen beyond which there were more roses. Once again Mackintosh called on the early article in *The Studio* in which Baillie Scott set out "The Decoration of the Suburban House" in which "The use of stencilling may be suggested for the frieze, and in the 'Rosebush' design this method is adopted. The leaves here are green, the stems greyish-black, and the roses red."[103] Mackintosh's preference for a lower register allowed his treillage to be complemented by a slim ebonised ladder-back chair. One recalls Eastlake's observation that the best bedroom chairs "are the rush-bottomed 'nursery chairs' of which the woodwork is stained black, with low seats and high backs." Eastlake also held to the view that "as a rule, our modern bedrooms are too fussy in their fitting up,"[104] whereas in Mackintosh's bedrooms (216) the fittings "are formed as simple boxes with complete suppression of division or filling and are enamelled white," with decoration of silver or colored glass or "very small parts painted with lively colours so that they gleam out like gems."[105] Given Mackintosh's regulated layout one can accept Muthesius's conclusion that "The furniture of Mackintosh is an organic part of the room."[106]

The hall also bears analysis. By the entrance porch there was access to Mr. Blackie's business room and library, where the shelves were packed with the firm's publications whose bindings gleamed like mother-of-pearl. Muthesius, that keen observer of British mores, recognized that, in the British country house, libraries "are merely used by the man of the house for writing letters, as a room to which he can retire to read and to rest." He also recognized the social requirement that the business room should be "so placed that the visitor...having no connection with the family, need not enter the inner part of the house,"[107] which was understood by Mackintosh, who elevated the main hall so that it was not "as is too often treated as only a vestibule, but it is properly a rendezvous"[108] and it could, as Stevenson wished, "resume its medieval character, as the chief room for the occupation of the family and guests, and for receptions, games and dances, with advantage."[109]

211. The Hill House (*overleaf*)

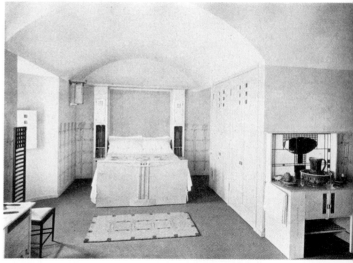

212. The Hill House, *Academy Architecture* (*top left*)

213, 214, 215. The Hill House, master bedroom (*top right*), entrance hall (*bottom left*), and drawing room (*bottom right*), *Deutsche Kunst*

216. The Hill House,
master bedroom and plan

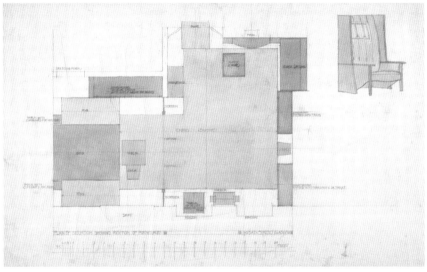

217. The Hill House, upper hall

When it came to the practicalities Mackintosh, as so often, seems to have heeded Baillie Scott when he opined, "The solid constructive character of heavy timber beams and posts will also help to suggest the same heavy simplicity," (217) preventing an "arbitrary division between construction and decoration of such a house."[110] But what of the decoration? The thickset oak table and chairs are devoid of decoration, of leaf or bud, the wall panels gray, topped by stencils patterned blue with dried flower heads and seeds while from the lampshades hang winter's honesty seeds. Pale winter to the glorious summer drawing room, where the tree of life rises by the fireplace while above and all around roses bloom, their petals cascading down the painted palisade that enfolds this secret garden, the abode of Sleeping Beauty—a gesso panel by Margaret Macdonald Mackintosh. (218) "I saw a large and extensive garden, entirely surrounded by a high, crenellated wall. There were roses in profusion … There were buds."[111]

218. *Sleeping Beauty*, Margaret Macdonald

Thus the words of the medieval romance. Yet in 1905 the gesso panel was not in place. Was it original to the theme, or is its later arrival and subject matter adventitious?

Whatever their symbolic significance The Hill House interiors were very different from those derided by Stevenson. "The lobby will be painted in imitation of marble or granite; the dining-room with a plain tint of bright green, and a white washed ceiling; the drawing-room paper of the last fashionable pattern; and the bedrooms as commonplace as those of an hotel; the carpets attempting to look an uneven surface of holes one would stumble in, and bunches of flowers one would crush in walking over; the furniture a mass of unmeaning curves; the pictures mere furniture and no part of architecture."[112] For The Four, as Muthesius saw it, there was another agenda. "The central aim of these members is the room as work of art, as a unified organic whole embracing colour, form and atmosphere."[113] ▪▪

I n 1906 Charles and Margaret Mackintosh removed from their tenement flat in the city center to the leafy suburb of Hillhead. It had developed as an independent burgh on the western edge of Glasgow, its verdant slopes rising over the river Kelvin meandering past farms, mills, and terraces, and below Scott's new university buildings, toward working-class Partick with its gasworks and grain mills at the confluence with the river Clyde. Before its absorption by the city of Glasgow in 1891 Hillhead had "its own administration, police, fire-brigade, and so on," and afterward it retained the gentility "of villas in their gardens, of a period previous to that of the rows of self-contained dwellings and tenements," where "something of the rural survived in a dairy farm or two, on the bank of the Kelvin." Many of the incomers "did not wish to be identified with a common Street, and nearly every street was divided up into Terraces, Places, Buildings."[1]

One consequence of the growth of the western suburbs of Hillhead and Kelvinside was "the lessened demand for houses in the Park district,"[2] where in 1895 a terrace house was on the market "at the reduced upset price of four thousand five hundred pounds."[3] James Salmon, however, could write in 1900: "We have practically got a £3,000 house to build in University Gardens" in Hillhead.[4]

If it was true of the Park area that "Glasgow society centers there,"[5] Hillhead was not without its own social delights. "From Hillhead and Kelvinside," it was reported in 1895, "we hear that the coming season will be the most fashionable that we have yet had, and, but for the gloomy outlook on the Clyde, this would be one of the cheeriest winters on record. Balls and parties are booked all through the season, the number of hostesses who are doing things on a lavish scale being greatly on the increase."[6]

One of the hostesses was the future Lady Jebb, the American wife of the professor of Greek at the university who was one of the first to take up residence in Scott's buildings. "Glasgow," Lady Jebb wrote, "is near the prettiest scenery in Great Britain, and living three miles out of town, the distance of the New University buildings, we shall escape much of the smoke and dirt." Driving out to view her new home she found "the largest house I have yet called my own, with handsome windows, plate glass, large square hall, broad stairs, etc. indeed so imposing in size that my soul shudders at the amount of furniture it would take to make it habitable."[7]

It was inevitable perhaps that one American should entertain a fellow exile. Bret Harte was invited to dinner. "With Principal Caird on one side of me, I was kept in constant anxiety for fear my country man might say something *too broad* for a clergyman's ears, let alone mine."

He insisted on smoking, "which nobody ever does here, until after they have finally parted from the ladies, because of the odour, I suppose." Worse—he was known to be flirting outrageously with a Mrs. MacLier, "a fast woman known to me and most people by sight, but not in any other way."[8] Another social occasion some weeks later gave rise to other thoughts. "Last week we went to a musical evening ... Our hosts were Mr. and Mrs. Mirrlees, very rich people, who went to America at the time of the Centennial. He had one of his railway locomotives on exhibition, a splendid thing, which they sold on the spot to some Cuban planter. They have twenty-five acres of land in the best neighbourhood in Glasgow. It makes me shudder to think what taxes they must pay."[9]

The Mirrlees's home, Redlands, was one of the "Mansions of our merchant princes"[10] lining the further streets of Great Western Road, which had a reputation as "the most fashionable Sunday afternoon resort around Glasgow. The West-End Park, the Queen's park and the Alexandra, not to speak of the Green, furnish the masses with ground for their Sunday outing ... who would look out of place among the silent company who adorn Great Western Road. No doubt some one or two common, even shabby people may be found there, but they are very exceptional,"[11] although in July 1885 a bequest meant that "the Botanic Gardens are this week open free of charge to the working classes ... many poor children, playing about in very obvious enjoyment of the unaccustomed playground. The children of the neighbourhood, being chiefly out of town, had made way for them entirely."[12]

The new home of Mr. and Mrs. Mackintosh was like many another, described by one local resident as "an ordinary house, of an ordinary terrace, in an ordinary street laid with cobbles and pavements of asphalt. In front of the house is a little plot, with a rhododendron in the center and lesser shrubs around it. The iron railings are relieved by a privet hedge. The gate opens to a path of big round 'chuckies' sunk in cement. Four broad steps lead up to the door ...

"The house is two-storeyed with attics. The dining-room windows look down upon the plot. At the rear is the kitchen and a room we call 'the parlour,' though more advanced Glasgow people may call it 'the morning room,' or even 'the breakfast-room.' From the parlour a glass-house, with a floor space some fifteen feet square, surrounded by shelves bearing plants, extends into the back green. We call it 'the conservatory', ...

"Upstairs is the drawing-room with which is connected a small apartment known as 'the ante-room' ...

"The drawing-room, with its big white marble mantelpiece and bright steel and brass fireplace ... The walls have a pale paper, its pattern suggesting 'watered silk' ... The woodwork is white; the panels of the doors and window-shutters have gold beadings."[13]

Such was the house to which the Mackintoshes had aspired. Yet, with "us middle class folk who have our removal term on the 28th May, and so often take advantage of it, to change our dwellings,"[14] one wonders why the Mackintoshes remained for as long as they did in their tenement flat. Of course, when deciding on a move their reasons would have been conscious and, as is so often the case, subliminal. There were friends—such as the Newberys—and colleagues such as John Keppie already settled in Hillhead, and on its eastern slope, where the social divide began as terraces gave way to tenements, the Macdonald family had a main door tenement flat that would become a refuge for the McNairs when they retreated to Glasgow. And Margaret Macdonald would surely have been aware of her husband's changed social role in society once he had entered into a partnership in one of the city's most distinguished practices.

Mackintosh's assumption as a partner had occurred in 1901. As he bought into the partnership it was not until 1904 that he is entered in the firm's books as sharing the profits with Honeyman and Keppie, although his were considerably lower but even so were twice as high as his salary of £240 in 1902. In 1905 the beneficiaries of the year's trading were Keppie and Mackintosh, with a "final payment" in November being entered against Honeyman's name.[15] He had settled in Bridge of Allan, a genteel spa resort to the east of Stirling where the firm had won the commission in 1894 for the local school and a hall at the parish church where, ten years later, the chancel was fitted out by Mackintosh—with a pulpit, to be of cypress or oak according to price.[16] Mackintosh would be invited to be in attendance at the Abbey Close Church (now demolished) in Paisley, which was to "be repainted and fitted with a system of Electric Light" and possibly, and contentiously, "a Carnegie Organ," all costing £600. In February 1905 it was reported that "Mr. Guthrie (Glasgow) was not the proper man" whereas Mackintosh "was willing to submit a scheme of decoration, take the oversight of all the work, design Organ case, and draw plans for reading desk etc. for a fee of £25." After an estimate of £1,200 was presented it was agreed that "the old pewter plates be gifted to the architect Mr. Mackintosh," with £10 given later for "the extra work and supervision which have fallen on the architect's shoulders."[17]

Mackintosh's last church designs, when considered in the context of works at Queen's Cross Church, must be seen as retro—perhaps in deference to a client's wishes. One is aware that here is the progenitor of the carved and pierced pendants in the School of Art library but without the fugitive historicism of ogee curves, crockets, and mouchettes, which in Mackintosh's drawings of the previous decade are as candles shedding holy light on swirling anthropomorphic shapes. Yet the minor works at Bridge of Allan and at Paisley can only have a poignant interest when set against the disappointment of not winning the Liverpool Cathedral competition. True, the second phase of the Glasgow School of Art was about to come on stream, although that would create tensions within the firm as when, doubtless, the biographical notice of John Keppie in

Who's Who in Glasgow in 1909 gave him the credit for the "*Glasgow Herald*, Mitchell St. buildings, and those of the *Daily Record*, Glasgow School of Art,"[18] without mentioning his partner. Of course, for as long as Honeyman was active within the firm a balance seems to have been held between the philosophies of the partners, for although officially retired Honeyman still retained a connection with his erstwhile firm allowing him to remain committed to his antiquarian interests. In 1907 he published a paper on the transepts of his beloved Glasgow Cathedral and in 1912, two years before his death, his last published essay was a history of the chancel pulpit.

A major interest in these last years was the state of the ruinous and abandoned medieval cathedral on the island of Iona. Doubtless as a promotional exercise, "alterations," showing a reroofed choir and transepts, were drawn up by the firm in 1891[19] from survey drawings by Alexander McGibbon.[20] When restoration did get under way in the next decade the day-to-day direction rested with the Edinburgh author and architect Thomas Ross. The firm's accounts show a payment to Annan in 1905 for photographs, and Iona again appears in the books two years later when McGibbon was paid four guineas for a perspective,[21] which would be the one published in *Academy Architecture* as a flyer for the firm to

219. Department store, Sauchiehall Street, *Academy Architecture*

220. Dineiddwg, *Academy Architecture*

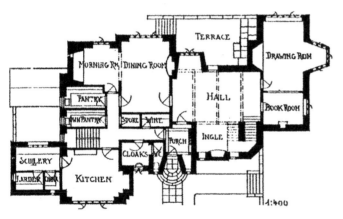

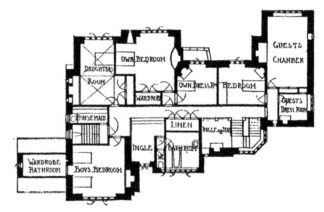

oversee the reerection of the nave against the resurrected choir and transepts.

Yet after Honeyman's formal departure from the firm the fissiparous tendencies of the remaining partners came to the fore, demonstrated clearly in successive issues of *Academy Architecture*, the bellwether of architectural trends. In 1906 The Hill House was lavishly featured, with plans and views of

the exterior and the master bedroom, together with the Scotland Street School, both of which were at odds with Keppie's Sauchiehall Street department store (219), which, with its stacked insignia of pediments, arches, and heraldic labels, was a flamboyant precursor of the Renaissance habiliments of the Parkhead Savings Bank with mahogany and veined marble interiors. Similarly loaded with the artifacts of history was

221. Auchenibert, perspective design and plans, *Academy Architecture*

Dineiddwg (220) not far from Auchenibert (221), a Mackintosh job that, to suit the whim of the owner's English wife, was a Cotswold manor but wearing steel casements so that, unlike Windyhill or The Hill House, it was, as one who was in the office at the time noted, "alien to the climate and to the country."[22] Mackintosh's involvement at Auchenibert ceased when the client had to fetch him of an afternoon from the local inn.

From the pages of *Academy Architecture* one senses that Mackintosh's star was on the wane. And it must be telling that the published perspective of Auchenibert bears the inscription "A. G. Henderson, delt.," an up-and-coming draughtsman in the firm.[23] More disturbing was the failing of Glasgow's economic fortunes affecting the business community so that in 1899 James Salmon wrote, "Unfortunately for Scotland the firm of J. S. and S. is doing very little just now."[24] One can understand a note in the office archive, "C.R.M. to Belfast £6:18:0," once the conditions for the Belfast University competition had arrived in the office in the summer of 1910.[25] In the early years of the Keppie—Mackintosh partnership previous commissions meant a continuation of fees for completion works or alterations, which soon became little more than a dribble. Fifteen guineas for St. Silas Church, an early Honeyman job; four guineas for Kelvinside Academy; "£21 adjudication Bowes Museum"; "Wellesley Tea Room £21." The biggest commissions were Keppie jobs—the Sauchiehall Street store and the Parkhead Savings Bank. Fortunately for Mackintosh, Miss Cranston was still an active and loyal patron, putting work in the firm's way. Not that there were new tearooms to be fitted out, only alterations to the existing ones.

After the conversion of the basement of the Argyle Street premises into the Dutch Kitchen, Miss Cranston turned her attention to her establishment at Ingram Street, where the acquisition of an adjacent shop allowed for its conversion into the galleried Oak Room while other adaptations allowed for the creation of the Chinese and Cloister Rooms. These last, in particular, invite questions as to Mackintosh's position as a modernist in the early twentieth century. In the Dutch Kitchen the multitudinous black-and-white squares,

superimposed by emerald green chairs, can be viewed with ever useful hindsight as a precursor of the later postwar jazz age. But the Chinese and Cloister Rooms—the one encased in vibrant turquoise-colored lattice screens inset with colored plastic and mirror glass in curved niches; the other vaguely Moorish—force us to ask just who selected the disparate themes and why. Was it the flamboyant Miss Cranston, who was driven into town of a morning in a carriage laden with flowers for the tables of her tearooms? Or was it her architect? A side of his character that has not been sufficiently commented upon was his theatricality, which could be displayed to the full in the Edwardian passion for fancy dress as at the long remembered Art Club Ball in the St. Andrew's Halls when E. A. Walton as Hokusai had proposed to Butterfly. At the 1895 "Art Exhibition and Grand Fancy Fair" to raise funds for the Lady Artists' Club, with "Miss Jessie Keppie" as one of the organizing committee, Mackintosh "as stage manager, tapped with a stick in true French fashion when the curtain was to be drawn."[26] In 1909 the formal opening of the second phase of the School of Art building was to be celebrated with "A Symbolic Masque in five designs and an Allegory entitled 'The Birth and Growth of Art.' Book by Mr. Newbery," concluding with "The Art of Today. Mrs. Macnair and Mr. Greiffenhagen ... Mr. Mackintosh to design the Stage."[27] In the previous year in a charity historical pageant at Glasgow University the photographer Craig Annan acted as King Arthur with Mrs. Mackintosh as "a resplendent Queen Morgan le Fay" (222), Graham Henderson as a Knight of the Realm, and even members of the Davidson family.[28]

Perhaps the commissions, especially the later ones, for Miss Cranston may be viewed as tableaux. Lacking a design relationship to one another, they are, therefore, without the subtle psychological dramas inherent in Robert Adam's compositions, where plans converge with one another unlike, say, at the Ingram Street premises, which became a warren of unconnected rooms without an obvious planning rationale. Was such willfulness a hallmark of the commissioning patroness? All is a contrast to her architectural designer, who set flower niches in the studio doorways in the School of Art and in whose Hill House the drawing room, as Baillie Scott put it, was "for tea and music, and is characterized by a certain daintiness of treatment which bears a feminine relation to the masculine ruggedness of the hall."[29] If that was true at The Hill House then why not at Ingram Street?

It was a measure of her "great originality of mind and outlook," as a contemporary saw it, that when Miss Cranston wanted a makeover of her own home, Hous'hill, she turned once more to Mackintosh as one who "from the beginning understood him and gave him a free-hand"[30] even to the ordering of the counterpanes and wash basins and water jugs in the bedrooms.[31]

222. Margaret Macdonald as Queen Morgan le Fay

The long-demolished Hous'hill was "pleasantly situated in the parish of Paisley and county of Lanark" and "built about the beginning of the century, is a comfortable residence,"[32] being a Regency addition to a much older property. (223) The Regency frontage was two storys high and three bays long with the extremities marked off by pilasters. A Grecian tetrastyle entrance porch was a fashionable touch, as was the rounded bow containing a dining-room on the ground floor and what became the music room above. With its classical cornice and eighteenth-century furniture the dining room (224) became a stylistic hybrid once the lower walls were stenciled and ceiling lamps were hung,[33] for "the Mackintoshes like to stick to the box shapes of the old style lantern … The boxes are applied to the ceiling in groups in a soldier-like order and are therefor a main motive in the architecture of the room." True enough, except that the Hous'hill dining room, overfurnished from another century, gave a patina of wealth and luxury that would have been at odds with Mackintosh's own desires. "Furniture," as Muthesius reported, "has a completely independent or special position in the art of the Mackintoshes. One can say that it is most conspicuous by its absence,"[34] and also, it should be said, by its absorption into the overall design concept as in the music room (225), where one can see, though only in photographs, the precepts of Baillie Scott being worked out once more.

The window bow was replicated by a curved openwork screen with a top rail tied into the wall picture rail, below which open shelving was suspended above wall couches. Such built-in furniture had developed from the inglenooks that had become de rigueur by the fireplaces of designer houses and been used by Baillie Scott to clear away the flotsam and jetsam of furniture and bric-a-brac crowding the floors of rooms to achieve "a positive void,"[35] as interior space should be open, which was not possible in a public tearoom but could be constructed within the intimacy of the Hous'hill music room as an enclosed bower. Mackintosh had introduced built-in furniture at Dunglass Castle and at The Hill House but not so elaborately as in the music room although that exercise—taut as it was—could not be deemed

wholly successful for there was an insufficient floor area to be subdivided satisfactorily. For Howarth the screen was a forerunner of the curved ebony room divider in Mies van der Rohe's Tugendhat House in Brno in 1930. That, however, may be a misjudgment. Perhaps a truer comparison could be drawn from the Willow Tea Room, where the curved back of the cashier's chair incorporates a spreading tree. In the music room screen there is a coppice of lesser struts and an occasional leaf with the solids becoming topiary around a bosquet edged by seating arbors. That may be fancy. Yet in the School of Art library the pierced gallery pendants are the forest canopy in an oak wood; at Ingram Street in the Oak Room the gallery struts are a leafless arboreal avenue. And a tree stands by the fireplace

in the drawing room of The Hill House. Was Mackintosh giving expression to a question posed by Maeterlinck? "Does a transparent tree exist within us, and are all our actions and all our virtues only its ephemeral flowers and leaves?"[36] Such a hypothesis would elevate the music room to the same intellectual and emotional plane as the Room de Luxe in the Willow Tea Room.

The glitziest interior at Hous'hill must have been the card room for six tables, for which there is a printed description. "The walls were gold, the fireplace surrounded with thick crystals. The card-tables were of mother-of-pearl inlay and matched the chairs. The principal feature ... was a set of gorgeous panels by Mrs. Mackintosh entitled *The Four Queens*,"[37] of which two are known from illustrations.

223. Hous'hill (demolished)

224, 225. Hous'hill, dining room
and drawing room, *The Studio*

Such riches, of course, were not affordable by the Mackintoshes in their home in Hillhead, 6 Florentine Terrace (226), the last house in a short terrace with a gable overlooking a service lane and, farther south, the university buildings. The house was the customary three storys and any external architectural pretension came from such sub-Thomson features as the distyle porch and the treatment of the attic floor as a continuous wall plane. Unlike in the earlier parts of Hillhead the house lacked a service basement and, indeed, the overall accommodation (227–232) was scarcely greater than in the Mains Street flat except that it was arranged vertically, with the usual division of a drawing room (with a white marble chimney-piece) above a dining room (with a black marble chimney piece). Mackintosh adhered to the conventions in the usage of these rooms and in his color schemes, installing furnishings and fittings from Mains Street. It was at Mains Street that the Mackintosh domestic interior came into being with little deviation in later decorative programs. Muthesius had analyzed the Mains Street flat where "the key-note is a spacious, grandiose, almost mystical repose ... achieved by the use of broad, unarticulated forms and a neutral background colour, such as grey, white or a dark-brownish grey ... Patterned materials are taboo, as is all mechanically produced ornament ... The decorated areas are usually coloured in bright green, dark pink or purple ... Mackintosh has enormously enriched the repertoire of ideas affecting interior decoration. Whether such enhancement is appropriate to our everyday rooms is another question."[38] Indeed, for "wealthy people ... Their fine large house is furnished in the style that makes other Glasgow people dining there look round a room and tot up in their minds the price of the curtains, carpets, chandeliers, pictures, inlaid cabinets, etc., etc."[39]

In the Mackintosh house there were no such indicators of wealth. Neither were there telltales of the past for the internal fabric's ornamentation had been stripped out, just as Mackintosh specified in 1907 for the Lady Artists' Club for which he listed a "New Porch with double doors outside and single door inside ... Panelling on walls of Vestibule staircase and waxed. Remove center flower on ceiling." The staircase would have "new brown paper. Stencilling decoration in gold, rose and purple, painting balustrade gold, handrail dark ebony." The dining room modifications would have been minor, unlike in the drawing room. "Take away marble

mantelpiece and marble step at front of mirror." The ceiling rose was to go along with the chandelier and brass curtain rail with "Flax silk for wall panels, rose, purple or grey."[40] In the event only the new entrance door and hall and staircase decoration were given the go-ahead but only after an explosive row leading to the resignation of the convener of the decoration committee.[41] Such are the ways of art clubs!

Mackintosh's time in his home in Hillhead was short. An entry in the firm's cash book on June 8, 1914, records a payment to the firm's lawyers for a "dissolution charge," which ended the partnership although it may have effectively ceased earlier when Mackintosh was credited with a final payment of £1.[42] Before then Mackintosh's jobs had been winding down. In the autumn of 1912 he had been called back to The Hill House

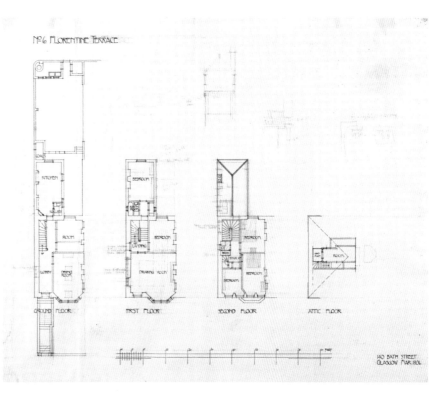

to list some necessary refurbishments, mostly in the drawing room. "Wall decoration as at present but to be touched up—ceiling and frieze to be painted dark—shade to be a plum colour—grey with stippled rose madder." Woodwork was to be repainted; lamps were to be resilvered. "Furniture to be touched up when injured," and the seating was to be recovered with corduroy, a favorite choice of Mackintosh. A year later there was another inconsequential exercise at Cloak at Kilmacolm. On a November morning Mackintosh went out to Paisley where his plans were accepted by the local building authority. He then went over the hill to Kilmacolm to the site and "found the water in the Court yard covered to a depth of over 2 feet. The new Portion in front of Kitchen Entrance door seems to me to be quite the best possible idea. This will give quite a distinction to the old entrance gable and add I am sure a new element of picturesque to the gable."[43] Sadly, the proposed tower with its saddleback roof was not to be.

A greater disappointment would have been the outcome of a competition for a teacher training college, a demonstration school, and a students' residential hostel to be sited on the western outskirts of Glasgow. This would be a major public commission at a time when such an opportunity was becoming rare. After much negotiation it was settled that the complex was to cost £132,000, with the professional fees being set at £8,100, a great lure. A list of six local architectural firms, including Honeyman, Keppie and Mackintosh, H. and D. Barclay, and John Burnet and Son, was chosen. Their nominated partners, Mackintosh among them, assembled in February 1913 and got an agreement "to extend the time for receiving the competition designs to 15th May 1913." A month later and the decision was announced to award the three buildings to three firms, with Honeyman, Keppie and Mackintosh given the demonstration school, costing £34,000.[44] However, when the working

227. 6 Florentine Terrace plan

226. 6 Florentine Terrace (demolished and resited)

228. 6 Florentine Terrace, entrance hall

229, 230. 6 Florentine Terrace,
dining room and drawing room

231. 6 Florentine Terrace, master bedroom

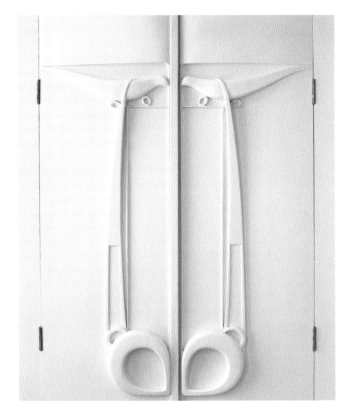

232. 6 Florentine Terrace, master bedroom (*top*)

233. *The Building Committee of the Glasgow School of Art*, Francis Newbery (*bottom*). Newbery is seated on the right. Mackintosh stands on the left. The setting is the School's board room.

drawings were submitted in December it was by Keppie, who "explained the details of the plans," and by July 1914 the firm was represented by Graham Henderson.[45] Mackintosh, having failed to produce a coherent scheme, had been frozen out.

In his last years in Glasgow Mackintosh enjoyed a public role as governor of the Glasgow School of Art, being re-elected in June 1913 as a representative of the Glasgow Institute of Architects.[46] At a board meeting, which Mackintosh had attended some weeks before, there was a discussion about the appointment of a head of sculpture and modeling. Jacob Epstein's name had come up. However, the sculptor of the controversial nude figures on the British Medical Building in London's Strand did not find favor with Newbery, who rated him "a stylist, whose work is so personal, that it could not be made a reliable vehicle for education."[47]

It would have been at this time that Mackintosh's portrait by Newbery was being painted. When it was publicly exhibited in February 1914 it was pronounced to be "something in the nature of pictorial genesis; the study of a fuller work,"[48] which was Newbery's group portrait of the members of the building committee of the Glasgow School of Art with the addition, once an extra strip of canvas was sewn in, of a copy of the portrait of the architect of the building clasping his plans for the school. (233) A month after the unveiling of the group portrait in May 1914[49] Mackintosh attended what would be his final governors' meeting.

It must have been about this time that Walter Blackie, at the request of Mackintosh's wife, called on the architect in his office, where he found him "sitting at his desk, evidently in a highly depressed frame of mind ... He said how hard he found it to receive no general recognition; only a very few saw merit in his work and the many passed him by." He spoke of the termination of the partnership and of the demonstration school, the plans for which "had that very day been accepted in part and now he himself would have no superintendence of the construction ... He was leaving Glasgow."[50] In July the Mackintoshes went on holiday to Walberswick in Suffolk. Mackintosh would never return to Glasgow. ▪

Much has been made of Mackintosh's break with Keppie. Undoubtedly, there came to be a strained personal relationship exacerbated by a diminishing workload and compounded by Mackintosh's dilatoriness in producing the drawings for the teaching college competition. Yet the collapse of Mackintosh and his withdrawal from architecture may have had as much to do with psychological causes as any others. Recollections by those who knew him tell of a man apart, a man ridden by demons. As Howarth recorded when engaged in his pioneering research: "I've been surprised at the lack of enthusiasm shown by his contemporaries and their unwillingness to discuss him."[1] There was his excessive drinking, which seems to have been a lifelong addiction with all-night drawing sessions in the office and in the mornings heaps of drawings and a discarded, empty whiskey bottle to be cleared away by a disgruntled junior employee.

Mackintosh was certainly difficult. Few, perhaps, could or would tolerate or exist with his unyielding, obsessive personality. So it was but the truth when Jessie Keppie wrote in her old age to Howarth of Mackintosh saying that she "always felt that architecture was to him the important thing in his life"[2] so that, as another correspondent remembered, "He had no hobby so far as I know."[3] The critic who commented on "the myriads of tiny squares" in the Dutch Kitchen[4] may have been most perceptive than since there would never have been any question of Mackintosh passing a design to an assistant to be worked up, since each new design concept for Miss Cranston, for example, required that not only the design envelope but coat hooks, umbrella stands, light fittings—each had to receive as much attention as a wall surface divided meticulously into a mathematical grid. As a friend had noted: "Mackintosh once asked me why he should design for my use an armchair like that of someone else."[5]

A psychiatrist would have seen in Mackintosh a creative artist ensnared in a midlife crisis for "there is certainly a consensus among observers writing from very different theoretical standpoints that, somewhere around the thirties or early forties, changes in attitude take place among many human beings which are often accompanied by emotional upheavals," and these can be more extreme for creative persons. Psychiatrists would see three periods in the life of a creative person with the learning period followed by mastery of the art. However, many artists do not reach the third stage because of an early death or the onset of a fallow period of inactivity, which can be characterized by the adoption of a secondary artistic pursuit[6] such as, with Mackintosh, flower painting.

Mackintosh traveled to Walberswick seeking recuperation. Aside from physical exhaustion (and perhaps he had

234. *A Cord,* Francis Newbery

never fully recovered from a bout of pneumonia two years before[7]) there was the cessation of confidence in oneself and, with that, the shriveling of artistic endeavor, which is to be remarked upon in the turning away from the symbolism of the Room de Luxe to the formulaic rationalism of the Dutch Kitchen, from "the inner world of the imagination and the outer world of fact."[8]

Mackintosh had first visited Walberswick in the late summer of 1897. The north Suffolk coast—flat, treeless, and devoid of architectural features save for the pylonlike church towers rising above the gleaming mud banks—was a draw for artists, those seeking to portray unsophisticated marine and local life or those desiring to catch the aqueous light glancing off staithes, the flat coastal reaches along the estuary of the river Blyth dividing Walberswick, with its single street, windmill, ruined church, and two public houses, from the larger, more bourgeois Southwold on the northern shore.

In 1897 Mackintosh sketched the rood screen, the oak door panels, and the fifteenth-century tower of Southwold Church.[9] The resort was a holiday destination and the termination for a narrow-gauge railway that traveled from the main London line along the Blyth valley with a small station at Walberswick, which was also connected with its larger and smarter neighbor across the water by a ferry that was painted by Newbery using a monochromatic palette to render the dun-colored tonality of the crossing and the flat shoreline of sable and ocher. (234) Mackintosh was probably first introduced to the locality by Newbery, who was unusual among the visiting artists in having a permanent home there, which was a destination for visitors from Glasgow such as Maurice Greiffenhagen and E. A. Walton who, with his family, engaged in tennis parties at which the Mackintoshes were present.[10]

Like Newbery, Mackintosh rented a fishing-tackle shed by the river as a studio where he could work on a planned series of watercolors of flowers—each in its season—*Larkspur* (235) in August 1914, and *Petunia* (236) and *Winter Stock*, then *Japanese Witch Hazel* and *Jasmine* in the winter. These studies are different from the pencil drawings

of flowers of ten years before although they do have the same familial characteristics in the placing of each specimen flat on the page without shading or perspective. There is the same forensic observation of the botanical formation of calyx, stamens, buds, and blossom—often with a single bloom placed at the side to allow for greater exploration of its parts. Now the use of color in thick washes gives a sheen on a petal or a glaucous leaf. These studies follow in the tradition of the botanical artist who would depict the whole plant—its roots, its seeds—whereas Mackintosh selects a sprig that is labeled, albeit occasionally misspelled, and dated within a cartouche, which is integral to the overall design, a device that he may have absorbed from

235. *Larkspur*, Charles Rennie Mackintosh

Christopher Dresser's influential text on Japanese art and architecture in which he commended Japanese drawing for "its crispness of touch,"[11] as displayed in Mackintosh's unerring draughtsmanship. It may have been that Mackintosh was gathering illustrations for a book to be published in Germany,[12] a project that was aborted by the outbreak of war with Germany in August 1914.

The onset of war changed much. According to Margaret Macdonald, when writing a gossipy letter in January 1915 to Anna Geddes, the wife of Patrick Geddes, she and Mackintosh had journeyed to Walberswick in mid-July 1914, "coming then just for our holiday and then the war broke out and I induced Toshie to just stay on and get the real rest cure that he has so badly needed for quite two years. It struck me as the right thing to do. There will be nothing really doing till the war is over for one thing and for another it is too dangerous to go on—when a man is overworked he must rest or something serious will happen . . . we are going to have a real Wander Jahr. Already Toshie is a different being and evidently at the end of the year he will be quite fit again and by that time we hope the war will be over and then perhaps he can have a hand in rebuilding the beautiful cities which are lost to us." She concluded, "We had a postcard from Professor Geddes from Bombay."[13] Margaret Macdonald's optimism for the well-being of her husband was to prove unfounded, for six months later Mackintosh—a stranger in Walberswick, given to solitary walks, sketchbook in hand—was reported to the local military authorities as a German spy, the house was searched, correspondence from Viennese architects was found, and he was ordered to move away from the locality.

Mackintosh's troubles were compounded by money worries. On the last day of 1914 Keppie, about to depart for Kirkcudbright, "bringing in the New Year as usual with Hornel," wrote about a debt of £397:3:9, "and if you cannot pay up the interest is now due."[14] As Mackintosh's plight worsened come the summer he complained to his former patron William Davidson that the war "has nearly finished me off." He was sending Davidson some watercolor drawings. "They

are quite straightforward and have been much thought of by the artist men who have seen them—E. A. Walton, Bertram, Priestman and others." His suggested prices were "from £10:10 to £7:7 each," with larger work being "a much larger consideration." Adding to his woes was an order from the military authorities "to leave here on Thursday."[15] The next day he dispatched a further plea to Davidson as "I find I am in a much worse plight than I imagined" and asking "will you please lend me one pound."[16]

When he next wrote Mackintosh was in London but without his wife who was so stressed "that the doctor would not let her travel."[17] It was indeed "an awful time." He had been at the Home Office for three hours seeking a revocation of the expulsion order, although he was still under suspicion

236. *Petunia*, Charles Rennie Mackintosh

"because since I came to London 2 detectives have followed my movements from day to day."[18] However, he had hopes that an interview with Lord Curzon, the foreign secretary, would clear their names, though if Davidson had not sent "£10 for the picture I don't know how I could have got our case forward at all."[19] Davidson had also offered some work and Mackintosh was "glad to make the stencils for your bedroom—I think there are 3 stencils and my charge would be either £7 or £9. On that basis could you let me have a cheque for £5 ... If you have the number of Dekorative Kunst with your house in it could you send it to me."[20]

In London Mackintosh had met up with Patrick Geddes, sociologist, environmentalist, and a pioneer of modern town planning. Not only was Geddes an admirer of the architecture of Mackintosh[21] but the families had been acquainted in Scotland, perhaps through a love of pageants and an interest in botany. Certainly they had many mutual friends and indeed it may be that Geddes provided some philosophical basis for the thinking of The Four when writing in 1895 of "Life the green leaf ... and Art the flower," phrases that, when transposed, Mackintosh would adopt almost as a motto. For Geddes, "All the great flowers of literature and art rise straight from their great root stocks, each deep within its soil." With such beliefs "our aesthete develops as never before ... and given this wealth of impressions, this perfection of sensibility, new combinations must weave themselves in the fantasies of reverie," creating "gardens of desire."[22]

Geddes in London was running a summer vacation school at King's College on the social problems of the Great War and its aftermath.[23] Mackintosh found his lectures "full of interest and enthusiasm."[24] Geddes had offered practical help to Mackintosh by giving him the share of a room in King's College, where his colleague found his presence uncongenial because, as he recollected, "his aroma was suffused with the alcoholic potations to which he was addicted." Mackintosh was "doing some plans and elevations ... Were these drawings of something Geddes wanted to take back to India with him ... The elevation of a building with a kind of pergola reminded me of Wright."[25]

In India, from which he had recently returned, Geddes had been looking at the need for the reconstruction of its cities[26] and from which, doubtless, came the proposition to Mackintosh of "an offer from the Indian Government to go out there for some six months starting in October to do some work in reconstruction schemes where they want me to do the architecture ... They offer to pay my passage and give me £5 a day while I am there."[27] But it was not to be.

There is then a gap in the records until July 1916 when the dramatist and critic George Bernard Shaw declined a luncheon invitation from Mrs. Mackintosh.[28] Is it a coincidence that at this time Wenman Bassett-Lowke, a friend of Shaw, was writing to Mackintosh that "all the drawings have safely arrived and the work is in hand. I have obtained possession of the house today and my friends are commencing the work."[29] Bassett-Lowke was an engineer. His company specialized in the manufacture of narrow-gauge model railway engines, which could carry passengers about the countryside. Before the war such precision engineering brought him into contact with German technology; during the war the firm prospered on government orders for working models of guns and ships.[30] Now Bassett-Lowke was marrying and his home was to be 78 Derngate, Northampton. He was fortunate, when new building work was prohibited under wartime regulations, that he could utilize his own labor force for house improvements and could obtain scarce materials. How and when contact was made with Mackintosh is unknown. He could have read of him in German design magazines although it is more likely that in his search for an architect who was not run of the mill he was led to Mackintosh. According to Bassett-Lowke, "I met a friend from Glasgow who held forth to me on the merits of the artist-architect, Charles Rennie Mackintosh ... On my return I made contact with Mr. Mackintosh."[31]

Once again Mackintosh had a patron who was shrewd in business and, while sympathetic to Mackintosh's ideas, had an eye for shapes, patterns, and materials (he had spent time in an architect's office) so that he could reject his architect's proposed hall floor. "It appears to me from your

drawings of the carpet it is hardly necessary to have this covered with oak as so little will be seen," and he wanted the carpet to be "the standard 22″ wide as you cannot get it 2 ft."[32]; carpet runners were to be "a natural grey hair colour as I think they would show the dust rather less than plain black."[33] As he could provide "one of my works draughtsmen to make you a 1″ scale drawing of all the walls in the hall so that you can proceed with your decorative scheme,"[34] one doubts if Mackintosh ever needed to pay a site visit while receiving thoughtful advice from a client knowledgeable about the latest technical and material innovations. Mackintosh had used plastic inlays in the Chinese Room and in Bassett-Lowke he had an enthusiast for a synthetic industrial material—Erinoid—sending booklets on Erinoid and asking, "Have you ever thought of using this in the decoration of furniture" because of "the ease with which the material can be worked and the various colours and forms which it can be obtained in."[35]

Bassett-Lowke had been given by his father a three-story redbrick house in a Georgian terrace. With a street frontage of fifteen feet more space was to be gained only by throwing out bay windows, which, on the rear elevation, carried balconies. Internally, the staircase by the front door was reset athwart the middle of the ground floor, effectively becoming a room divider between the rear dining room and the enlarged hall lounge, itself a new term.

The abolition of the old rigidities of internal division and the bursting out of the rear elevation into balconies was paralleled on the continent by architects such as Gropius and Mies van der Rohe. While the rear elevation is akin to the street frontage of the Willow Tea Room it is without surface modeling or the abstractions in glass and metal of nature's forms. Here, instead, are window boxes and hanging baskets although these are minor emphases since nature is everywhere else abolished. Thus in the guest bedroom there

would be no pastel tints or frieze of roses but black-and-white stripes—thick as arrows—springing up from behind the bedheads and flying across the ceiling. (237) Here indeed, as in the brilliant ultramarine and emerald green of the bed coverings, is a precursor of the jazz age. And is it so in the hall lounge? (238) Or are the black walls and furnishings enclosed by a golden stenciled frieze a throwback to the ebonized aesthetic interiors of the last quarter of the nineteenth century? Yet the hall lounge is a paradox. At The Hill House the drawing room is white and silver with drooping roses; at Derngate, the hall lounge is black enclosed within golden pleached foliage. Yet what was the spring for the metamorphosis from the romance of a lady's retreat overlooking a garden to a man's mechanistic place of business overlooking a street? Was the hall lounge a casino, its formal decoration a reinterpretation of the wintry stems and orb of leaves atop the Secession House?

Although in 1920 *Ideal Home* magazine devoted a long article, without mentioning the architect's name, to "the unique transformation that Mr. W. J. Bassett-Lowke has effected in his house," which was seen as "almost a house of the future,"[36] Derngate would prove to be Mackintosh's

238. Derngate, hall lounge

237. Derngate, guest bedroom as reconstructed in the Hunterian Art Gallery, University of Glasgow

last significant architectural commission so that the years after 1917 must have been bleak indeed. In 1917 he was again writing to William Davidson because "I find myself at the moment very hard up" and offering "one of my flower paintings or landscapes for £20 or £30 or you could take it in pawn for 2 or 3 months when I shall be able to repay you as I am just about to start some work that will bring me in a fair remuneration by that time . . . I shall be glad to hear from you this week as my rent of £16 is overdue and I must pay or leave."[37] In August things were no better and Mackintosh was even more importunate, asking "could you please wire me £7 this week as I have a tax to pay that must be settled at once or the law will move."[38] Not only did Davidson send the money but he purchased *Begonias* (239), a very loose arrangement quite unlike the meticulous flower studies of earlier times. Even so, Mackintosh would still "need to go begging elsewhere, a job I abhor."[39] Yet the future was not entirely hopeless for there was the prospect of selling the house in Glasgow, which had been tenanted. As Margaret, who seems to have had the business matters in her hands, wrote to Davidson: "It was bought for £975 and was then in a dreadful state . . . the bills were over £800."[40] That the house had no basement was now an advantage in the changed social circumstances in the aftermath of the war. "Evidently the servant difficulty is the same there as here—for here—houses with basements will neither sell nor let and houses without one are snapped up with a large premium."[41]

Meanwhile, Mackintosh was producing drawings and still lifes of cut flowers but could not understand "why these things don't sell. They are always much admired by all our friends but then these are mostly struggling artists or comparatively poor people." Another venture was textile designs. (240) "I get very good prices for them and I am almost certain to sell a good many to one manufacturer."[42]

It must have been with a sense of optimism that at the commencement of 1920 Mackintosh began a diary as an aide-mémoire for his increasing professional activities.[43] On January 8 he noted: "Harold Squire instructed me to

239. Begonias, Charles Rennie Mackintosh

prepare sketch plans of proposed Studio and dwelling in Glebe Place," which was where the Mackintoshes had settled, leasing lodgings from Squire and studios—£8 a quarter was the rent for Mackintosh's one—although he complained in summer that "the heat in these top-lighted studios is almost unbearable"[44] while Margaret compared hers to "an orchid-house."[45]

For the Mackintoshes Chelsea was, in a sense, almost a home from home for, as a bohemian quarter, it had long been attractive to artists so that when George Henry had removed from Glasgow it was to settle in Glebe Place.[46] Prominent in the tight-knit artistic community was the Scottish colorist, J. D. Fergusson, who had known Mackintosh in Glasgow. Fergusson's partner, the dancer Margaret Morris, recorded, "One day the bell rang, I went down, opened the door and found old Toshie—Charles Rennie Mackintosh—

with a delightful happy smile, holding a small flowerpot with two slim, intertwined twigs, two leaves at near the bottom, and two more at the top. He laughed and said—'I saw this on a barrow and had to bring it to you, *it's so like you.*' "[47]

Another Glasgow connection was the sculptor F. Derwent Wood, who had taught at the Glasgow School of Art and given the city some of its liveliest and most innovative sculpture in association with James Salmon. Augustus John, having known the McNairs in Liverpool, now came into contact with Mackintosh, "whose friendship I enjoyed in Chelsea."[48] Another who became an engaging companion was the draughtsman and theatrical designer Randolph Schwabe. Also around was the musician Eugène Goossens and the composer Arnold Bax. Such was the set with whose ploys the Mackintoshes quickly became involved, including the idea by Fergusson to have art exhibitions for the London Salon of the Independants "in Army huts with glass roofs on one of the walks in Hyde Park … Charles Rennie Mackintosh had that part in hand" as one of the group's management committee. Others were some of the most forward-thinking artists in London. That the Mackintoshes were drawn into such circles would have been through their established contact with Fergusson.[49] A favorite rendezvous, especially of an evening, was a local restaurant, the Blue Cockatoo, where the Mackintoshes dined at the end of February with the photographer E. O. Hoppé and his wife, when the conversation could have turned from their mutual friend J. Craig Annan, the renowned Glasgow photographer, to Hoppé's visit to Maurice Maeterlinck in his hometown of Ghent.[50]

Hoppé was a renowned society photographic portraitist whose sitters included Mackintosh. The camera study, which dispensed with the usual background props, reflected Mackintosh's view of himself as the successful, well-connected professional artist about to make a mark on the London architectural scene. (241) The photograph, when exhibited, was on display between that of the Duchess of Northumberland and the celebrated theatrical designer Gordon Craig, another member of Mackintosh's circle. Yet within a few days of the dinner date Mackintosh was

forced to borrow ten shillings from his wife, although it was not so long since he had received a final payment from Hoppé who, having made a modest extension to his weekend cottage at East Grinstead, was now contemplating building a new house for which Mackintosh had left the plans while at East Grinstead.[51]

Both couples were members of The Plough, a club founded in 1917 "for the purpose of stimulating interest in good art of an unconventional kind."[52] Hoppé had allowed his large house in London to be the club's headquarters, where the main reception room with its black walls and touches of jade green and clover purple and the purple carpet could have interested Mackintosh, who was a committee member in 1918

240. Textile design, Charles Rennie Mackintosh

and indeed by May 1919 she was relaying the news to Glasgow that "The Plough had its last meeting in our studios."[56]

To set himself up in London as a practicing architect Mackintosh "Ordered writing paper with printed heading," purchased envelopes, a diary, job estimate books, a roll of cartridge paper, "Bannister Fletcher's Building Acts of London" (different from those in Scotland), as well as "3 various pencils" and "3 sheets tracing," noting the modest prices and concluding with "Sent subscription to RIBA [Royal Institute of British Architects] £16:16:0," giving him recognition as a registered architect. Rather charmingly, prior to all that expenditure, he "Bot. Pot of hyacinths."

While the architectural commissions were coming in Mackintosh was reliant on selling textile designs receiving in early February "cheques value £57 for 6 designs for Mr. Sefton," followed some months later by his sending "6 designs for handkerchiefs and 1 box top to Mr. Sefton £46," although more lucrative would have been the "24 designs for Mr. Foxton,"[57] the day after dispatching "drawings of Triptych to Mr. Newbery," and, later, "drawings of Lady Chapel." A welcome bonus at the end of the year would have been the cheque for £6:6:0 from the fashion store of Liberty.

No sooner was Mackintosh instructed to prepare drawings for Harold Squire's intended studio dwelling than a similar commission came from the American artist Arthur Blunt. Next Derwent Wood's wife called, whereupon Mackintosh "sketched plan of her husband's proposed studio." (242) In and around Glebe Place there were possibilities for demolition and the acquisition of a large building plot, which could be utilized by the Arts League of Service, in which Fergusson and Margaret Morris were prime movers and which would construct studios and flats that "were a practical proposition because there was such a need for them that they were let in advance." When the project stalled it was, according to Margaret Morris, because the planning authority wanted "a few Greek columns, or swags of fruit or flowers,"[58] which Mackintosh refused to supply although he touched on another cause when he noted laconically, "It was left to me to proceed with plans for Minister of Housing and get grant if possible."

along with, among others, the sculptor Jacob Epstein and the poet Laurence Binyon, best remembered for his lament for the war dead with its oft-repeated lines beginning, "They shall not grow old, as we that are left grow old."[53] A distant member of The Plough was William Davidson[54] to whom Margaret wrote of the club's financial difficulties. "The members are mostly artists and musicians and other mad hatters—full of enthusiasm but not of money and productions cost a lot. It is felt better to stop than lower the standard,"[55]

241. Charles Rennie Mackintosh, photographed by E. O. Hoppé

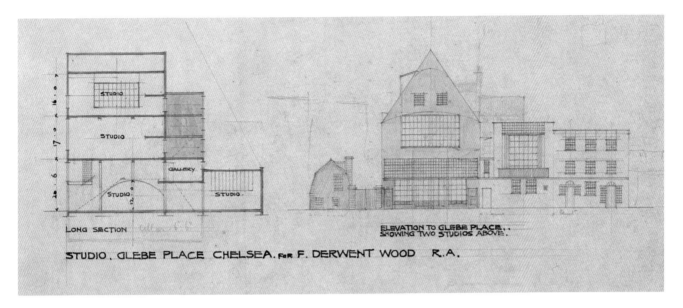

STUDIO . GLEBE PLACE . CHELSEA. for F. DERWENT WOOD R.A.

LONG SECTION

ELEVATION TO GLEBE PLACE.
SHOWING TWO STUDIOS ABOVE.

242. Studio design for Derwent Wood, Charles Rennie Mackintosh

Another ongoing project was an intended theater for Margaret Morris since Mackintosh felt "the converted hall in Flood Street was unworthy of me and my work,"[59] even although "I had no hope of getting it built."[60] Such was the economic reality. Thus Squire, who had been introduced to the Mackintoshes through the Arts League,[61] asked if the price of his studio development "could be reduced to say £6,000" and by lopping off one floor the price was set at £4,353, whereupon Mackintosh was instructed to proceed with building at once. However, when the drawings were laid before the local surveyor Mackintosh was told that "my elevations are not architectural enough and must be more elaborate." Worse was to come when both the studio block and the theater "were deemed as unsuitable buildings for the locality" so that, despite much feverish activity and high hopes, all that was erected was Squire's studio block, which he reckoned "had a magnificence which no other in London possessed."[62] Sadly, it has since been much modified.[63]

Of the many artists' studio dwellings in west London most were of a harsh weather-resistant redbrick with a white neo-Georgian trim—such was the acceptable norm. Mackintosh had offered angularity, mechanical lines, flat facades beneath sharp gables, where the interest is in the balance of part against part, of a grid against smooth planes, of glazing against white render, of a complexity that is accomplished way beyond the gaucheries at Windyhill, which as with the Glasgow School of Art and the medieval closes in the city's High Street are the begetters of these last unbuilt architectural projects.

It is an interesting reflection that, despite Mackintosh's perceived reputation of being difficult, his chief Glasgow patrons each turned to him for advice and help in the days of his exile from Glasgow. Even that most demanding of patrons Miss Cranston was prepared to call on Mackintosh's services at a remove when it came to converting a basement addition to the Willow Tea Room. Called the Dug-Out, because of its underground location and as a reference to "The Great European War Between the Allied Nations and the Central Powers" whose flags emblazoned the chimney piece, the Dug-Out was artificially lit and painted black with splashes of brilliant primary colors as at Derngate.[64]

Another who turned to Mackintosh was Walter Blackie who, as a publisher, reminded Mackintosh at the close of 1921 that he had earlier "prepared designs for two series entitled

'The Rambler Travel Books' and 'Rambles Through Our Industries.' " Now Henty's titles were to be reissued and Blackie was "sending a 'dummy' volume to show show the size of the projected volumes," which, as he explained in a succeeding letter, were "books for boys, they are generally historical romances" whose author was "one of the foremost writers of the 19th century," comparable even to Walter Scott; these books "make for high ideals of courage, manliness, directness and honourable conduct, so the cover should be manly and full of courage," which should have recommended Mackintosh to take up reading Henty.[65] Sadly, that was Mackintosh's last communication with Glasgow.

In 1923 the Mackintoshes, with their finances bolstered by the sale of their former home and an inheritance, left London for France, traveling south, almost to the Spanish border, to Amélie-les-Bains in the Pyrenees Orientales.[66] At first they seem to have intended to replicate something of their life in Chelsea by renting studios and accommodation but soon their existence became peripatetic as they moved from one hilltop base to another. They kept

in touch with artist friends such as Fergusson who, with Margaret Morris, may have been among those who, from their own experience of sojourning in France, would have recommended a change of location to a warmer and more equable climate in a country where the lower cost of living had always been an attraction for the impecunious or financially embarrassed British. In early 1925 Mackintosh wrote to Fergusson: "We are now settled in our beloved Ille-sur-Têt ... We shall be here until the end of May then we go to Mont Louis for 2 months and then back here," or perhaps to Montpellier where Patrick Geddes had set up his Scots College in 1924.[66]

Mont Louis, high in the hills, was cooler in summer and became an alternative to Port-Vendres, where the couple settled in 1925 within walking distance of Collioure—an established artists' colony. Perhaps the Mackintoshes preferred to be apart from other artists, perhaps they were escaping from the flies, "which are increadible [sic] at Collioure."

243. *Port Vendres*, Charles Rennie Mackintosh

Port-Vendres was lively. From their balconies above the quayside there was a panoramic view of the deep-sea steamers bringing in cargoes of wine, wood, and copper, which "seem suitable merchandice [*sic*] to bring into this our beautiful sunlit harbour . . . there must be one hundred men and women working." (243) Occasionally naval vessels appeared from which "young sailor lads—hundreds and hundreds of them had made a feeble-hearted French effort to paint the town red—white and blue."

In May 1927 Margaret returned to London, partly to seek medical attention and also to settle financial matters. It was then that in her prolonged absence, the first in almost thirty years of marriage, Mackintosh wrote to her "a sort of chronacle [*sic*]," which is the most important source of information for the time in France.[68] To ward off the depression brought on by the separation Mackintosh tried to fill his days with activity—except on Sundays, which his Scottish Presbyterian upbringing dictated should be a day of rest from labor. "Have had my closes [*sic*] on all day and am glad to-morrow is Monday when I can get back to my normal cord-u-roys" and to his day's painting, for there was an exhibition in the offing for which he had to produce fifty paintings. The venue was to be the Leicester Galleries in London,[69] which would be a great coup as they were foremost in the promotion of contemporary art. However, the production of watercolors while working *en plein air* was not without its irritations, whether it was a gaggle of curious schoolboys or, more frequently, "The number of insects of every description that one meets if you are working on a sheet of paper either indoors or out of doors is incredible—I am shooing them aside on this sheet now." And then there were the near gale force winds, "howling and shrieking," so that "I could not hold my cardboard steady enough to draw properly." As the days went by he felt that he was underachieving for "really the last month has been about as bad as winter—not so much for wind as for the terrific thunderstorms—rain—and sea fogs."

In Walberswick Mackintosh had begun to compose landscapes. For most of his working life buildings were recorded in isolation from their surroundings because they could have a potential use in the future. Thus sketches were marked up with notes on moldings or materials and often provided with thumbnail sketches of brackets, latches, and such like. Sometimes a design would emerge many years after an initial sketch. When the Mackintoshes holidayed at Cintra in Portugal in 1908 Mackintosh was intrigued by a well, around which were curved benches, ideas that reappeared some years later when called upon to design a memorial fountain.[70] In his middle years Mackintosh would sometimes produce a more finished drawing (244), as in 1909 when he and Margaret were staying at Newton Castle in Perthshire.[71] In the south of France Mackintosh,

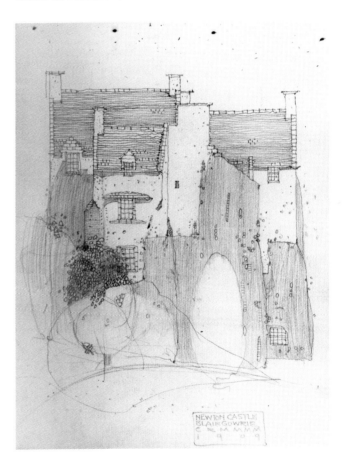

244. *Newton Castle, Perthshire*, Charles Rennie Mackintosh

now a full-time painter, opened up in a letter to Newbery, as perhaps he would not have done to anyone else, saying "I am struggling to paint in watercolour—soon I shall start in oils—but I find I have a great deal to learn or unlearn. I seem to know far too much and this knowledge obscures the really significant facts, but I am getting on."[72] As he did, for the later watercolors are as intricate as musical exercises and sometimes made more so by tweaking the scenery as if it was not challenging enough with its scarred, outlandish geological outcrops, striations, and escarpments, where dwellings are huddled around a church or below a hilltop fortress. (245) These intellectual abstractions are akin not only to the massing of the castle on Holy Island but to the spatial complexities of the Room de Luxe or an advertising label for Bassett-Lowke (246) or a stencil design for his hallway at Derngate. In the watercolors one sees the architect's training—not the artist's emotive response to the waywardness of nature but the acceptance and delight in the repetitions of buildings and the rendering of materials, preferring to forget about the bustle of a commercial port or the seduction of coastlines. He is more content in the hills where he can be alone for a few hours before returning at mealtimes to his hotel and to people. With the absence of people Mackintosh's views are like an Arthurian vision that seems to exist only in the imagination.

In London Margaret was trying to place "my drawings of Fetges and Port Vendres," with the hope, too, that one of the flower pieces, *Pinks* or *Anemones*, would be placed on the cover of *Homes and Gardens* magazine, although Mackintosh thought that "some of the smaller drawings like the Peonie etc. or even the conventional bouquet would be more suitable for the outside cover of a magazine."

Mackintosh told his wife that he was "basking here in the pink of health and only depressed because you are not near me" so that he was longing for her return when "the necessity of chronyce [*sic*] writing is over. I prefer a more intimate form of intercourse." Meanwhile he had underestimated the first appearance of symptoms in his physical condition. "My tongue is swollen—burnt and blistered," after which there appeared "a big 'button' growing on the right hand side of the point of my nose." In the autumn after

245. *The Village of La Llagonne*, Charles Rennie Mackintosh

good sign; others were less sanguine. For his convalescence Mackintosh sought a garden where he could sit "under a tree." Margaret found, on the southern edge of Hampstead Heath in Willow Road, a furnished house with a garden and a tree beneath which Mackintosh sat for much of the summer of 1928.[75] One visitor was Margaret Morris, who taught him vocal exercises.[76] When "some trouble with the landlady" occurred and as they had no place to go to Chapman-Huston took the Mackintoshes into his own home in Porchester Square as his guests. There they had use of the top floors of the Victorian stucco terrace house filled with books and pictures and overlooking the square's gardens. Soon Mackintosh could not cope with the stairs, whereupon his host made over his dining room on the ground floor, which had a balcony out on to the gardens.

As Mackintosh's plight worsened he was transferred to a nearby nursing home.[77] At this time the Leicester Galleries were showing some of the watercolors. Chapman-Huston, having purchased one of the harbor at Port-Vendres and one of the hills behind, took them into the nursing home and at Mackintosh's bedside asked him to sign them. "He sat up in bed and signed them for me—the last time he held a pencil."[78] Mackintosh died on December 10, 1928, and was cremated next day in a "Chapel that is dismal and so was the Service." To please Margaret, Chapman-Huston had the coffin draped with "lovely silver-grey velvet" on which were placed "lots of finely coloured flowers—so the last glimpse Margaret had of him was quite lovely."[79]

After further years of unsettled wandering on the continent and in England Margaret died in London on January 7, 1933, and was cremated in the same dismal chapel.

Once Mackintosh had copied into a notebook the following lines.

> Though young I was my Youth
> Could not withstand nor me protect
> From Death's impartial hand
> Life's but a Cobweb be it ever so gay
> And Death the Broom that Sweps [sic] us all away.[80]

a consultation with the local doctor he was advised to return to Britain. On arriving in London the couple were met by Mrs. Newbery who arranged for Mackintosh to be admitted to the Westminster Hospital, where the diagnosis was cancer of the tongue,[73] which had been attacked by a lethal combination of whiskey and pipe tobacco. Margaret contacted another friend from their Glasgow days, Desmond Chapman-Huston.[74] She was staying at a club in Pimlico to be near her ailing husband. By some special arrangement she prepared, cooked, and brought him his food in the hospital. After much painful medical treatment Mackintosh was discharged, which he took to be a

246. Advertising label for W. Bassett-Lowke, Charles Rennie Mackintosh

When the second phase of the Glasgow School of Art was opened in 1909 Mackintosh was described as being "in his prime being in his 42nd year ... Mr. Makintosh's work is conspicuous in Glasgow ... His work is also much admired abroad," in part through exhibitions in Moscow, Budapest, Dresden, and Berlin and before these in Vienna and Turin.[1] Yet how soon the fall!

Throughout the 1890s every Mackintosh commission was featured in the architectural journals of the day. Yet in the decade after his departure from Glasgow there was almost total oblivion. Perhaps it was symptomatic that his name was omitted (for whatever reasons by Bassett-Lowke) from the feature in 1920 by *Ideal Home* on 78 Derngate. Some restitution was made in 1924 when Charles Marriott in *Modern English Architecture* hailed the Glasgow School of Art as "important because of the great influence of Mr. Mackintosh's work on the Continent—in Germany, Holland and Sweden. It is hardly too much to say that the whole modernist movement in European architecture derives from him and the Glasgow School of Art, as an early and successful attempt to get architecture out of building, making decorative features of structural forms, goes far to explain the reason why."[2] Surely that was an overstated case since the School of Art had never been written about in the journals and no illustration of the exterior would be published until 1930, and no plans until 1950.

With his death in 1928 there was some belated interest once again in Mackintosh although as John Betjeman observed the obituary notice in *The Times* was "about as long as that given to the obscurest and dottiest of peers."[3] As was to be expected the *Glasgow Herald* was more fulsome although the contributor did crib his assessment of

the School of Art from Marriott. Another contributor wrote: "What strikes me most is the European reputation of your Glasgow architect, Mackintosh ... His name is a household word in Vienna, Buda-Pest, in Turin and Munich, in Paris and all over Holland."[4] This was much the same line as that taken by the professional journals. "The Glasgow School of Art contains in its external treatment and in many characteristics of its interior detail, the germ of themes today familiar through the work of men like Hoffman, Behrens, Gropius or Le Corbusier."[5] The *Architectural Review* saw Mackintosh "as the originator of many of the best things in the sober 'functional' styles of today."[6] Also in 1929 Bruno Taut's *Modern Architecture*, although classifying Mackintosh as English, did include illustrations of the library and of the attic studio, but using turn-of-the-century photographs, which show the studio not yet reduced in width by the introduction of the corridor between the east staircase and the hen run.

When Betjeman wrote about Mackintosh in the following year in a piece on the history of interior decoration he viewed Mackintosh as one "whose work influenced modern Continental architecture more than any past architect" but without advancing supporting evidence from Europe.[7] As Betjeman was discussing interior decoration he restricted himself to Miss Cranston's Willow Tea Room, although by then it and the Buchanan Street tearoom were no longer functioning.

In 1933 following the death of Margaret Macdonald Mackintosh and the subsequent Memorial Exhibition, there was a shift of emphasis in the perception of Mackintosh. He became "A Neglected Genius" with the *Architectural Review* insisting that "Mackintosh, unknown and ignored in England, has long been honoured in Scotland and in Europe," doubtless because the School of Art was without "unnecessary decorations and the using of structural lines as the dominant motif in a building."[8] However, in *Twentieth Century Houses* by Raymond McGrath the school was held to be "without question Scottish in quality and feeling. The tall growth of the overhanging windows puts one in mind of the top structure of Craigievar," the early-seventeenth-century castle in the northeast of Scotland. It was McGrath who incorrectly pronounced, "From 1910 to 1915 Mackintosh was architect head of the Glasgow School of Art."[9]

In a lengthy piece in the *Architectural Review* in 1935 Morton Shand pointed out that following on the Memorial Exhibition the Scottish National Portrait Gallery had purchased Newbery's portrait of Mackintosh and that the city of Glasgow had bought two watercolors, which, for Morton Shand, "evince a timeless modernity and an essentially architectural quality of abstract design such as none of his buildings or furniture approaches." That Mackintosh was so flawed was because of his wife. It was the "florid coarseness of her wholly inferior decorative talent ... that too often led him into an uxorious ornamental vulgarity."[10]

The definitive reputation of Mackintosh as one in the pantheon of the heroes of modernism was finally established by the German art historian Nikolaus Pevsner in 1936 in his seminal *Pioneers of the Modern Movement from William Morris to Walter Gropius*. It was Pevsner who, by his authoritarian didacticism, would stamp for following generations the role of Mackintosh, one that would be adopted by Howarth in the subtitle of his 1952 biography. Indeed, in discussing the Glasgow School of Art there is often little difference between the texts of the two scholars.

Pevsner was setting out the wares of modernism. Therefore, Mackintosh was "one of the most imaginative and brilliant of all young European architects ... the real forerunner of Le Corbusier." As for the School of Art—Pevsner denied Mackintosh his position as a student of nineteenth-century historicism. "Not a single feature here is derived from period styles. The façade leads on to the twentieth century ... no curves are admitted." In the school's library, "Curves have completely disappeared" before "an overwhelmingly full polyphony of abstract form." Was Pevsner unaware or did he overlook Mackintosh's interest in symbolism? Externally, as Pevsner saw it, there was "a squareness and precision in the high narrow windows. It seems that Dutch architects especially have derived benefit from Mackintosh's style."[11] But how, since no continental magazine had published details?

Pevsner's essay was republished in 1960 and it has since become one of the standard texts. Mackintosh's place in modernism was ensured by placing his School of Art on the cover along with the Eiffel Tower and the Fagus factory by Gropius. It was, of course, inevitable that there would be a reaction to the Pevsnerian concept so that today Mackintosh can be considered a latter-day master of the Arts and Crafts, a symbolist and the progenitor of the Glasgow Style which was the antithesis of modern—for Pevsner at least. Nevertheless, Mackintosh does not sit comfortably among his Arts and Crafts peers. In the early work there are gestures to overt constructional techniques but these are abandoned in favor of smooth uninterrupted lines, whether in furniture or in buildings, which when combined with the inherent symbolism defines Mackintosh's work as without parallel in the early twentieth century. ▪▪

N⚬TES

PREFACE

1 Royal Australian Institute of Architects to T. Howarth, 12 Dec. 1946. University of Toronto, Special Collections, B96-0028/017 (01).
2 W. Moyes to T. Howarth, 29 April 1947 *et seq.* University of Toronto, Special Collections, B96-0028/017 (14).
3 Miss H. Swaisland to T. Howarth, 123 Tilehurst Rd., London SW3, 25 Jan. 1946. University of Toronto, Special Collections, B96-0028/017 (21).
4 Post Office Glasgow Directories.
5 *Old Country Houses of the Old Glasgow Gentry,* 2nd edn. (1878), pp. 127–28.
6 T. Howarth, *Charles Rennie Mackintosh and the Modern Movement* (1952), p. 2.
7 A. Somerset, "Mackintosh's Sisters," p. 5.
8 A. Moffat, *Remembering Charles Rennie Mackintosh* (1989), p. 23.
9 Howarth, *op. cit.,* p. 33.
10 GLAHA 52368.
11 For background on the Macdonald and McNair families see J. Helland, *The Studios of Frances and Margaret Macdonald* (1996).
12 "We the undersigned members of staff . . . Frances MacNair, J. Herbert MacNair." GSAA, B8/7, 19 May 1910.
13 W. Rothenstein, *Men and Memories,* vol. II (1932), p. 5.
14 A. John, *Finishing Touches* (1966), p. 60.
15 C. Reilly, *Scaffolding in the Sky* (1938), p. 90.
16 GLAHA 52360.
17 Moffat, *op. cit.,* pp. 23–24.
18 B. E. Kalas, "De La Tamise a la Spree" (1905). Reprinted in *1933 Memorial Exhibition, A Reconstruction* (1983), p. vii.

Chapter 1
LET GLASGOW FLOURISH

1 A. F. Weber, *The Growth of Cities in the Nineteenth Century* (1899, reprinted 1968), pp. 60, 64; C. A. Oakley, *"The Second City"* (1967), pp. 31, 113; G. Gordon, "The Changing City," *Perspectives of the Scottish City* (1985), pp. 4, 10.
2 Lord Esher, *Conservation in Glasgow* (1971), p. 1.
3 *The Bailie,* no. 56, 12 Nov. 1873. For an assessment of Glasgow's sculpture see *Glasgow Revealed* (1988) and its fuller successor R. McKenzie, *Sculpture in Glasgow* (1999).
4 *Scottish Art Review,* vol. I, no. 1, June 1888, pp. 93–94; C. Cunningham, *Victorian and Edwardian Town Halls* (1981).
5 G. G. Scott, *Lectures on the Rise and Development of Medieval Architecture,* vol. II (1879), pp. 200–202.
6 *The Bailie,* vol. XLVIII, 26 Aug. 1896.
7 GSAA, Governors' Minutes, vol. 4, 21 Oct., 1896.
8 GLAHA 41425–6.m.
9 Senex (R. Reid), *Glasgow Past and Present* (1884), vol. I, p. xlviii.

10 *Ibid.,* vol. I, p. xviii; J. Pagan, *Glasgow Past and Present* (1851), vol. I, p. 13.
11 Senex, *op. cit., vol.* I, p. xxii.
12 Quoted by A. Noble, "Urbane Silence," *Perspectives,* pp. 85–87. See also A. Slaven, *The Development of the West of Scotland, 1750–1960* (1975), p. 150 and I. Maver, *Glasgow* (2000), pp. 85–87.
13 T. M. Devine, *The Tobacco Lords* (1990), p. 108; Slaven, *op. cit.,* pp. 6, 21–23; Maver, *op. cit.,* p. 18.
14 W. Forbes of Pitsligo, *Memoirs of a Banking House* (1859), p. 27; A. Gibb, *The Making of a City* (1983), p. 61, quoting Slaven, *op. cit.,* p. 23. Maver, *Ibid.*
15 J. Denholm, *History of the City of Glasgow* (1804), p. 531; Devine, *op. cit.,* pp. 34–35, 46, 61–65.
16 Senex, *op. cit.,* vol. II, pp. 46–47; Devine, *op. cit.,* pp. 114–16.
17 Senex, *op. cit.,* vol. III, p. 176, quoting Denholm, *op. cit.,* p. 423.
18 W. M. Wade, *The History of Glasgow* (1821), p. xxvi.
19 T. Garnett, *Observations on a Tour of Scotland* (1810), vol. II, p. 190.
20 J. Kohl, *Scotland, Glasgow, the Clyde to the Lakes* (1844), p. 26.
21 R. Rodger, "Employment, Wages and Poverty in the Scottish Cities, 1841–1914," *Perspectives,* p. 35; Maver, *op. cit.,* p. 44.
22 Gibb, *op. cit.,* p. 90; Slaven, *op. cit.,* pp. 82 and 133; Maver, *op. cit.,* p. 41.
23 Kohl, *op. cit.,* pp. 19–20.
24 Oakley, *op. cit.,* p. 73.
25 Weber, *op. cit.,* p. 61.
26 J. R. Kellett, *Glasgow, A Concise History* (1967), pp. 27–28.
27 Weber, *op. cit.;* Slaven, *op. cit.,* pp. 120–21.
28 *The Bailie,* "Men You Know," nos.1530, 12 Feb. 1902; 1620, 16 Dec. 1903. Maver, *op. cit.,* pp. 120–21.
29 Gibb, *op. cit.,* p. 116.
30 Senex, *op. cit.,* vol. III, p. 176, quoting Denholm, p. 423.
31 Kellett, *op. cit.,* p. 31; Slaven, *op. cit.,* p. 11; Maver, *op. cit.,* pp. 113–18. In the spring of 1893 it was reported that "affairs on the Clyde do not look satisfactory in the meantime. Last month there were only some 24,000 tons of shipping launched on the river. This is less than half the work done a year ago." Nevertheless the statistics at the end of the year showed that "of the 988,402 tons of shipping built during the year, the Clyde is accountable for 280,160." *Quiz,* vol. XXV, 6 April 1893, and vol. XXVI, 28 Dec. 1893.
32 F. M. Walker, *The Song of the Clyde* (1984), pp. 22, 168–69; Slaven, *op. cit.,* pp. 127–29.
33 Walker, *op. cit.,* p. 26.
34 *Ibid.,* pp. 172–73.

35 *The Bailie*, no. 662, 24 June 1885.

36 Walker, *op. cit.*, pp. 47–48.

37 *The Bailie*, nos. 638, 7 Jan. 1885; 789, 30 Nov. 1887; 819, 27 June 1888.

38 Glasgow School of Art, Governors' Minutes, vol. 2 (1882–87). Report of Meeting in March 1882.

39 *Ex inf.* F. M. Walker. A. Sloan with G. Murray, *James Miller, 1860–1947* (1993), pp. 30–31.

40 R. Rodger, *op. cit.*, p. 49. "In Glasgow there are 31,032 one-roomed houses, with 100,298 persons living in them." *Quiz*, vol. XXVII, 30 Aug. 1894.

41 R. McFadzean, *The Life and Works of Alexander Thomson* (1979), pp. 91–95.

42 H. Muthesius, *Die Englische Baukunst der Gegenwart* (1900), p. 114.

43 *The Builder*, vol. LXXIX, 18 Aug. 1900, p. 160.

44 *Quiz*, vol. XIX, 21 March 1890.

45 Wade, *op. cit.*, pp. 159–60. For a discussion of Glasgow's urban form see p. Reed (ed.), *Glasgow: The Forming of the City* (1993), especially chaps. 5 and 6.

46 C. Dickens, *Pickwick Papers* (1986), p. 534.

47 F. J. Sinclair (ed.), *Charles Wilson Architect, 1810–1863* (1995), pp. 16, 18–19.

48 Kellet, *op. cit.*, p. 20.

49 Senex, *op. cit.*, vol. II, p. 77.

50 P. Reed, "The Victorian Suburb," *Glasgow*, pp. 59–75; Maver, *op. cit.*, pp. 94–95.

51 *Quiz*, vol. XXIV, 2 Feb. 1893.

52 B. Dicks, "Choice and Constraint," *Perspectives*, p. 104, quoting M. A. Simpson and T. Lloyd, *Middle Class Housing in Britain* (1977), p. 50. The Kelvinside estate was purchased in 1839 by two Glasgow lawyers, Matthew Montgomerie and John Park Fleming, in association with James Neilson, the inventor of the hot-blast furnace. He and Fleming were among the first occupants of Kirklee Terrace. It was Fleming who drew up the partnership agreement between Samuel Cunard and the Burns family. *Kelvinside* (1894), pp. 1, 4, and 16.

53 E. Williamson, A. Riches, and M. Higgs, *Glasgow* (1990), p. 308.

54 H. B. Morton, *A Hillhead Album* (1973).

55 Williamson et al., *op. cit.*, pp. 314–5, 346.

56 G. McCrone, *Wax Fruit* (reprinted 1993), pp. 128–29.

57 A. Blackie, *Blackie and Son, 1809–1959* (1959), pp. 2–3.

58 *Ibid.*, pp. 27–28; B. Edwards, "Glasgow Improvements, 1866–1901," *Glasgow*, p. 86.

59 A. Briggs, *Victorian Cities* (1968), p. 227.

60 *Memoirs and Portraits of One Hundred Glasgow Men* (1886), vol. I, pp. 37–38; W. G. Blackie, *Concerning Blackie and Son* (1897), pp. 91–94; A. Blackie, *op. cit.*, p. 28; Maver, *op. cit.*, pp. 172–73.

61 McFadzean, *op. cit.*, pp. 204–5; B. Edwards, "Alexander Thomson and the Glasgow Improvement Scheme," *"Greek" Thomson* (G. Stamp and S. McKinstry, eds.) (1994), pp. 135–50.

62 Briggs, *op. cit.*, p. 232.

63 *The Builder*, vol. LXXV, 9 July 1898, p. 21.

64 Obituary, *North British Daily News*, 13 Feb. 1873, among the Blackie MSS, Business Record Archive, University of Glasgow. See also W. G. Blackie, *op. cit.*, p. 101.

65 "Proposed New Church for Hillhead, Botanic Gardens and Downhill Districts, Glasgow." Blackie MSS, Business Record Archive, University of Glasgow.

66 W. W. Blackie, *John Blackie, Senior (1782–1874)* (1933), p. 46.

67 W. W. Smith, *Kelvinside Church* (1937), pp. 8, 11–12.

68 Alexander Thomson to George Thomson, 20 Sept. 1872 (*ex inf.* Dr. G. Stamp); T. Gildard, lecture to the Glasgow Philosophical Society, 30 June 1888, p. 30.

69 Typed obituary notice, Blackie MSS; A. Blackie, *op. cit.*, p. 21.

70 GSA, Governors' Minutes, vol. 2 (1882–87), 24 April and 19 May 1855.

71 A. Blackie, *op. cit.*, p. 30; McFadzean, *op. cit.*, pp. 177–79.

72 W. G. Blackie, *op. cit.*, p. 107.

73 *Ibid.*, p. 126; McFadzean, *op. cit.*, pp. 273–74.

74 W. G. Blackie, *op. cit.*, p. 104; *Free Westbourne Church. Calendar and Directory* (1894), pp. 8, 29, 36.

75 J. Macaulay, " 'Greek' Thomson's Literary and Pictorial Sources," *"Greek" Thomson*, pp. 51–59.

76 G. Law, "Greek Thomson," *Architectural Review*, vol. CXV (May 1954), p. 316.

77 P. Kinchin and J. Kinchin, *Glasgow's Great Exhibitions* (1988), p. 19; Maver, *op. cit.*, pp. 179–80.

78 *Scottish Art Review*, vol. I, no. 1 (June 1888), pp. 4–5, 33–35, 58; Kinchin, *op. cit.*, pp. 21, 23, 26, 32.

79 Mackintosh sketchbook. National Gallery of Ireland, 2009 TX11.

80 *Quiz*, vol. XVII, 8 March and 26 April 1889.

81 McKenzie's intention was to join Keppie and Mackintosh in Honeyman's office. Instead, he went out to India to assist his father in the family's cabinet-making business. McKenzie had had some experience in cabinet making in 1884 and '85 before becoming an apprentice architect in 1886. There is a family tradition that in India McKenzie had a set of chairs made in teak to a design by Mackintosh.

Was Hugh McNab the architect William H. McNab who studied at the Glasgow School of Art between 1881 and 1886, where he was registered as an architectural draughtsman? McKenzie, Keppie, and McNab were seen off from Glasgow by Bob Wallace, a grocer, who attended the Glasgow School of Art in the session 1887–88. Andrew Prentice had studied at the Glasgow School of Art between 1883 and 1887.

Ex inf. Dr. George Rawson.

Chapter 2
"NEW ART"

1 W. J. Smith, "An Architectural Anthology," *Proceedings of the Royal Philosophical Society of Glasgow*, vol. 57 (1951), part 6, p. 58.

2 "Scotch Art Notes," *The Studio*, vol. I (1893), p. 161.

3 *Ibid.*, vol. I, p. 14.

4 *Ibid.*, vol. I, p. 234.

5 *Ibid.*, vol. I, pp. 5, 49; W. Crane, *Ideals in Art* (1892), p. 263.

6 *The Studio*, vol. II (1893), pp. 38–39.

7 *Ibid.*, vol. IV (1894), p. 19.

8 S. Bing, "The Art of Utamaro," *The Studio*, vol. IV, pp. 137, 139.

9 *The Bailie*, vol. XLVI, 24 July 1895.

10 *Quiz*, vol. XXVII, 2 Aug. 1894.

11 F. MacSporran, *Edward Arthur Walton, 1860–1922* (1987), p. 44.

12 R. Billcliffe, *The Glasgow Boys* (1985), p. 7.

13 *Quiz*, vol. III, 31 March and 7 July 1882.

14 W. Buchanan, *Mr. Henry and Mr. Hornel Visit Japan* (1979), p. 8.

15 *Quiz*, vol. XVIII, 24 May 1889.

16 J. P. MGillivray, "Japanese Sword Guards," *Scottish Art Review*, vol. I (1888), pp. 129–31.

17 *Quiz*, vol. XXV, 23 March 1893.

18 Billcliffe, *op. cit.*, p. 256.

19 *Quiz*, vol. XXIV, 9 Feb.1893. Henry had been unwell for a long time before setting off for Japan. *Quiz*, vol. XXIV, 3 Nov. 1892 and 15 Dec. 1892.

20 G. Henry to E. A. Hornel, Kai Ki Kwan, 6 Oct. 1893. 3/1, Hornel Library, National Trust for Scotland.

21 Do. to do., n.d. 3/11 Hornel Library, NTS.

22 Do. to do., 136 Wellington St., Glasgow, 17 Oct., 1894. 3/12, Hornel Library, NTS.

23 *Quiz*, vol. XXVII, 7 March 1895.

24 E. A. Hornel, "Japan." A printed version of the lecture is in the Hornel Library, NTS. Buchanan, *op. cit.*, pp. 13, 17. On 7 March 1895 it was reported that Henry, as Hornel's "brother artist and adventurer will tonight tell the members of the Art Club and their friends a few of his reminiscences among the Japanese." Henry "again assented to read another paper on the same subject" at the Art Club, which "was a great success. The lantern illustrations were very fine, and the lecture itself sparkled with wit and humour." He was still lecturing on "Japan and the Japanese" in 1889. *The Bailie*, vol. XLVII, 16 and 23 Sept. 1896, and vol. LIII, 25 Jan. 1899.

25 *Quiz*, vol. XXVIII, 2 May 1895.

26 Hornel, *op. cit.*

27 The drawings, dated 1909, are in the Hornel Library, NTS.

28 Buchanan, *op. cit.*, p. 58.

29 Billcliffe, *op. cit.*, p. 266.

30 *Ibid.*, p. 252.

31 *Quiz*, vol. XXX, 6 Feb. 1896.

32 "The Exhibition of the Glasgow Institute of the Fine Arts," *Scottish Art Review*, vol. I, pp. 243–45.

33 *Glasgow Herald*, 8 April 1895.

34 Billcliffe, *op. cit.*, 38.

35 *Scottish Art Review*, vol. I, p. 317.

36 J. Guthrie to E. A. Hornel, 7 Woodside Place, Glasgow, 10 June 1891. Hornel Library, NTS.

37 *Quiz, vol.* XIX, 16 May 1890.

38 R. Billcliffe, *The Royal Glasgow Institute of the Fine Arts, 1861–1989* (1991), vol. 2, pp. 324–26; vol. 3, pp. 90, 93, 139, 155; see also J. Helland, *The Studios of Frances and Margaret Macdonald* (1996).

39 T. Neat, *Part Seen, Part Imagined* (1994), pp. 14, 18; A. Crawford, *Charles Rennie Mackintosh* (1995), pp. 19, 27, 89, 189.

40 R. Billcliffe, *Architectural Sketches and Flower Drawings by Charles Rennie Mackintosh* (1977), p. 12.

41 *Quiz, vol.* XXVIII, 15 Nov. 1894; E. Bird, "Ghouls and Gas Pipes: Public Reaction to Early Work of 'The Four,' " *Scottish Art Review*, vol. XIV, no. 4 (1975), pp. 13–16, 28.

42 Mitchell Library, Royal Glasgow Institute of the Fine Arts, Minute Book, 1891–99.

43 N. Munro, *Erchie and Jimmy Swan* (1993), pp. 116–18.

44 *Quiz*, vol. XXVIII, 28 March 1895.

45 *Supra*, n. 41.

46 "Recent Architecture in the West of Scotland," *Scottish Art Review*, vol. II (1889), p. 114.

Chapter 3
THE MENTORS

1 Honeyman and Keppie Job Book, 1852–65. University of Glasgow, Hunterian Art Gallery, Mackintosh Collection, GLAHA 53056. D. Walker, "The Architect of the Restoration of Brechin Cathedral. An Outline of the Career of John Honeyman (1831–1914)," *Society of Friends of Brechin Cathedral. Book of the Society*, no. 41 (1992). For the history of the firm that became John Honeyman and Keppie, see D. Stark, *Charles Rennie Mackintosh and Co.* (2004).

2 *Who's Who in Glasgow in 1909* (1909), pp. 91–92; *The Bailie*, vol. XLVIII, 26 Aug. 1896.

3 *Transactions of the Aberdeen Ecclesiological Society*, vol. II (1890–93), p. v, and III (1894–6), p. 12.

4 NAS, MW/1/194. *The Bailie*, Ibid. G. Eyre-Todd (ed.), *The Book of Glasgow Cathedral* (1898), pp. 443–44.

5 GLAHA 41418.

6 *Ibid.*

7 *Supra*, n. 2.

8 *Supra*, n.1

9 J. L. Aikman, *Historical Notices of the United Presbyterian Congregations in Glasgow* (1875), p. 203.

10 J. Ruskin, *The Seven Lamps of Architecture. The Works of John Ruskin*, vol. VIII (1903), p. 12.

11 G. Scott, *Lectures on the Rise and Development of Medieval Architecture* (1879), vol. I, p. 15.

12 C. Eastlake, *A History of the Gothic Revival* (1872), pp. 292–93.

13 Aikman, *op. cit.*, p. 206. The trade estimates in June 1862 amounted to £2,040:13:9. GLAHA 53056.

14 Glasgow City Archives, Mitchell Library, CH3/662/1.

15 A. Gomme and D. Walker, *Architecture of Glasgow* (1987), pp. 115, 172–73.

16 *Supra*, n. 2.

17 Job Book, 1852–65, pp. 70–72. 117. GLAHA 53056.

18 Job Book, 1874–82, p. 115. "U.P. Church, Infirmary Square, October 1878." The estimate of £12,199:13:4 included £300 for statuary and £200 for stained glass. GLAHA, 53058.

19 *Westbourne Free Church Calendar and Directory* (1894), pp. 7–8.

20 GCA/CH3/1412/18. The original costs had been: mason £4,254; joiner £1,736; slater £96, which is £6,086. GLAHA, 53058.

21 *Supra*, n. 20. Michael Honeyman was an accountant who lived in Hamilton Drive. *Post Office Directory, 1892–93* (1892), p. 329.

22 Aikman, *op. cit.*, pp. 206–7.

23 *British Architect*, 22 Nov. 1889. Gomme and Walker, *op. cit.*, p. 263.

24 W. Blair to T. Howarth, 25 Feb. 1946. University of Toronto, Special Collections, B89–0014/001.

25 Alexander Thomson to George Thomson, Glasgow 20 Sept. 1872. *Ex inf.* Dr. Gavin Stamp. Job Book, 1861–76. GLAHA 53057.

26 Job Books, 1852–65 and 1861–76. "Messrs. Burns £568:19:5" included McConnell's iron beams and iron castings from McElroy Brothers. GLAHA 53056 and 53057.

27 Of the ninety-six entries in the job books for the 1870s twelve are in Skelmorlie. Honeyman was at Stroove in Skelmorlie from 1872 to 1879. *Supra*, n. 2.

28 D. MacGibbon and T. Ross, *The Castellated and Domestic Architecture of Scotland* (1990), vol. III, pp. 63–75.

29 *Scottish Art Review*, vol. I, no. 1 (June 1888), p. 31.

30 A. Graham, *Memories of a Highland Estate* (1993), pp. 63–70. There are two entries in the job books. For Skipness Castle in June 1867, the year after the acquisition of the estate by new owners, prices are as follows: mason £3,450; wright £2,178; plasterer £449; slater £199:10:0; plasterer £459. Twelve years later trade prices are much the same but with addition of gas fitting at £90:8:11. Perhaps an earlier project to rehabilitate the medieval castle was considered and then rejected.

31 Auchamore House may have been built in stages. An entry in the job books covers the years 1881–83 when J. and W. Guthrie supplied stained glass. Major works occurred in 1896. Prices in the job books are: joinery £3,317:5:8; slater £542:5:41/2; plasterer (G. Rome) £655:1:8; plumbing £584:4:6; tiles £102:9:61/2. A small entry is for photographs by Annan paid for by Honeyman and Keppie. The painter work was by J. and W. Guthrie. Hutcheson and Grant's account for joinery was in excess of the estimate because of oak flooring £135; oak stair £45; oak finishings £769; porch £49; belfry £4; ironmongery £10; marble steps £22. Plumbing included "Hydrants, 250 feet hose with copper couplings, £22 and copper roof of belfry and vane £35." GLAHA 53059 and 53060. *Academy Architecture*, 1897, pt. I, pp. 70, 77 shows the finished house. Following on a fire it was considerably reduced in size.

32 *The Bailie*, vol. XCV, 31 March 1920.

33 Mackintosh's application for fellowship of the RIBA was signed and witnessed on 20 September 1906, approved by the RIBA council on 5 November, and accepted at the business meeting on 3 December. The RIBA signatories were T. Collcutt and Leonard Stokes.

34 John Keppie wrote of the death of Sellars in 1888: "He was my apprentice master and if he had lived I would have been his partner." J. Keppie, *The Story of the Glasgow Institute of Architects* (1921), p. 18.

35 From a peak of ninety-six entries in the job books in the 1870s, the entries for 1880–89 are sixty of which a third were additions or alterations to earlier work.

36 A. G. Henderson, *RIBAJ*, Sept. 1945.

37 *Quiz*, vol. XXV, 15 June 1893.

38 D. L. Sayers, *Five Red Herrings* (1972), p. 48.

39 *Evening News*, 3 June 1893.

40 Drawings by Honeyman, Keppie and Mackintosh Architects, 4 Blythswood Square, Glasgow, Jan. 1909. Hornel Library, NTS.

41 J. Keppie to C. R. Mackintosh, 31 Dec. 1914. GLAHA 41394.

42 J. Keppie to E. A. Hornel, Glasgow 10 Dec. 1930 and 16 Dec. 1931. Hornel Library, NTS.

43 *Glasgow Weekly Herald*, 28 Oct. 1933. W. Buchanan, "The Mackintosh Circle, Part III, Mackintosh, John and Jessie Keppie," *Charles Rennie Mackintosh Society Newsletter*, no. 32 (1982).

44 *The Architect*, 14 Feb. 1890.

45 Anderson's College Medical School Minute Book, Glasgow University Archives, DC 244/1/4.

46 GCA, Royal Glasgow Institute of the Fine Arts Minute Book.

47 *Quiz*, vol. V, 31 Aug. 1883.

48 Minute Book of the Fairfield Shipbuilding and Engineering Co. Ltd. GCA, UCS/2/1/1. In 1890 "the Principal Entrance of New Offices" was exhibited at RGIF. R. Billlcliffe (ed.), *The Royal Glasgow Institute of the Fine Arts*, vol. 2 (1991), p. 245.

49 Job Book, 1881–94. GLAHA 53059. John Honeyman gave a lecture, "Recent Alterations in the Choir of Glasgow Cathedral," to the Philosophical Society of Glasgow, which was reported in the *Building News*, vol. 58, 26 Dec. 1890.

50 Mackintosh Sketch Book. National Gallery of Ireland, 2009, TX 18, 19. The wooden drill hall of 1863–64 was burned down in March 1889. A. F. Jones, *Cardross. The Village in Days Gone By* (1985), p. 80.

51 Cash Book, 1889–1917. GLAHA 53079.

52 *British Architect*, 31 Oct. 1890.

53 Howarth, *op. cit.*, p. 40.

54 Job Book, 1861–76. GLAHA 53057.

55 Howarth, *op. cit.*, p. 6.

56 J. B. McNair, *McNair, McNear and McNeir Genealogies* (1923), p. 26. *The Old Country Houses of the Old Glasgow Gentry* (1878).

57 *Statistical Account of Scotland, 1791–99* (1973), vol. VII, p. 340.

58 J. Hopkirk, "A Statistical Account of the Barony Parish of Glasgow, 1836." Glasgow University, Special Collections.

59 *Catalogue of Plans of Abandoned Mines*, vol. V (Scotland) (1931).

60 Howarth, *op. cit.*, pp. 18–19.

61 *Ibid.*, p. 21. It is now accepted that the interior showing the Mackintosh frieze was at 27 Regent Park Square, which was the eventual Mackintosh family home after removing from Dennistoun. R. Billcliffe, *The Complete Furniture, Furniture Drawings and Interior Designs* (1980), p. 35.

62 GSAA.

63 Keppie, *op. cit.*, pp. 7–8.

64 T. Gildard, "The 'Alexander Thomson' Memorial." GCA.

65 Glasgow Institute of Architects, Minute Book, Alexander Thomson Memorial.

66 *The Bailie*, vol. XXVI, 17 Sept. 1890. Also *Building News*, 29 Nov. 1889.

67 *Supra*, n. 65. *Building News*, 26 Sept. 1890.

68 P. Robertson (ed.), *Charles Rennie Mackintosh. The Architectural Papers* (1990), pp. 226–34.

69 GCA, F. Newbery, News Cutting Book, "Scotch Art Students' Work in London," 27 July 1891.

70 *Supra*, n. 65.

Chapter 4
ITALY

1 T. Howarth, *Charles Rennie Mackintosh and the Modern Movement* (1952), p. 7.

2 A. McLaren Young, *Charles Rennie Mackintosh, 1868–1928* (1968), p. 18.

3 *British Architect*, 13 Nov. 1891. L. Douglas Penman studied architecture at the Glasgow School of Art from 1884–89 when he was an apprentice architect.

4 K. Clark, *The Gothic Revival* (1962), p. 176.

5 J. Ruskin, *The Seven Lamps of Architecture* (1903), p. 258.

6 J. Ruskin, *Lectures on Painting and Architecture* (1907), p. 103.

7 *Ibid.*

8 Ruskin, *The Seven Lamps of Architecture*, p. 27.

9 *Ibid.*, preface to the 2nd edition, p. 11.

10 *Ibid.*, p. 255.

11 C. Eastlake, *A History of the Gothic Revival* (1872), p. 269.

12 Ruskin, *The Stones of Venice*, vol. II (1904), p. 279.

13 G. G. Scott, *Remarks on Secular and Domestic Architecture* (1858), p. vii.

14 *Ibid.*, p. 48.

15 *Ibid.*, p. 113.

16 G. McKenzie, "Diary."

17 C. R. Mackintosh, "Diary of a Tour in Italy," *Charles Rennie Mackintosh. The Architectural Papers* (P. Robertson, ed.) (1990) p. 110. Mackintosh's manuscript is in the Mackintosh Collection, HAG.

18 Robertson, *op. cit.*, p. 91.

19 *Ibid.*, p. 90. "Geo. Murray" is described in the GSA records for 1881–82 as a lithographic draughtsman. George W. Murray won prizes for modeling in 1879–80. He may have worked in the textile trade, then a major employer in Glasgow. Robertson thought he may have been in the office of Honeyman and Keppie but cites no evidence.

20 *Ibid.*, p. 92.

21 *Ibid.*

22 *Ibid.*, p. 93.

23 *Ibid.*, p. 111.

24 *Ibid.*, p. 92.

25 *Ibid.*, p. 93.

26 *Ibid.*, pp. 95–98. One can presume that "Maggie" and "Billy" were Mackintosh's sister Margaret (1870–1924) and brother William (1866–1902). Even allowing for the formality of the Victorian age one wonders about the reference to "Mr. Keppie."

27 *Ibid.*, p. 97.

28 *Ibid.*, p. 113.

29 *Ibid.*, p. 96.

30 McKenzie, *op. cit.*

31 Robertson, *op. cit.*, p. 95.

32 McKenzie, *op. cit.*

33 Robertson, *op. cit.*

34 McKenzie, *op. cit.*

35 *Ibid.*

36 *Ibid.*

37 Robertson, *op. cit.*, p. 107.

38 *Ibid.*, p. 98.

39 McKenzie, *op. cit.*

40 Robertson, *op. cit.*, pp. 98–99. "Paxton and a fellow Dods" could have been James Paxton and R. S. Dods. The former was a student at the Glasgow School of Art from 1886–87 and is described as an assistant architect. In 1887 he won a prize for building construction, as did Mackintosh. Dods was a New Zealander who trained in Edinburgh and London. In 1898 he met Robert Lorimer in Oxford and would later work for him. In 1896 he went to Brisbane, Australia. p. Savage, *Lorimer and the Edinburgh Craft Designers* (1980), p. 164; *Directory of British Architects, 1834–1914*, vol. 1, p. 546.

41 *Ibid.*, p. 99.

42 McKenzie, *op. cit.*

43 Scott, *op. cit.*, p. 77.

44 Robertson, *op. cit.*, p. 102.

45 *Ibid.*, p. 103.

46 McKenzie, *op. cit.*

47 Ruskin, *The Seven Lamps of Architecture*, p. 175.

48 *Ibid.*, p. 10.

49 *Ibid.*, p. 114.

50 Ruskin, *The Stones of Venice*, vol. II, p. 212.

51 Minute Book, Alexander Thomson Memorial, Glasgow Institute of Architects.

52 *Building News*, 12 June 1891; *Architect*, 13 June 1890.

53 *British Architect*, 9 Sept. 1892; *Architect*, 9 Sept. 1892.

54 *British Architect*, 21 March 1890.

55 *Building News*, 26 Dec. 1890.

56 *British Architect*, 26 Dec. 1890.

57 *Building News*, 29 Nov. 1890.

58 *British Architect*, 20 Feb. 1891; *Architect*, 20 Feb.1891.

59 NAS, MW/1/194. *Architect*, 27 Oct. 1893. The sculptor of the reredos was James Young. It was paid for by Lady Maxwell of Calderwood in memory of her husband, the tenth baronet. G. Eyre-Todd, *The Book of Glasgow Cathedral* (1898), p. 443.

60 *Architect*, 10 Jan. 1890.

61 *The Bailie*, vol. XXXV, 22 Jan.1890.

62 *Ibid.*, 23 April 1890.

63 *Ibid.*, 6 Aug. 1890.

64 *British Architect*, 27 Feb. 1891.

65 *The Bailie*, vol. XXXVIII, 10 June 1891.

66 *Building News*, 10 June, 14 Aug., 4 and 11 Sept. 1891; *Architect*, 11 Sept. 1891.

67 *Building News*, 11 and 18 Dec. 1891, 8 and 22 April 1892; *Architect*, 18 Dec. 1891 and 22 April 1892; *British Architect*, 8 and 22 April, 11 June

1892; *The Bailie*, vol. XXXIX, 3 Feb. 1892. Howarth, *op. cit.*, p. 9, says that there were three schemes from Honeyman and Keppie, one classical and the other two English and Scottish Renaissance.

68 *Who's Who in Glasgow in 1909* (1909).

69 Howarth, *op. cit.*, p. 11; A. Crawford, *Charles Rennie Mackintosh* (1995), p. 18.

70 *Building News*, 29 July 1892.

71 *Ibid.*, 22 Jan. 1892; *British Architect*, 22 Jan. 1892.

72 Job Book, 1881–94. GLAHA 53059.

73 *Supra*, n. 70.

74 *Supra*, n. 71.

75 GSAA. Robertson, *op. cit.*, p. 83.

76 *Builder*, 23 April 1892.

77 *The Bailie*, vol. XLVI, 1 May 1895; D. Martin, *The Glasgow School of Painting* (1897), intro. by F. Newbery, p. 30; A. Tanner, *Helensburgh and the Glasgow School* (1972), p. 21.

78 *British Architect*, 13 Jan. 1893.

79 *Ibid.*, 17 Feb. 1893.

80 Drawings held by William Hardie Ltd., Glasgow, are dated 1879 and give the office address as 266 St. Vincent Street.

81 GSAA.

82 *British Architect*, 8 Feb. 1895. Drawings held by William Hardie Ltd. are dated from 1893 to 1896. *Academy Architecture* (1894), p. 89.

83 *Builder*, vol. LXXV, 9 July 1898, p. 25.

84 *Supra*, n.82.

85 GAC, Minute Book No.1 (1887–92), 27 Nov. 1891.

86 *Ibid.*, 15 Dec. 1891.

87 *Ibid.*, 22 April 1892.

88 *Ibid.*

89 GAC, Minute Book No. 2 (1892–99), 17 May 1892.

90 *Ibid.*, 6 July 1892.

91 *Studio*, vol. I, p. 161.

92 *The Bailie*, vol. XLII, 7 June 1893.

93 *Supra*, n. 91.

94 *Supra*, n. 92.

95 Robertson, *op. cit.*, pp. 201, 206–8. See also D. Walker, "Mackintosh on Architecture," in Robertson, *op. cit.*, pp. 166, 168.

96 GAC, List of Members.

97 GAC, Artist Candidates Nomination Book.

98 Letter to the author from Thomas Howarth.

99 Job Book, 1881–94. GLAHA 53059.

100 *Supra*, n. 95.

101 *Studio*, vol. III, pp. 71, 79.

102 *The Glasgow Style* (1984), p. 24.

103 *Evening Times*, 5 June 1893; *Glasgow Herald*, 6 June 1893.

Chapter 5
"THIS LITTLE GROUP OF GLASGOW WORKERS"

1 Prospectus: Session, 1904–5, p. 7. GSAA.

2 A Crawford, *Charles Rennie Mackintosh* (1995), p. 9.

3 G. Ramsay, *Allan Glen's School and Technical Education* (1888), pp. 7–8.

4 Glasgow School of Art: Prospectus 1893–94, p. 5. GSAA.

5 F. Newbery, "On the Training of Architectural Students," *Proceedings of the Philosophical Society of Glasgow*, vol. XIX (1887–88), pp. 176–80, 186.

6 Prospectus, 1904–5, p. 27.

7 Prospectus, 1893–94, pp. 14–15.

8 G. Scott, *Lectures on the Rise and Development of Medieval Architecture* (1879), vol. I, p. 14.

9 *Ibid.*, vol. I, p. 6.

10 *Ibid.*, vol. I, p. 209.

11 *Ibid.*, vol. I, p. 25.

12 *Ibid.*, vol. I, pp. 201–2.

13 National Gallery of Ireland, MS 2009.TX 93.

14 Prospectus, 1893–94, p. 14.

15 Prospectus, 1904–5, p. 30

16 Annual reports. GSAA.

17 *Quiz*, vol. IV, 2 Aug. 1889.

18 Annual reports. GSAA.

19 P. W. Davidson, "Memories of Mackintosh," *Charles Rennie Mackintosh Society Newsletter*, no. 22 (Summer 1979), pp. 5–6.

20 *Quiz*, vol. XXII, 19 Feb. 1892; *The Bailie*, vol. XLI, 23 Nov. 1892.

21 Prospectus, 1893–94, p. 6.

22 *Ibid.*, p. 11.

23 *Ibid.*, p. 23.

24 *The Bailie*, vol. LVII, 28 Nov. 1900.

25 GCA, F. Newbery, News Cutting Book.

26 Prospectus, 1893–4, p. 21.

27 Most of Mackintosh's sketchbooks are in the Mackintosh Collection, HAG.

28 *Quiz*, vol. XIV, 7 Oct. 1887.

29 *British Architect*, 22 Nov. 1895.

30 *Ibid.*, 8 Nov. 1895.

31 *Supra*, n. 29.

32 *Supra*, n. 30.

33 *Supra*, n. 29.

34 N. Pevsner, *North Somerset and Bristol* (1958), p. 31.

35 *Supra*, n. 30.

36 J. Stewart to T. Howarth, 23 Feb. 1946. University of Toronto, Special Collections, B89–0014/001. J. Gaff Gillespie (1870–1926) had been a student at Glasgow School of Art where he shared the Glasgow Institute of Architects prize with Mackintosh in 1889. He joined the Salmon practice in 1891. R. O'Donnell, *James Salmon, 1873–1924* (2003), p. 36.

37 *The Bailie*, vol. XXXIII, 24 Oct. 1888.

38 E. A. Taylor, "A Neglected Genius, Charles Rennie Mackintosh," *The Studio*, vol. CV (1933), pp. 350–51.

39 T. Howarth, *Charles Rennie Mackintosh and the Modern Movement* (1952), p. 58.

40 *The Bailie*, no. 2476, 31 March 1920.

41 *Ex inf.* Mr. Chris Allan.

42 *Supra*, n.36.

43 *Ex inf.* Mr. Robin Hume.

44 G. R. Stewart, *Bret Harte, Argonaut and Exile* (1931), pp. 268, 284.

45 P. Morrow, *Bret Harte* (1972), p. 11.

46 B. Harte, *The Complete Works*, vol. 2 (1881), pp. 162–63.

47 *Ibid.*, p. 104.

48 D. MacGibbon and T. Ross, *The Castellated and Domestic Architecture of Scotland*, vol. III (1889), p. 498.

49 *Ibid.*, p. 504.

50 National Gallery of Ireland, MS 2010. TX.

51 Taylor, *op. cit.*, pp. 349–50.

52 *Studio*, vol. III (1894), pp. 38–39.

53 E. Grogan, *Beginnings: Charles Rennie Mackintosh's Early Sketches* (2002), pp. 142–43.

54 R. Billcliffe, *Charles Rennie Mackintosh. The Complete Furniture, Furniture Drawings and Interior Designs* (1980), pp. 32, 35, says that Jessie Keppie was deserted by Mackintosh in 1896. T. Neat, *Part Seen, Part Imagined* (1994), pp. 17, 88, says that Mackintosh and Jessie Keppie were formally engaged by 1892, that the engagement was terminated in 1894, and that the jewel casket was an offer of propitiation.

55 Howarth, *op. cit.*, p. 25.

56 GSAA.

57 W. Moyes to T. Howarth, n.d. "He had no hobby so far as I know and limped when he walked." H. Swaisland to T. Howarth, 25 Jan. 1946. "He was a very distinguished looking gentleman in spite of his club foot and his defective eye." University of Toronto, Special Collections, B96–0028/017 (01) and (19).

58 Howarth, *op. cit.*, p. 19.

59 *Ibid.*, p. 20.

60 H. Muthesius, *The English House* (1979), p. 51.

61 G. White, "Some Glasgow Designers and their Work," *The Studio*, vol. XI (1897), p. 227.

62 *The Bailie*, vol. XLIII, 28 Feb. 1894; vol. XLVII, 23 Sept. 1896. *The Glasgow Boys*. Part two. The History of the Group and Illustrations (1968), p. 17.

63 Howarth, *op. cit.*, p. 40.

64 White, *op. cit.*, p. 87.

65 *The Glasgow Style* (1984), p. 43.

66 GSAA, Governors' Minutes, 30 Jan. 1893; *The Glasgow Style*, pp. 9–10.

67 Victoria and Albert Museum, National Art Library, AAD/1/74–1980.

68 AAD/1/43–1980.

69 *Quiz*, vol. XIX, 30 May 1890.

70 *The Bailie*, vol. XXV, 15 Jan. 1890.

71 *The Glasgow Style*, p. 6.

72 *Quiz*, vol. XIX, 7 March 1890.

73 AAD/1/75–1980.

74 AAD/1/76–1980.

75 AAD/1/82–1980.

76 AAD/1/87—1980.

77 AAD/1/86—1980.

78 *Studio*, vol. IX (1896), pp. 203—4.

79 "Die Glasgower Kunstbewegung: Charles R. Mackintosh und Margaret Macdonald Mackintosh," *Dekorative Kunst*, vol. 9 (1902), p. 201.

80 T. Morris, "Concerning the work of Margaret Macdonald, Frances Macdonald, Charles Mackintosh and Herbert McNair—An Appreciation," Kelvingrove Art Gallery and Museum, E46—5x.

81 H. Muthesius, *The English House* (1979), p. 51.

82 AAD/1/806—1980.

83 *Quiz*, vol. XXVIII, 11 April 1895.

84 *Glasgow Herald*, 8 April 1895; K. Moon, *George Walton, Designer and Architect* (1993), pp. 38—39. The *Catalogue of the Arts and Crafts Exhibition* lists all the exhibitors in two classes—amateur and professional—and indicates the prices of those works for sale. *Ex inf.* Pamela Robertson.

85 *Quiz*, vol. XXXII, 10 Dec. 1896.

86 J. S. Gibson, "Artistic Houses," *Studio*, vol. I (1893), p. 215.

87 *Ibid.*, vol. IV (1894), p. 24.

88 G. White, "Some Glasgow Designers and their Work" (Part II), *Ibid.*, vol. XI (1897), pp. 227—29.

89 H. P. Putnam, "Hasbrouck and the Rose." *Ex inf.* M. Sloman.

90 White, *op. cit.*, p. 227.

91 *Ibid.*, p. 229.

92 GSAA.

93 Neat, *op. cit.*, appendix 1.

94 A. Raeburn, "Round the Studios, The Magazine," 1893. GSAA.

95 Morris, *op. cit.*

96 C. R. Mackintosh, "Cabbages in an Orchard, The Magazine," 1894. GSAA.

97 *Ibid.*, 1896.

98 *The Bailie*, vol. XLV, 14 Nov. 1894.

99 Morris, *op. cit.*

100 White, *op. cit.*, p. 228.

101 *Quiz*, vol. XXXVI, 11 April 1894; vol. XXXIX, 13 June 1895.

102 *The Bailie*, vol. XLI, 15 March 1897.

103 *Ibid.*, vol. XLV, 16 Jan. 1895.

104 Newbery, *op. cit.* E. Bird, "Ghouls and Gas Pipes: Public Reaction to Early Work of 'The Four,' " *Scottish Art Review*, vol. XIV, no. 4 (1975), p. 16.

105 White, *op. cit.*, pp. 98—9.

106 Morris, *op. cit.*

107 *Glasgow Herald*, 28 June 1898; GLAHA 52931. Also in 1898 Margaret Macdonald was elected a member of the Royal Scottish Society of Painters in Water-Colours. She was one of two successful candidates, out of fourteen; the other was Stott of Oldham. *The Bailie*, vol. LI, 9 March 1898.

108 Morris, *op. cit.*

109 Muthesius, *op. cit.*

Chapter 6
"ART IS THE FLOWER—
LIFE IS THE GREEN LEAF"

1 Mackintosh Collection, HAG.

2 *Architect*, vol. 47, 15 April 1892.

3 A. Moffat, *Remembering Charles Rennie Mackintosh* (1989), p. 33.

4 P. Robertson (ed.), *Charles Rennie Mackintosh. The Architectural Papers* (1990).

5 *Ibid.*, p. 201.

6 *Journal of Proceedings of the RIBA, vol.* VIII, N.S. 11 Feb. and 30 June 1892.

7 Robertson, *op. cit.*, p. 183.

8 *Ibid.*

9 *Ibid.*, p. 181.

10 *Ibid.*, p. 182.

11 *Ibid.*, p. 187.

12 *Supra*, n.9.

13 *Ibid.*, p. 189.

14 *Ibid.*, p. 196.

15 *Ibid.*

16 *Ibid.*, p. 201.

17 *Ibid.*, p. 202.

18 *Ibid.*, p. 206.

19 *Ibid.*, p. 207.

20 G. Scott, *Lectures on the Rise and Development of Medieval Architecture* (1879), vol. I, p. 356.

21 G. Scott, *Remarks on Domestic and Secular Architecture* (1858), p. 46.

22 *Ibid.*, p. 109.

23 Robertson, *op. cit.*, p. 186.

24 *Ibid.*, p. 51.

25 *Ibid.*, pp. 49—50.

26 *Ibid.*, p. 52.

27 Scott, *op. cit.*, p. 14.

28 Robertson, *op. cit.*, p. 63.

29 *Ibid.*, p. 141.

30 *Ibid.*, p. 145.

31 *Ibid.*, pp. 141—42.

32 *Ibid.*, p. 143.

33 *Ibid.*, p. 207.

34 *Ibid.*, pp. 204—5.

35 *Ibid.*, p. 206.

36 *Ibid.*, p. 224.

37 The surviving drawings for the Conservative Club, Helensburgh, dated 1894, show that the ornamental detail was worked up later.

38 *Supra*, n. 32.

39 *The Bailie*, vol. XIL, 9 Dec. 1896.

40 J. H. Muir, *Glasgow in 1901* (2001), p. 28.

41 *The Bailie*, vol. XXXVI, 16 April 1890.

42 *Building News*, 29 Nov. 1889.

43 Muir, *op. cit.*, pp. 21, 23—24.

44 *The Bailie*, vol. XLVI, 7 Aug. 1895.

45 J. Pagan, *Glasgow, Past and Present, vol.* I (1851), p. 20.

46 *Glasgow Evening News*, 20 June 1893; *Academy Architecture*, 1894, p. 79.

47 *Quiz*, vol. XXIV, 13 Oct. 1892.

48 *Supra*, n. 46.

49 Job Book, 1891—94. GLAHA 53060.

50 *The Bailie*, vol. XIL, 25 Nov. 1896.

51 *Ibid.*, 21 Oct. 1896.

52 *The British Architect*, 5 July 1895; *Academy Architecture*, 1894, p. 79.

53 Job Books, 1881—94 and 1891—4. GLAHA 53059 and 53060.

54 Donald Mackay Stoddart (1875—1930) was articled to Honeyman and Keppie from 1892—97 when he attended the Glasgow School of Art. From 1900 he worked for Campbell, Douglas and Paterson. When he was proposed for a LRIBA in 1910 one of his sponsors was John Keppie. *Directory of British Architects, 1834—1914* (2001), vol. 2, p. 709.

55 GUA, DC 233/2/22/18 and 19.

56 GUA, DC 233/2/1/1/8.

57 GUA, DC 233/2/6/1/3. Job Book, 1874—82 records, "H. W. Bell, Esq. House. Great Western Road, 22 March 1875. [£]4862:1:5." GLAHA 53058.

58 *Supra*, n. 56.

59 *Supra*, n. 57.

60 GUA, DC 233/2/1/1/7.

61 *Quiz*, vol. XXIV, 13 Oct., 10 Nov., and 1 Dec. 1892.

62 *Supra*, n. 57.

63 GUA, DC 233/2/20/1/3; *Academy Architecture*, 1895, pp. 70, 148.

64 *Ibid.*

65 *Ibid.*

66 Professor Thomas Bryce, 28 April 1933. GLAHA 52374.

67 Westbourne Free Church, *Calendar and Directory* (1894), pp. 20—23.

68 GCA/CH3/1412/18.

69 G. E. Philip, *Free St. Matthew's Church*, Glasgow (1898), p. 155.

70 *Ibid.*, pp. 125—26.

71 *Ibid.*, p. 156.

72 GCA/CH3/971/17.

73 C. Marriott, *Modern English Architecture* (1924), p. 93.

74 C. Eastlake, *A History of the Gothic Revival* (1872), p. 372.

75 Marriott, *op. cit.*, p. 96.

76 *Ibid.*, p. 102.

77 J. Newman and N. Pevsner, *Dorset* (1993), pp. 20, 72.

78 C. R. Mackintosh, "Wareham and Its Churches," *British Architect*, 8 Nov. 1895, pp. 326, 332—33.

79 *Glasgow Herald*, 9 Sept. 1899. See GLAHA 53069—53074.

80 W. Lethaby, *Architecture, Nature and Magic* (1956), p. 144.

81 *Transactions of the Glasgow Ecclesiological Society* (1895), pp. 7, 10.

82 *Academy Architecture*, 1898, p. 65.

83 *Ibid.*, 1901, p. 78. Job Book, 1881—94. GLAHA 53059.

84 Minute of 29 Sept. 1897. Brechin Cathedral archive.

85 "Proposed Restoration of Brechin Cathedral." BCA.

86 "Brechin Cathedral. Restoration of and Additions to. Digger and Mason Work." BCA.

87 John Honeyman to Alexander Philip, 12 Jan. 1899. BCA.

88 Do. to do., 17 July 1900. BCA.

89 Macfarlane and Erskine, Lithographers, Engravers and General Printers, 14 and 19 St. James Square, Edinburgh, 26 Jan. 1898. BCA. *Academy Architecture*, 1898, p. 52. In March 1898 Alexander McGibbon was paid ten guineas for "Brechin Cath. and Edinburgh Church perspectives." Cash Book, 1889–1917. GLAHA 53079.

90 J. Honeyman, Minewood, Bridge of Allan, 13 Feb. 1899. BCA.

91 J. Honeyman to A. Philip, 140 Bath St., Glasgow, 23 Jan. 1902. BCA.

Thomas Taylor (1880–1946) was apprenticed to Honeyman and Keppie and studied at the Glasgow School of Art from 1897 to 1902. An assistant with James Miller from 1904–5 and afterward with Rowand Anderson, he set up in practice with D. B. Hutton from 1906. GSAA, Alphabetical Register, 1892–93; *Directory of British Architects, 1834–1914*, vol. 2, p. 774.

92 J. Honeyman to A. Philip, 3 Jan. 1902. BCA.

93 Honeyman and Keppie, 17 Dec. 1901, and J. Honeyman to A. Philip, 12 Feb. 1902. BCA. The statues were to be returned for adjustments "to Mr. Kellock Brown 152A Renfrew St. Glasgow." Job Book, 1894–1904. GLAHA 53061.

94 "New Board Schools in Glasgow," *Builder*, vol. XXXIII, 27 March 1875, p. 274.

95 GCA, D-ED 1/1/3/9; *Academy Architecture*, 1896, pp. 80, 85.

96 GCA, D-ED 1/1/8/1.

97 GCA, D-ED 1/1/12.

98 *Builders' Journal and Architectural Engineer*, 28 Nov. 1906, p. 268, and 26 Dec. 1906, p. 323. G. Stamp, "School Lessons," *Architects' Journal*, vol. 187, no. 14, April 1988, pp. 42–53.

99 RIBA Fellowship Paper.

100 HAG. R. Billcliffe, *Architectural Sketches and Flower Drawings by Charles Rennie Mackintosh* (1977), pp. 10, 59, 64.

101 *Academy Architecture*, 1897, p. 85.

102 N. Pevsner, *Pioneers of Modern Design* (1960), p. 214.

103 GCA, D-ED 1/1/12/20.

104 GCA, D-ED 1/1/12/21.

105 GCA, D-ED 1/1/12/22. See also D-ED 1/1/1/8, Education Committee Minutes, 1904–5, pp. 217–18, 222, 233. In D-ED 1/1/12/23 there is a reference on 27 December 1906 "to the conversation which the Board's Master of Works had with your Mr. Moyes today."

William Moyes entered the Glasgow School of Art in 1897 where he was a student until 1901. He was in the office of Honeyman and Keppie for ten years but left Glasgow in 1907 for the New Hebrides and then settled in Australia. Moyes wrote to Howarth on 22 July 1947, "Regarding perspective of Scotland Street Public School I may have set up the perspective in pencil for Mr. Mackintosh but he would have completed it in ink and added the master touches." University of Toronto, Special Collections, B96–0028/017 (01) and (14).

106 L. Sullivan, *Kindergarten Chats and Other Writings* (1979), p. 191.

107 Eastlake, *op. cit.*, p. 293.

108 Lethaby, *op. cit.*, p. 20.

109 *Ibid.*, p. 87.

Chapter 7
A PLAIN BUILDING

1 GSA, Governors' Minutes, vol. 2 (1882–87), 25 October 1882.

2 *Ibid.*, 30 Nov. 1882.

3 *Ibid.*, 18 Dec. 1882.

4 *Ibid.*, 2 March 1885.

5 *Ibid.*, 5 and 20 March 1885.

6 *Ibid.*, 24 April 1885.

7 *Ibid.*, 11 and 19 May 1885. For an account of Newbery's time at the Glasgow School of Art see G. Rawson, *Fra H. Newbery, Artist and Art Educationist, 1855–1946* (1996).

8 *Ibid.*, 16 Oct. 1885.

9 *Ibid.*, 14 April 1882.

10 F. Niven, *Justice of the Peace* (1914), p. 346.

11 *Studio*, vol. XIX (1900), p. 51.

12 GSA, Governors' Minutes, *vol. 4*, 6 June 1895.

13 *Ibid.*, vol. 2, 23 Oct. 1885.

14 *Ibid.*, 22 Dec. 1885.

15 *Ibid.*, *vol. 3*, 26 Jan. 1888 and 5 Feb. 1889. Morris was an examiner at the South Kensington Schools for many years after 1877. J. W. Mackail, *The Life of William Morris* (1995), vol. 1, p. 374.

16 W. Morris, 14 Jan. and 6 Feb.1889. GSAA.

17 *Ibid.*, 22 Sept. 1890.

18 *Ibid.*, 11 May 1887.

19 *Ibid.*, 27 Oct. 1888 and 30 Nov. 1891.

20 "Report of Deputation," *Procs. of the Philosophical Society of Glasgow*, March 1893, p. 3.

21 *Ibid.*, p. 6.

22 *Ibid.*, pp. 9–10.

23 Governors' Minutes, vol. 3, 16 March and 4 April 1894.

24 *Ibid.*, 28 Jan. 1895. *Glasgow Herald*, 7 March 1895.

25 *Ibid.*, vol. 4, 6 Sept. 1895.

26 *Ibid.*, 16 March 1896

27 Building Committee Minute Book, 1896–99, 28 May 1896.

28 GSAA. H. Ferguson, *Glasgow School of Art, the History* (1995), pp. 66–73, reproduces the surviving set of competition drawings.

29 Building Committee Minute Book, 1896–9, 1 June 1896.

30 Governors' Minutes, vol. 4, 12 Aug. 1896.

31 *Ibid.*, 27 Aug. 1896.

32 Building Committee Minute Book, 1896–99, 17 Dec. 1896.

33 Governors' Minutes, vol. 4, 13 Jan. 1897.

34 Building Committee Minute Book, 1896–99, 27 Jan. 1897.

35 Governors' Minutes, vol. 4, 11 Oct. 1897.

36 *Ibid.*, 2 May 1898.

37 *Ibid.*, December 1899.

38 *Scotia*, 6 Jan. 1900.

39 *Glasgow Herald*, 26 May 1898.

40 Governors' Minutes, vol. 4, 12 May 1899.

41 *Ibid.*, 30 April 1900.

42 Governors' Minutes, vol. 5, 18 Sept. 1901 and 8 Jan. 1902.

43 Box A/12, GSAA.

44 *The Herald*, 3 April 1995.

45 J. Thomson, "Report on Ventilation and Heating of Bute Hall, 21 December 1878," *A Collection of Glasgow Tracts*, vol. XCV (n.d.).

46 Governors' Minutes, vol. 5, 11 Oct. 1897.

47 *Studio*, vol. XIX (1900), pp. 51–56.

48 H. Muthesius, "Die Glasgower Kunstbewegung: Charles R. Mackintosh und Margaret Macdonald Mackintosh," *Dekorative Kunst*, vol. IX (108), p. 208.

49 *Ibid.*, p. 216.

50 Governors' Minutes, vol. 5, 20 Nov. 1903.

51 *Ibid.*, 15 March 1904.

52 *Ibid.*, 3 June 1906.

53 *Ibid.*, 25 Feb 1907.

54 Building Committee Minute Book, 1906–7, 22 Jan. 1907.

55 *Ibid.*, 7 March 1907.

56 Letter Book, 1907–10, 13 and 15 March 1907.

57 *Ibid.*, 9 Oct. 1907.

58 Building Committee Minute Book, 1906–7, 7 Feb.1908.

59 Letter Book, 1907–10, 5 Feb. 1908.

60 Building Committee Minute Book, 1906–7, 26 Feb. 1908.

61 *Ibid.*, 17 March 1908.

62 Letter Book, 1907–10, 30 April 1908.

63 *Ibid.*, 9 Nov. 1908.

64 J. Dunlop to W. Davidson, 20 April 1933. GLAHA 52438.

65 Building Committee Minute Book, 1908–10, 26 Jan. 1909.

66 Letter Book, 1907–10, 2 Feb.1909.

67 Building Committee Minute Book, 1908–10, 24 Sept. and 21 Oct. 1909.

68 Letter Book, 1907–10, 7 March 1910.

69 B8/7, GSAA.

70 Building Committee Minute Book, 1908–10, 6 Oct.1910.

71 C. Voysey, "The English Home," *The British Architect*, 27 Jan. 1911, p. 60.

72 W. Crane, *The Bases of Design* (1898), p. vii.

73 W. R. Lethaby, *Architecture, Nature and Magic* (1956), p. 109.

74 J. Macaulay, "Elizabethan Architecture," *Charles Rennie Mackintosh. The Architectural Papers* (P. Robertson, ed.) (1990), p. 134.

75 *RIBA Journal*, vol. VIII, N.S., 30 June 1892.

76 Lethaby, *op. cit.*, p. 16.

77 *Ibid.*, pp. 106, 119.

78 W. R. Lethaby, *Architecture, Mysticism and Myth* (1974), p. 39.

79 *Ibid.*, pp. 34–35.

80 G. White, "Some Glasgow Designers and Their Work," *Studio*, vol. XI, (1897), pp. 87–88, 91.

81 *Ibid.*, pp. 92, 98, 230, 234.

82 *The Norse Myths* (intro. K. C. Holland) (1980), p. 123.

83 J. G. Frazer, *The Golden Bough* (1890), vol. I, p. 58.

84 Crane, *op. cit.*, p. 248. The interpretation of the library of the Glasgow School of Art as a three-dimensional Tree of Knowledge was first put forward by the author in *Glasgow School of Art* (1993). See also "Symbolism in the Glasgow School of Art," *Mac Journal*, vol. 2 (1995), pp. 19–27.

85 J. Summerson, *The Turn of the Century: Architecture in Britain around 1900* (1976), p. 24; J. Summerson, *The Unromantic Castle* (1990), pp. 240–41.

86 *The Glasgow Boys: Part One: The Artists and their Work* (1968), p. 52.

87 N. Pevsner, *Pioneers of the Modern Movement* (1936), pp. 158, 160, 165.

88 *Ibid.*, p. 160.

89 Crane, *op. cit.*, p. 249.

90 W. R. Lethaby, *Architecture, Nature and Magic*, p. 147.

91 *Ibid.*, p. 63.

Chapter 8
THE SCOTTISH SECESSIONIST

1 GCA, TD 1309/A/111.

2 L. Sullivan, *Kindergarten Chats and Other Writings* (1979), p. 27.

3 *Ibid.*, p. 52.

4 *Ibid.*, p. 207.

5 *Ibid.*, p. 206.

6 *Ibid.*, p. 121.

7 *British Architect*, 15 Nov. 1895. The other competing firms were Burnet, Son and Campbell, and Thompson and Sandilands, who were given the commission. *Academy Architecture*, 1895, p. 56. Honeyman and Keppie received a premium of £50. Cash Book, 1889–1917. GLAHA 53079.

8 J. Belcher and M. Macartney, *Later Renaissance Architecture* (1901), vol. I, p. 5.

9 *Who's Who in Glasgow in 1909* (1909), p. 171.

10 *Quiz*, vol. XVII, 8 March 1889.

11 *The Bailie*, vol. LVIII, 1 May and 14 Aug. 1901.

12 *Ibid.*

13 Job Book, 1894–1902. GLAHA 53061.

14 W. Buchanan, *The Art of the Photographer. J. Craig Annan, 1864–1946* (1992), pp. 12–16, 25. *The Bailie*, vol. LXIV, 31 Aug. 1904.

15 D. C. L. Dewar, *History of the Glasgow Society of Lady Artists' Club* (1950), p. 25.

16 Cash Book, 1889–1917. GLAHA 53079

17 *The Bailie*, vol. XLIV, 21 Sept. 1892. The architect was W. Boston.

18 K. Moon, *George Walton, Designer and Architect* (1993), pp. 30–31.

19 *Supra*, n.11.

20 Job Book, 1902–1908. GLAHA 53062. The statues cost £100 and each corbel was £3. The painter work was by George Walton and Co. Ltd. *Builders' Journal and Architectural Engineer*, 28 Nov.1900, p. 263.

21 *Glasgow Herald*, 30 Jan. 1959.

22 G. Gordon, "The Morphological Development of Scottish Cities from Georgian to Modern Times," *The Built Form of Western Cities* (ed.) T. R. Slater) (1985), p. 221.

23 R. O'Donnell, *James Salmon, 1873–1924* (2003), pp. 75–77, 113–5.

24 *The Bailie*, vol. XLI, 28 Sept. 1892; *Academy Architecture*, 1893, p. 11.

25 R. Rodger, "Employment, Wages and Poverty in the Scottish Cities, 1841–1914," *Perspectives of the Scottish City* (ed. G. Gordon) (1985), p. 38.

26 *Supra*, n.7.

27 Glasgow International Exhibition, 1901. Minutes, Mitchell Library.

28 GSAA.

29 P. and J. Kinchin, *Glasgow's Great Exhibitions* (1988), p. 60.

30 *Studio*, vol. 23 (1901), pp. 45, 48.

31 *Building News*, 13 and 27 Sept. and 1 Nov. 1901.

32 *Builder*, 20 July 1902.

33 *British Architect*, 13 March 1903, p. 186.

34 T. Howarth, *Charles Rennie Mackintosh and the Modern Movement* (1952), pp. 184–87.

35 GSAA.

36 H. Muthesius, *The English House* (1979), p. 51.

37 *Dekorative Kunst*, vol. 1 (1898), p. 50.

38 *Ibid.*, vol. 3 (1898), p. 48.

39 *Ibid.*, vol. 9 (1902), p. 196.

40 H. Muthesius, *Die Englische Baukunst der Gegenwart* (1900), pp. 60–61.

41 J. D. Kornwolf, *M. H. Baillie Scott and the Arts and Crafts Movement* (1972), pp. 216–22.

42 R. J. Clark, "Olbrich and Mackintosh," *Mackintosh and His Contemporaries in Europe and America* (ed. p. Nuttgens) (1985), p. 103.

43 *American Architect and Building News*, vol. LXXXV (24 Sept. 1904), pp. 103–4.

44 *Meister Der Innen Kunst. Charles Rennie Mackintosh*, a copy presented to the Glasgow School of Art by C. R. Mackintosh, 14 Oct. 1908. GSAA.

45 *Dekorative Kunst*, vol. 7 (1901), p. 171.

46 *Ibid.*; p. Vergo, *Vienna 1900* (1983), pp. 23–32, 40–45.

47 *Quiz*, vol. XXVII, 2 Aug. 1894.

48 A. Crawford, *C. R. Ashbee, Architect, Designer and Romantic Socialist* (1985), p. 411.

49 E. Sekler, "Mackintosh and Vienna," *The Anti-Rationalists* (eds. J. M. Richards and N. Pevsner) (1973) p. 138; P. Vergo, "Fritz Waerndorfer and Josef Hoffmann," *Burlington Magazine*, no. 964 (July 1983), p. 403; E. Sekler, *Josef Hoffmann, The Architectural Work* (1985), pp. 38–39; R. Billcliffe and P. Vergo, "Charles Rennie Mackintosh and the Austrian Art Revival," *Burlington Magazine*, no. 896 (Nov. 1999), pp. 739–45; R. Franz, "A Tale of Two Cities," *Charles Rennie Mackintosh Society Journal*, no. 85 (Winter 2003), pp. 5–8.

50 University of Toronto, Special Collections, B96-0028/017 (15). Also A. S. Levetus, "Scottish Artists in Vienna," *Glasgow Herald*, 29 May 1909.

51 A. Moffat, *Remembering Charles Rennie Mackintosh* (1989), p. 67.

52 *Dekorative Kunst*, vol. 7 (1901), pp. 181–82.

53 *Ibid.*, vol. 4 (1899), pp. 78–79

54 Sekler, "Mackintosh and Vienna," p. 136.

55 *Ibid.*

56 *Dekorative Kunst*, vol. 9 (1902), p. 204.

57 *Studio*, vol. 26 (1902), p. 46.

58 AAD/1/98—1980, National Art Library, Victoria and Albert Museum.

59 GSAA. See *Torino 1902. Le Arti Decorative Internazionali del Nuovo Secolo.*

60 *Studio*, vol. 26 (1902), p. 95.

61 Turin Exhibition, 1902, vol. I. GSAA.

62 *Ibid.*, items xiv and xv.

63 *Ibid.*, item xi.

64 *Ibid.* C. G. Generi to F. Newbery, 15 May 1902.

65 *Studio*, vol. 26 (1902), p. 93.

66 *Supra*, n. 61.

67 *Ibid.*

68 *Studio*, vol. 26 (1902), p. 97.

69 Vergo, *op. cit.*, p. 404.

70 Clark, *op. cit.*, p. 106.

71 *Supra*, n.66.

72 *Deutsche Kunst und Dekoration*, vol. 10 (Aug. 1902), p. 578.

73 M. N. Sturrock, Eastgate, Corfe Castle, Dorset, to T. Howarth, 30 June [1944]. University of Toronto, Special Collections, B96–0028/017 (22). See also Moffat, *op. cit.*, p. 64.

74 F. Newbery to "Signor" Generi, 20 May 1902. Turin Exhibition, 1902, vol. I.

75 *Ibid.* Generi to Newbery, 16 May 1902.

76 *Supra*, n.59.

77 P. Robertson, "Margaret Macdonald Mackintosh: The Seven Princesses," *Ein Moderner Nachmittag* (2000), p. 50.

78 F. Newbery, "News Cutting Book," Mitchell Library, Glasgow.

79 *Studio*, vol. 26 (1902), p. 94.

80 *Ibid.*, pp. 96–97.

81 *Deutsche Kunst und Dekoration*, vol. 10 (Aug. 1902), pp. 570, 581–82.

82 Turin Exhibition, 1902, vol. I, item vii.

83 *Dekorative Kunst*, vol. 10 (1902), pp. 400–6.

84 Turin Exhibition, 1902, vol. I, item xi.

85 *Ibid.*, item vii. Generi to Newbery, 5 June, 7 Aug., and 25 Oct. 1902.

86 *Ibid.*, items ix and i.

87 *Ibid.*, item vii.

88 *Ibid.*, items xii and iv. C. R. Mackintosh to J. Groundwater, secretary of the Glasgow School of Art, 19 Jan. 1903.

89 *Ibid.*, item vii. Generi to Newbery, 20 Sept. 1902.

90 *Studio*, vol. 31 (1904), p. 56; R. Billcliffe, *Charles Rennie Mackintosh. The Complete Furniture, Furniture Drawings and Interior Designs* (1980), pp. 151–52.

91 *Ibid.*, pp. 178–80.

92 W. Brumfield, "The Decorative Arts in Russian Architecture: 1900–1907," *Journal of Decorative and Propaganda Arts* (Summer 1987), pp. 20–22; C. Cooke, "Shekhtel in Kelvingrove and Mackintosh on the Petrovka," *Scottish Slavonic Review* (Spring 1988), pp. 196–99. According to D. Chapman-Huston, a Mackintosh friend, it was the Grand Duke Serge of Russia who, having visited the Turin exhibition, invited Mackintosh to exhibit in Moscow. The Grand Duke was the husband of the Grand Duchess Elizabeth. *Artwork* (1930), p. 29.

93 Clark, *op. cit.*, pp. 107 and 109.

94 Sekler, *op. cit.*, p. 141.

95 *Studio*, vol. 23 (1901), p. 46.

96 C. Cooke, "Fedor Shekhtel," *The Twilight of the Tsars. Russian Art at the Turn of the Century* (1991), pp. 51–53.

97 Levetus, *op. cit.*; Vergo, *op. cit.*, p. 403.

98 Sekler, *op. cit.*, p. 139.

99 Levetus, *op. cit.*; *Studio*, vol. 57 (1912), pp. 71–72; Billcliffe and Vergo, *op. cit.*, p. 743.

100 Sekler, *op. cit.*, p. 140. See also Toronto University, Special Collections, B96–0028/017 (15).

101 E. Muthesius and J. Posener, *Hermann Muthesius, 1861–1927* (1979), p. 31.

102 Generi to Newbery, 8 Sept. and 5 Oct. 1902. Turin Exhibition, 1902, vol. I.

103 *The Bailic*, vol. LXI, 28 Jan. 1903.

104 G. Rawson, *Fra H. Newbery, Artist and Art Educationist* (1996), p. 12.

105 Vergo, *Vienna 1900*, p. 44.

106 Sekler, *ibid.*; Franz, *op. cit.*, pp. 6–7.

107 *Ibid.*

108 *Studio*, vol. 21 (1901), p. 114.

109 Billcliffe and Vergo, *op. cit.*, p. 740.

110 Howarth, *op. cit.*, p. 280.

111 E. Grogan, "Charles Rennie Mackintosh's Antwerp Sketches," *Charles Rennie Mackintosh Society Journal*, no. 85 (Winter 2003), p. 14.

112 Billcliffe and Vergo, *op. cit.*, p. 744.

113 Vergo, "Fritz Waerndorfer and Josef Hoffmann," p. 408.

114 Sekler, *op. cit.*, p. 141.

Chapter 9
"A BENEFICIENT REVOLUTION"

1 G. White, "Some Glasgow Designers and Their Work (Part I)," *The Studio*, vol. XI (1897), pp. 89–92.

2 *The Bailie*, vol. XXXV, 2 Oct. 1889.

3 J. J. Waddell, "Some Recent Glasgow Tea-Rooms," *Builders' Journal and Architectural Record*, 15 April 1903. See also p. Robertson, "Catherine Cranston," *Journal of the Decorative Arts Society*, vol. 10 (1985), pp. 10–17.

4 *The Bailie*, vol. XLVII, 19 Aug. 1896.

5 *Supra*, n. 2.

6 *Quiz*, vol. XIII, 11 March 1887.

7 *Supra*, n.2.

8 *The Bailie*, vol. XXXIV, 9 Oct. 1889.

9 Cash Book, 1889–1917. GLAHA 53079.

10 *The Bailie*, vol. XLV, 1 May 1895.

11 *Quiz*, vol. XVII, 10 May 1889.

12 *The Bailie*, vol. LI, 17 Nov.1897.

13 *Supra*, n. 11.

14 *The Bailie*, vol. XLVIII, 19 Aug. 1896.

15 *Quiz*, vol. XXVIII, 19 Aug.1896.

16 *Ibid.*, vol. II, 7 Oct. 1881.

17 *The Bailie*, vol. XLIII, 21 Dec. 1893.

18 *Quiz*, vol. XXV, 22 June 1893. H. D. Walton (1862–1919) trained in Glasgow and London where latterly, 1886–87, he was an assistant to William Young, then working on the Glasgow City Chambers, after which he set up his own practice in Glasgow. *Directory of British Architects, 1834–1914*, vol. 2 (2001), p. 909.

19 *Quiz*, vol. XXIV, 15 Dec. 1892.

20 *The Bailie*, vol. XLI, 21 Dec. 1892.

21 *Supra*, n. 3.

22 *Quiz*, vol. X, 13 Nov. 1885.

23 *Ibid.*, vol. XII, 21 Jan. 1887.

24 *The Bailie*, vol. LI, 20 Oct. 1897.

25 *Quiz*, vol. XXVIII, 15 Nov. 1894.

26 *The Bailie*, vol. LXXVIII, 26 July 1911.

27 J. J. Bell, *I Remember* (1932), p. 34.

28 *Post Office Directory*.

29 *The Bailie*, vol. XXXII, 22 Aug.1882.

30 *Quiz*, vol. XVI, 18 Jan. 1889.

31 D. Mays, "A Profile of George Washington Browne," *Architectural Heritage*, vol. III (1992), pp. 56–57.

32 *The Royal Scottish Academy Exhibitions, 1826–1900* (ed. C. B. Laperriere), vol. I, (1991), p. 211.

33 *Academy Architecture*, 1896, p. 68 and (1897, Pt. I), p. 72; *The British Architect*, 28 Feb. 1896, p. 148; *Builder*, vol. LXXV (9 July 1898), pp. 23–9; Waddell, *op. cit.*

34 White, *op. cit.*, p. 94.

35 J. Taylor, "Modern Decorative Art at Glasgow. Some Notes on Miss Cranston's Argyle Street Tea House," *Studio*, vol. 39 (1907), p. 33.

36 White, *op. cit.*, p. 99.

37 *Scottish Art Review*, vol. I (1889), p. 304.

38 *Quiz*, vol. XVII (5 July 1889).

39 D. Martin, *The Glasgow School of Painting* (intro. by F. H. Newbery) (1897), pp. xi, xii.

40 *The Bailie*, vol. LI, 26 Jan. 1898.

41 P. M. Chalmers, "Art in Our Society," *Philosophical Society of Glasgow* (1896), p. 25.

42 White, *op. cit.*, p. 88.

43 *Ibid.*, p. 87.

44 K. A. Morrison, *English Retail Shops and Shopping* (2003), p. 140.

45 White, *op. cit.*, p. 95.

46 *Ibid.*, p. 92.

47 M. H. Baillie Scott, "The Decoration of the Suburban House," *Studio*, vol. V (1895), p. 18.

48 *The Bailie*, vol. L, 5 May 1897.

49 W. R. Lethaby, *Architecture, Mysticism and Myth* (1974), introduction.

50 K. Crossley-Holland, *The Norse Myths* (1980), p. xxiii.

51 J. G. Frazer, *The Golden Bough* (1890), vol. I, p. 82.

52 L. Guillaume and J. de Meun, *The Romance of the Rose* (1994), pp. 3, 19, 70.

53 White, *op. cit.*, p. 95.

54 W. Crane, "Notes on Gesso Work," *Studio*, vol. I (1893), p. 45.

55 *Ibid.*, p. 53.

56 P. Robertson, *Ein Moderner Nachmittag* (2000), p. 46.

57 W. S. Moyes to T. Howarth, n.d. University of Toronto, Special Collections, B96–0028/017 (14). See also T. Neat and G. McDermott, *Closing the Circle* (2002), p. 101.

58 *Dekorative Kunst*, vol. 7 (1901), p. 180.

59 C. Percy and J. Ridley (eds.), *The Letters of Edwin Lutyens to His Wife Lady Emily* (1985), pp. 49–50, 56–57.

60 *Quiz*, vol. XXXIV, 1 July 1897.

61 "Ein Mackintosh Tee-Haus in Glasgow," *Dekorative Kunst*, vol. XIII (1905), p. 259.

62 Job Book, 1902–8. GLAHA 53062.

63 *The Bailie*, vol. LXIII, 4 Nov. 1903.

64 A. S. Levetus, "Glasgow Artists in Vienna," *Glasgow Herald*, 29 May 1909.

65 *Studio*, vol. XXII (1901), p. 235.

66 *Ibid.*, p. 264.

67 *Supra*, n. 57.

68 GLAHA 16/F/11.

69 G. Fuchs, "Mackintosh und die Schule von Glasgow in Turin," *Deutsche Kunst und Dekoration*, vol. 10 (1902), p. 570.

70 "Ein Mackintosh Tee-Haus in Glasgow," p. 264.

71 C. Voysey, "Remarks on Domestic Entrance Halls," *Studio*, vol. XXI (1901), p. 246.

72 "Ein Mackintosh Tee-Haus in Glasgow," p. 259.

73 *Ibid.*, p. 266.
74 *Ibid.*, p. 258.
75 *Ibid.*, p. 257.
76 *Ibid.*, p. 266.
77 W. Crane, *The Claims of Decorative Art* (1892), p. 159.
78 *Ibid.*, p. 10.
79 *Ibid.*, p. 112.
80 *Ibid.*, p. 11.
81 *Ibid.*, p. 113.
82 16/F/08, HAG.
83 N. Munro, *Erchie and Jimmy Swan* (1993), p. 101.
84 *Quiz*, vol. XVI, 18 Jan. 1889.
85 Waddell, *op. cit.*, p. 127.
86 GLAHA 16/F/09.
87 Job Book, 1902–8. GLAHA 53062.
88 Taylor, *op. cit.*, pp. 35–36.
89 "Ein Mackintosh Tee-Haus in Glasgow," p. 578.
90 *Supra*, n. 68.
91 Crane, *op. cit.*, p. 7.
92 *Ibid.*, p. 6.
93 "Ein Mackintosh Tee-Haus in Glasgow," p. 258.

Chapter 10
"HERE IS THE HOUSE"
1 *Studio*, Special Summer Number (1901), p. 3.
2 *Ibid.*, "Prospectus."
3 B. E. Kalas, "De La Tamise a la Spree" (1905). Reprinted in the *1933 Memorial Exhibition, A Reconstruction* (1983), pp. v–vi.
4 C. Reilly, *Scaffolding in the Sky* (1938), p. 90.
5 Augustus John to William Rothenstein, 4 St. James' Rd., Liverpool in W. Rothenstein, *Men and Memories* (932), p. 5; A. John, *Finishing Touches* (1966), pp. 60–61.
6 G. White, 'Some Glasgow Designers and Their Work', *The Studio*, vol. XI (1897), p. 90.
7 *Ibid.*, vol. XIX (1900), p. 128.
8 *Ibid.*, vol. XXXVIII (1906), p. 72.
9 *Ibid.*, vol. XX (1900), p. 95.
10 *Ibid.*, vol. XXIV (1902), p. 287.
11 *Supra*, n.1, pp. 110–19.
12 *Supra*, n.6.
13 T. Morris, "Concerning the Work of Margaret Macdonald, Frances Macdonald, Charles Mackintosh and Herbert McNair—An Appreciation." Kelvingrove Art Gallery, E46-5x.
14 *Studio*, vol. XIX (1900), p. 173.
15 *Ibid.*, vol. XXV (1902), p. 90.
16 *Ibid.*, vol. XVII (1899), p. 178.
17 *Ibid.*, vol. II (1894), p. 29.
18 *Ibid.*, vol. VII (1896), pp. 15–21.
19 *Ibid.*, vol. III (1894), p. 150.
20 Job Book, 1861–76. GLAHA 53057.
21 *The Bailie*, vol. XXXVII (8 Oct. 1890).
22 G. Henry to E. A. Hornel, 113 West Regent St., Glasgow., n.d. Hornel Library, 1/8.
23 Do. to do. Hornel Library 2/6.
24 Do. to do. Hornel Library, 1/22.
25 Do. to do. Hornel Library, 2/7.

26 Do. to do. 132 West Regent St., Glasgow, 8 July 1892. Hornel Library, 2/7.
27 As recorded in the Job Books, GLAHA 53059 and 53060, there was an extensive building program of extensions and a stable block at Craigie Hall in 1892–93, with ornamental work commissioned in 1898.
28 *British Architect*, vol. 33, 21 March 1890.
29 R. Billcliffe, *The Royal Glasgow Institute of the Fine Arts, 1861–1989*, vol. 2 (1991), p. 245. *Building News*, 4 Dec. 1891; *Academy Architecture*, vol. III (1893).

    Dunloe was commissioned by N. B. Stewart, whose father had been one of the four guarantors for the erection of the Institute of Fine Art galleries in 1878. Mitchell Library, Royal Glasgow Institute of the Fine Arts, Minute Book, 3 Dec. 1891.
30 Job Book, 1894–1904. GLAHA 53061. *Academy Architecture*, 1900, pt. 1.
31 RIBA Fellowship application.
32 Job Books 1881–1894 and 1891–1894, GLAHA 53059 and 53060. *Academy Architecture*, 1900, Pt.1.
33 G. Cinnamon, "Talwin Morris, Blackie and the Glasgow Style," *The Private Library*, 3rd series, vol. 10:1 (1987), pp. 3–5.
34 White, *op. cit.*, p. 232.
35 P. Robertson (ed.), *Charles Rennie Mackintosh. The Architectural Papers* (1990), p. 51.
36 *Ibid.*, p. 53.
37 *Ibid.*, p. 63.
38 Cash Book, 1889–1917. GLAHA 53079.
39 H. Muthesius, "Die Glasgower Kunst bewegung: Charles R. Mackintosh und Margaret Macdonald Mackintosh," *Dekorative Kunst*, vol. 9 (1902), pp. 215–16.
40 In 1982 the drawings were listed as being with Strathclyde Regional Council Renfrewshire. H. Kimura, "Charles Rennie Mackintosh: Architectural Drawings Catalogue, Part One," Mackintosh School of Architecture, Glasgow, pp. 35–36, 136–40.
41 GLAHA 52388–9. H. R. Davidson, "Memories of Charles Rennie Mackintosh," *Scottish Art Review*, vol. XI, no. 4 (1968), pp. 2–5, 29.
42 Letters of James Salmon to H. A. Salmon. NMRS.
43 *Studio*, vol. XI (1897), p. 23. D. Simpson, *C. F. A. Voysey, An Architect of Individuality* (1979), pp. 26–77; W. Hitchmough, *C. F. A. Voysey* (1995), pp. 36–39.
44 Muthesius, *op. cit.*, p. 215.
45 *Studio*, vol. XXVII (1902), pp. 13, 24.
46 H. Muthesius, *The English House* (1979), p. 43.
47 GLAHA 53012, ff.42–3.
48 *Charles Rennie Mackintosh Society Newsletter*, no. 64 (Spring 1994), p. 15.
49 For an account of the expansion of the steading that became Melsetter House see T. Garnham, *Melsetter House* (1993).

50 Muthesius, "Die Glasgower," pp. 214–15.
51 R. Kerr, "Plan" in *The Principles and Practice of Modern House Construction* (ed. G. L. Sutcliffe) (1899), vol. I, p. 31.
52 C. R. Mackintosh to W. Davidson, 12 June 1901. GLAHA 52389.
53 *Supra*, n. 51.
54 Muthesius, *The English House*, p. 51.
55 *Studio*, vol. IV (1894), pp. 127–32.
56 *Ibid.*, vol. V (1895), p. 16.
57 *Ibid.*, vol. XII (1898), p. 172.
58 *Ibid.*, vol. V (1895), p. 17.
59 *Supra*, n. 57.
60 *Supra*, n. 55.
61 *Ibid.*, vol. IX (1897), p. 31.
62 J. Bruce, *Charters and Other Writs of the Lands of Kirkmichael, Stuckleckie, Milligs and Drumfad* (1925), p. 10.
63 R. Chapman, *The Topographical Picture of Glasgow* (1820), vol. I, pp. 361–62.
64 S. Green, "William Leiper's Houses in Helensburgh," *Architectural Heritage*, vol. II (1992), pp. 32–42.
65 *British Architect*, 2 Sept. 1887, p. 183. *Inf. ex* Professor Pamela Robertson.
66 Muthesius, *op. cit.*, p. 27.
67 *Studio*, vol. VII (1896), p. 29.
68 *Ibid.*, p. 147.
69 J. D. Kornwolf,. *H. M. Baillie Scott and the Arts and Crafts Movement* (1972), p. 202.
70 *Supra*, n. 54.
71 *Quiz*, vol. XXXII (3 Dec. 1896).
72 *The Bailie*, vol. LVII (21 Nov. 1900).
73 T. Morris, Sketchbook, Dunglass, Bowling, 1895. Kelvingrove Art Gallery and Museum, 77–13ac.
74 *Studio*, vol. XVIII, Special Winter Number, 1899–1900, p. 28.
75 *Inf. ex* Mrs. Ruth Hedderwick (née Blackie) per Mrs. A. Ellis.
76 W. W. Blackie, "Memories of Charles Rennie Mackintosh," *Scottish Art Review*, vol. XI, no. 4 (1968), pp. 6–7.
77 *Ibid.*, p. 8.
78 J. J. Stevenson, *House Architecture*, vol. I (1880), p. 3.
79 *Ibid.*, vol. I, p. 5.
80 *Ibid.*, vol. I, p. 7.
81 *Ibid.*, vol. I, p. 377.
82 *Ibid.*, vol. I, p. 378.
83 *Ibid.*, vol. I, p. 28.
84 *Ibid.*, vol. I, p. 54.
85 *Ibid.*, vol. I, p. 56.
86 *Ibid.*, vol. I, p. 57.
87 *Ibid.*, vol. I, p. 65.
88 *Ibid.*, vol. I, p. 67.
89 *Ibid.*, vol. I, p. 70.
90 *Ibid.*, vol. I, p. 73.
91 Kerr, *op. cit.*, pp. 37, 39.
92 *Ibid.*, p. 38.

93 *Ibid.*, p. 41.
94 *Ibid.*, p. 36.
95 *Ibid.*, p. 45.
96 *Ibid.*, p. 32.
97 C. Wood, *Burne-Jones* (1998) p. 6.
98 F. Agnoletti, "The Hill-House Helensburgh," *Deutsche Kunst und Dekoration*, vol. VI (1905), p. 359.
99 *Supra*, n. 75.
100 "Inventory and Valuation of House Furniture and Plenishing, 1934." Blackie MSS.
101 "The Hill-House Helensburgh," pp. 341–59, *passim*.
102 G. de Lorris and J. de Meun, *The Romance of the Rose* (1994), pp. 3, 9.
103 *Studio*, vol. V (1895), p. 18.
104 C. Eastlake, *Hints on Household Taste* (1986), p. 201.
105 Muthesius, "Die Glasgower Kunstbewegung," p. 206.
106 *Ibid.*, p. 213.
107 Muthesius, *The English House*, p. 89.
108 Kerr, *op. cit.*, p. 17.
109 Stevenson, *op. cit.*, p. 118.
110 *Supra*, n. 56.
111 *The Romance of the Rose*, p. 4.
112 Stevenson, *op. cit.*, p. 16.
113 Muthesius, *op. cit.*, p. 51.

Chapter 11
AND THE MANY PASSED HIM BY

1 J. J. Bell, *I Remember* (1932), pp. 13–14.
2 *Quiz*, vol. V, 16 March 1882.
3 *Ibid.*, vol. VIII, 10 Oct. 1884.
4 Letters from James Salmon to H. A. Salmon, Rowantreehill, 2 Feb. 1900. NMRS.
5 *Supra*, n.2.
6 *Quiz*, vol. XXX, 5 Dec. 1895.
7 M. R. Bobbit, *With Dearest Love to All* (1960), pp. 113–14.
8 *Ibid.*, pp. 165–6.
9 *Ibid.*, p. 168.
10 *The Bailie*, vol. liv, 31 May 1899.
11 *Quiz*, vol. XII, 11 Feb. 1887.
12 *Ibid.*, vol. IX, 17 July 1885.
13 Bell, *op. cit.*, pp. 109–10.
14 *Quiz*, vol. XII, 25 Feb. 1887.
15 Cash Book, 1889–1917. GLAHA 53079.
16 Job Book, 1881–1894. GLAHA 53059.
17 NRAS, CH3/465/17.
18 *Who's Who in Glasgow in 1909* (1909), p. 107.
19 Job Book, 1881–1894. *Academy Architecture*, 1901, pt. I, p. 78.
20 *Builder*, vol. 65 (1893), pp. 336–40. One would imagine that the accompanying unsigned account of the history of the site and the ecclesiastical remains nearby was by Honeyman.
21 Cash Book, 1889–1917.
22 W. S. Moyes to T. Howarth, 22 July 1947. University of Toronto, Special Collections, B96–

0028/017 (14). T. Neat and G. McDermott, *Closing the Circle* (2002), p. 99.
23 *Academy Architecture*, 1906, pt. I, p. 72.
24 J. Salmon, Rowantreehill, 10 Feb. 1899.
25 Cash Book, 1889–1917.
26 D. C. L. Dewar, *History of the Glasgow Society of Lady Artists' Club* (1950), p. 14.
27 GSAA, Building Committee Minute Book, 1908–10.
28 N. G. Bowe and E. Cumming, *The Arts and Crafts Movements in Dublin and Edinburgh, 1885–1925* (1998), pp. 37, 44. See also *Charles Rennie Mackintosh Society Newsletter*, no. 73 (Summer 1998), p. 11.
29 M. H. Baillie Scott, "A Country House," *Studio*, vol. XIX (1900), p. 31.
30 D. Chapman-Huston, "Charles Rennie Mackintosh," *Artwork* (1930), pp. 22, 24.
31 Job Book, 1902–8. GLAHA 53062.
32 *Old Country Houses of the Old Glasgow Gentry* (1878), pp. 137–38.
33 *Studio Yearbook* (1907), p. 59.
34 H. Muthesius, "Die Glasgower Kunstbewegung: Charles R. Mackintosh und Margaret Macdonald Mackintosh," *Dekorative Kunst*, vol. 9 (1902), p. 213.
35 J. D. Kornwolf, *M. H. Baillie Scott and the Arts and Crafts Movement* (1972), p. 115.
36 M. Maeterlinck, *The Treasure of the Humble*, 4th edition (1903), p. 70.
37 Chapman-Huston, *op. cit.*, p. 29.
38 H. Muthesius, *The English House* (1979), p. 52.
39 C. Carswell, *The Camomile* (1987), p. 169.
40 *Inf. ex* the late Mrs. Ailsa Tanner. The specification is among the Macaulay Stevenson MSS, East Dunbartonshire Archives, GD1998.
41 Dewar, *op. cit.*, p. 23.
42 Cash Book, 1889–1917.
43 F. A. Walker, "The Mysterious Affair at Cloak," *Charles Rennie Mackintosh Society Newsletter*, no. 31 (Winter/Spring 1981–82), pp. 2–4.
44 Minutes of Meetings, Glasgow Provincial Committee for the Training of Teachers, 1912–13, pp. 4, 8, 9, 21, 197. University of Strathclyde, JCE/1/1.
45 Minutes, 1913–14, pp. 9, 10, 12, 199. University of Strathclyde, JCE/1/1.
46 GSAA, Minute Book No. 9, March 1913 till June 1914.
47 *Ibid.*
48 *Glasgow Herald*, 14 Feb. 1914.
49 *Supra*, n.45.
50 Walter Blackie must have been mistaken when he put the date of the meeting with Mackintosh in the late autumn of 1915. "At any rate it was in the early days of the Great World War." W. W. Blackie, "Memories of Charles Rennie Mackintosh," *Scottish Art Review*, vol. XI, no. 4 (1968), p. 8.

Chapter 12
"A REAL WANDER JAHR"

1 T. Howarth to W. S. Moyes, 17 July 1947. University of Toronto, Special Collections, B96–0028/017 (14).
2 J. Keppie to T. Howarth, 29 Nov. 1949. University of Toronto, Special Collections, B96–0028/017 (13).
3 *Supra*, n. 1.
4 J. Taylor, "Modern Decorative Art at Glasgow," *The Studio*, vol. XXXIX (1907), p. 36.
5 D. Chapman-Huston, "Charles Rennie Mackintosh," *Artwork* (1930), p. 24.
6 A. Storr, *Churchill's Black Days and Other Phenomena of the Human Mind* (1988), p. 146.
7 M. M. Mackintosh to A. Geddes, 6 Florentine Terrace, Hillhead, Glasgow, c.1912. University of Strathclyde archives, T-GED 9/2174.
8 *Ibid.*, p. 236.
9 GLAHA 53013.
10 R. Scott, *The Walberswick Enigma* (1994), pp. 24–25. See also F. MacSporran, *Edward Arthur Walton, 1860–1922* (1987), p. 76.
11 C. Dresser, *Japan: Its Architecture, Art, and Art Manufactures* (1882; reissued 1977), p. 286.
12 Chapman-Huston, *op. cit.*, p. 30
13 M. M. Mackintosh to A. Geddes, Millside, Walberswick, Suffolk. National Library of Scotland, MS. 10582, f.16.
14 J. Keppie to C. R. Mackintosh, 257 West George Street, Glasgow, 31 Dec. 1914. GLAHA 41394.
15 C. R. Mackintosh to W. Davidson, Millside, Walberswick, by Southwold, Suffolk, n.d. GLAHA, 52534.
16 Do. to do. 19 June 1915. GLAHA, 52505.
17 Do. to do., n.d. GLAHA, 52536.
18 Do. to do. University Hall of Residence, 10 Carlyle Square, Chelsea, London, 29 July 1915. GLAHA 52537.
19 *Supra*, n. 17.
20 *Supra*, n. 18.
21 P. Kitchen, *A Most Unsettling Person* (1975), p. 149.
22 P. Geddes, "The Sociology of Autumn," *The Evergreen* (1895), pp. 31, 36.
23 P. Mairet, *Pioneer of Sociology* (1951), p. 169.
24 *Supra*, n.17.
25 P. Mairet to W. A. M. Grigor, 2 March 1967. Copy in GLAHA 52373. See V. M. Welter, "Arcades for Lucknow: Patrick Geddes, Charles Rennie Mackintosh and the Reconstruction of the City," *Architectural History*, vol. 42 (1999), pp. 316–22.
26 Mairet, *op. cit.*, pp. 148, 155, 162.
27 C. R. Mackintosh to W. Davidson, Paultons Square, Chelsea, 5 Aug. 1915. GLAHA, 52538.
28 GLAHA 52363.
29 W. Bassett-Lowke to C. R. Mackintosh, 31 July 1916. GLAHA 41411.

30 L. Campbell, "A Model Patron: Bassett-Lowke, Mackintosh and Behrens," *Journal of the Decorative Arts Society*, vol. 10 (1985), pp. 1–2; M. Miers, "78 Derngate, Northampton," *Country Life* (23 Sept. 2004), pp. 120–23. See also R. Fuller, *The Bassett-Lowke Story* (1984), pp. 67–71.

31 A. Moffat, *Remembering Charles Rennie Mackintosh* (1989), p. 100.

32 *Supra*, n. 29.

33 W. Bassett-Lowke to C. R. Mackintosh, Kingswell Street, Northampton, 11 Jan. 1917. GLAHA 52327.

34 Do. to do., 2 Nov. 1916. GLAHA 41414.

35 Do. to do., 12 Jan. 1917. Mackintosh used plastic insets in dining room furniture, which he designed in 1918 for Candida Cottage, the weekend retreat of Bassett-Lowke. GLAHA 41542.

36 "Now and Then. A Transformation," *The Ideal Home* (Aug. and Sept. 1920), pp. 53–55, 92–95.

37 C. R. Mackintosh to W. Davidson, 2 Hans Studios, 43a Glebe Place, Chelsea, S.W.3, 1 April 1919. GLAHA, 53539.

38 Do. to do., 12 Aug. 1919. GLAHA, 52541.

39 Do. to do., 23 Aug. 1919. GLAHA, 52543.

40 M. M. Mackintosh to W. Davidson, 43a Glebe Place, Chelsea, S.W.3, 26 Feb. 1919. GLAHA, 52530.

41 Do. to do., 13 March 1919. GLAHA, 52531.

42 C. R. Mackintosh to W. Davidson, 15 Aug. 1919. GLAHA, 52542.

43 GLAHA 52408.

44 *Supra*, n.42.

45 M. M. Mackintosh to W. Davidson, 25 May 1919. GLAHA, 52532.

46 W. Buchanan, *Mr. Henry and Mr. Hornel Visit Japan* (1979), p. 14.

47 M. Morris, *The Art of J. D. Fergusson* (1974), p. 206.

48 A. John, *Finishing Touches* (ed. D. George) (1966), p. 61.

49 J. D. Fergusson, *Modern Scottish Painting* (1943), pp. 95, 98.

50 T. Pepper, *Camera Portraits of E. O. Hoppé* (1978), p. 6.

51 A pencil sketch and plan of "Little Headgecourt, East Grinstead, for E. O. Hoppé" is dated 15 March 1919. GLAHA 53015. R. Gradidge, "The Last of Mackintosh," *The Field* (8 Dec. 1984), pp. 11–13.

52 The Plough, prospectus, 1991. *Ex inf.* Mr. F. Hoppé.

53 Pepper, *op. cit.*, pp. 4–5.

54 *Supra*, n. 52.

55 *Supra*, n. 40.

56 *Supra*, n. 46.

57 W. Foxton to T. Howarth, 19 June 1945. University of Toronto, Special Collections, B96–0028/017 (08).

58 M. Morris, *The Art of Ferguson*, p. 132.

59 M. Morris, *My Life in Movement* (1969), p. 35.

60 *Supra*, n. 57.

61 H. Squire to T. Howarth, "The Hundred," Henfield, Sussex, 26 Jan. 1946. University of Toronto, Special Collections, B96–0028/017 (21).

62 *Ibid.*

63 B. Cherry and N. Pevsner, *London, North-West* (1991), p. 576.

64 The fullest account of the Dug-Out is in R. Billcliffe, *The Complete Furniture, Furniture Drawings and Interior Designs* (1980), pp. 235–38.

65 W. Blackie to C. R. Mackintosh, 17 Stanhope Street, Glasgow, 29 Dec. 1921 and 12 Jan. 1922. GLAHA 52358, 52359.

66 For accounts of the Mackintoshes' time in France see p. Robertson and p. Long, *Charles Rennie Mackintosh in France* (2005), and R. Crichton, *Monsieur Mackintosh* (2006).

67 C. R. Mackintosh to J. D. Fergusson, Hotel du Midi, Ille-Sur-Têt, Pyrenees Orientales, 1 Feb. 1925. GLAHA 52505.

68 *The Chronycle. The Letters of Charles Rennie Mackintosh to Margaret Macdonald Mackintosh—1927* (ed. p. Robertson) (2001), p. 49.

69 Chapman Huston, *op. cit.*, p. 30. See also M. M. Mackintosh to W. Blackie, 12 Porchester Square, London, W.2, 26 Feb. 1929. Blackie MSS.

70 University of Strathclyde, archives, T/GED 22/1/1413.1.

71 GLAHA, Mackintosh Collection, A5. Newton Castle was a property of Macpherson of Cluny and Blairgowrie. In 1909 it was let. The tenant was Charles Ogilvie. A painting student at the Glasgow School of Art between 1893 and 1899 he became a member of staff in 1911 until his death early in 1933 shortly after retiring because of ill health. *Ex inf.* Sir William Macpherson of Cluny.

72 C. R. Mackintosh to F. Newbery, Hotel du Commerce, Port Vendres, Pyrenees Orientales, 28 Dec. 1925 (National Library of Scotland). Moffat, *op. cit.*, pp. 112–13.

73 *Ibid.*, p. 149.

74 Neat and McDermott, *op. cit.*, p. 132.

75 D. Chapman-Huston to T. Howarth, 31 Jan. 1946. University of Toronto, Special Collections, B96–0028/003 (11).

76 Moffat, *op. cit.*, p. 152.

77 *Supra*, n. 73.

78 D. Chapman-Huston to T. Howarth, 27 Oct. 1944. University of Toronto, Special Collections, B96-0028/003 (11)

79 *Supra*, n. 73.

80 GLAHA 53012.

EPILOGUE

1 *Evening Times*, 15 Dec. 1909.

2 C. Marriott, *Modern English Architecture* (1924), p. 129.

3 J. Betjeman, "Still Going Strong," *Architectural Review*, May 1930.

4 *Glasgow Herald*, 15 Dec. 1928.

5 *RIBAJ*, vol. 56, 12 Jan. 1929.

6 *Architectural Review*, Jan. 1929.

7 Betjeman, *op. cit.*

8 *Architectural Review*, May 1933.

9 R. McGrath, *Twentieth Century Houses* (1934), pp. 78–79.

10 P. Morton Shand, "Scenario for a Human Drama," *Architectural Review*, Jan. 1935.

11 N. Pevsner, *Pioneers of the Modern Movement* (1936), pp. 158–65.

BIBLIOGRAPHY

BOOKS

Aikman, J. Logan. *Historical Notices of the United Presbyterian Congregations in Glasgow*, Glasgow, 1875.

Belcher, John and Macartney, Mervyn. *Later Renaissance Architecture*, 2 vols., London, 1901.

Bell, J. J. *I Remember*, Edinburgh, 1932.

Billcliffe, Roger. *Architectural Sketches and Flower Drawings by Charles Rennie Mackintosh*, London, 1997.

Billcliffe, Roger. *Charles Rennie Mackintosh. The Complete Furniture, Furniture Drawings and Interior Designs*, 2nd edn., Guildford, 1980.

Billcliffe, Roger, *The Glasgow Boys*, London, 1985.

Billcliffe, Roger, *The Glasgow Institute of the Fine Arts, 1861–1989*, 2 vols., Bearsden, Glasgow, 1991.

Blackie, Agnes. *Blackie and Son, 1809–1959*, London and Glasgow, 1959.

Blackie, W. G. *Concerning Blackie and Son*, London and Glasgow, 1897.

Blackie, W. W. *John Blackie, Senior (1782–1874)*, London and Glasgow, 1933.

Bobbit, Mary R. *With Dearest Love to All. The Life and Letters of Lady Jebb*, London, 1960.

Bowe, Nicola, and Cumming, Elizabeth. *The Arts and Crafts Movement in Dublin and Edinburgh, 1885–1925*, Dublin, 1998.

Briggs, Asa. *Victorian Cities*, Harmondsworth, 1968.

Bruce, John. *Charters and Other Writs of the Lands of Kirkmichael, Stuckleckie, Milligs and Drumfad*, Helensburgh, 1925.

Buchanan, William. *The Art of the Photographer J. Craig Annan, 1864–1946*, Edinburgh, 1992.

Buchanan, William. *Mr. Henry and Mr. Hornel Visit Japan*, Edinburgh, 1979.

Carsewell, Catherine. *The Camomile*, 1922, republished London, 1987.

Catalogue of Plans of Abandoned Mines, 5 vols., West Lothian, 1931.

Chapman, Robert. *The Topographical Picture of Glasgow*, 3 vols., Glasgow, 1820.

Charles Rennie Mackintosh. The Chelsea Years, Glasgow, 1994.

Cherry, Bridget and Pevsner, Nikolaus. *London, North-West*, London, 1991.

Clark, Kenneth. *The Gothic Revival*, 1928, republished Harmondsworth, 1964.

Crane, Walter. *The Bases of Design*, London, 1898.

Crane, Walter. *The Claims of Decorative Art*, London, 1892.

Crane, Walter. *Ideals in Art*, London, 1905.

Crawford, Alan. *Charles Rennie Mackintosh*, London, 1995.

Crawford, Alan. *C. R. Ashbee, Architect, Designer and Romantic Socialist*, New Haven and London, 1985.

Crichton, Robin. *Monsieur Mackintosh*, Edinburgh, 2006.

Cumming, Elizabeth. *Hand, Heart and Soul. The Arts and Crafts Movement in Scotland*, Edinburgh, 2006.

Cunningham, Colin. *Victorian and Edwardian Town Halls*, London, 1981.

De Lorris, Guillame, and de Meun, Jean. *The Romance of the Rose*, Oxford, 1994.

Denholm, James. *History of the City of Glasgow*, 3rd edn., Glasgow, 1804.

Devine, Thomas M. *The Tobacco Lords*, Edinburgh, 1990.

Dewar, de Courcy L. *History of the Glasgow Society of Lady Artists' Club*, Glasgow, 1950.

Dickens, Charles. *The Pickwick Papers*, Oxford, 1986.

Directory of British Architects, 1834–1914, 2 vols., London and New York, 2001.

Dresser, Christopher. *Japan: Its Architecture, Art, and Art Manufactures*, London, 1882, reprinted New York, 1977.

Eastlake, Charles. *Hints on Household Taste*, 4th revised edition, 1878, republished New York, 1986.

Eastlake, Charles, *A History of the Gothic Revival*, London, 1872.

Egger, Hanna; Robertson, Pamela; Trummer, Manfred; Vergo, Peter. *Ein Moderner Nachmittag. Margaret Macdonald Mackintosh und der Salon Waerndorfer in Wien*, Wien, 2000.

Esher, Lord. *Conservation in Glasgow*, Glasgow, 1971.

Eyre-Todd, George (ed.). *The Book of Glasgow Cathedral*, Glasgow, 1898.

Ferguson, Hugh, *Glasgow School of Art, the History*, Glasgow, 1995

Fergusson, John D. *Modern Scottish Painting*, Glasgow, 1943.

Forbes, William, of Pitsligo. *Memoirs of a Banking House*, Edinburgh, 1859.

Frazer, James G. *The Golden Bough*, 2 vols., London, 1890.

Free Westbourne Church, Calendar and Directory, Glasgow, 1894.

Fuller, Roland. *The Bassett-Lowke Story*, London, 1984.

Garnham, Trevor. *Melsetter House*, London, 1993.

Garnett, Thomas. *Observations on a Tour of Scotland Through the Highlands and Parts of the Western Isles of Scotland*, 2 vols., London, 1810.

Gibb, Andrew. *The Making of a City*, London, 1983.

The Glasgow Boys, Edinburgh, 1968.

The Glasgow Style, Glasgow, 1984.

Gomme, Andor, and Walker, David. *Architecture of Glasgow*, 1968, 2nd revised edn., London, 1987.

Gordon, George (ed.). *Perspectives of the Scottish City*, Aberdeen, 1985.

Graham, Angus. *Skipness: Memories of a Highland Estate*, Edinburgh, 1993.

Grogan, Elaine. *Beginnings: Charles Rennie Mackintosh's Early Sketches*, Oxford, 2002.

Harte, Bret. *The Complete Works*, 2 vols., London, 1881.

Helland, Janice. *The Studios of Frances and Margaret Macdonald*, Manchester and New York, 1996.

Hitchmough, Wendy. *C. F. A. Voysey*, London, 1995.

Howarth, Thomas. *Charles Rennie Mackintosh and the Modern Movement*, London, 1952.

John, Augustus. *Finishing Touches* (Daniel George ed.), London, 1966.

Jones, Arthur F. *Cardross. The Village in Days Gone By*, Dumbarton, 1985.

Kellett, John R. *Glasgow, A Concise History*, London, 1967.

Kelvinside, Glasgow, 1894.

Keppie, John. *The Story of the Glasgow Institute of Architects*, Glasgow, 1921.

Kinchin, Perilla. *Tea and Taste, The Glasgow Tea Rooms, 1875–1975*, Wendlebury, 1991.

Kinchin, Perilla and Kinchin, Juliet. *Glasgow's Great Exhibitions*, Wendlebury, 1988.

Kitchen, Paddy. *A Most Unsettling Person. An Introduction to the Ideas and Life of Patrick Geddes*, London, 1975

Kohl, Johann G. *Scotland, Glasgow, the Clyde to the Lakes*, London, 1844.

Kornwolf, James D. *M. H. Baillie Scott and the Arts and Crafts Movement*, Baltimore and London, 1972.

Laperriere, Charles B. (ed.). *The Royal Scottish Academy Exhibitions, 1826–1900*, 2 vols., Calne, 1991.

Lethaby, William R. *Architecture, Mysticism and Myth*, London, 1974.

Lethaby, William R. *Architecture, Nature and Magic*, London, 1956.

MacGibbon, David, and Ross, Thomas. *The Castellated and Domestic Architecture of Scotland*, 5 vols., Edinburgh 1887–92, reissued Edinburgh, 1990.

Mackail, John W. *The Life of William Morris*, London, 1899, republished New York, 1995.

MacSporran, Fiona, *Edward Arthur Walton 1860–1922*, Glasgow, 1987.

Maeterlinck, Maurice, *The Treasure of the Humble*, 4th edn., London, 1903.

Mairet, Philip, *Pioneer of Sociology. The Life and Letters of Patrick Geddes*, London, 1957.

Marriott, Charles, *Modern English Architecture*, London, 1924.

Martin, David, *The Glasgow School of Painting*, London, 1897.

Maver, Irene, *Glasgow*, Edinburgh, 2000.

Mavor, James, *My Windows on the Street of the World*, 2 vols., London, Toronto and New York, 1923

McCrone, Guy. *Wax Fruit*, 1947, republished Edinburgh, 1993.

McFadzean, Ronald. *The Life and Works of Alexander Thomson*, London, 1979.

McGrath, Raymond, *Twentieth Century Houses*, London, 1934.

McKenzie, Ray. *Sculpture in Glasgow*, Glasgow, 1999.

McNair, James B. *McNair, McNear and McNeir Genealogies*, Chicago, 1923.

Memoirs and Portraits of One Hundred Glasgow Men, Glasgow, 1886.

Moffat, Alistair. *Remembering Charles Rennie Mackintosh*, Lanark, 1989.

Moon, Karen. *George Walton, Designer and Architect*, Oxford, 1993.

Morris, Margaret. *The Art of J. D. Fergusson. A Biased Biography*, Glasgow and London, 1974.

Morris, Margaret. *My Life in Movement*, London, 1969.

Morrow, Patrick D. *Bret Harte*, Boise, Idaho, 1972.

Morton, Henry B. *A Hillhead Album*, Glasgow, 1973.

Muir, James Hamilton. *Glasgow in 1901*, Glasgow, 1901, reissued Oxford, 2001.

Munro, Neil. *Erchie and Jimmy Swan* (Osborne, Brian D., and Armstrong, Ronald eds.), Edinburgh, 1993.

Muthesius, Eckhart, and Posener, Julius. *Hermann Muthesius, 1861–1927*, London, 1979.

Muthesius, Hermann. *Die Englische Baukunst der Gegenwart*, Leipzig and Berlin, 1900.

Muthesius, Hermann. *The English House*, London, 1979.

Neat, Timothy. *Part Seen, Part Imagined*, Edinburgh, 1994.

Neat, Timothy, and McDermott, Gillian. *Closing the Circle. Thomas Howarth, Mackintosh and the Modern Movement*, Aberdour, 2002.

Newman, John, and Pevsner, Nikolaus. *Dorset*, Harmondsworth, 1993.

Niven, Frederick. *Justice of the Peace*, London, 1914.

The Norse Myths (intro. by Kevin Crossley-Holland), New York and London, 1980.

Nuttgens, Patrick (ed.). *Mackintosh and His Contemporaries in Europe and America*, London, 1988.

Oakley, Charles A. *The Second City*, Glasgow and London, 1967.

O'Donnell, Raymond. *The Life and Work of James Salmon, Architect, 1873–1924*, Edinburgh, 2003.

Old Glasgow Houses of the Old Glasgow Gentry, 2nd edn., Glasgow, 1878.

Pagan, James. *Glasgow, Past and Present*, 3 vols., Glasgow, 1851.

Pepper, Terence. *Camera Portraits of E. O. Hoppé*, London, 1978.

Percy, Clayre and Ridley, Jane (eds.). *The Letters of Edwin Lutyens to His Wife, Lady Emily*, London, 1985.

Pevsner, Nikolaus. *North Somerset and Bristol*, Harmondsworth, 1958.

Pevsner, Nikolaus. *Pioneers of Modern Design from William Morris to Walter Gropius*, Harmondsworth, 1960.

Pevsner, Nikolaus. *Pioneers of the Modern Movement*, London, 1936.

Philip, George E. *Free St. Matthew's Church*, Glasgow, Glasgow, 1898.

Post Office Directory, 1892–93, Glasgow, 1892.

Ramsay, George. *Allan Glen's School and Technical Education*, Glasgow, 1888.

Rawson, George. *Fra H. Newbery, Artist and Art Educationist, 1855–1946*, Glasgow, 1996.

Reed, Peter. *Glasgow: The Forming of the City*, Edinburgh, 1993.

Reid, Robert (Senex). *Glasgow Past and Present*, 3 vols., Glasgow, 1884.

Reilly, Charles. *Scaffolding in the Sky*, London, 1938.

Richards, James M., and Pevsner, Nikolaus (eds.). *The Anti-Rationalists*, London, 1973.

Roberson, Pamela (ed.). *Charles Rennie Mackintosh, The Architectural Papers*, Wendlebury, 1990.

Robertson, Pamela (ed.). *The Chronycle. The Letters of Charles Rennie Mackintosh to Margaret Macdonald Mackintosh, 1927*, Glasgow, 2001.

Robertson, Pamela (ed.). *Doves and Dreams. The Art of Frances Macdonald and James Herbert McNair*, Aldershot and Burlington, 2006.

Robertson, Pamela, and Long, Philip. *Charles Rennie Mackintosh in France*, Edinburgh, 2005.

Rothenstein, William. *Men and Memories*, 2 vols., London, 1931–32.

Ruskin, John. *Lectures on Architecture and Painting Delivered at Edinburgh in November 1853*, London, 1907.

Ruskin, John. *The Seven Lamps of Architecture. The Works of John Ruskin*, 9 vols., London, 1903.

Ruskin, John. *The Stones of Venice. The Works of John Ruskin*, 9 vols., London, 1904.

Savage, Peter. *Lorimer and the Edinburgh Craft Designers*, Edinburgh, 1980.

Sayers, Dorothy L. *Five Red Herrings*, 1931, new edn., London, 1972.

Scott, George G. *Lectures on the Rise and Development of Medieval Architecture*, 2 vols., London, 1879.

Scott, George G. *Remarks on Secular and Domestic Architecture*, London, 1857.

Scott, Richard. *The Walberswick Enigma: Artists Inspired by the Blyth Estuary*, Ipswich, 1994.

Sekler, Eduard. *Josef Hoffmann, The Architectural Work*, Princeton, 1985.

Simpson, Duncan. *C. F. A. Voysey, An Architect of Individuality*, London, 1979.

Simpson, Michael A., and Lloyd, Terence. *Middle Class Housing in Britain*, Newton Abbot, 1977.

Sinclair, Fiona J. *Charles Wilson Architect, 1810–1863*, Glasgow, 1995.

Sinclair, John. *Statistical Account of Scotland, 1791–99*, 21 vols., Edinburgh, 1973.

Slater, Terry R. (ed.). *The Built Form of Western Cities*, Leicester, 1990.

Slaven, Anthony, *The Development of the West of Scotland, 1750–1960*, London, 1975.

Sloan, Audrey, with Murray, Gordon, *James Miller, 1860–1947*, Edinburgh, 1993.

Smith, William W. *Kelvinside Church*, London and Glasgow, 1937.

Stamp, Gavin, and McKinstry, Sam (eds.). *"Greek" Thomson*, Edinburgh, 1994.

Stark, David. *Charles Rennie Mackintosh and Co.*, Ayrshire, 2004.

Stevenson, John J. *House Architecture*, 2 vols., London, 1880.

Stewart, George R. *Bret Harte. Argonaut and Exile*, Boston and New York, 1931.

Storr, Anthony. *Churchill's Black Days and Other Phenomena of the Human Mind*, London, 1988.

Sullivan, Louis. *Kindergarten Chats and Other Writings*, New York, 1979.

Summerson, Sir John. *The Turn of the Century: Architecture in Britain around 1900*, Glasgow, 1976.

Summerson, Sir John, *The Unromantic Castle*, London, 1990.

Sutcliffe, G. Lister (ed.). *The Principles and Practice of Modern House Construction*, 6 vols., London and Glasgow, 1899.

Tanner, Ailsa. *Helensburgh and the Glasgow School*, Helensburgh, 1972.

The 1933 Memorial Exhibition, A Reconstruction, Glasgow, 1993.

Vergo, Peter. *Vienna 1900*, Edinburgh, 1983.

Wade, William M. *The History of Glasgow*, Glasgow, 1821.

Walker, Fred M. *The Song of the Clyde. A History of Clyde Shipbuilding*, Cambridge, 1984.

Weber, Adna F. *The Growth of Cities in the Nineteenth Century*, New York and London, 1899, reprinted Ithaca, New York, 1968.

Westbourne Free Church Calendar and Directory, Glasgow, 1894.

Who's Who in Glasgow in 1909, Glasgow and London, 1909.

Williamson, Elizabeth; Riches, Anne; and Higgs, Malcolm. *Glasgow*, London, 1990.

Wood, Christopher. *Burne-Jones*, London, 1998.

Young, Andrew M. *Charles Rennie Mackintosh 1868–1928*, Edinburgh. 1968.

ARTICLES

Agnoletti, Fernando. "The Hill-House, Helensburgh," *Deutsche Kunst und Dekoration*, vol. VI, 1905.

Baillie Scott, M. H., "A Country House," *Studio*, vol. XIX, 1900.

Baillie Scott, M. H., "The Decoration of the Suburban House," *Studio*, vol. V, 1895.

Betjeman, John, "Still Going Strong," *Architectural Review*, vol. 72, May 1930.

Billcliffe, Roger, and Vergo, Peter. "Charles Rennie Mackintosh and the Austrian Art Revival," *Burlington Magazine*, vol. CXIX, no. 896, 1977.

Bing, Samuel, "The Art of Utamaro," *The Studio*, vol. IV, 1894.

Bird, Elizabeth, "Ghouls and Gas Pipes: Public Reaction to Early Work of 'The Four,' " *Scottish Art Review*, vol. XIV, no. 4, 1975.

Blackie, Walter W. "Memories of Charles Rennie Mackintosh," *Scottish Art Review*, vol. XI, no. 4, 1968.

Brumfield, William. "The Decorative Arts in Russian Architecture, 1900–1907," *Journal of Decorative and Propaganda Arts*, Summer 1987.

Buchanan, William. "The Mackintosh Circle, Part III, John and Jessie Keppie," *Charles Rennie Mackintosh Society Newsletter*, no. 32, 1982.

Campbell, Louise. "A Model Patron: Bassett-Lowke, Mackintosh and Behrens," *Journal of the Decorative Arts Society*, vol. 10, 1985.

Chalmers, P. MacGregor. "Art in Our Society," *Philosophical Society of Glasgow*, 1896.

Chapman-Huston, Desmond. "Charles Rennie Mackintosh," *Artwork*, 1930.

Cinamon, Gerald. "Talwin Morris, Blackie and the Glasgow Style," *Private Library*, 3rd Series, vol. 10:1, Spring 1987.

Cooke, Catherine. "Shekhtel in Kelvingrove and Mackintosh on the Petrovka: Two Russo-Scottish Exhibitions at the Turn of the Century," *Scottish Slavonic Review*, Spring 1988.

Cooke, Catherine. "Fedor Shekhtel," *The Twilight of the Tsars, Russian Art at the Turn of the Century*, London, 1991.

Crane, Walter. "Some Notes on Gesso Work," *Studio*, vol. I, 1893.

Davidson, Hamish R. "Memories of Charles Rennie Mackintosh," *Scottish Art Review*, vol. XI, no. 4, 1968.

Davidson, Peter, W. "Memories of Mackintosh," *Charles Rennie Mackintosh Society Newsletter*, no. 22, Summer 1979.

"Ein Mackintosh Tee-Haus in Glasgow," *Dekorative Kunst*, vol. XIII, 1905.

Franz, Rainald. "A Tale of Two Cities. Vienna, Glasgow and the 100th Anniversary of the Founding of the Wiener Werkstatte," *Charles Rennie Mackintosh Society Journal*, no. 85, Winter 2003.

Fuchs, Georg. "Mackintosh und die Schule von Glasow in Turin," *Deutsche Kunst und Dekoration*, vol. 10, 1902.

Geddes, Patrick. "The Sociology of Autumn," *Evergreen*, 1895.

Gibson, J. S. "Artistic Houses," *Studio*, vol. I, 1893.

"Die Glasgower Kunstbewegung Charles R. Mackintosh und Margaret Macdonald Mackintosh," *Dekorative Kunst*, vol. 9, 1902.

Gradidge, Roderick. "The Last of Mackintosh," *Field*, 8 Dec. 1984.

Green, Simon. "William Leiper's Houses in Helensburgh," *Architectural Heritage*, vol. II, 1992.

Grogan, Elaine. "Charles Rennie Mackintosh's Antwerp Sketches," *Charles Rennie Mackintosh Society Journal*, no. 85, winter 2003.

Law, Graham. "Greek Thomson," *Architectural Review*, vol. CXV, May 1954.

Levetus, Amelia S. "Scottish Artists in Vienna," *Glasgow Herald*, 29 May 1909.

Macaulay, James. "Symbolism in the Glasgow School of Art," *Mac Journal*, vol. 2, 1995.

McGillivray, J. Pittendrigh. "Japanese Sword Guards," *Scottish Art Review*, vol. I, 1888.

Mackintosh, Charles Rennie. "Wareham and Its Churches," *British Architect*, vol. XLIV, 1895.

Mays, Deborah. "A Profile of Sir George Washington Browne," *Architectural Heritage*, vol. III, 1992.

Miers, Mary. "78 Derngate, Northampton," *Country Life*, 23 Sept. 2004.

Muthesius, Hermann. "Die Glasgower Kunst bewegung Charles R. Mackintosh und Margaret Macdonald Mackintosh," *Dekorative Kunst*, vol. 9, 1902.

"New Board Schools in Glasgow," *The Builder*, vol. XXXIII, 1875.

Newbery, Francis H. "On the Training of Architectural Students," *Proceedings of the Philosophical Society of Glasgow*, vol. XIX, 1887–88.

"Now and Then. A Transformation," *The Ideal Home*, Aug. and Sept. 1920.

Robertson, Pamela. "Catherine Cranston," *Journal of the Decorative Arts Society*, vol. 10, 1985.

Shand, P. Morton. "Scenario for a Human Drama," *Architectural Review*, vol. 77, 1935.

Smith, William J. "Architectural Anthology," *Proceedings of the Royal Philosophical Society of Glasgow*, vol. 75, part 6, 1951.

Stamp, Gavin. "School Lessons," *Architects' Journal*, vol. 187, no. 14, 1988.

Taylor, Ernest A. "A Neglected Genius, Charles Rennie Mackintosh," *Studio*, vol. CV, 1933.

Taylor, John. "Modern Decorative Art at Glasgow. Some Notes on Miss Cranston's Argyle Street Tea House." *Studio*, vol. XXXIX, 1907.

Thomson, John. "Report on Ventilation and Heating of Bute Hall, 21 December, 1878," *A Collection of Glasgow Tracts*, vol. CXV, n.d.

"Torino 1902," *Le Arti Decorative Internazionali del Nuovo Secolo*.

Vergo, Peter. "Fritz Waerndorfer and Josef Hoffmann," *Burlington Magazine*, vol. CXXXV, no. 964, 1983.

Voysey, Charles A. "The English Home," *The British Architect*, vol. 75, 1911.

Voysey, Charles A. "Remarks on Domestic Entrance Halls," *Studio*, vol. XXI, 1901.

Waddell, Jeffrey J. "Some Recent Glasgow Tea-Rooms," *Builders' Journal and Architectural Record*, 15 April 1903.

Walker, David. "The Architect of the Restoration of Brechin Cathedral. An Outline of the Career of John Honeyman (1831–1914)," *The Society of Friends of Brechin Cathedral. Book of the Society*, no. 41, 1992.

Walker, Frank, A. "The Mysterious Affair at Cloak," *Charles Rennie Mackintosh Society Newsletter*, no. 31, Winter/Spring 1981–82.

Welter, Volker M. "Arcades for Lucknow: Patrick Geddes, Charles Rennie Mackintosh and the Reconstruction of the City," *Architectural History*, vol. 42, 1999.

White, Gleeson. "Some Glasgow Designers and Their Work," *Studio*, vol. XI, 1897.

MAGAZINES

Academy Architecture
American Architect and Building News
Architect
Bailie
British Architect
Builder
Builders' Journal and Architectural Engineer
Building News
Dekorative Kunst
Deutsche Kunst und Dekoration
Evening News
Evening Times
Glasgow Herald
Glasgow Weekly Herald
Quiz
Royal Institute of British Architects' Journal
Scottish Art Review
Studio
Transactions of the Aberdeen Ecclesiological Society
Transactions of the Glasgow Ecclesiological Society

THESIS

Edwards, Brian. "Glasgow Improvements, 1866–1901," Ph.D. thesis, Glasgow University, 1990.

COLLECTIONS OF PAPERS

Blackie MSS, University of Glasgow
Brechin Cathedral archive
Glasgow Art Club
Glasgow City Archives, Mitchell Library
Glasgow Institute of Architects
Hornel Library, National Trust for Scotland
Howarth MSS, University of Toronto, Special Collections
Kelvingrove Art Gallery, Glasgow
Mackintosh Collection, Hunterian Art Gallery, University of Glasgow
National Gallery of Ireland
Victoria and Albert Museum, National Art Library

CHRONOLOGY

1868 Mackintosh born in Glasgow

1883 Architectural apprentice; enrolls as a part-time student at the Glasgow School of Art

1888 Apprenticeship ends; enters office of John Honeyman

1889 John Keppie becomes a partner of John Honeyman; J. H. McNair enters office of John Honeyman and Keppie; Mackintosh's design for a Mountain Chapel published in *Building News*

1890 Redclyffe, the first architectural commission; awarded silver medal from South Kensington for Science and Art Museum; design for a public hall in the early classic style; wins Thomson Travelling Scholarship; lecture on "Scotch Baronial Architecture"

1891 Mackintosh in Italy; Glasgow Art Gallery competition

1892 Design for a chapter house; awarded gold medal, South Kensington; design work on Glasgow Cathedral and Glasgow Art Club; bedroom suite for David Gauld; lecture on Italy to the Glasgow Architectural Association

1893 Glasgow Art Club opens; details published in *The Bailie*; Canal Boatmen's; Institute; *Glasgow Herald*; Craigie Hall; design for a railway station terminus published in *British Architect*; contributes to The Magazine

1894 *Harvest Moon*; *The Tree of Influence*; Royal Insurance competition; Queen Margaret Medical College; Conservative Club, Helensburgh

1895 Account of tour in Hampshire, Dorset, and Somerset published in *British Architect*; drawings from West Kilbridge and Arran; wallpaper designs in Glasgow Arts and Crafts exhibition; Martyrs School; McNair opens his own studio

1896 Poster for the *Scottish Musical Review*; exhibits at the London Arts and Crafts Exhibition Society include a hall settle and *Part seen, imagined part*; furniture for Argyle Street tearoom; mural designs for Buchanan Street tearoom; competition for a purpose built Glasgow School of Art

1897 Articles in The Studio on The Four; Queen's Cross Church; phase one of the new Glasgow School of Art begins

1898 Article in *Dekorative Kunst*; designs a concert hall and industrial hall for Glasgow's forthcoming International Exhibition; interiors at Craigie Hall; McNair becomes instructor in decorative design in Liverpool

1899 Interior in Munich; exhibits oak chairs at the London Arts and Crafts Exhibition Society; Ruchill Church halls; phase one of the Glasgow School of Art opened; mural decorations at St. Serf's Church, Dysart, Fife; J. H. McNair and Frances Macdonald marry

1900 Mackintosh marries Margaret Macdonald; sets up home in Mains Street; *Daily Record*; Windyhill, Kilmacolm; interiors at Dunglass Castle; interiors Ingram Street tearoom; Vienna Secession exhibition

1901 Mackintosh becomes a partner in Honeyman and Keppie; designs for a Town House for an Artist and a Country Cottage for an Artist; House for an Art Lover competition; the Wassail and the May Queen gesso panels by Mackintosh and his wife for the Ingram Street tearoom illustrated in *Academy Architecture*

1902 Article on Charles and Margaret Mackintosh in *Decorative Kunst*; The Hill House, Helensburgh; Liverpool Cathedral competition; Rose Boudoir by Mackintosh and his wife and the Writing Room by Herbert and Frances McNair for the Turin exhibition of decorative art; music room for Fritz Waerndorfer, Vienna

1903 Scotland Street School; Ingram Street tearoom—ladies' room, luncheon room; Willow Tea Room; internal alterations and furnishings for Hous'hill; exhibitions in Dresden, Moscow

1904 Dining room in Berlin; internal additions to Holy Trinity Church, Bridge of Allan

1905 Articles on The Hill House and the Willow Tea Room in *Deutsche Kunst und Dekoration* and *Dekorative Kunst*; Argyle Street tearoom—Dutch Kitchen; internal alterations to Abbey Close Church, Paisley

1906 Charles and Margaret Mackintosh move to Ann Street, Hillhead

1907 Phase two of the Glasgow School of Art begins; Ingram Street tearoom—Oak Room

1908 Lady Artists' Club—doorway and decorations; designs for Auchenibert published in *Academy Architecture*

1909 Phase two of the Glasgow School of Art is opened; Ingram Street tearoom—Oval Room and Ladies' Rest Room; McNairs leave Liverpool and return to Glasgow

1911 Ingram Street tearoom—Chinese and Cloister Rooms

1912 The Hill House refurbished

1913 Cloak; Kilmacolm; Mackintosh portrait painted by Newbery

1914 Charles and Margaret Mackintosh leave Glasgow for Walberswick, Suffolk

1915 Charles and Margaret Mackintosh settle in London

1916 Mackintosh commissioned to produce designs for 78 Derngate, Northampton

1917 The Dug Out, Ingram Street tearoom; Charles and Margaret Mackintosh are founder members of The Plough

1918 Candida Cottage, Northamptonshire

1919 The Plough is wound up; cottage at East Grinstead, Sussex; textile designs

1920 Designs studios, studio flats, and theater; textile designs

1921 Death of Frances McNair

1922 Book cover designs for W. W. Blackie

1923 Charles and Margaret Mackintosh leave London to settle in the south of France

1927 Mackintosh writes the Chronycle; returns to London for medical treatment

1928 Mackintosh dies

1933 Margaret Macdonald Mackintosh dies; Memorial Exhibition in Glasgow

INDEX

architectural projects of, 16, 29, 78–80, *79, 80,* 82–83, 96, 97, 99, 104, 132, 136, 180, 181, 186, 225, 226, 247–48, *248,* 249, 250, 259
   Honeyman and, 49, 77, 82
   Mackintosh and, 55, 68, 77, 94, 100, 105, 114–15, 181, 262, 264
Keppie family, 111, 133
Kerr, Robert, 231, 236
Kibble Fine Art Palace, 22–23
Kilmacolm, 228, 255
Kincardineshire, 175
King, Jessie M., 194
Kirkcudbright, 55, 63, 78, 264
Kirkcudbright Free Church, 132
Kirklee Terrace, Glasgow, 38, *38*
Klimt, Gustav, 199
Knox, Archibald, 96
Koch, Alexander, 52, 194

Ladbroke Grove Free Library, London, 173, *174,* 187
Lady Artists' Club, 250, 254–55
Lansdowne Church, Glasgow, 69–70, *70,* 72, 132
Larkspur (Mackintosh), 263, *263*
Later Renaissance Architecture (Belcher and Macartney), 179–80
Lavery, John, *48,* 117, 133
Le Corbusier, 278, 279
Lectures on the Rise and Development of Medieval Architecture (Scott), 111
Leicester Galleries, 273, 275
Leiper, William, 30, 52, 54, 157–58, 159, 179, 233
Lethaby, William R., 118, 128, 129, 140, 172, 175, 206, 229
Liberty, 206, 270
Liège Arts and Crafts Exhibition, 157
Lilybank House, 37, 40
Lime Street Terminus, Liverpool, 99–100
Linlithgow, 97, *97*
Lion Chambers, Glasgow, 181, 182
Lister, Lord, 22
Livadia (Russian imperial yacht), *28,* 29, 30, 46
Liverpool, 99–100
   McNairs in, 19, 125, 218–19, *219*
Liverpool Cathedral design competition, 186–87, *186, 187*
Liverpool School of Art, 218–19
Liverpool University, 218–19
Logan, George, 194
London, 46, 57, 118, 140, 171, 173, 187
London Salon of the Independents, 269
Loretto School, 132
Louise, Princess, Duchess of Argyll, 198, 208
Lovers, The (McNair), 106, 123
Lowe, Peter, 79–80
"Luck of Roaring Camp, The" (Harte), 115
Lusitania, RMS, 30
Lutyens, Edwin, 198, 208–9

Macbeth, Ann, 194
MacBrayne, David, 30
MacBrayne family, 34
McColl, D. S., 197
Macdonald, Charles, 125, 226–27
Macdonald, Frances (Mrs. McNair), 18, 55, 63–64, *64,* 106, *107,* 112, 113, 115, 117, *117,* 118, 119, 121, 124, 171, 187, 191, 202, 247, 250
   in Liverpool, 19, 125, 194, 218–19, *219,* 269
   marriage of, 125, 191, 218
   suicide of, 19, 117
   in Turin Exhibition, 16, 194, 196, 197, *197*
   see also Four, The
Macdonald, Margaret (Mrs. Mackintosh), 22, 55, 61, 63–64, *64,* 105, 106, *107,* 112, 113, 115, 116–17, *117,* 118, 119, 121, 137, 173, 181, 187, 188, 191, 197, 202, 206, 207–8, 210, 212, 219, 250, *251,* 265
   death of, 275, 278
   Florentine Terrace residence of, *245,* 246–47, 254–55, *255, 256, 258, 259*
   in France, 272–73
   letters of, 16, 264, 268, 270
   in London, 268–72, 273, 274–75
   Mains Street residence of, 16, 19, 125, 131, 181, 191, 194, 218, 219, *221*
   marriage of, 18, 125, 131, 191, 199, 218, 259, 263, 264, 268–69, 272–75
   in Turin Exhibition, 194–95, 196, *197,* 198
   see also Four, The
Macdonald family, 18, 247
Macfarlane, Walter, 29, 34, *34, 37,* 38, 41, 84, 131
McGibbon, Alexander, 46, 82, *83,* 110, 111, 128, 140, 157, 158, 228, 248
MacGibbon, David, 94, 111, 115, 138
Macgillivray, J. Pittendrigh, 79–80, 117, 175, 180, 185
McIntosh, Margaret Rennie, 16, 18
McIntosh, William, 16, 17, 18, 91
McKenzie, George, 48–49, *49,* 90, 91, 111
Mackintosh, Charles Rennie, *15, 49, 113, 117, 270,* 279
   apprenticeship of, 68, 72
   architectural credo of, 129–30, 152
   birth of, 16–17, 22
   death of, 275
   English sketching tour of, 113–14
   European influence of, 199
   Florentine Terrace residence of, *245,* 246–47, 254–55, *255, 256, 258, 259*
   flower paintings and drawings by, 116, *116,* 262, 263–64, *263, 264,* 268, *268,* 274
   furniture by, 19, 52, 55, 118, 119, 121, 171, 191, 194–95, 197, 219, *221,* 237, 251
   gesso work by, 191, 207–8
   Glasgow School of Art and, 110–12
   Honeyman and, 26, 68, 77
   at Honeyman and Keppie, 77, 82, *83,* 84

Italian tour of, 42, 48, 90–91, 93–94, 96, 106, 107, 110, 111, 128, 186–87, 199
Japanese influence in, 53–54, 221
Keppie and, 55, 68, 77, 94, 100, 105, 114–15, 181, 262, 264
lectures by, 94, 128–30, 227
in London, 265, 267–72, 275
McNair and, 68, 84, 90, 91
marriage of, 18, 125, 131, 191, 199, 218, 259, 263, 264, 268–69, 272–75
money problems of, 264–65, 268, 269
nature as inspiration for, 130, 152, 171–72
1933 Memorial Exhibition for, 16, 278
paintings by, *51, 52,* 61, 63, *63,* 64, 68, *87,* 90, 93, 97, *97, 109,* 123, 194, *261, 272,* 273, 275, 279
in partnership with Honeyman and Keppie, 52, 147, 171, 182, 209, 226, 247, 255, 259
posters and graphics by, 64, 109, *109,* 124, *125,* 274, *275*
Ruskin's influence on, 88–90, 91, 93–94
Secession House exhibit of, 188, 191, 193, *194,* 198, 199, 208, 212, 215, 267
sketches and drawings by, 48, *49,* 63, *67,* 68, *82,* 89, 90, 91, 93, *93,* 100, *101,* 106, 107, 113–14, 115, *115,* 116, *116,* 138, *138,* 147, *152,* 229
symbolist aesthetic of, 106, 172–73, 175, 210–11, 212, 228, 243, 279
textile designs by, 268, *269,* 270
Thomson Studentship awarded to, 42, 85, 89, 94
in Turin Exposition, 12, 194–97, *197,* 198, 210, 212, 215
in Walberswick, 259, 262–64, 273
see also Four, The
Mackintosh, Charles Rennie, architecture and interior design of:
   Abbey Close Church, 247
   Auchenibert, *249,* 250
   chapter house design, *96,* 97
   City Gallery competition, 96, *97, 98,* 99
   Country Cottage for an Artist, 229
   Craigie Hall, 221, *222, 223,* 225–26, *225*
   Daily Record offices, 152, 178–79, *178, 179,* 180–81, 247–48
   Dunloe, 225–26, *225, 226,* 227
   Florentine Terrace residence, *245,* 246–47, 268, 272
   Glasgow Art Club, 104–7, *104, 105, 107,* 132, 199
   Glasgow Herald extension, 16, 72, 100–101, *100, 101, 103,* 107, 128, 132, 180, 187, 188, 228, 247–48
   Glasgow School of Art, 43, 61, 64, 77, 99, 110, 114, 128, *155,* 158–59, 161, *161, 162, 163, 164,* 166, *166, 167,* 168–69, *168, 169,* 171–75, *171, 173, 174,* 178, 182, 199, 207, 212, 215, 221, 247–48, 250–51, 252, 271, *277,* 278–79

THE GLASGOW ARCHITECTURAL ASSOCIATION

CHAS. R. MACKINTOSH